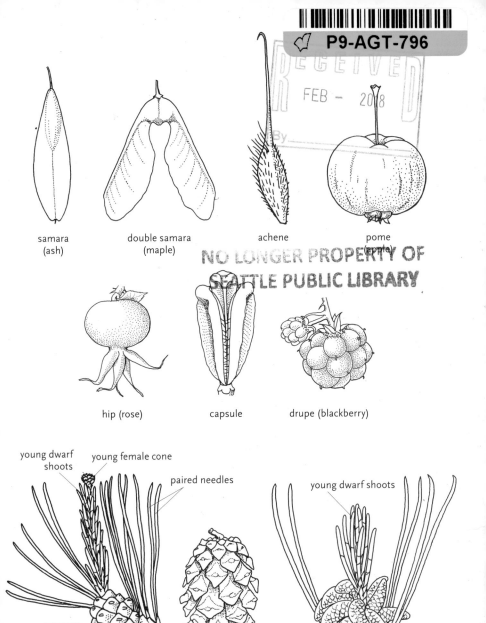

samara
(ash)

double samara
(maple)

achene

pome
(apple)

hip (rose)

capsule

drupe (blackberry)

young dwarf
shoots

young female cone

paired needles

young dwarf shoots

green immature cone

woody
mature cone

male cone

seed (female) cones

pollen (male) cones

FRUITS AND SEEDS

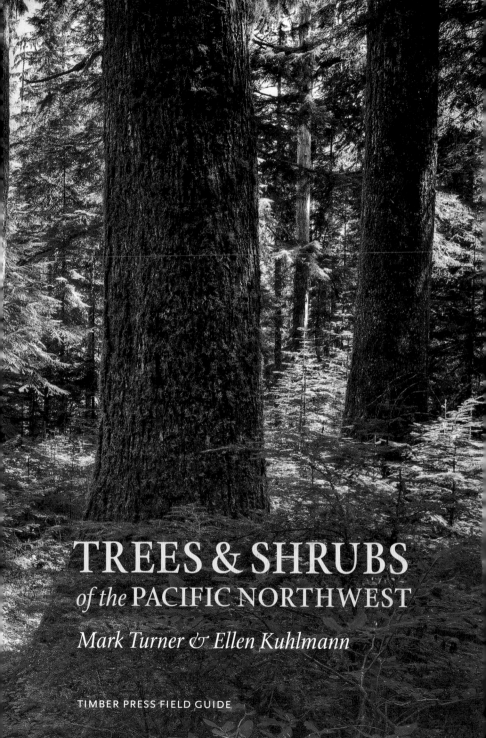

TREES & SHRUBS
of the PACIFIC NORTHWEST

Mark Turner & Ellen Kuhlmann

TIMBER PRESS FIELD GUIDE

To two lifelong learners—

Al Hanners, who mastered the willows and sedges after turning 60,
and **Marie Hitchman,** who at midlife decided to learn plant biology
and coastal ecology so she could intelligently contribute
to environmental issues.

They have shown us that much is attainable
when you put your mind to it.

Copyright © 2014 by Mark Turner and Ellen Kuhlmann. All rights reserved.
Photographs by Mark Turner unless otherwise noted.

Published in 2014 by Timber Press, Inc.

The Haseltine Building
133 S.W. Second Avenue, Suite 450
Portland, Oregon 97204-3527
timberpress.com

Printed in China
Book design by Susan Applegate
Endpaper drawings by Alan Bryan

Second printing 2016

Library of Congress Cataloging-in-Publication Data

Turner, Mark, 1954 April 8–
    Trees and shrubs of the Pacific Northwest/Mark Turner and Ellen
Kuhlmann.—[First edition].
        pages cm—(Timber Press field guide)
    Includes bibliographical references and index.
    ISBN 978-1-60469-263-1
    1. Trees—Northwest, Pacific—Identification. 2. Trees—Northwest,
Pacific—Pictorial works. 3. Shrubs—Northwest, Pacific—Identification. 4.
Shrubs—Northwest, Pacific—Pictorial works. I. Kuhlmann, Ellen E. (Ellen
Elizabeth), 1963– II. Title. III. Series: Timber Press field guide.
    QK144.T73 2014
    582.1609795—dc23   2013036236

CONTENTS

PREFACE

Anyone who has spent time outdoors in the Pacific Northwest has likely marveled at a giant old-growth Douglas-fir and cursed a thicket of devil's club. Alpine explorers may have been surprised to stumble upon dwarf willows no taller than the toe of their boot.

Trees and shrubs are almost everywhere in the Northwest. Maybe we take them for granted. We know that we once did, lumping understory shrubs into one homogenous "boring shrub layer" while searching for wildflowers or barreling up a trail in pursuit of an alpine summit. But the reality is that there is a great deal of diversity among our trees and shrubs, thanks in large part to the wide range of growing conditions in the Northwest. A few species, like Douglas-fir, western serviceberry, chokecherry, and common snowberry, are found in almost every county or regional district. Others, like our two rockmats, are very narrow endemics found in only a few places. The Klamath-Siskiyou Range is home to more conifer species than almost any other similar-size chunk of geography in the world.

When we began the journey that resulted in this book, we knew there were a lot of trees and shrubs to cover. Some—particularly those of the North Cascades, where we live—were familiar friends to revisit on each hike. Others, like the willows, had a vague familiarity but were often passed over because they were challenging to learn. Neither of us started on this book knowing everything we would discover along the way.

It stands to reason that our largest trees grow where the most rain falls each season. It takes a lot of water to produce a coast redwood, Sitka spruce, western redcedar, or Douglas-fir. Go east of the mountains to the Columbia Plateau or the Great Basin and you'll find a landscape dominated by sagebrush, bitterbrush, rabbitbrush, and other small shrubs. In this arid part of the Northwest, what passes for old growth may be barely shoulder high.

Chaparral only touches the Northwest, with its northernmost examples just crossing the border from California into Oregon. It's a dense, nearly impenetrable shrub environment with many oaks, manzanitas, and ceanothus that were new to both of us.

We joked at the outset of writing and photographing this book that it was our excuse to learn the willows. That notoriously challenging genus taxed our powers of observation and frustrated us with the great variability within many of the species. We even thought about skipping them because they're hard, but that would have been a disservice to you, our readers. We hope we haven't led you astray because even after the time we've spent with the willows we're far from experts. That takes nearly a lifetime of study.

This book would not have been possible without the work of numerous botanists and plant explorers who came before us. Their journeys and study laid the foundation. Some of them are memorialized in the names of trees and shrubs, people like David Douglas, Archibald Menzies, John Scouler, and George Engelmann.

While a few readers may gripe about the size and weight of this volume, we chose to err on the side of clarity and include at least a pair of photographs for most of the 568 taxa that have a main entry. We relied on the much larger, and much heavier, regional floras to identify specimens in the field and as primary sources for our descriptions. Books like *Flora of the Pacific Northwest*, its big brother *Vascular Plants of the Pacific Northwest*, and both the 1993 and 2012 editions of the *Jepson Manual* are well-thumbed references, in some cases held together by duct tape.

We also relied on several online resources, sometimes pulling up websites like Cal-Flora on a smartphone, seemingly in the middle of nowhere, to help identify a shrub. Mark relied on herbarium records, mapped through Google maps, to guide him to known locations for many species, following a line of red dots on the screen in the palm of his hand.

Botany is undergoing many changes, with taxonomists challenging old relationships and discovering new ones, often based on DNA research rather than the morphological observations of old. We've used the most up-to-date names (as of January 2013) as the primary entry, using one or more older names as synonyms. For our older readers, many of whom learned their plant names from Hitchcock and Cronquist, join us in learning the newer names as well.

Come along on this journey of exploration. Stop cursing the dense shrubs in your path and learn their names and characteristics. Knowing that it's devil's club (*Oplopanax horridus*) blocking your path won't make it any less prickly, but the knowledge just might add a bit to your enjoyment when you see its giant leaves backlit under the forest canopy and spires of red berries beacon-like across a wet slope.

May your copy of this book become dog-eared and pollen-stained, favorite pages marked by sticky tabs.

ACKNOWLEDGMENTS

Trees and Shrubs of the Pacific Northwest would have been impossible without the help of many people who generously offered their time, expertise, and patience.

Our families put up with long absences during the field work and photography. When we were home we spent nearly every waking hour holed up in our offices with computers, reference books, and thousands of photographs. Ellen was blessed with the unwavering support of her mother, Mary, and siblings, Ann and Mike. We both wish to thank Natalie, Zach, and Ian, Mark's wife and sons. Without your support and encouragement we wouldn't have made it. Zach updated the script (which he originally wrote for *Wildflowers of the Pacific Northwest*) that generated the distribution maps from our database records. Ian helped with numerous computing tasks that made managing the massive amount of data and photographs easier. Natalie helped proofread and gave endless support, advice on language, and opinions on photo selection.

Many Native Plant Society field trip participants pointed out nice specimens along the trail, offered suggestions and feedback about what plants should be included and how they should be treated, and were patient with a photographer who just can't spend less than 15 minutes on a plant. Additional thanks to the organizers of the field trips at both WNPS and NPSO annual meetings and study weekends, as well as to those responsible for Botany Washington.

Several individuals spent time in the field with Mark, helping to locate and identify specimens, or providing directions to prime habitat locations. Don Knoke, Paul Slichter, and Jennifer and Lance Barker became friends when Mark was photographing *Wildflowers* and provided invaluable assistance for this volume as well. Jennifer and Lance also provided a place to stay and homegrown meals when Mark was in central Oregon. Michael Kauffmann, author of *Conifer Country*, helped with locations in northern California. Barbara Coatney lent her guest bedroom in Etna, California. Marla Knight, botanist, Klamath National Forest, pointed out several Siskiyou County locations. Ken Kilborn assisted with locations around Redding. Carol and C J Ralph hosted Mark in Arcata and shared many Humboldt County sites. Karen Phillips, Frank Callahan, and Lee Webb directed Mark to several southern Oregon locations. Steve Walters and Cheryl Lisin shared their home, a meal, and shrub locations near the Lost Coast in southern Humboldt County. Phyllis and Dick Gustafson provided several nights' lodging, meals, and coffee stops as well as encouragement to continue the journey that resulted in this book. Phyllis did preliminary sketches for the endpaper illustrations as well.

Other folks provided photos for certain aspects of plants not captured by Mark in the field; these individuals are listed separately on page 426 at the back of the book. Then there were the people encountered along the way, whose names were not recorded, that helped Mark find plants. One of those was a U.S. Forest Service employee who sent Mark to the summit of Lake Mountain to find foxtail pines.

Almost every trip Mark made into the mountains since moving to Washington in 1990 became an opportunity to photograph plant specimens, long before this book was conceived. Many of these were hikes or climbs with friends in the Bellingham branch of The Mountaineers or as a leader of Bellingham Troop 3 Boy Scout outings. Thank you for your patience and understanding when you were in a hurry to move on down the trail.

David Giblin at the University of Washington Herbarium provided invaluable assistance with taxonomic questions, helping us sort out the numerous name changes between older references and current practice. He and Ben Legler, also with the UW Herbarium, additionally helped to identify locations to photograph several species. Ellen is especially thankful to Barry Wendling and Don Knoke, who cast critical and expert eyes on the text. Barry reviewed the plant families chapter, and Don the plant profiles. Both provided valuable suggestions and corrections.

Finally, this book would not be in your hands without the talented support of the people at Timber Press. Tom Fischer, acquisitions editor, encouraged us to propose the book as a sequel to *Wildflowers of the Pacific Northwest*. Susan Applegate created the page design, building elegantly on our rough original concept and accepting our input into a collaborative process that is rare in publishing.

This book has been our life for two and a half years. Thank you to each and every one of you who touched upon it during that time. Thank you too, dear reader, for choosing to carry our book on your journey in search of Northwest trees and shrubs.

HOW TO USE THIS BOOK

Trees and Shrubs of the Pacific Northwest is designed to be easy to use in the field to help you identify the woody plants you find. It includes color photographs, clear and concise descriptions, and range maps for 568 trees and shrubs of all sizes found from southern British Columbia to northern California. Additional related species are mentioned in the text.

Our goal in selecting plants was to include as many as possible that you are likely to find while exploring all parts of our large territory. Almost all native species, some well-established non-natives, and a few rare and endemic plants are here. Trees and shrubs that show up only occasionally in the wild as garden escapees are excluded; in other words, in urban areas and around old homesteads you may encounter a lilac or other plant that is not in this book.

As you look up the trees and shrubs you find, be sure to use all the information provided. The text and photographs complement each other. The range maps show the county (in the United States) or regional district (in British Columbia) where the plant is documented to have been found. Keep in mind that habitat, not shown on the individual maps, is also critically important.

Learning About New Plants

It is very easy to miss a critical detail about a plant you are identifying if you don't adopt a systematic way of looking. While we're usually attracted first to the flowers and their shape and color, or the leaves, the rest of the plant is also important.

Start by getting an overall impression of the plant. How big is it? Does it grow like a vine, form a mat on the ground, have stems clumped together, or have a single stem that stands by itself? Are the stems stiff and strong or are they weak? Are there any spines, prickles, or hairs? What does the bark look like?

Examine the leaves. Are they mostly right at the ground (basal) or do they grow along the stem? Some plants have both basal and stem leaves. What shape are the leaves? Leaf shapes are pictured inside the back cover. Stem leaves can be opposite each other, arranged alternately, or whorled. Leaves can be attached to the stem with a long petiole, clasp the stem, have little appendages at the attachment point (stipules), or appear to have the stem growing through the leaf. Many plants have simple leaves, but some have compound leaves with several leaflets. You may need to count the leaflets and note how they're arranged. Leaf texture is another clue. Are they soft, leathery, hairy on one or both sides, or spiny?

Study the flowers. Identification usually requires a close look at the color, arrangement, and number of the flowering parts. Color is obvious, but it may change as the flowers age or vary among individuals of the same species. Sometimes petals have spots or blotches of a second color. Count the petals, if there are any. Some flowers don't have any petals, or they are very small and inconspicuous. Count the sepals, usually located at the base of the flower. For many plants, this will be enough to make an identification. However, you may also need to look closely to see how many stamens there are. Sometimes you need to see whether these sex parts are longer or shorter than the petals. For a few flowers you have to look closely to see how dense the hairs are inside and outside the flower. A 10× hand lens is useful for this close level of examination, can add a lot to your enjoyment, and doesn't add much weight to your pack. The visual glossary inside the front and back covers can help you with any technical terms you haven't yet learned.

Observe the habitat. Does the plant grow in the forest or out in the open? What is the soil like? What else is growing around your plant? Are you at the seashore, in the mountains, or somewhere in between? All these clues will help you learn about new plants.

Organization

The trees and shrubs in this book are organized into four main groups. First are the conifers (broken into three families), followed by plants with simple leaves, plants with compound leaves, and finally those with no leaves or insignificant leaves. Within each of those three last leaf groups, plants are broken down into further leaf types: alternate, opposite, and basal or whorled leaves; or, in the case of those with no leaves, into shrubs and cactus. Within each of these sections, plants are listed by family, genus, and species.

The fastest way to look up an unknown plant is to look at the leaves. Are they needle-like (conifers), simple, or compound (divided into leaflets)? For all but the conifers, look to see if the leaves are attached to the twig in pairs across from each other (opposite) or staggered (alternate). Then turn to the appropriate section and leaf through the pages until you come to plants that look similar to the one you're examining. Study the photographs and read the descriptions until you find a match. Use the maps to tentatively eliminate plants that don't grow where you are; however, you may be lucky enough to have discovered a range extension or found a plant not included in this book. Once you have a preliminary identification, you may want to re-read the description as you study the plant carefully a second time.

Some plants are easier to recognize than others. The willows, manzanitas, shrubby oaks, and ceanothus are especially challenging and may require consulting a technical manual for additional information if you need positive identification. Even experts have trouble telling some of them apart.

If you recognize the family of your plant, it may be faster to turn to the plant families chapter first and go to the descriptions from there. Each family is described briefly, followed by page references for the family members.

The index includes the common and scientific names for the taxa featured in the book. If you know a plant's name but aren't sure what it looks like, then turn to the index to find it quickly.

Photographs

In most cases there is more than one photograph for each plant. The photos were selected to show as many important identifying characteristics as possible; use them to get a general feel for what the plant looks like, then read the description.

Plant Names

Each plant has a unique scientific name, a binomial, of two parts: genus and species. In some cases there are also subspecies and varieties, but for the most part these are lumped together under the main species. Because plant names can change over time, we've listed scientific synonyms for some plants (in parentheses). The first name listed is the accepted name at the time of publication; in general, these follow the names in the *Flora of North America*. In a few cases where there was disagreement, we chose to follow the *Washington Flora Checklist* or the *Jepson Manual* (Baldwin et al. 2012). Names given in the standard technical keys are listed as synonyms if they are different from the currently accepted name. We wish that scientific names for plants were not undergoing so much and such rapid change and that there could be universal agreement among professional taxonomists about how plants are classified. Unfortunately, that's not the case and we hope you'll come along with us as we learn new names for some of the plants we've known for a long time.

Each plant also has one or more common names. The same plant may be called by different names in different places, or the same name may refer to different plants in different places. Some plants have so many common names, we couldn't list them all.

Descriptions

Each plant entry gives the plant's height, relative abundance, bloom time, habitat, and whether it is native or non-native. Each description is written in a consistent style so you can quickly scan for individual characteristics. The descriptions start with a general overview of the plant habit, such as tree or shrub. Leaves are next, followed by details about flowers and fruit. Finally, you'll find information about the plant's ecology.

Height. Plant heights, in inches or feet, are for typical mature specimens under normal growing conditions. You may find individuals that are taller or shorter than the figures given, but if you're looking at a plant that is only a foot tall and the description gives a range of 5–15 feet, there's a good chance you need to reconsider your identification. For help with converting units, see the table on page 434 and the ruler on the edge of the back cover.

Habit. In general, trees are defined as woody plants with one main stem at least 3 in. across at breast height (4.5 ft. above ground level), with a crown of foliage and over 20 ft. tall at maturity. Shrubs tend to be shorter, with multiple, narrower stems. Subshrubs are woody only at the base of the plants; sometimes the woody portion is below ground. Subshrub herbage may die back to the soil surface each year, depending on the species and the climate in which it grows.

Almost all the plants in this book are perennial. We've included a few woody vines and even non-woody annuals that have shrub-like growth habit because even though they're not true shrubs, they look like they are.

Abundance. The abundance of a plant is another clue you can use to identify it. Botanists speak of populations of plants, which simply means a group of individual specimens of one species growing in close proximity to one another. A population can have very few individuals, be a dense stand covering the ground, or anything in between. We've used the terms *rare*, *scattered, uncommon, locally common,* and *common* to describe plant populations. The terms refer to how likely you are to find the plant in our region. Some plants that are uncommon or rare here are prolific in other parts of the continent.

You'll also see the term *endemic* in some descriptions. An endemic plant has a limited geographic range. Within that range you may find many populations with lots of individual plants, as with Crater Lake currant, which thrives on rocky sites at high elevations in Oregon. Another easily found endemic is California pipevine, which grows prolifically in wooded areas of the Sacramento River basin. By contrast, Chelan rockmat is found only in a very few places along the Columbia River near Wenatchee, Washington. Areas that have the largest number of endemic species covered in this book are the Olympic, Siskiyou, Steens, Wallowa, and Wenatchee mountains and the Columbia Gorge.

Using the term *rare* to describe a plant generally means the species has few known populations, often but not always small in size, across a defined area. Plants may be rare within an ecoregion, state, region, or globally. A species may be rare in one state and common in another. We are categorizing a plant's abundance as rare in accordance with lists compiled by state, federal, and provincial authorities, and the California Native Plant Society. If a plant is both rare and common within the area covered by this book, both abundance levels are noted: the one which corresponds to the condition in a larger portion of the book's geographic range is listed at the top, the second level is noted near the end of the species' description, in the section on ecology. Many rare plants are threatened or endangered. Be especially respectful of any rare species you are lucky enough to find.

We consider a plant to have *scattered* distribution when you're likely to find a few individuals here and there within its habitat and range. Species with scattered abundance tend to have a broad geographic distribution and are not considered rare or uncommon because they have many populations. Spotting plants of a species with a scattered distribution may take a keen eye as the plants are spread throughout the communities in which they grow.

Uncommon plants are just that. They may be found across a wide range, but there aren't very many populations. You could find fairly large numbers of individual plants in a particular spot but only find them in a few places. Or there could be only a few plants in each of many places.

Locally common plants have a wide range and in some places you'll find large numbers of individuals. These species often have specific habitat requirements that limit the types of places where they will grow successfully. Lewis's mock-orange and California wild grape are both locally common; in the areas where they grow, you're likely to find many plants and many populations.

Common plants are found in large numbers in many habitats and locations. Oceanspray is found from sea level to fairly high in the mountains. Serviceberry is found in every county and regional district covered in this book.

Bloom time. Most plants bloom only for a fairly short period each year. We've subdivided spring and summer into early, mid, and late. Few of our shrubs or trees bloom in autumn and even fewer in winter or year-round. The bloom times are related more to weather conditions than to calendar dates and should be used with caution. For high-elevation plants that bloom following snowmelt, there's really only one season: summer.

In general, early spring begins in mid March at low elevations, although you may find flowers as early as February in warm, exposed locations such as the Washington side of the Columbia Gorge and sun-baked sites along Puget Sound. Mid spring comes with the leafing out of the bigleaf maples. Late spring arrives as the Garry oak leaves attain full size.

Early summer runs up through the solstice, or immediately after the snow melts at high elevations. In mid summer the alpine meadows are at their lush maximum growth. By late summer the soil has mostly dried out and blooms are slowing down. Autumn is short as seeds mature and foliage dies back.

Habitat. In real estate, it's location, location, location. For plants, it's habitat, habitat, habitat. The subject is so important we've given it a section all its own, in the next chapter.

Elevation. We've used the terms *low, mid,* and *high,* as well as *subalpine* and *alpine,* to describe the elevation range where a plant is most likely to be growing. Because the Northwest is so diverse, these terms are necessarily vague. In general, a plant will be found at lower elevations in the northern or coastal part of its range than in the south or hundreds of miles inland. Low elevations range from sea level to about 2000 feet but can also include valley floors in mountain-ous regions. Mid elevations range from 2000 to 5000 feet and include the high plains of eastern Washington and Oregon, as well as montane forests below the subalpine zone that begins around timberline. High elevations include everything above about 5000 feet, including the treeless alpine and transitional subalpine zones.

Maps

Plants are mapped by the counties in which they have been found in the United States and by regional districts in British Columbia. Dark shading indicates a plant has been found in the county. The maps are designed to give you a general idea about where each plant grows. You need to take habitat into consideration as well as geographic distribution.

The maps are based on herbarium specimen records from sources in Canada, Washington, Oregon, and California. An herbarium specimen is a pressed, dried plant collected by an individual and placed in a library of such specimens. They are usually first identified by the plant collector. Sometimes, but not always, they are reviewed and checked by another botanist. In some cases, specimens may have been identified incorrectly or the location written down wrong. Plant names can also change over the years.

Herbarium specimens span over 100 years of plant collecting in the Northwest. In a few cases, a plant was collected once many decades ago and hasn't been seen since. Some areas have been more popular for plant collecting than others. The west side of the Cascades, the national parks, and places where an individual was particularly interested in the plants are better represented with herbarium specimens than some eastern counties, which have fewer people and more land in agriculture.

In short, the maps should be used as a guide, not absolute gospel.

The distribution data for the maps was provided by CalFlora, Oregon Flora Project, University of Washington Herbarium, e-Flora BC, and the Pacific Northwest Herbaria Consortium. Complete citations are in the bibliography.

Serendipity

For the most part, plants don't grow in isolation. Often, when you stop along the trail to identify a plant that catches your eye you'll discover several other interesting specimens lurking nearby. Take the time to look around and explore. Over time, you'll begin to learn which plants often grow together and form communities. You may also find interesting plants growing in unexpected places.

Keep your eyes open to the tree and shrub possibilities that surround you almost anywhere you go. From sidewalk cracks to roadside ditches to pristine mountain meadows, the Northwest is blessed with an incredible diversity of trees and shrubs. With this book in your pack, pocket, or glove compartment you'll be prepared to identify and learn about them. In time, many of these plants will become like old friends you want to visit again and again.

CLIMATE, GEOGRAPHY, AND PLANT HABITATS

Washington, Oregon, northern California, and southern British Columbia—the area encompassed by this field guide—share major climatic and physical features that affect vegetation. Within the region there is also great habitat diversity, each habitat creating the conditions for different plant communities to thrive. Weather, landforms, soils, elevation, and disturbance all affect our diverse environments. As a result, the Northwest is blessed with thousands of vascular plant species, from herbaceous wildflowers and grasses to the many subshrubs, shrubs, and trees, some the largest and oldest in the world, that are the focus of this book.

The Pacific Ocean is the chief determinant of the weather patterns throughout the region. It is the source of the precipitation for which the Northwest is famous, and it moderates temperatures year-round, although its influence diminishes east of the mountains. West of the Coast Range, and to a large extent in the broad valleys immediately to the east, winters are cool and rainy with little snowfall. As the jet stream swings north in the summer, generally moderate and dry conditions prevail. Summer temperatures are warmer in the southern and interior parts of the region than in the north or along the coast.

Rainfall is greatest along the north coast, diminishing to the south and east. Along the southern Oregon and northern California coastline, summer fog contributes to the moisture required by coast redwoods and the plants that grow in the understory beneath them. To the north the coastal forest is dominated by Sitka spruce, transitioning inland to Douglas-fir, western hemlock, and western redcedar. This temperate coniferous rainforest along the coast from southeast Alaska to northern California is unique in the world, with the greatest biomass per acre of any place on earth.

The second important influence, the mountains, modifies the weather coming in off the ocean. Two major mountain ranges form north–south ridges parallel to the coast. The Coast Range, broadly defined to include the spine of Vancouver Island, the Olympic Mountains, and extending south into northern California's Klamath Mountains, catches massive amounts of precipitation during the winter months. Along the mountain crest deep moisture-laden snow typically doesn't melt out until mid July in the Olympics, a little earlier in the Klamaths. East of the Coast Range a "rain shadow" dramatically reduces the precipitation on the east side of Vancouver Island, the Sunshine Coast, the Puget Sound lowlands and Willamette Valley, and in the intermountain valleys of southern Oregon and northern California. Rainfall rises rapidly again as the clouds push up against the Cascades.

The larger Cascade Mountain Range, the backbone of our region, is characterized by high peaks and deep valleys. Studded by a string of volcanoes that rise above the rest of the summits, the Cascades catch nearly all the remaining moisture blowing in from the coast. Dense snow piles up from November to April, taking months to melt the following spring and summer. The major volcanic peaks can even make their own weather as winds are pushed up and around them. The northern Cascades are home to the largest number of glaciers in the lower 48 states, a testament to record-setting snowfall. Even where the glaciers have melted away, their former presence is obvious from the U-shaped valleys left in their wake.

In the basin east of the Cascades, conditions are generally dry year-round with what little precipitation that falls coming mostly in the winter months. This vast area, hundreds of miles east of the ocean, is also characterized by cold winters and hot summers. While Forks, on Washington's coast, averages almost 120 inches of rainfall annually, the area around Kennewick, 280 miles to the east in central Washington, receives less than 8 inches in an average year.

This intermountain area includes the east slopes of the Cascades, the Okanogan Valley, Columbia Plateau, and the basin and range province of southeastern Oregon. Forested mid elevations are dominated by ponderosa pine, Douglas-fir, and lodgepole pine. Valleys, including the immense channeled scablands of the Columbia Plateau in central Washington, have sagebrush and grasses as their major vegetation. Most wildflowers bloom in early spring before the topsoil layer dries out from summer's blistering heat, while shrubs may bloom at any time, as they are less dependent on surface moisture.

The northern Rocky Mountains extend into northeastern Washington and southeastern British Columbia, rising from the Columbia Plateau. Precipitation increases with elevation, but this far inland there is less of it, the air is colder, and the winter snow is lighter and drier. Even so, the climate is marine-influenced and many of the same species found in the Cascades also grow in the Northern Rockies.

The Blue Mountains stretch across north-central and eastern Oregon into southeast Washington and include the Strawberry, Greenhorn, Elkhorn, Aldrich, and Maury ranges, and the Ochoco and Wallowa mountains. This region is also dominated by conifer forests, grading into shrub-steppe habitats in the lower elevations.

In addition to the influence the mountains have on precipitation and temperature, the rocks from which they are built determine the composition of the soils on their slopes and in the valleys between them. Volcanic peaks and the Columbia River basalt flow are the best-known and most common source of rock in the Northwest, but they are not uniform throughout the region. In fact, Northwest geology is quite complex. Besides the widespread basalt, there are areas of sandstone, limestone, granite, and serpentine.

Plants are sensitive to soil depth as well as to its mineral composition and moisture content. Thin ridgetop soils support plants that have adapted to harsh conditions while excluding species that need to sink their roots deeper or have greater water requirements. Where the living is easier, the competitive balance shifts, and the plants that thrive under tough conditions are often edged out by species that more effectively exploit the better soils and increased water availability. Challenging environments are often home to a greater diversity of plant species while the habitats well within most species' growing requirements tend to be occupied by large numbers of a smaller set of species.

Ecoregions

The relationships of precipitation, geology, physiography, vegetation, climate, soils, land use, wildlife, and hydrology can be used to paint a broad picture of the ecology of any one geographical area. Within each ecoregion or biogeoclimatic zone, a visitor can expect to find comparable populations of plants and animals. The first part of this chapter has introduced the major influences that define the ecoregions of the Northwest. This section will explore each of these areas of ecological similarity. A basic understanding of the ecoregional concept helps to explain the relationships between habitats and the plants that grow there.

Ecoregion definitions vary somewhat depending on the agency and researcher that developed them. Each system starts with a very broad grouping and progresses to ever-finer distinctions and smaller geographical areas. The U.S. Forest Service definitions, first presented by Robert G. Bailey in 1978, differ from the U.S. Environmental Protection Agency (EPA) definitions, based on the work of James M. Omernik. In British Columbia a similar classification system was developed by Dennis A. Demarchi. The important concept they have in common is describing the interrelationships among the ecological elements and providing a framework for predicting the flora and fauna to be found within the ecoregion. The descriptions here follow EPA Level III Ecoregions and the Ministry of Sustainable Resource Management's Ecoregions of British Columbia. They are described from north to south and west to east. Some B.C. ecoregions have been combined for the sake of clarity and drawing a more cohesive cross-border picture. Although the map shows hard boundary lines, in reality ecoregion boundaries are wide and diffuse.

Coast Range. Running the length of the region, the Coast Range is characterized by high rainfall and productive conifer forests dominated by Sitka spruce with a mixture of western hemlock, western redcedar, Alaska yellow-cedar, and Douglas-fir in inland areas. A majority of the precipitation falls between November and April. Along the coast and in adjacent valleys, summer fog and relatively cool temperatures significantly affect the climate, ameliorating drought conditions. Redwoods dominate near the coast in the southern portion of the Coast Range. Much of the area has been heavily logged and the original forest mosaic replaced with intensively managed Douglas-fir plantations. The hills and mountains are relatively low. Streams typically originate as deeply incised, steep-gradient drainages that eventually feed large, low-gradient river systems on the coastal plain. The coastal plain can be as much as 20 miles wide and is composed of glacially deposited sediment and rock. Coastal bluffs often have soil derived from wind-deposited material (loess). Wetlands are common. Western Vancouver Island is the northern extension of the Coast Range.

Pacific Ranges. These high and rugged mountains, the southernmost part of the Coast Mountains in British Columbia, rise abruptly from deep fjords and numerous islands in the Strait of Georgia. Canada's

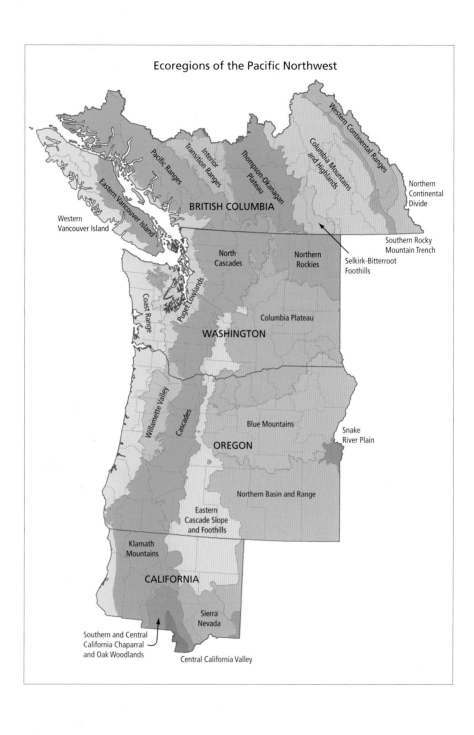

Ecoregions of the Pacific Northwest

Pacific Ranges

Transition Ranges

Interior Transition Ranges

Thompson-Okanagan Plateau

Western Continental Ranges

Columbia Mountains and Highlands

Northern Continental Divide

Eastern Vancouver Island

BRITISH COLUMBIA

Western Vancouver Island

Southern Rocky Mountain Trench

North Cascades

Northern Rockies

Selkirk-Bitterroot Foothills

Coast Range

Puget Lowlands

WASHINGTON

Columbia Plateau

Willamette Valley

Cascades

Blue Mountains

Snake River Plain

OREGON

Northern Basin and Range

Eastern Cascade Slope and Foothills

Klamath Mountains

CALIFORNIA

Sierra Nevada

Southern and Central California Chaparral and Oak Woodlands

Central California Valley

largest trees grow in this maritime climate. Forests cover a majority of the ecoregion. Low to mid elevations are a mix of western hemlock, western redcedar, and Pacific silver fir in wetter areas, with drier forests a mix of western hemlock and Douglas-fir. The forest composition changes above 3000 feet to mountain hemlock and Pacific silver fir with some Alaska yellow-cedar. Subalpine fir is dominant at higher elevations just below treeline. Major wetland types are bogs, fens, and swamps.

Puget Lowlands. Much of this ecoregion lies in the rain shadow of the Olympic Mountains and Vancouver Island, and rainfall varies accordingly. It includes the many islands, peninsulas, and bays around Puget Sound and the Strait of Georgia as well as glacial outwash plains and river floodplains. The climate is mild year-round due to the maritime influence. A majority of the ecoregion was once occupied by forests dominated by Douglas-fir. The region is now predominantly urbanized or agricultural, and many non-native species can be found here. Western hemlock is a significant component of undisturbed forests (hemlock seedlings thrive in shade), and western redcedar and Sitka spruce are often found along streams and in wet areas. Common tree species in forested areas near the Puget Sound shoreline are madrone and shore pine. Prairie systems dominated by herbaceous species, once common, are now relatively rare, as are the associated Garry oak woodlands. Included here are the Eastern Vancouver Island, Georgia-Puget Basin, and Lower

COAST RANGE Sitka spruce (*Picea sitchensis*), enveloped in coastal fog at Patrick's Point State Park, California.

PACIFIC RANGES Subalpine firs (*Abies lasiocarpa*) and mountain hemlocks (*Tsuga mertensiana*) frame Black Tusk in Garibaldi Provincial Park, British Columbia.

PUGET LOWLANDS Second-growth Douglas-firs (*Pseudotsuga menziesii*), western redcedars (*Thuja plicata*), and red alders (*Alnus rubra*) surround Lost Lake in the Chuckanut Mountains a few miles south of Bellingham, Washington.

Mainland ecoregions, which experience the highest level of annual sunshine and mildest average annual temperature in British Columbia.

Willamette Valley. Situated between the Coast Range and the Cascades, the Willamette Valley is a fairly level alluvial plain with scattered basalt hills. It has mild, wet winters, and warm, dry summers. Historically the area was home to rolling prairies, mixed deciduous/coniferous forests, and extensive wetlands. Native Americans frequently set fires throughout the valley to maintain a mosaic of grasslands, oak savannas, wet meadows, and other habitats. Forests were concentrated on the edges of the ecoregion, with Douglas-fir, grand fir, and western redcedar the major tree species. Like the Puget Lowlands, much of the Willamette Valley has been converted to agri-

culture and urban environments. Only fragments of the original vegetation remain.

Klamath Mountains. In southern Oregon and northern California the Coast Range transitions into the physically and biologically diverse Klamath Mountains, a predominantly east–west range in a region oriented north–south. The Klamaths, which include the Siskiyous, are highly dissected and folded with a mix of igneous, sedimentary, and some metamorphic rock. This ecoregion is considerably drier than the adjacent Coast Range and experiences a lengthy summer drought. It is a transition zone with a mix of northern California and Pacific Northwest conifers and a high number of endemic species. The Klamaths have the largest number of cone-bearing tree species of any like-sized area in the world. The Cascade-Siskiyou National Monument,

WILLAMETTE VALLEY Garry oaks (*Quercus garryana*) covered in lichens form a dense stand in the Willamette Valley, Oregon.

KLAMATH MOUNTAINS In early May the northern California hills explode with color. This roadside slope at the corner of Poker Bar Road and Highway 299 near Lewiston has manzanitas, western redbud (*Cercis occidentalis*), buckbrush (*Ceanothus cuneatus*), and ponderosa pine (*Pinus ponderosa*).

set aside for its biological diversity, is along the Oregon-California border at the eastern edge of the Klamath Mountains.

North Cascades. This is the most rugged and least disturbed ecoregion in the Northwest south of British Columbia. High mountains contrast with deep valleys, and the underlying rocks are more sedimentary and metamorphic than those in the adjacent Cascades ecoregion to the south. With a wide range of elevation zones from lowland forests to high alpine summits, the North Cascades have an equally wide range of climate zones, from a humid, mild, and cloudy marine-influenced climate in the west to a continental climate in the east, with greater swings in temperature and humidity, and fewer clouds. Forests domi-nated by Douglas-fir with varying amounts of western hemlock and western redcedar carpet lower elevations. Stands which have long been undisturbed will usually be dominated by western hemlock. Pacific silver fir and mountain hemlock often predominate at middle and high elevations, with subalpine fir a significant presence in the subalpine. Above timberline, alpine heaths, meadows, and fell fields are interspersed with rock, ice, and snow. Special habitats include riparian areas, wetlands, and avalanche chutes dominated by vine maple and Sitka alder. The North Cascades are home to the largest number of glaciers in the conterminous United States, which have left deep valleys in their wake as they retreated from their maximum extent some 10,000 years ago. There is extensive subalpine and

NORTH CASCADES Mountain hemlocks (*Tsuga mertensiana*) and subalpine firs (*Abies lasiocarpa*) frame Picture Lake and Mount Shuksan. Cascade blueberries (*Vaccinium deliciosum*) and sedges cover the ground between the trees. Mount Shuksan is in North Cascades National Park; Picture Lake is at Heather Meadows in the Mount Baker–Snoqualmie National Forest east of Bellingham, Washington.

alpine habitat beginning at about 4000 feet elevation. North Cascades National Park and the mountainous portion of Olympic National Park are both in this ecoregion. In British Columbia the Cascade and Okanagan ranges, including Manning Provincial Park, share most characteristics of the North Cascades.

Cascades. Running from approximately Snoqualmie Pass south to northern California, the Cascades are predominantly volcanic in origin and are home to numerous volcanoes today, both active and dormant. As in the North Cascades, mountains here have experienced significant alpine glaciation, but alpine and subalpine habitats are less extensive, especially in the southern part of the ecoregion, where a high-elevation montane forest is more common. The climate is moist and temperate, supporting an exten-

sive and productive fir and hemlock forest. The east slopes are characterized by a high plateau, while the west slopes have steep ridges and deep river valleys. Mount Rainier and Crater Lake National Parks are located in the Cascades ecoregion, as is the Mount St. Helens National Volcanic Monument.

Interior Transition Ranges. This mountainous region lies on the east side of the Pacific Ranges as they slope down toward the Thompson-Okanagan Plateau. Rainfall is higher in the north and west, with the southern and eastern portions of the region experiencing more of a rain shadow effect. Subalpine forests at higher elevations are predominantly Engelmann spruce, subalpine fir, and lodgepole pine. Downslope to the east is a montane forest with white spruce, quaking aspen, lodgepole pine, and Douglas-fir. At the lowest elevations is

CASCADES Mount Rainier from Paradise, framed by subalpine firs (*Abies lasiocarpa*) and a wildflower meadow. Mount Rainier National Park, Washington.

an open mix of scattered ponderosa pines, bunchgrasses, and sagebrush grasslands. The Fraser and lower Thompson River valleys have significant amounts of agriculture.

Eastern Cascade Slopes and Foothills. The rain shadow of the Cascades is a dominant influence on the Eastern Cascade Slopes and Foothills. Like the Interior Transition Ranges to the north, this ecoregion experiences greater temperature extremes and receives less precipitation than the mountainous regions to the west. Coniferous forest communities dominate this region. At higher elevations, moist areas typically host subalpine fir, mountain hemlock, or Pacific silver fir; drier areas may have lodgepole pine, Douglas-fir, western larch, or grand fir as dominant trees. Mid- to low-elevation areas usually are a combination of Douglas-fir, ponderosa pine, and western larch. Garry oak woodlands appear in the southern half of the ecoregion at lower elevations. These forests are highly susceptible to wildfire, historically the dominant natural form of disturbance. High elevation and moist areas typically had infrequent fire events of high intensity and severity, resulting in high rates of tree mortality; mid- to low-elevation areas had more frequent fires of lower intensity and severity due to a combination of factors, including plant community structures that limited fire spread, plant adaptations that increased fire resistance and resilience, and low fuel buildup due to the relatively frequent burns. Shrub-steppe communities appear on some south-facing slopes and ridgetops, usually dominated by either bitterbrush or big sagebrush. Special habitats include wetlands such as seeps and wet meadows, alpine communities, subalpine parklands, grasslands, and serpentine outcrops. In southern Oregon this ecoregion includes the Klamath Basin and the mountains and high plateaus that surround it.

Sierra Nevada. This region of rugged mountains and deep valleys has the greatest biological diversity in California, with a large number of endemic species. Much of the range is built of granite and has been heavily glaciated, in contrast to the mostly sedimentary Klamath range to the west and the Cascades to the north. Ponderosa pine on the west side and lodgepole pine on the east side dominate lower elevations, with fir and spruce found higher on the mountains below the alpine zone. The great majority

EASTERN CASCADE SLOPES AND FOOTHILLS White fir (*Abies concolor*) forms an open forest on the slopes at the far eastern edge of the Eastern Cascade Slopes and Foothills ecoregion in the Warner Mountains east of Alturas, California.

of the Sierra Nevada lies south of the range of this book. Two other California ecoregions—Southern and Central California Chaparral and Oak Woodlands, and Central California Valley—just touch our area between the Klamath and Sierra Nevada mountains.

Thompson-Okanagan Plateau. One of the driest and warmest ecoregions in Canada, this rain shadow area ranges from open ponderosa pine forest, grassland, and sagebrush in the river valleys to moist subalpine forests of Engelmann spruce, subalpine fir, and lodgepole pine. Precipitation generally rises with elevation, falling as snow in the winter and short thunderstorms in the summer. Temperatures are more extreme in this continental region, with both colder winters and warmer summers than the more marine-influenced areas to the west. The Okanagan and Thompson rivers have cut into the gently rolling glacial deposits that cover much of this region.

Columbia Plateau. This vast and relatively flat ecoregion dominates central and eastern Washington and extends into northern Oregon and the Okanagan Highland in British Columbia. The Columbia Plateau

SIERRA NEVADA Mountain whitethorn (*Ceanothus cordulatus*), green manzanita (*Arctostaphylos patula*), incense cedar (*Calocedrus decurrens*), and western white pine (*Pinus monticola*) along Highway 36 in the Sierra Foothills east of Chester, California.

COLUMBIA PLATEAU Few trees grow on the arid Columbia Plateau. Instead, small shrubs like showy phlox (*Phlox speciosa*) grow among the grasses and wildflowers. Most bloom in the spring, when the soil is still moist and the air has begun to warm, then nearly disappear in the hot, dry summer. This view is on Ginkgo Petrified Forest State Park at Vantage, Washington.

is the result of millennia of basalt flows, which produced the nearly 2-mile-thick layer of basalt that underlays it. Soils are mainly derived from wind-deposited material (loess). During the Pleistocene, a series of tremendous floods caused by periodic release of glacial meltwater from Lake Missoula scoured much of the Columbia Plateau, removing soils and rock while creating coulees, dry falls, mesas, and buttes. These features are collectively called the Channeled Scablands. The driest part of the Northwest, the Columbia Plateau receives as little as 6 inches of precipitation annually. Vegetation is predominantly sagebrush and bunchgrasses, highlighted most springs by immense displays of wildflowers. Extensive grazing, the introduction of cheatgrass, and agricultural use through irrigation and dry land wheat farming have altered significant areas of this ecoregion. A variety of seasonal wetlands dot the Columbia Plateau, some of which are dry for a number of years until enough moisture occurs for plant growth and development. Other special habitats in the Columbia Plateau include perennial wetlands and lakes, sand dunes, talus slopes, grasslands, and pockets of ponderosa pine or Douglas-fir forest. The least disturbed area is the buffer zone around the Hanford Nuclear Reservation, as public access is restricted.

Blue Mountains. Cutting a wide swath across central and northeastern Oregon, the Blues are a complex of mountains that are generally lower and more open than either the Cascades or the Northern Rockies. Except

BLUE MOUNTAINS The Grand Ronde River cuts a deep channel through the Wallowa Mountains in the northeast corner of the Blue Mountain complex. Ponderosa pines (*Pinus ponderosa*) are the dominant conifer here, with alders and willows just beginning to leaf out near the river. Wallowa-Whitman National Forest, Oregon.

for the higher peaks in the Wallowa and Elkhorn ranges, the Blue Mountains are volcanic in origin. Within the Blue Mountain ecoregion are many subregions reflecting a diversity of habitats from the broad valleys of the Grand Ronde, Wallowa, and Baker rivers to the high peaks of the Wallowas. This ecoregion also includes the John Day area, with low precipitation and wide temperature swings both daily and annually. The wettest part of the region receives precipitation coming up the Columbia River Gorge and lies east and south of Pendleton, Oregon, and Walla Walla, Washington. Grasslands and shrubfields cover a significant percentage of the landscape. Mountain and big sagebrush often dominate the shrub-steppe communities, especially in overgrazed areas. These plant communities are often interspersed with open forest stands dominated by ponderosa pine or Douglas-fir. Grand fir is a significant component of many of these forests. Higher elevations have conifer forests with subalpine fir and Engelmann spruce as the main tree species.

Northern Basin and Range. A large portion of southeastern Oregon, northern Nevada, and far northeastern California are within the Northern Basin and Range ecoregion. This arid land contains tablelands, scattered mountains, intermontane basins, and dissected lava plains. Sagebrush-steppe vegetation is common in the areas without mountains but is impacted by grazing in many places. The semiarid uplands and partially forested Steens Mountain are included in this region, as are the extensive wetlands of the Malheur and Warner lakes areas.

Snake River Plain. This ecoregion, bordering the upper Snake River primarily in Idaho,

touches eastern Oregon. It is a dry intermontane basin and range area that is considerably lower and more gently sloping than surrounding ecoregions. The natural vegetation is primarily sagebrush and bunchgrasses, but much of the region has been altered by grazing and irrigated agriculture.

Selkirk-Bitterroot Foothills. This is a transition zone between the relatively dry areas to the west and the higher and wetter Columbia Mountains and Canadian Rockies to the east. Vegetation of this ecoregion is similar to the Northern Rockies across the border to the south.

Northern Rockies. Despite being hundreds of miles inland, the Northern Rockies have

NORTHERN BASIN AND RANGE Wide-open country with broad valleys alternating with mountain ridges characterize the Northern Basin and Range ecoregion. Here, timberline sagebrush (*Artemisia rothrockii*), a California endemic, dominates the landscape near Litchfield.

SNAKE RIVER PLAIN Bartonberry (*Rubus bartonianus*) is endemic to the Snake River canyon on the Oregon-Idaho border. Here, at the mouth of Sawpit Creek in Hell's Canyon, it is growing along a small stream with blue elderberries (*Sambucus nigra* ssp. *cerulea*).

NORTHERN ROCKIES White spruce (*Picea glauca*) ring a high-elevation marsh at Vermilion Lakes in Banff National Park, Alberta. Mount Rundle is the reflected mountain in the distance. This rugged environment is on the far eastern edge of the territory covered by this book.

a climate and vegetation that are marine-influenced. Like the Cascades, Douglas-fir, subalpine fir, Engelmann spruce, western redcedar, western hemlock, and grand fir grow here, as does ponderosa pine. The range is neither as high nor as snow-covered as the Canadian Rockies to the north and east, although in the highest elevations, alpine and glacial lakes abound. Lewis and Clark traversed this rugged range over 200 years ago as they crossed from the Missouri River to the Columbia. Unlike the other ecoregions visited by Lewis and Clark, the Northern Rockies is still home to all the species present during their expedition, even though there has been substantial logging, mining, and development in the intervening centuries.

Habitats and Local Environments

Ecoregions describe the conditions for numerous plant communities in broad terms. A visitor can expect to find many of the same plants growing in similar conditions throughout each ecoregion. But as useful as ecoregions are for picturing the overall ecology of large areas, more localized sets of conditions—habitats and even microhabitats—largely determine the actual mix of species to be found.

All plants need nutrients, water, and light to grow and bloom. But they vary greatly as to how much of these essential factors they need, and how they obtain and store them. This variation, combined with climate and plant migration over time, leads to formation of plant communities, plants that grow together and interact with each other. Within reason, the same habitats in different ecoregions will house species that have similar characteristics.

Different species have a range of require-ments for soil, which anchors plants in place as well as providing a nutrient source. Some need deep, rich soil, while others eke out an existence in thin, rocky habitats. For example, big sagebrush requires deeper soils to grow and thrive, while rigid sage prefers thin, rocky soils. Soils differ in pH, and some soils have relatively high salt levels, which selects for plants that can tolerate the amount of salt present. Soils derived from serpentine substrates are infertile and contain levels of magnesium and heavy metals many plants cannot tolerate. Those that can tolerate or thrive in serpentine soils enjoy an advantage in these areas.

Annual precipitation greatly influences whether an area supports giant trees or modest shrubs. Some species, like Douglas-fir, will grow in areas with widely differing rainfall but attain much greater size when they receive 40 or more inches of rain compared to 20. Cottonwoods and many willows grow along watercourses where their roots can find sufficient moisture, even in areas that receive only a small amount of rain. Conversely, shrubs like sagebrush and rabbitbrush are adapted to dry conditions and would be crowded out by more moisture-loving species with greater precipitation levels. These dryland plants survive by having a deep taproot and by doing some of their growth during the winter, when most rainfall occurs. Even in areas with more annual precipitation, conifers and broadleaf evergreens take advantage of winter moisture by photosynthesizing during mild periods in the colder months. In mountainous areas where almost all precipitation falls as snow, growth is limited to the short period between one winter's snowmelt and the next winter's accumulation.

As for the essential factor of light, mature

trees grow tall and spread their branches to capture as much of it as possible. Down below, very little may grow in the deep shade on the forest floor. Some trees, like western hemlock, have seedlings that are quite shade-tolerant. They grow slowly, waiting for a disturbance to open a hole in the canopy and let in more light. Then they begin growing much more quickly, reaching for the sky themselves. Understory species like vine maple, salal, and huckleberries grow much more vigorously and produce more fruit at forest edges, along trails, and along roads, where gaps in the canopy allow more light to reach the ground. East of the mountains in the shrub-steppe where plants get plenty of sunshine, water and summer heat are the limiting factors, and some plants lose their leaves and go dormant during the hot, dry season.

Each plant entry in this field guide includes notes on what growing conditions the tree or shrub prefers and the most likely places to find it.

Coastal. The coastal environment encompasses several smaller and more specific habitats, including sandy beaches and dunes, salt marshes, and rocky shores. The dense coastal forest often grows right down to kiss the high tide line. Coastal habitats are found both on the outer Pacific Ocean coast and along the hundreds of miles of Puget Sound, Hood Canal, Strait of Juan de Fuca, and Strait of Georgia shoreline.

Coastal habitats occupy a narrow strip where the land meets salt water. Plants that grow here may have to develop tolerance to salt, drifting sand, or thin and rocky soils. Both sandy beaches and rocky shores support very little terrestrial plant life due to the constant and vigorous action of the tides. Just shoreward, out of reach of all but the largest waves, sand gives way to soil, and one

COASTAL Sitka spruce (*Picea sitchensis*) frame a sheltered bay at Sand Point on the Pacific Coast in Olympic National Park, Washington.

begins to find wildflowers and subshrubs like gumweed. Huckleberries, elderberries, coast willow, and salal grow right down to the edge of the beach, forming a dense understory beneath the forest canopy. Rocky headlands and sea stacks are often home to nearly impenetrable shrub communities.

Sand dunes are found along the coast between northern Washington and southern Oregon but are most common between Coos Bay and Florence. The active dune area usually supports few plants, but more stable dune areas are home to a variety of native species, including Pacific crabapple and beach knotweed. Salt marshes, found along inland shores with little surf, are productive habitats for wildflowers, but you'll find few shrubs or trees.

West-side forest. The dense forests on the west slopes of the Coast Range, Cascades, and Northern Rockies are a mosaic of mostly coniferous trees with numerous streams and rivers. Dominant tree species, depending on moisture and elevation, include Sitka spruce, coast redwood, western hemlock, western redcedar, Douglas-fir, and mountain hemlock. Where undisturbed at lower elevations, trees often grow to massive sizes. Unfortunately, most of this old growth has been cut for timber, and much of the forest is now second- or third-growth.

Mosses, ferns, and lichens abound in the understory, as do huckleberries, oceanspray, and devil's club. Forest edges and openings often have large stands of thimbleberries, and rocky outcrops may be dotted with

WEST-SIDE FOREST Giant old-growth Douglas-firs (*Pseudotsuga menziesii*) and western hemlocks (*Tsuga heterophylla*) once dominated the forest landscape at lower elevations west of the Cascades. Stands like this one, near the Nooksack River in the Mount Baker–Snoqualmie National Forest east of Bellingham, can still be found.

serviceberries or stunted trees. Elevation makes a big difference in the forest plant communities, as do local variations in soils and precipitation. Even within this generally moist habitat, you'll find both wet and dry pockets. Boggy depressions are fairly common at all elevations.

East-side forest. Much drier and more open than the west-side forest, the east-side forest is dominated by ponderosa and lodgepole pines, although you'll also find Douglas-fir and grand fir here. Grasses are more common in the understory than ferns and mosses. Mature east-side trees never reach the immense size of the largest west-side trees, although ponderosa pines on a good site can be 130 feet tall and over 3 feet in diameter. The east-side forest encompasses all the forested regions east of the Cascades except for the Northern Rockies in northeast Washington and portions of the Blue and Wallowa mountains where increased precipitation allows west-slope species to grow.

The open understory supports a wide range of species, although usually not in large quantities at any one site. Roses, snowberries, bitterbrush, currants, honeysuckles, sagebrush, and many other shrubs find a home under the pines. Wet and boggy areas are less frequent than on the west side. Look for bog cranberry, hardhack, black twinberry, cottonwood, aspen, and other moisture-loving plants near bogs, streams, and lakeshores. Microhabitats and variations in soils affect vegetation in the

EAST-SIDE FOREST Quaking aspens (*Populus tremuloides*) and willows begin to turn golden in early autumn in the Fremont National Forest above Lakeview, Oregon. The conifers are ponderosa pines (*Pinus ponderosa*), characteristic of forests east of the Cascade crest.

east-side forests as much as they do elsewhere in the Northwest. Latitude and elevation also play a role. Similar species grow at higher elevations in northern California than in southern British Columbia.

Subalpine. A short growing season and ample precipitation, mostly in the form of winter snow, characterize this habitat found at the upper limits of tree growth. The forest here is dominated by subalpine fir, Engelmann spruce, and mountain hemlock, with deciduous larches also found near and east of the Cascade crest. Craggy whitebark pines are sometimes found on drier or harsher sites. Open meadows, both wet and dry, are interspersed with rocky outcrops and pockets of forest. The subalpine is a transition zone between the forests at lower elevations and the treeless alpine zone above. Hurricane Ridge in the Olympics, Heather Meadows in the North Cascades, Paradise and Sunrise at Mount Rainier, and the rim drive at Crater Lake are all easily accessible subalpine areas. The shrub layer includes mountain ashes, heathers, and huckleberries. Wildflowers bloom right next to the melting snow during the short summer season, as does spreading phlox, a subshrub.

Alpine. Some of the harshest growing conditions in the Northwest are found in the true alpine zone, which rises above timberline on the mountain crests. Snow lingers deep and late, and soils are usually thin and rocky. Wind howls across the ridges, and flowering

SUBALPINE Mount Shuksan, mountain hemlocks, (*Tsuga mertensiana*), and subalpine firs (*Abies lasiocarpa*) are reflected in Picture Lake at Heather Meadows in the Mount Baker–Snoqualmie National Forest east of Bellingham. This area can see up to 100 feet of snowfall each winter.

plants often seek protection in the micro-habitats behind larger rocks or krummholz trees. Most plants are perennial and take a cushion form so the wind flows over them. Look for heathers, ground-hugging dwarf willows, and dwarfed conifers among the rocks of the alpine zone.

Shrub-steppe. Spanning vast tracts of the Columbia Basin in central Washington and the high plains of central and south-eastern Oregon, the shrub-steppe can be underwhelming at first glance. Trees are practically nonexistent in this arid region. Big sagebrush, bitterbrush, and rabbit-brush dominate the shrub layer, cover-ing 10–60% of the ground. Undisturbed shrub-steppe has very little bare ground; the space between plants is occupied by crypto-gamic crust, a protective coating of mosses, lichens, algae, and bacteria, and bunch-grasses and forbs are common. With dis-turbance, particularly grazing, sagebrush coverage increases, and the highly flamma-ble and invasive annual cheatgrass often replaces native perennial bunchgrasses. As with other Northwest habitats, differ-ences in moisture, soils, and exposure cre-ate microhabitats that favor specific plants. Most shrub-steppe wildflowers bloom in the spring; penstemons follow later, and the shrubs (rabbitbrush, sagebrush, and others) often bloom in summer and fall.

Chaparral. This plant community just enters the area covered by this guide, although it is

ALPINE In alpine areas like this one above Maple Pass in the Okanogan National Forest in Washington, trees give way to a barren, rocky landscape with a sparse covering of low-growing shrubs like pink mountain-heather (*Phyllodoce empetriformis*) and white heather (*Cassiope mertensiana*). Black Peak is in the distance above Wing Lake.

SHRUB-STEPPE Spiny hopsage (*Grayia spinosa*) in a typical Columbia Plateau shrub-steppe habitat on The Nature Conservancy's Moses Coulee Preserve in Washington. Big sagebrush (*Artemisia tridentata*) is the dominant shrub in the valley at the base of the basalt cliff.

a dominant one farther south in California. Chaparral is characterized by dense shrub thickets, a mix of evergreen and drought-deciduous species. Herbaceous plants are few, soils are mostly shallow, and the climate is mild in winter and hot and dry during the summer. Most chaparral shrubs photosynthesize through the winter and often go dormant during the summer to minimize water loss. Drought-deciduous species drop their leaves during the dry season; evergreen species conserve water by having thick leaves with a waxy protective coating. Many chaparral plants have a dual root system, with shallow roots to capture rainwater, and deep taproots to survive the summer drought. Fire is a frequent natural disturbance, due in part to the dense structure of the plant communities and the resins in plant tissues. Most chaparral species are adapted to recover after fire, either by resprouting from the base or through seeds designed to germinate post-fire. Chamise, scrub oak, birchleaf mountain mahogany, California flannelbush, toyon, ceanothus, and the manzanitas are common chaparral plants.

Rocky sites. Some of the more interesting trees and shrubs grow on rocky hilltops in thin soils called lithosols, and they tend to be among the earliest bloomers. Such plants as narrowleaf goldenweed are able to push their roots down into the cracks in the rocks, where they can stay cool and pockets of moisture remain, while above ground everything looks completely dry. In addition to lithosol ridges, rocky sites can include talus slopes and basalt cliffs. Threetip sagebrush, coyote mints, and rockmats make their home in these tough conditions.

Serpentine. Serpentine-derived soils are relatively infertile, with high concentrations of magnesium and nickel and low amounts of calcium and nitrogen. Serpentine is most common regionally in the Klamath-Siskiyou Range in northwestern California and southwestern Oregon, and in central Washington's Wenatchee Mountains and the Twin Sisters, near Mount Baker. A high number of endemic plants grow on serpentine. Where serpentine is present, plant cover is often sparse, and bare soil or rock is generally exposed. Soil develops slowly. The plants that tolerate these tough conditions tend to have root systems that seek out moisture in the cracks and crevices of the rock. Trees and shrubs grow more slowly on serpentine, and their ultimate size is smaller in many cases than the same species growing on granitic or other more nutrient-rich soils. Not all serpentine habitats are dry. Wet serpentine can take the form of a fen, generally a sloping meadow with water slowly flowing through it, or seeps that drip down the face of rock cliffs.

Vernal-wet. Winter rains accumulate in shallow pools where relatively thin soils lie directly over a layer of impervious rock, usually basalt. Successive rings of flowers bloom around the edges as the pools dry up in spring and early summer. Examples of this vernal-wet habitat may be found throughout the Columbia Plateau and on top of Table Rocks in the Rogue River valley of southern Oregon. Sometimes the vernal (spring) pools will be interspersed with hummocks that have entirely different vegetation. Occasionally you'll find a cottonwood in the middle of a vernal pool. Defined a bit more broadly, vernal-wet habitats can be any place that is wet early in the season and dry by late spring or early summer. Even drying roadside ditches can be considered vernal-wet.

Bog/fen/wetland. Year-round water creates several habitats, depending on how much water is flowing through. These range from bogs, with almost no water flow, to fens with running water. Bogs are generally acidic and low in essential nutrients. They often support a thick layer of sphagnum mosses, with flowering plants, small shrubs, and trees growing on slightly higher hummocks and around the edges. Many coastal bogs that originally supported native cranberries have been converted to commercial cranberry production. Other bog plants are Labrador tea, bog rosemary (barely coming south of the Canadian border), and western swamp laurel.

Fens differ from bogs in that they always have water flowing through them, may be found on hillsides, and may be either acidic or basic. Southwestern Oregon and northwestern California are home to particularly interesting and accessible fens, just off Highway 101 north of Florence, Oregon, and off Highway 199 in Del Norte County, California. At the edge of these fens, with slightly drier conditions, look for western azaleas, Jeffrey pines, and incense cedars. Fens are very sensitive environments that should be observed only from the solid ground around their edges.

SERPENTINE Serpentine habitats are characterized by red-orange soil and sparse vegetation. Here leather oaks (*Quercus durata*) and manzanitas grow on a serpentine slope in the Shasta-Trinity National Forest near Hayfork, California, with Jeffrey and gray pines, *Pinus jeffreyi* and *P. sabiniana*.

Lake-pond. The shallow edges of freshwater lakes and ponds are home to a great many aquatic species that are not covered in this book. Many are rushes and sedges; others grow primarily submerged and are not particularly showy. However like other edge habitats, lakes and ponds have a variety of shrubs and trees that take advantage of the light present at the water's edge.

Streambanks. Moist, cool soils adjacent to streams large and small, often in the shade of the forest canopy but sometimes out in full sun, provide a productive habitat for many plants with a long growing season or a late bloom period. Plants that grow here like plenty of water, but don't want their roots as wet as those that thrive in the water itself.

While some of these streambanks may technically be defined as wetlands, you're not as likely to get your feet soggy, at least after the spring rains have passed. Streambanks are found at all elevations from the coast to alpine areas. Look for currants and gooseberries, black cottonwood, aspens, salmonberry, willows, and vine maples among many other plants along streams.

Meadows. Any area that is devoid of significant tree or shrub cover can be considered a meadow. What grows within a meadow is very dependent upon the elevation, soils, and precipitation. We've used the term *meadow* to differentiate plants that grow out in the open from those that live under the forest canopy. Shrubs and trees invade

A wet meadow in Washington's Methow Valley, with pearhip roses (*Rosa woodsii* var. *ultramontana*) in the foreground.

drier meadows, and often thrive at the meadow-forest ecotone (transitional area), where light levels are higher than in the forest proper.

Disturbed. Roadsides, vacant lots, cropland, grazing areas, gardens, and clearcuts are all examples of disturbed sites. Many of the plants growing in these areas are commonly thought of as weeds, and a large proportion are originally from Europe or Asia. Some are particularly noxious and invasive, such as Scotch broom, Russian olive, and white willow.

Putting It Together

Pacific Northwest plant habitats are affected by large factors such as the weather coming off the Pacific Ocean and the rise of the major mountain ranges. They're also impacted by soil and the rocks from which it is derived. Elevation, light exposure, available moisture, and relationships with surrounding plants also play a role in defining habitat. Within similar environments you can expect to find the same or similar species, whether you're looking across broad ecoregions or among localized microhabitats.

DISTURBED Russian olive (*Elaeagnus angustifolia*) is a common sight in disturbed areas, particularly near streams, in the Columbia Plateau. This specimen is along the Old Vantage Highway, Kittitas County, Washington.

EXPLORING FOR TREES AND SHRUBS

Trees and shrubs are all around us—along city sidewalks, beside the highway, and in more pristine environments from coastal bluffs to subalpine meadows. In this book, we've included almost all the woody plants you'll encounter, from towering coast redwoods down to diminutive subshrubs no more than a few inches tall. Also included are a few nonwoody species commonly mistaken for shrubs or subshrubs. From early spring until autumn you're likely to find something in bloom almost anywhere you look in the Pacific Northwest. Look for plants in fruit as well as in bloom, and enjoy our many conifers any time of the year.

Searching for plants you've never seen before can be a good excuse to take a trip to the mountains, beach, or sagebrush plains. So can going to visit old friends in the plant community. Some people return to a few nearby haunts throughout the seasons to watch each plant bloom and ripen its fruit.

Although trees and shrubs are found almost everywhere, some locations have a higher concentration of species. It's not our goal to lead you to specific sites, a subject that has filled several books already. Rather, we'll give you some hints about the kinds of places that will be most productive to look. The previous chapter goes into detail about plant environments.

Access, Fees, and Permits

Plants have no need to respect property boundaries. They grow wherever the conditions are right, regardless of whether their roots are sunk into public or private land. Many landowners are justifiably concerned about strangers traipsing across their property even if it's just to look at what's growing there. Ask permission before going onto private land. Remember to leave gates the way you found them and to walk softly.

Public lands are generally open to exploration, but entrance or parking fees may be required. These charges can change from year to year and are not consistent from one state or province to another. Before venturing out, it's worth checking with the land management agency to find out whether you'll be charged. The fees help maintain the parking areas and may also help with trail construction.

Private preserves, such as those owned by The Nature Conservancy or local conservation groups, also vary in their access restrictions. Usually there is no fee, but donations are gratefully accepted.

Learning About Trees and Shrubs

We're glad you chose to take this book with you on your journey. It's packed with information about most of the trees and shrubs you're likely to encounter in the Northwest. We couldn't include everything you might want to learn about each species, however, so you may want to use some additional resources.

Technical books. Serious botanists rely on technical keys to positively identify the plants they find. These books can be intimidating to the first-time user but go into much greater detail than is possible in a book like this one. Technical floras are thick and heavy and may call for you to use a hand lens, take flowers apart, or examine the hairs on a leaf to see distinguishing characteristics. You'll find yourself turning to the glossary frequently, and even then being baffled on occasion. Visit your library or local herbarium to look up plants in these books before you invest in a copy.

At the time this book was written, there were three major floras for the region, with a new volume for Oregon in the works to replace *A Manual of the Higher Plants of Oregon* by Morton E. Peck. In British Columbia, consult *Illustrated Flora of British Columbia* by George Douglas et al., an eight-volume set. Washington and Oregon as far south as Roseburg are covered in *Flora of the Pacific Northwest* by Hitchcock and Cronquist. Southern Oregon shares many plants with northern California, for which you need the *Jepson Manual* (Baldwin et al. 2012). See the bibliography for full publication information.

Like-minded explorers. It's more fun to go looking for plants with people who share your interest. There are native plant societies in each state and province. Local chapters sponsor field trips to prime locations throughout the season and welcome non-members who want to learn more about their flora. Sometimes you'll find announcements of these field trips in your newspaper. Each state or provincial group also has a website with links to local chapters and field trips. Use "native plant society" and your state or province name in your favorite online search engine to find them.

Some other groups that lead plant hikes and field trips include parks and recreation departments, Sierra Club, and Audubon

Native Plant Society of Oregon members on a field trip to explore Chenowith Table near The Dalles.

Society groups. Check your newspaper or the organization's newsletter or website for information.

Websites. Many websites have a wealth of information about native plants. Use your favorite search engine and the scientific name of the plant you want to learn more about as the search term. As with all Internet searches, there will be some irrelevant results, and you need to evaluate the source of the page before deciding how reliable it is likely to be. Now that smartphones can connect to the Internet anywhere there's a cell signal, you may be able to look up more information about a plant while it's still in front of you.

Grow by the Inch, Die by the Foot

Sometimes we get so carried away with the excitement of finding new and interesting plants that we forget to pay attention to the impact we're making on their environment. You've heard the adage, "Take nothing but pictures and leave nothing but footprints." Often even our lightest footprints do significant damage. Park rangers like to remind us that plants "grow by the inch and die by the foot." Our footsteps easily break delicate woody stems that take years to grow back, particularly in subalpine and alpine environments with short growing seasons. They compact the soil, reducing the air and water reaching roots, and they form social paths that other hikers follow. Even the roots of giant old-growth Douglas-firs can be impacted by too much foot traffic.

We can minimize our impact by following Leave No Trace principles. They're designed to protect wild lands, but LNT principles apply equally to heavily traveled areas: 1) plan ahead and prepare, 2) travel and camp on durable surfaces, 3) dispose of waste properly (pack it in, pack it out), 4) leave what you find, 5) minimize campfire impacts, 6) respect wildlife, and 7) be considerate of other visitors. For more information, visit lnt.org.

Perhaps most important for the plant explorer is to travel on durable surfaces. You don't want to be responsible for destroying the very plants you've come to find and enjoy. If there is an established trail, stay on it. In some cases, as in heavily visited national parks, you absolutely must stay on established trails, and rangers will remind you of the policy when they find that you have strayed. You'll often find more examples of a plant that's a bit too far off the trail to examine just by hiking a little farther up the trail.

"Don't hike here" sign from a revegetation project in North Cascades National Park.

In areas where there are no trails, you don't want to create a "user trail" that will encourage others to follow in your footsteps. Think about where you're walking and consider the consequences of your actions. Perhaps you can step from rock to rock. If not, grasses and sedges handle footsteps better than woody plants like heathers and huckleberries. When hiking with a group, practice "meadow walking." That means spreading out and hiking side by side rather than following the leader in a single-file line.

When you come to an interesting plant that you want to study, be aware of what you're trampling as you move around your subject. Be careful where you set your pack down. And when it's time for lunch, choose a rock, log, or grassy area to sit down.

With rare exceptions, you don't need to pick a flower or leaf to identify the species. Leave the plant collecting to the professionals who have learned the techniques for preserving specimens and have received permission to collect from land managers.

Safety

Searching for trees and shrubs is generally a low-risk activity, but there are a few hazards you should be aware of.

Weather. What starts as a beautifully warm and sunny day can quickly turn cold, windy, and rainy. Dress appropriately for the conditions and be prepared for unexpected changes, especially at high elevations.

Poisonous plants. In some areas poison-oak (page 372) or poison-ivy (page 373) are thick; learn to recognize their distinctive three leaves and woody stems. Stinging nettles are another irritant to watch out for, although the effects don't last as long. And while eating fruits and other plant parts

along the trail is one of the joys of exploring, use caution whenever you consume a wild edible. Be certain of your indentification; some plants look similar, with one having edible fruit and the other not. It is a good idea to eat only a small portion, then wait 30 minutes to an hour. If there are no ill effects, it is likely safe to eat. Avoid plants along roadsides or other areas that may receive chemical treatment. The fruits we've noted as edible in the descriptions are generally safe, but some people are more sensitive than others.

Rattlesnakes. Watch where you step and where you place your hands throughout the drier parts of our region. Rattlesnakes will usually sound their distinctive warning rattle before you get too close, but you don't want to surprise or corner one. They're not particularly common and you're unlikely to see one of these generally shy reptiles, but be cautious when you're in their territory.

Ticks. Ticks are common in parts of our region, especially in tall grasses and weeds. They usually take several hours to attach themselves, so you have time to do a thorough tick check when you return to your car or home.

Traffic. Many trees and shrubs grow at the side of roads. Find a safe place to pull over and park, making sure you're out of the travel lane. Walk on the left, facing traffic. Stay well out of the road when examining the plants. Even on lightly traveled forest roads, you should expect vehicles to come by while you're stopped.

Rockfall. You don't want to be either the cause or the victim of falling rock. Many areas with interesting trees and shrubs are on or near cliffs. Volcanic rock, our most common geologic formation, is often fractured and loose. Even on trails, it is easy to kick rocks down on the people hiking the switchbacks below you. If you do happen to dislodge a rock, call out "Rock!" to warn others of the potential hazard.

Rising tide. There aren't a lot of trees or shrubs right on the beach, but several species do grow just above the high tide line or on top of coastal sea stacks. If you climb one, make sure you don't get trapped by a rising tide. Consult a tide table just as you would before exploring the tide pools that are often nearby.

Your own limits. Be realistic about how far you can hike in a day and at what elevation. Know how much elevation you can climb (and descend). As you approach or exceed your limits, you're more likely to have an accident.

Have Fun

Searching for and learning about our trees and shrubs is a lot of fun, whether you're a beginner or a certified Hitchcock-carrying plant nut. There's always a new place to go or a new plant to find. You can go out intentionally searching for plants, or you can casually enjoy and learn about them as you go backpacking, kayaking, or visiting historic sites. There are enough trees and shrubs in the Northwest to keep you busy for years if you choose to try to find them all. Explore the trails through your neighborhood or travel to an exotic corner of our region. The choice is yours. Wherever you go, whatever the season, you're likely to find something—a tree in bloom, a shrub lit up by fall color—that will stop you in your tracks.

Washington Native Plant Society members take time on a North Cascades subalpine slope to key out a plant, part of the fun when you get seriously interested in our region's flora.

PLANT FAMILIES

There are an estimated 400,000 plant species worldwide, a number in constant flux as species are discovered or rediscovered, "split or lumped," or go extinct. In order to make sense of this dizzying array of biodiversity, coming and going, botanists depend upon a centuries-old classification system of scientific names, which not only impose order but help explain evolutionary relationships among plants. Scientific names are binomials, consisting of two parts: the first is that of a closely related group, or genus (pl. genera), the second is that of a specific species in that genus. Take, for example, the scientific name for Douglas-fir, *Pseudotsuga menziesii*. The genus, as always, is capitalized and written in italic (*Pseudotsuga*), and the species epithet, as always, is written entirely in lowercase italic (*menziesii*). A scientific name is recognized worldwide, as opposed to common names, which are regional. Although the scientific name can and does change, it allows for conversation about a plant with minimal confusion.

Genera are grouped into families, the highest botanical classification level in common usage. Plants in the same family share many characteristics, and learning these characteristics can make identification of an unknown plant more manageable. For example, if you know that members of the mint family (Lamiaceae) have simple, opposite leaves, square stems, tubular flowers, and nutlet fruits, then when you see a plant with these features, you know you are looking at a mint, one like purple sage (*Salvia dorrii*).

The species within any one genus share more morphological and genetic traits than does the larger family and often become easier to recognize with time and practice. What constitutes a species is sometimes a murky concept, but in general a species is defined as a group that can freely interbreed and form fertile offspring. Species can be further divided into subspecies (ssp.) and varieties (var.), entities that have some morphological and genetic differences but are considered closely enough related to be part of the same species.

Learning the plant families and their major characteristics is one tool you can use to help identify the various plants you find. Some families are large, with many genera; others have few, or even a single genus. Each of the families treated in this field guide, beginning with the conifers (or gymnosperms) and followed by the flowering plants (or angiosperms), is described here in alphabetical order.

Conifer Families

CUPRESSACEAE—CYPRESS FAMILY. Leaves scalelike, occasionally somewhat needlelike, opposite or whorled. Male and female reproductive structures on the same plant or on separate plants. Seed cones small, woody or fleshy, cone scales opposite or in 3s. Trees and shrubs. Page 89.

EPHEDRACEAE—MORMON-TEA FAMILY. Leaves scalelike, opposite, ephemeral. Flowers unisexual, sexes usually on separate plants. Cones oval to egg-shaped, seed cones 2–4 at nodes, scales several, red and fleshy at maturity or brown and dry. Shrubs, subshrubs, and rarely herbaceous perennials. Page 420.

PINACEAE—PINE FAMILY. Leaves needle-like, borne singly, in bundles, or on short lateral branches. Male and female reproductive structures on the same plant or on separate plants. Seed cones small to large, woody, cone scales spirally arranged. Trees, occasionally shrubs. Page 58.

TAXACEAE—YEW FAMILY. Leaves linear, spreading from the branch surface in 2 opposite rows. Male and female reproductive structures on separate plants. Seeds single, covered by a fleshy to leathery covering (aril). Trees and shrubs. Page 104.

Flowering Plant Families

ADOXACEAE—ELDERBERRY FAMILY. Leaves opposite, simple or compound. Flowers bisexual, tubular or saucer- to bell-shaped, petal lobes 4–5, sepal lobes 2–5, stamens mostly 5, attached to petals. Fruit a berry or stone fruit, mostly fleshy, sometimes dry. Shrubs, trees, and herbaceous plants. Pages 301, 410.

AIZOACEAE—FIG-MARIGOLD FAMILY. Leaves generally opposite, often fleshy. Flowers bisexual, saucer- to bell-shaped, hypanthium present, sepals usually 5, often unequal and petal-like, petals 0 to many, linear, in whorls, stamens 1 to many, the outer often petal-like, ovary superior or inferior. Fruit a berry, capsule, or nut. Herbaceous annuals and perennials, shrubs and subshrubs. Page 303.

AMARANTHACEAE—AMARANTH FAMILY. Leaves alternate or opposite, simple. Flowers bisexual or unisexual, if unisexual the sexes on the same or different plants. Flowers saucer-shaped or tubular, tepals 3–5 or 0, fused at base or separate, stamens 2–5 and opposite the tepals, ovary superior. Fruit a dry, 1-seeded inflated sac. Herbaceous perennials and annuals, some shrubs and subshrubs. Page 106.

ANACARDIACEAE—SUMAC FAMILY. Leaves alternate, simple or compound, with resinous or milky sap that contains irritants. Flowers small, usually unisexual, sepals 5, fused at base, petals 5, sometimes absent, stamens 5–10 inserted in a disc, ovary superior. Fruit a stone fruit. Shrubs and trees. Pages 111, 370.

AQUIFOLIACEAE—HOLLY FAMILY. Leaves alternate, simple, often toothed or lobed. Flowers mostly unisexual, on the same or different plants. Sepals and petals mostly 4, can be 5 or 6, fused at base, stamens 4–6, ovary superior. Fruit berrylike or stone fruit. Trees and shrubs. Page 111.

ARALIACEAE—GINSENG FAMILY. Stems branched. Leaves alternate, simple or compound. Flowers small, in clusters, flower parts in 5s, sepals small, fused at base, petals separate, alternating with the stamens, ovary inferior. Fruit a berry or stone fruit. Shrubs, trees, woody vines, and herbaceous perennials. Pages 112, 419.

ARISTOLOCHIACEAE—BIRTHWORT FAMILY. Leaves alternate, simple, heart-shaped. Flowers solitary in leaf axils, sepals 3, partly fused into bowl shape, petals absent or reduced, stamens 6–12, filaments often distinct, may be fused to the style. Fruit a capsule, seeds with fleshy appendages. Herbaceous perennials, vines, shrubs, and rarely trees. Page 113.

ASTERACEAE—ASTER FAMILY. Leaves various. Flowers composite, with many small flowers crowded together giving the impression of being one. Flowers of two types: ray flowers with one of the petals long and strap-like, and disk flowers that are tubular, all petals the same size. Heads can have both ray and disk flowers, or one type. Fruit an achene. Herbaceous annuals, biennials, perennials, subshrubs, shrubs, and trees. Pages 113, 350, 374.

BERBERIDACEAE—BARBERRY FAMILY. Leaves alternate, simple or compound. Sepals and petals in several multiples of 6(4), alike or dissimilar, sometimes absent, stamens same number as petals. Fruit a small pod or berry. Shrubs, trees, and herbaceous perennials, often rhizomatous. Page 377.

BETULACEAE—BIRCH FAMILY. Leaves alternate, simple, edges toothed, deciduous. Flowers unisexual, both sexes on the same plant, mostly clustered into catkins, male catkins always drooping. Perianth lacking or tepals 3–4, stamens mostly 1–4, ovary inferior. Fruit a nut, nutlets, or samara. Trees and shrubs. Page 137.

BORAGINACEAE—BORAGE FAMILY. Leaves alternate or opposite, simple to compound. Flowers tubular or funnel-shaped, petals and sepals 5, stamens 5, attached to petals, ovary superior, 4-lobed. Fruit a nutlet. Herbaceous annuals, perennials, and shrubs. Pages 146, 304.

CACTACEAE—CACTUS FAMILY. Stems fleshy, succulent, with clusters of spines, leaves absent or ephemeral. Flowers with many sepals, petals, and stamens, hypanthium present, ovary inferior. Fruit berrylike to leathery, many-seeded. Trees, shrubs, subshrubs, and vinelike plants. Page 421.

CALYCANTHACEAE—STRAWBERRY-SHRUB FAMILY. Leaves opposite, simple. Flowers solitary, bisexual, tepals 15–30, spirally arranged, outer bractlike, inner petal-like, stamens many, filaments shorter than anthers, spirally arranged, outer fertile, inner sterile. Fruit, many achenes enclosed in leathery capsule-like structure. Shrubs and small trees. Page 304.

CAPRIFOLIACEAE—HONEYSUCKLE FAMILY. Leaves opposite, simple. Flowers solitary or in clusters, bisexual, bell-shaped or snapdragon-like, sepals 3- to 5-lobed, petal lobes mostly 5, stamens attached to petals, mostly 5, ovary inferior. Fruit, mostly berries or berrylike. Woody shrubs and vines. Page 305.

CELASTRACEAE—STAFF-TREE FAMILY. Leaves opposite or alternate, simple. Flowers in leaf axils, sepals and petals 4–5, stamens same number as sepals or twice as many, attached to disc. Fruit a capsule, small pod, stone fruit, or schizocarp, seeds often with fleshy appendage. Shrubs and trees. Page 311.

COMANDRACEAE—TOADFLAX FAMILY. Leaves alternate, sometimes reduced, simple. Flowers bell-shaped, petals absent, sepals 4- to 5-lobed, stamens same number as sepals, attached to hypanthium, ovary inferior. Stone fruit. Herbaceous perennials and subshrubs, many parasitic. Page 147.

CONVOLVULACEAE—MORNING-GLORY FAMILY. Leaves alternate, simple, with milky juice. Flower parts in 5s, sepals separate, petals funnel- or bell-shaped, stamens attached to petals, ovary superior. Fruit a capsule. Herbaceous annuals and perennials, subshrubs. Page 147.

CORNACEAE—DOGWOOD FAMILY. Leaves usually opposite, sometimes alternate or whorled, veins prominent, appear parallel. Flowers small, bisexual or unisexual, petals 4(5 or 0), separate, sepals 4(5), separate, stamens same number as petals, anthers curved inward, flower cluster usually surrounded by large white petal-like bracts. Fruit a berry or stone fruit. Trees, shrubs, and herbaceous perennials. Pages 312, 351.

CROSSOSOMATACEAE—CROSSOSOMA FAMILY. Leaves generally alternate, simple, ephemeral, deciduous. Flowers bisexual or unisexual, sepals and petals 5, separate, petals white, usually short-lived, stamens 4–50. Fruit, small pods. Shrubs. Page 150.

ELAEAGNACEAE—OLEASTER FAMILY. Leaves alternate, opposite, or whorled, plants with scaly and/or star-shaped hairs. Flowers bisexual, or if unisexual the sexes on separate plants. Petals absent, sepals 4, joined into funnel-shaped tube, stamens 4 or 8, attached near top of tube, ovary superior. Fruit berrylike. Trees and shrubs. Pages 151, 316.

ERICACEAE—HEATH FAMILY. Leaves usually alternate, simple and evergreen, sometimes deciduous, or leaves reduced. Flowers saucer-, funnel-, or urn-shaped, petals and sepals in 5s, sometimes 4s, occasionally 2–3 in wind-pollinated species, joined or separate. Stamens mostly equal to number of petals or twice as many (reduced in wind-pollinated plants), opening by pores or slits. Fruit a capsule, berry, or stone fruit. Herbaceous perennials, shrubs, and trees. Pages 154, 317, 351.

FABACEAE—PEA FAMILY. Leaves mostly alternate and compound, often with tendrils. Sepals and petals in 5s, often in the characteristic pea shape consisting of 1 larger upper petal (banner), 2 side petals (wings), and 2 lower petals (keel), which are often fused. Stamens mostly 10, joined or separate. Ovary superior. Fruit a pod, usually opening at maturity. Herbaceous annuals and perennials, subshrubs, shrubs, and trees. Pages 184, 381.

FAGACEAE—BEECH FAMILY. Leaves alternate, simple, often lobed. Flowers unisexual, male and female flowers on the same plant, in spikes or catkins. Tepals 4- to 7-lobed, stamens 4–20, ovary inferior. Fruit a nut, mostly with a cup-like cap (acorn). Trees and shrubs. Page 187.

GARRYACEAE—SILK-TASSEL FAMILY. Leaves opposite, simple, evergreen. Flowers unisexual, in drooping catkinlike clusters, sexes on separate plants. Flowers with cup-like bracts or bracts absent, male flowers with 4 stamens, female flowers with an inferior ovary. Fruit berrylike, becoming dry as it matures. Shrubs and small trees. Page 320.

GROSSULARIACEAE—GOOSEBERRY FAMILY. Leaves alternate, simple, often mapleleaf-shaped. Stems with spines, prickles, or unarmed. Flowers saucer-shaped, flower parts mostly in 5s, hypanthium present, ovary inferior. Fruits mostly berrylike. Shrubs. Page 200.

HYDRANGEACEAE—HYDRANGEA FAMILY. Leaves opposite, simple. Flowers bisexual, sometimes sterile, petals and sepals mostly 4–5, petals often white. Stamens mostly numerous, ovary inferior or partly inferior. Fruit a capsule. Shrubs and trees. Page 322.

JUGLANDACEAE—WALNUT FAMILY. Leaves usually alternate, compound. Flowers unisexual, mostly both sexes on same plant. Male flowers in drooping catkins, tepals 4 or absent, stamens 3–40. Female flowers in erect catkins, flowers few to many, tepals 4 or absent, ovary inferior. Fruit a nut in husk or winged nutlets. Trees, rarely shrubs. Page 388.

LAMIACEAE—MINT FAMILY. Plants aromatic, stems square. Leaves opposite, simple. Flowers tubular, tubes sometimes with lips, sepals and petals 5, stamens 2–4, attached to petals, ovary superior. Fruit, nutlets. Herbaceous annuals and perennials, subshrubs, and shrubs, rarely trees or vines. Page 323.

LAURACEAE—LAUREL FAMILY. Leaves usually alternate, sometimes opposite, simple, plants aromatic. Flowers generally bisexual, tepals 6–9, joined at base but appear separate, stamens mostly 9, ovary superior. Fruit a berry or stone fruit. Trees and shrubs, rarely herbaceous. Page 214.

LINNAEACEAE—TWINFLOWER FAMILY. Leaves opposite, mostly simple. Flowers bisexual, funnel-shaped or snapdragon-like, sepal lobes mostly 5, petal lobes 5, stamens 4, attached at two different levels, ovary inferior. Fruit, capsules or achenes. Subshrubs, shrubs, and small trees. Page 328.

MALVACEAE—MALLOW FAMILY. Leaves alternate, simple, often lobed and somewhat maple-like. Flowers bowl-shaped, sepals and petals 5, stamens 5 to many, fused at base forming a tube, ovary superior. Fruit a capsule or schizocarp, rarely berrylike. Herbaceous annuals and perennials, subshrubs, shrubs, and trees. Page 215.

MORACEAE—MULBERRY FAMILY. Leaves generally alternate, sometimes opposite, simple, sometimes lobed. Flowers unisexual, sexes in separate flowers on the same or different plants. Male flowers usually with 4(2–6) tepals, tepals cup-shaped, stamens same number as tepals, female flowers with 4–5(8) tepals or absent, stamens 1–5, ovary superior. Fruit an achene, often clustered with a fleshy coating, or stone fruit. Trees, shrubs, and vines, rarely herbaceous, often with milky juice. Page 217.

MYRICACEAE—BAYBERRY FAMILY. Leaves alternate, simple, gland-dotted, aromatic. Flowers unisexual, male and female flowers on the same plant or on separate plants, in catkinlike clusters. Perianth absent, male flowers with 2–9 stamens. Fruit a nut, achene, or stone fruit. Shrubs and trees. Page 218.

MYRTACEAE—MYRTLE FAMILY. Leaves opposite or alternate, evergreen, plants glandular, aromatic. Sepals and petals 4–5, sometimes fused, hood-shaped, white, stamens showy, many, hypanthium present, ovary mostly inferior. Fruit a berry, capsule, or nut. Trees, shrubs, and subshrubs. Page 219.

OLEACEAE—OLIVE FAMILY. Leaves mostly opposite, simple or compound. Flowers usually bisexual, if unisexual the sexes on the same or different plants. Sepals cup-shaped, 4- to 15-lobed, very small, rarely absent, petals usually 4 to many and fused, rarely absent, stamens 2, ovary superior. Fruit a samara, berry, capsule, or stone fruit. Trees, shrubs, and herbaceous perennials. Page 412.

PAPAVERACEAE—POPPY FAMILY.
Leaves alternate or basal, rarely opposite, simple but often deeply lobed, with colored or milky sap. Flowers bisexual, saucer-shaped or bilaterally symmetrical, sepals 2–3, often ephemeral, petals mostly 4, stamens many, ovary superior. Fruit a capsule. Herbaceous annuals and perennials, subshrubs, shrubs, and small trees. Page 220.

PHRYMACEAE—LOPSEED FAMILY.
Leaves opposite, simple. Flowers bisexual, sepals and petals 5, tubular, petal lobes 2-lipped, stamens mostly 4 in 2 pairs, ovary superior. Fruit often capsules, can also be achenes or berrylike. Herbaceous annuals, perennials, subshrubs, and shrubs. Page 329.

PLANTAGINACEAE—PLANTAIN FAMILY.
Leaves basal, alternate, or opposite, rarely whorled, simple. Flowers unisexual or bisexual, sepals 4–5, fused at base, petals mostly 5-lobed, rarely 4, fused, often snapdragon-like, stamens 2 or 4, sterile stamens 0–2, ovary superior. Fruit are capsules. Herbaceous annuals, perennials, subshrubs, and shrubs. Page 330.

PLATANACEAE—SYCAMORE FAMILY.
Leaves alternate, simple, lobed. Bark peeling in patches, giving trunk a mottled appearance. Flowers unisexual, both sexes on same plant, small, in round heads. Sepals 3–7, cup-shaped, petals 3–7, tiny or absent, stamens 3–7, ovary superior. Fruit an achene. Trees. Page 221.

POLEMONIACEAE—PHLOX FAMILY.
Leaves opposite or alternate, simple or compound. Flowers trumpet-shaped, solitary or in clusters. Petals and sepals 5, stamens 5, attached to floral tube, alternate with petal lobes, ovary superior. Fruit are capsules. Herbaceous perennials and annuals, shrubs, and vines. Pages 222, 335.

POLYGALACEAE—MILKWORT FAMILY.
Leaves mostly alternate, simple. Flowers pea-like, sepals 5, petals 3–5, stamens 4–10. Fruit usually a capsule, sometimes a stone fruit, samara, berry, or nut. Herbaceous perennials, subshrubs, shrubs, rarely trees, vines, or annuals. Page 222.

POLYGONACEAE—BUCKWHEAT FAMILY. Leaves basal or alternate, sometimes with a papery sheath around the node where the petiole attaches to stem. Flowers small, tepals mostly 6, can be 5, often with cuplike bracts below. Stamens usually 5–9, ovary superior. Fruit an achene or nutlet. Herbaceous annuals and perennials, subshrubs and shrubs, rarely trees. Pages 223, 352.

PRIMULACEAE—PRIMROSE FAMILY.
Leaves alternate, opposite, or whorled, simple. Flowers saucer-shaped or tubular, sepals, petals, and stamens mostly 5(4), ovary usually superior, can be partially inferior. Fruit a capsule, berry, or stone fruit. Herbaceous perennials and annuals, subshrubs. Page 367.

RANUNCULACEAE—BUTTERCUP FAMILY. Leaves can be basal, alternate, or opposite, simple or compound. Flowers saucer-shaped or tubular, occasionally bilateral, sepals and petals mostly 5, petals sometimes absent and then tepals 4 to many, stamens usually many, pistils 5 to many, ovary superior. Fruit are usually aggregated achenes or small pods, rarely berrylike or capsules. Herbaceous annuals and perennials, vines, and sometimes shrubs. Page 414.

RHAMNACEAE—BUCKTHORN FAMILY. Leaves alternate or opposite, simple. Flowers often small, hypanthium present, sepals mostly 5(4), cup-shaped, petals mostly 5(4), stamens 5(4), alternate with sepals, ovary superior to inferior. Fruit usually a capsule or berrylike, sometimes a stone fruit. Shrubs and trees. Pages 225, 340.

ROSACEAE—ROSE FAMILY. Leaves mostly alternate or basal, simple to compound, bracts usually present at petiole base. Flowers often saucer-shaped, hypanthium present, sepals and petals mostly in 5s, number of stamens and pistils various, ovary superior or inferior. Fruit an achene, stone fruit, pome (applelike), capsule, drupelet (raspberrylike), or small pod. Shrubs, subshrubs, trees, and herbaceous perennials and annuals. Pages 235, 389.

RUBIACEAE—BEDSTRAW FAMILY. Leaves whorled or opposite. Flowers small, mostly bisexual, sepals and petals mostly 4-lobed, can be 3 or 5, fused at base, sepals sometimes absent. Stamens attached to petals and alternate with lobes, ovary inferior. Fruit a berry, stone fruit, or nutlets, rarely capsules. Trees, shrubs, subshrubs, and herbaceous annuals and perennials. Pages 344, 368.

RUTACEAE—RUE FAMILY. Leaves usually alternate, can be whorled, simple or compound, glandular. Flowers generally bisexual, sepals and petals 4–5, joined at base or separate, stamens 2–4 times more than number of petals, ovary inferior. Fruit a schizocarp, berry, stone fruit, or capsule. Herbaceous perennials, shrubs, and trees, often aromatic. Page 408.

SALICACEAE—WILLOW FAMILY. Leaves alternate, simple. Flowers mostly unisexual, often grouped into catkins, can be reduced to a single flower, male and female flowers usually on separate plants. Perianth mostly absent, each flower with a bract, stamens (1)2 to many, pistil 1, stigmas 2–4. Fruit a capsule, berry, or stone fruit. Shrubs and trees. Page 260.

SAPINDACEAE—SOAPBERRY FAMILY. Leaves opposite or alternate, simple or compound, if simple often lobed. Flowers unisexual or bisexual, sepals and petals 4–5, sepals sometimes fused, petals separate, occasionally lacking, stamens usually 8, attached to lobed disc, ovary superior. Fruit a schizocarp or capsule, rarely berry, stone fruit, or nut. Trees, shrubs, and woody vines. Pages 345, 417.

SCROPHULARIACEAE—FIGWORT FAMILY. Leaves alternate or opposite, usually simple. Flowers mostly tubular, lobes similar or sometimes liplike, petals 4–5, sepals 3–5, stamens usually 4 in 2 pairs, sometimes with a 5th sterile stamen, or reduced to 2, ovary superior. Fruit a capsule, stone fruit, or schizocarp. Trees, shrubs, subshrubs, and herbaceous perennials and annuals. Page 349.

SMILACACEAE—CATBRIER FAMILY. Leaves alternate, simple. Flowers unisexual, male and female flowers on separate plants, tepals 6, mostly separate, stamens 6, ovary superior. Fruit a berry. Vines, sometimes herbaceous perennials. Page 291.

SOLANACEAE—NIGHTSHADE FAMILY. Leaves mostly alternate and simple, sometimes compound. Flowers saucer- to bell-shaped, petals, sepals, and stamens

5, stamens attached to and alternate with petal lobes, ovary superior. Fruit a berry, capsule, or schizocarp. Shrubs, subshrubs, herbaceous annuals and perennials. Page 292.

STAPHYLEACEAE—BLADDERNUT FAMILY. Leaves opposite, simple or compound. Flowers bisexual or unisexual, sepals 5, joined at base or not, petals 5, separate, stamens 5, ovary superior to partially inferior. Fruit a capsule, occasionally a small pod, stone fruit, or berry. Shrubs, trees, rarely herbaceous perennials. Page 418.

STYRACACEAE—STORAX FAMILY. Leaves alternate, simple, often with star-shaped hairs. Flowers bisexual, sepals cup- to bell-shaped, lobes mostly 4–5, sometimes 2–7, petals joined at base, seem separate, same number as sepals, stamens usually twice the petal number, attached to petals, ovary superior to inferior. Fruit mostly a capsule, can be nutlike or a stone fruit. Trees and shrubs. Page 294.

TAMARICACEAE—TAMARISK FAMILY. Leaves alternate, scalelike. Flowers bisexual or unisexual, small, solitary or in dense clusters, sepals and petals 4–5(6), separate, stamens same number as petals or twice as many, ovary superior. Fruit a capsule. Shrubs and small trees. Page 295.

THYMELAEACEAE—MEZEREUM FAMILY. Leaves alternate, opposite, or whorled, simple or compound, edges smooth. Flowers bisexual or unisexual, tubular to bell-shaped, petals often absent or reduced to 3–12 (commonly 5) scales, sepals 4- to 5-lobed, stamens 2 to many, ovary superior. Fruit a berry, achene-like, or stone fruit, not opening at maturity. Shrubs, sometimes trees, vines, or herbaceous. Page 296.

ULMACEAE—ELM FAMILY. Leaves alternate, simple. Flowers in leaf axils, bisexual or unisexual, tepals greenish, usually 4- to 9-lobed, stamens the same number as tepals or more, and opposite them, ovary superior. Fruit a samara or nutlet. Trees. Page 297.

VITACEAE—GRAPE FAMILY. Leaves alternate, simple or compound, usually with a tendril opposite the leaf. Flowers bisexual or unisexual, sepals usually 4–6 and highly reduced, petals 5, separate or joined at tips, stamens 4–6 and opposite petals, ovary superior. Fruit a berry. Woody vines, sometimes shrubs. Pages 300, 409.

TREES & SHRUBS
of the PACIFIC NORTHWEST

Abies amabilis
PINACEAE
PACIFIC SILVER FIR
Native, locally common, seed cones mature
in 1 year, 100–233 ft. West-side forest, east-
side forest, low to high elevation

Tree, crown oval to cone-shaped, trunk straight, bark whitish gray, thin, smooth with resin blisters when young, becoming scaly with age. Twigs hairy, needles spirally arranged but appear flat, longer needles projecting out to the side of the branch with shorter needles growing flattened against the branch top. **LEAVES** evergreen, single, needlelike, 0.3–1 in. long, shiny dark green above, grooved, whitish beneath, tip blunt, often notched. **CONES** pollen cones beneath on lower branches, red to reddish yellow. Seed cones erect on upper branches, purple, cylindric, 3–5 in. long, cone scales hairy, fan-shaped, falling apart at maturity. Seeds tan, 0.15 in. long, wing brownish, about same size as seed. **ECOLOGY** grows in dense, shady forests, commonly with western hemlock, noble fir, and Sitka spruce, usually at mid elevation inland but in coastal areas can grow near sea level. Highly shade tolerant, even of its own dense canopy; seedlings are sturdy, tol-

erating forest litter and snowfall better than competitors. Highly susceptible to fire but reseeds burned areas, replacing more fire-tolerant species after a few centuries if left undisturbed. Typically lives 300–500 years, succumbing thereafter to disease or insect attack. Rare in California.

Abies concolor (*Abies lowiana*)

PINACEAE

WHITE FIR, BALSAM FIR, SIERRA WHITE FIR

Native, locally common, seed cones mature
in 1 year, 133–200 ft. West-side forest, east-
side forest, mid to high elevation

Tree, crown spirelike, sometimes flattened with
age, trunk straight, bark brownish to gray, smooth
with resin blisters when young, with age becoming
thick and deeply furrowed, furrows exposing yellowish inner bark. Twigs non-hairy, needles somewhat
arranged in 2 rows, flat on lowest branches, otherwise
curving upward. **LEAVES** evergreen, single, needlelike,
0.5–2.5 in. long, surfaces with whitish stomatal bands,
tip blunt to pointed. **CONES** pollen cones yellow to dark
red. Seed cones erect on upper branches, olive- to yellowish green, cylindric, 3–5 in. long, cone scales hairy,
fan-shaped. Cones fall apart at maturity. Seeds tan,
to 0.5 in. long, winged, the reddish tan wing twice as
long as the seed. **ECOLOGY** grows on moist to dry sites
with a variety of conifer and hardwood species. Moderately shade tolerant and highly susceptible to fire
when young. Fire suppression has led to its expansion
into drier sites, where frequent fires historically would
have excluded it. Some authorities do not subdivide
this taxon, some separate it into 2 varieties, and others
grant trees found in the Sierra Mountains of California
specific status, as *A. lowiana*. Differences in appearance are slight, with var. *lowiana* needles having fewer
stomatal bands on the upper surface, and notched tips.

Abies grandis
PINACEAE
GRAND FIR
Native, common, seed cones mature in 1 year, 133–250 ft. West-side forest, east-side forest, low to mid elevation

Tree, crown cone-shaped to rounded, trunk straight, bark grayish to light brown, smooth with resin blisters when young, somewhat thick, furrowed, and scaly with age. Twigs hairy, needles arranged in 2 rows, one on each side of the branch, producing flat, spreading foliage, top of branch visible. **LEAVES** evergreen, single, needlelike, 1–2.5 in. long, shiny dark green above, grooved, 2 or more whitish stomatal bands beneath, tip blunt, mostly notched. **CONES** pollen cones oval to egg-shaped, yellowish. Seed cones erect on upper branches, yellowish green to purplish, cylindric, 2.5–5 in. long, cone scales hairy, fan-shaped. Cones fall apart at maturity. Seeds tan, 0.3 in. long, wing slightly longer, reddish tan. **ECOLOGY** grows on moist to dry sites with a variety of conifer and hardwood species. Fast growing, moderately shade tolerant. Mature trees have some resistance to low-intensity fire; however, the mortality rate is often high in dense stands and when low-hanging branches are present. Trees typically live about 250 years, susceptible to such conditions as heart rot (identify trees infected with the fungus by finding hoof-shaped conks, blackish above and with grayish spines beneath, on the trunk). Hybridizes with *A. concolor*, which has slightly upward-facing needles with whitish stomatal bands on both surfaces.

Abies lasiocarpa (*Abies bifolia*)
PINACEAE
SUBALPINE FIR
Native, common, seed cones mature in 1
year, 60–100 ft. West-side forest, east-side
forest, subalpine, mid to high elevation

Tree, crown tapered, spirelike, bark gray, thin, smooth,
with resin blisters when young, growing furrowed
with age. Branch whorls evenly spaced, branches often
extending to ground level, twigs reddish-hairy, needles
spirally arranged, mostly curved upward.

LEAVES evergreen, single, needlelike, about 1 in. long,
bluish green, whitish stomatal bands on both surfaces, smooth with the band appearing single above,
ridged with 2 bands below, tip blunt, often notched.

CONES pollen cones clustered, bluish to purple. Seed
cones erect, cylindric, 2–4 in. long, deep purple (rarely
green), often with a resinous coating, cone scales oval,
hairy, bract visible at pollination, scale growth hiding
it thereafter. Cones fall apart at maturity. Seeds brown,
0.3 in. long, wing longer than seed.

ECOLOGY grows in pure or mixed-species stands in
montane and subalpine forests, subalpine parklands,
and on alpine slopes. Shade tolerant and masterfully
adapted to windy, snowy, and cold habitats. Assumes a
variety of habits, from spires that prevent heavy snow
buildup on branches to squat alpine forms that minimize wind exposure. Branches near the ground and
those weighed down by snow can root and form new
shoots, creating a thicket. Highly flammable and susceptible to fire. Subalpine fir forests experience infrequent, stand-replacing fires. Trees grow slowly, typically live about 250 years, and are prone to heart rot.
Rare in California.

Abies magnifica
PINACEAE
CALIFORNIA RED FIR, RED FIR
Native, locally common, seed cones
mature in 1 year, 67–190 ft. West-side
forest, east-side forest, mid elevation

Tree, crown cone-shaped, bark grayish, thin and smooth when young, with age becoming thick, reddish brown, furrowed, with ridges up to 4 times wider than furrows, outer layers flake off, twigs yellow to tan, reddish-hairy first 1–2 years. **LEAVES** evergreen, single, needlelike, 1–1.5 in. long, bluish green, squarish (4-angled) in cross section, whitish stomatal bands on both surfaces, the topside smooth with 2 bands, the lower surface bluish to silvery green with 1 band, tip blunt, often notched, needles curved upward, hockey stick–shaped. **CONES** pollen cones clustered, purple to reddish brown. Seed cones erect, cylindric, 6–9 in. long, purple becoming yellow to greenish brown, scales hairy, bracts not extending beyond scale tip. Cones fall apart at maturity. Seeds reddish brown, 0.6 in. long, the rose-colored wing about the same length. **ECOLOGY** widespread in montane forests, growing in pure stands or more often with other conifers (white fir, sugar pine, Jeffrey pine), in places with cold, snowy winters and short, warm summers. Highly frost hardy, moderately tolerant of shade, fairly intolerant of drought, and quite fire resistant: its thick bark and needles do not burn easily. Fire often creates openings, which California red fir colonizes. Grows best on sunny spots with deep soils.

Abies magnifica var. shastensis

(Abies ×shastensis)

PINACEAE

SHASTA RED FIR

Native, locally common, seed cones mature in 1 year, 67–190 ft. West-side forest, east-side forest, subalpine, mid to high elevation

Tree, crown cone-shaped, bark grayish, thin and smooth when young, with age becoming thick, reddish brown to purplish black, furrowed, with ridges up to 4 times wider than furrows, outer layers flake off, twigs yellow to tan, reddish-hairy first 1–2 years.

LEAVES evergreen, single, needlelike, 1–1.5 in. long, bluish green, squarish (4-angled) in cross section, whitish stomatal bands on both surfaces, the top-side smooth with 2 bands, the lower surface bluish to silvery green with 1 band, tip blunt, often notched; needles resemble hockey sticks. **CONES** pollen cones clustered, purple to reddish brown. Seed cones erect, cylindric, 6–9 in. long, purple becoming yellow to greenish brown, scales hairy, bracts extend beyond scale tip. Cones fall apart at maturity. Seeds reddish brown, 0.6 in. long, wing about the same length, rosy.

ECOLOGY widespread in montane forests, growing in pure stands or more often with other conifers (white fir on warmer sites, mountain hemlock on cooler sites), in places with a cool, moist climate, tolerating short periods of hot, dry summer weather. Moderately shade tolerant and fairly drought intolerant; grows best on sunny spots with deep soils and often colonizes openings created by fire. Mature trees are fire resistant; their thick bark and needles do not burn easily. The similar *A. procera* usually has a groove on the needle's upper surface, and bark with furrows and ridges about the same width; *A. magnifica* differs in that the cone bracts do not extend beyond the scale tips.

Abies procera
PINACEAE
NOBLE FIR

Native, common, seed cones mature in 1
year, 133–233 ft. West-side forest, east-side
forest, subalpine, mid to high elevation

Tree, crown tapered, spirelike, symmetrical, bark grayish brown when young, becoming reddish brown and
furrowed with age, furrows and ridges similar widths,
outer layers flake off. Branches short and inflexible,
twigs hairy, needles curved upward, twisted at the
base, resembling a hockey stick. **LEAVES** evergreen, single, needlelike, 0.5–1 in. long, bluish green, squarish
(4-angled) in cross section, whitish stomatal bands on
both surfaces, grooved midvein, bands 2–4 above, 0–2
below, tip blunt, often notched. **CONES** pollen cones
reddish. Seed cones erect, cylindric, 4.5–8 in. long,
green, red, or purple when immature, cone scales
hairy, bracts extend beyond scale tip and are bent back.
Cones fall apart at maturity. Seeds reddish brown, 0.5
in. long, wing slightly larger than the seed.

ECOLOGY grows on cool, moist sites, often in mixed
conifer forests; common associates are Pacific silver fir,
western hemlock, mountain hemlock, and Douglas-fir.
Drought intolerant and less shade tolerant than other
firs; seedlings do not establish well in
shade but readily colonize burned or
otherwise disturbed sites. Usually lives
300–400 years, sometimes to 700 years.
Limited fire resistance. Can hybridize with the closely related *A. magnifica*, forming trees with intermediate
characteristics.

Larix lyallii
PINACEAE
SUBALPINE LARCH
Native, locally common, seed cones
mature in 1 year, 33–83 ft. East-side forest,
alpine, subalpine, high elevation

Tree, crown cone-shaped to irregular, bark thin, reddish to purplish brown, furrowed and platelike, plates
flaking off as thin scales, branches spreading and
often drooping, new twigs hairy, hairs long and tangled. **LEAVES** deciduous, bundled, needlelike, 1–1.5
in. long, spirally arranged, 30–40 per bundle on short
twig spurs, bluish green, squarish (4-angled) in cross
section, tip pointed. **CONES** pollen cones yellow, 0.5
in. long. Seed cones stalked, oval, about 1–2 in. long,
reddish brown when mature, cone scales roundish,
long-hairy underneath, edges irregularly toothed, bract
tip linear, extending beyond scale tip. Seeds purplish
or yellowish brown, 0.1 in. long, wing twice as long
as seed. **ECOLOGY** grows in rocky, subalpine to alpine
areas, in small pure stands at timberline, scattered
on rocky substrates, or mixed with subalpine fir and
other conifers. Deciduous habit limits winter water
stress, and trees can therefore colonize bare rock and
talus slopes, sites that are too harsh for other conifers.
Extremely cold tolerant but intolerant of shade or moisture stress. Grows slowly, and seed production is generally low. Seedlings develop special wintergreen needles that stay on the tree for a year or longer, helping
the young tree survive, as they are more drought resistant than deciduous needles. Typically lives 400–500
years but can live 1000 years or more. *Pinus albicaulis*
has a similar elevational range but prefers warmer and
drier sites.

Larix occidentalis
PINACEAE
WESTERN LARCH
Native, scattered, seed cones mature in 1 year,
100–183 ft. East-side forest, mid to high elevation

Tree, crown pyramid-shaped, trunk straight, branch-free through much of its length, bark reddish brown, thick, furrowed and platelike, plates flaking into orangish red scales, branches spreading and rarely drooping, twigs smooth or hairy, if hairy hairs short and not tangled. **LEAVES** deciduous, bundled, needlelike, 1–2 in. long, spirally arranged, 15–30 per bundle on short twig spurs, pale green, triangular in cross section, fairly stiff, tip pointed. **CONES** pollen cones yellow, 0.5 in. long. Seed cones stalked, egg-shaped, about 1 in. long, yellowish brown when mature, cone scales egg-shaped, edges smooth, bract tip linear and extending beyond scale tip. Seeds reddish brown, 0.1 in. long, wing twice as long as seed. **ECOLOGY** mixed conifer forests, montane, easy to spot on slopes in autumn, when the needles turn golden yellow. Common associates include Douglas-fir and ponderosa pine on drier sites, and firs and Engelmann spruce on cooler, moister sites. Long-lived, shade intolerant, and fast growing, this species is adapted to both survive fire and colonize open, burned areas; often, seed is available from nearby surviving trees. Fire-resistant traits include thick bark, branches absent near the ground, deep roots, and moisture-rich needles. Larch habitats have a history of periodic fire, and without fire, western larch eventually declines in abundance.

Picea breweriana
PINACEAE
BREWER SPRUCE, WEEPING SPRUCE
Native, locally common, seed cones mature
in 1 year, 80–133 ft. Chaparral, west-side
forest, subalpine, mid to high elevation

Tree, crown cone-shaped, trunk straight, flaring at the base and tapering upward, bark gray to brown, with long, irregularly rectangular scales. Branches drooping, all but topmost branches with tinsel-like, drooping branchlets, 4–8 ft. long, twigs hairy. **LEAVES** evergreen, single, stalked, needlelike, 0.5–1 in. long, flattened to triangular in cross section, rigid, dark green, with whitish stomatal bands above, stomatal bands absent below, tip blunt. Peglike leaf stalk remains attached to branch when needle is shed. **CONES** pollen cones dark purple, 0.75–1.25 in. long, scattered throughout the tree in leaf axils. Seed cones at branch tips, cylindric, dark green and erect when immature, becoming dark brown and drooping at maturity, 2.5–5 in. long, cone scales fan-shaped, rigid, edges mostly smooth. Seeds 0.1–0.2 in. long, wing 4 times longer than the seed. **ECOLOGY** endemic to the Klamath Mountains, growing in valley bottoms, ridges, and slopes in mixed conifer forests, montane chaparral, or in small pure stands. Common associates include red fir, white fir, and mountain hemlock. It grows on all aspects but prefers steep, north-facing slopes. Tolerates a wide range of soils, temperatures, and precipitation levels but tends to be found in shallow, rocky soils, and dislikes boggy conditions or prolonged moisture stress. Shade tolerant. Fire is frequent throughout its range, and the species suffers high mortality from even low-intensity ground fires.

Picea engelmannii
PINACEAE
ENGELMANN SPRUCE

Native, locally common, seed cones mature in
1 year, 50–167 ft. Streambanks, east-side forest,
alpine, subalpine, mid to high elevation

Tree, crown narrow, spirelike, tip erect, bark brownish red to purplish, thin, texture scaly, scales large and
loosely attached. Branches spreading to slightly drooping, twigs usually hairy. **LEAVES** evergreen, single,
stalked, needlelike, 0.5–1 in. long, squarish (4-angled)
in cross section, surfaces bluish green with stomatal
bands, tip sharply pointed. Peglike leaf stalk remains
attached to branch when needle is shed. **CONES** pollen
cones yellow to purple, 0.5 in. long. Seed cones dangling, oval, 1–3 in. long, yellowish brown, cone scales
oval to diamond-shaped, flexible, edges irregularly
toothed. Seeds winged, 0.1 in. long, wing 2–3 times
longer than seed. **ECOLOGY** moderately shade tolerant,
long-lived, and slow growing, often in cold places with
a heavy snowpack and short, cool summers. At timberline it can be found on drier sites; at lower elevations,
usually found near streams or wetlands. Assumes a
low, shrubby form in the alpine zone but below timberline tends to be taller than other tree species of
comparable age. Often infected with Cooley spruce
gall aphids, causing branch tips to swell and curve,
resembling deformed seed cones, green when immature, turning reddish brown after aphids emerge. Periodic disturbance, such as from fire, allows Engelmann
spruce to maintain a presence on sites that would
otherwise be dominated by subalpine fir, which has
greater shade tolerance. Rare in California.

Picea glauca

PINACEAE

WHITE SPRUCE

Native, locally common, seed cones mature in 1 year, 80–133 ft. East-side forest, low to mid elevation

Tree, crown narrow, spirelike, tip erect, trunk straight to bent, bark silvery brown, thin, texture scaly or smooth. Branches spreading to slightly drooping, twigs non-hairy. **LEAVES** evergreen, single, stalked, needlelike, 0.5–1 in. long, squarish (4-angled) in cross section, bluish green, stiff, tip very sharply pointed. Peglike leaf stalk remains attached to branch when needle is shed. **CONES** pollen cones light red. Seed cones dangling, oval, 1–2.5 in. long, yellowish brown, cone scales fan-shaped, stiff, edges smooth.

ECOLOGY grows on moist to dry forest slopes, along streams, and in bogs and fens in montane to subalpine areas. Slow growing and moderately shade tolerant. Fire historically had an important role in stand renewal, with mixed-severity fires killing some trees and skipping others, creating openings for seedling establishment. Seed is primarily wind-dispersed; it is a desired wildlife food for small mammals, particularly red squirrels, and birds such as chickadees, nuthatches, and pine siskins. The similar *P. engelman-*

nii tends to grow at higher elevations and has oval to diamond-shaped, flexible cone scales with ragged edges, and hairy twigs. Hybrids commonly form between the two species where their ranges overlap; seed cones of resulting plants are intermediate in character. Hybrids with *P. sitchensis* have also been reported.

Picea sitchensis

PINACEAE

SITKA SPRUCE

Native, locally common, seed cones mature
in 1 year, 133–267 ft. Coastal, streambanks,
west-side forest, low to mid elevation

Tree, tip erect, crown cone-shaped, bark thin, grayish
brown to purplish, texture scaly, scales flake off revealing reddish brown inner bark. Branches spreading
with drooping ends, twigs pinkish brown, non-hairy.
LEAVES evergreen, single, stalked, needlelike, 0.5–1
in. long, flattened or triangular in cross section, stiff,
surfaces yellowish to bluish green, tip very sharply
pointed. Peglike leaf stalk remains attached to branch
when needle is shed. **CONES** pollen cones red, 0.5–1
in. long. Seed cones dangling, egg-shaped, 2–3.5 in.
long, reddish to yellowish brown when immature,
becoming tan, cone scales roundish, tips irregularly
toothed. Seeds winged, 0.1 in. long, wing approximately 3 times longer than seed. **ECOLOGY** grows in
wet places or where humidity is high, coastal forests
and river terraces, sometimes in mountain foothills,
often beside a stream, in nutrient-rich soils. Seedlings
often grow on downed logs or stumps. Trunks on old
growth specimens reach 7 ft. in diameter or more. Can
be uprooted in high winds due to its shallow root system; other disturbances include fire (rarely) and logging. Trees with greater shade tolerance can replace
it over time, although this largest spruce species can
grow taller than its competitors. Does not tolerate prolonged drought. Often infected with Cooley spruce gall
aphids, causing branch tips to swell and curve, resembling deformed seed cones, green when immature,
turning reddish brown after aphids emerge.

Pinus albicaulis
PINACEAE
WHITEBARK PINE
Native, locally common, seed cones mature in 2
years, 17–70 ft. Rocky sites, west-side forest, east-
side forest, alpine, subalpine, mid to high elevation

Tree, can have shrubby form above timberline, crown
cone-shaped to spreading, trunk often contorted by
wind, bark whitish gray, smooth, becoming scaly with
age. **LEAVES** evergreen, in bundles of 5, needlelike, 1–3
in. long, dark yellowish green, often curved upward.
CONES pollen cones oblong to egg-shaped, 0.5 in. long,
bright red. Seed cones not stalked, roundish to egg-
shaped, 1.5–3 in. long, dark purple when immature.
Cones mostly remain closed and on the tree. Seeds
to 0.5 in. long, dark brown, wingless. **ECOLOGY** grows
in harsh environments, such as windy ridges and on
cold, high mountain slopes near timberline. Assumes
a sprawling, shrubby form in alpine habitats; at lower
elevations, it grows mixed with other tree species. Slow
growing and long-lived (individuals over 1000 years old
have been documented). Dispersal of seed is dependent on Clark's nutcrackers; the birds open the cones,
collect seed, and cache it in multiple locations for later
consumption. Seed in unused caches often germinate
and grow into trees. Squirrels collect whole cones and
store for later use; these caches are in turn raided by
bears. Has declined in abundance due to fire suppression, bark beetles, and white pine blister rust. Effectively colonizes burned-over slopes (fire often reduces
competition from more shade tolerant species); mature
trees survive low-intensity fire but are killed by more
severe burns.

Pinus attenuata
PINACEAE
KNOBCONE PINE, SCRUB PINE

Native, scattered, seed cones mature in 2 years, 30–80 ft. Serpentine, west-side forest, low to mid elevation Tree, sometimes a shrub, crown cone-shaped, trunks one to several, bark thin, grayish to dark brown, furrowed with loose, scaly plates, branches ascending, twigs reddish brown. **LEAVES** evergreen, in bundles of 3, needlelike, 2.5–6.5 in. long, sheath persistent at base of needles, surfaces yellowish green, tips pointed. **CONES** pollen cones egg-shaped, to 0.6 in. long, orangish brown. Seed cones typically whorled in groups of 4–5, lance- to egg-shaped, curved and asymmetrical, 3–6 in. long, yellowish brown, cone scale tips knoblike, = or > 1 in. long with a stout prickle. Cones remain closed when mature and stay on the tree. Seeds are egg-shaped, 0.3 in. long, blackish, wing about 3 times longer than seed. **ECOLOGY** grows in a transitional area between chaparral and oak woodlands, as well as in mixed conifer forests at higher elevations. Often found on serpentine. Shade intolerant, fast growing, and short-lived (60–100 years). Ecotonal populations tend to be small, with trees widely spaced; denser stands occur in mixed conifer forests. Fire is a key factor in reproduction. With rare exceptions, cones remain closed until a fire's heat melts the resin; the scales can then open and release seeds, which germinate and grow readily in the burned area, allowing knobcone pine to compete effectively and perpetuate itself.

Pinus balfouriana
PINACEAE
FOXTAIL PINE
Native, uncommon, seed cones mature in 2 years,
20–73 ft. Rocky sites, serpentine, west-side forest,
shrub-steppe, alpine, subalpine, high elevation

Tree, crown cone-shaped to irregular, trunk mostly
single, sometimes leaning, bark thick, gray, pinkish,
or orangish brown, with irregular furrows and plates,
branches contorted, reddish brown, resemble foxtails.
LEAVES evergreen, in bundles of 5, needlelike, 0.5–1.5
in. long, bluish or yellowish green, curved upward,
tips pointed. **CONES** pollen cones red, oval, to 0.4 in.
Seed cones egg-shaped, 2.5–3.5 in. long, purple when
immature, becoming reddish brown, resin amber-col-
ored, cone scale tips rounded, prickles mostly absent.
Cones open when mature, not persistent on tree. Seeds
oval, 0.4 in. long, brown with red patches, wing about
as long as seed. **ECOLOGY** endemic to California and
barely across the border in Oregon, occurring in the
Klamath and Sierra Nevada mountains, with separate
northern and southern populations. Northern specimens often grow in serpentine; southern populations,
in granitic soils. Also found near alpine meadows and
in rocky areas. Can grow in pure stands. Common
associates include lodgepole pine, Jeffrey pine, and

California red fir; at higher elevations,
whitebark pine or mountain hemlock.
Shade intolerant and slow growing, typically living over 1000 years, although
many have heart rot by that time. Close
relations *P. longaeva* and *P. aristata* are
fire resistant, but little is known of foxtail pine's relationship with fire.

Pinus contorta
PINACEAE
SHORE PINE, BEACH PINE
Native, common, seed cones mature in 2
years, 33–50 ft. Coastal, bog/fen/wetland,
west-side forest, low elevation

Tree, trunk straight to more often bent or twisted,
crown rounded to flat-topped, bark dark brown to grayish black, thick, furrowed and scaly, branches mostly
spreading, often bent. **LEAVES** evergreen, in bundles
of 2, needlelike, 1–3 in. long, dark green, straight or
curved. **CONES** pollen cones clustered, oval, 0.2–0.5 in.
long, reddish. Seed cones stalked or not, roundish to
egg-shaped, lopsided, 1–2.5 in. long, tan to light reddish brown. Cones scales open when seed is mature or
remain closed. Mature cones persist on the tree. Seeds
are reddish brown, egg-shaped, 0.2 in. long, winged.
ECOLOGY grows on rocky sites and in poor soils in
coastal lowlands and bluffs, sand dunes, swamps, and
bogs; colonizes burned or otherwise disturbed sites.
Shade intolerant but a prolific seed producer; trees
typically produce a cone crop every year, and the mixture of seed rain and seed protected
in cones gives the species a competitive advantage after disturbances such
as fire. Without disturbance, however,
more shade tolerant trees will eventually crowd out shore pine on many sites;
seedlings cannot grow under a dense
canopy.

Pinus contorta var. *latifolia*

PINACEAE
LODGEPOLE PINE

Native, common, seed cones mature in 2
years, 33–117 ft. West-side forest, east-side
forest, subalpine, low to high elevation

Tree, slender, crown narrow, rounded, trunk straight,
bark gray to reddish brown, thin, surface scaly, platelike, branches mostly spreading. Can assume a
shrubby form at high elevation. **LEAVES** evergreen, in
bundles of 2, needlelike, 2–3 in. long, yellowish green,
straight or curved. **CONES** pollen cones clustered, oval,
0.2–0.5 in. long, reddish. Seed cones stalked or not,
roundish to egg-shaped, lopsided, 1–2.5 in. long, tan to
light reddish brown. Cones scales open when seed is
mature or remain closed. Mature cones persist on the
tree. Seeds are reddish brown, egg-shaped, 0.2 in. long,
winged. **ECOLOGY** thrives on cold, dry sites and does
well in poor soils, often growing in pure, dense stands.
Mostly short-lived (80–100 years) but can live 300 years
or more under the right conditions. Shade intolerant,
fast growing, and produces seed prolifically, typically
a cone crop every year, giving the species a competitive advantage after disturbances such as fire. More
fire resistant than many *Abies* spp., often surviving a
light burn, and often benefits from more severe fires,
for although tree mortality is high, seed from adjacent
stands plus seed from fire-opened cones allow lodgepole pine to recolonize and dominate burned sites.
Without disturbance, more shade tolerant trees will
eventually replace it on most sites. Var. *murrayana* can
be distinguished by its upward-pointing branches and
symmetrical seed cones that fall off the tree.

Pinus flexilis

PINACEAE

LIMBER PINE

Native, locally common, seed cones mature
in 2 years, 13–50 ft. East-side forest,
alpine, subalpine, high elevation

Tree, crown rounded, irregular, trunk often bent or
twisted, bark gray when young, blackish brown, furrowed and scaly when older. Branches long, spreading to ascending, twigs hairy, light reddish brown.
LEAVES evergreen, in bundles of 5, needlelike, 1.5–3 in.
long, dark yellowish green, straight or curved upward.
CONES pollen cones oval, 0.5 in. long, light red to yellow. Seed cones stalked or not, lance- to egg-shaped,
3–6 in. long, green when immature, becoming light
brown, cone scale thin at tip, prickle absent. Cones
open when seed is mature, and soon after fall from
the tree. Seeds egg-shaped, 0.5 in. long, dark brown,
short-winged, wing usually remains attached to cone
scale. **ECOLOGY** grows on harsh sites, often on steep,
rocky slopes or ridges near timberline. Slow growing,
long-lived (to 500 years or more), and shade intolerant. Assumes a shrubby form in alpine habitats. Its
presence at lower elevations indicates poor soils or a
history of fire; at higher elevations it has little competition from other tree species. Often affected by bark
beetle attacks and afflicted with white pine blister
rust. Seed dispersal is largely bird-dependent; seed
in unused caches germinates in the right conditions.
Pinus albicaulis inhabits similar habitats; distinguish
limber pine by its larger cones, often lying intact near
the tree base, and cones green rather than purple when
immature.

Pinus jeffreyi
PINACEAE
JEFFREY PINE
Native, locally common, seed cones mature in
2 years, 80–177 ft. Serpentine, west-side forest,
east-side forest, subalpine, mid to high elevation

Tree, crown open, oval to rounded, branches whorled,
spreading, lower branches self-pruning as tree grows.
Trunk usually straight, bark thick, reddish brown, furrowed when young, with a surface of puzzlelike plates
that break off with age. Bark often smells like vanilla or
lemon, especially in the sun. **LEAVES** evergreen, in bundles of 3(2), needlelike, 5–11 in. long, bluish green with
a whitish waxy coating, tips pointed. **CONES** pollen
cones clustered, lance-shaped to oblong, 1–1.5 in. long,
yellow to purplish brown. Seed cones located at branch
tips, egg-shaped, 6–12 in. long, green to reddish purple when immature, light reddish brown at maturity,
scales arranged in a gentle spiral, both sides same
color, scale tip a slender bent prickle. Seed cone scales
open to release the grayish brown winged seed, seed
about 0.5 in. long. **ECOLOGY** grows on dry mountain
slopes, often at higher elevations than ponderosa pine.
Favors nutrient-poor soils such as serpentine. Seed
often cached by mammals and birds. Adapted to survive fire with its thick bark, self-pruning branches, and
protected buds; decreases in abundance with fire exclusion, while more shade tolerant tree species increase.
Similar to and can hybridize with *P. ponderosa*, but
hybrids rarely occur as the timing of pollen release differs between the two species. Distinguish Jeffrey pine
by its larger cones and longer, bluish green needles;
also, it tends to be shorter and with stouter branches
than ponderosa pine when the two grow together.

Pinus lambertiana
PINACEAE
SUGAR PINE
Native, locally common, seed cones mature
in 2 years, 100–200 ft. West-side forest, east-
side forest, subalpine, low to high elevation
Tree, crown flat-topped, trunk straight, bark dark gray
and smooth when young, becoming thick, cinnamon
to grayish brown, furrowed with platelike ridges that
flake off with age. Branches spreading to ascending
at the tip, twigs grayish green to reddish tan, hairy.
LEAVES evergreen, in bundles of 5, needlelike, 2–4 in.
long, flexible, bluish green, tips pointed. **CONES** pollen
cones clustered, yellowish brown, oval, 0.5 in. long.
Seed cones dangling at branch ends, shiny yellowish brown, cylindric, 10–20 in. long, cone stalks 2.5–6
in. long. Cone scales with thick, yellowish brown tips,
prickle absent. Seed winged, brown, egg-shaped, 0.5–1
in. long. **ECOLOGY** grows scattered in mixed conifer
forests, both moist and dry types; can be the dominant
species in certain circumstances. Shade intolerant and
long-lived, this is the largest pine, typically 3–6 ft. in
diameter, but majestic specimens are recorded to be
250 ft. tall and 11 ft. in diameter. Its thick, fire-resistant bark and high, open crown help it survive low- to
moderate-intensity fires. Fire exclusion has increased
stand density and stress on sugar pines in many places.
Increased stress, such as reduced water availability,
makes the species vulnerable to attack by bark beetles
and white pine blister rust. Native Americans collected
sugar pine seed and chewed its sweet resin as gum.

Pinus monticola
PINACEAE
WESTERN WHITE PINE
Native, locally common, seed cones mature
in 2 years, 100–167 ft. West-side forest, east-
side forest, subalpine, low to high elevation

Tree, crown narrowly cone-shaped to flattened, bark
gray and smooth when young, becoming checked
with squarish scales that flake off, exposing cinna-
mon-brown inner bark. Branches whorled, spreading to upturned, twigs light reddish brown, hairy and
sometimes glandular. **LEAVES** evergreen, in bundles of
5, needlelike, 1.5–4 in. long, light bluish green, slender
and flexible. **CONES** pollen cones clustered, yellow, oval,
0.5 in. long. Seed cones stalked, clustered, dangling,
oval to lance-shaped, 4–10 in. long, light brown to yellowish, opening when seed is mature and thereafter
falling intact from the tree. Cone scales thin at the tip,
prickle absent. Seeds winged, reddish brown, triangular to egg-shaped, 0.3 in. long. **ECOLOGY** grows in
moist or humid areas, from river bottoms or bog edges
to mixed conifer forests, often in poor soils. Tolerates
some shade and is relatively fast growing. Historically
it benefited from fire, which reduced the density of
competing trees and allowed its seed to colonize the
burned-over ground. Young trees are susceptible to
fire kill, while older trees sometimes survive low-intensity fire. Once heavily logged, then decimated by white
pine blister rust, the species is slowly resurging. Logging has been reduced, rust-resistant trees have been
planted, and natural rust resistance has been found in
some wild trees.

Pinus muricata
PINACEAE
BISHOP PINE
Native, locally common, seed cones mature in 3 years,
50–80 ft. Coastal, west-side forest, low elevation

Tree, crown rounded to flattened, often irregular and
sparse, bark thick, dark gray, furrowed with scaly
plates, branches ascending or spreading, often twisted,
twigs orangish to dark brown. **LEAVES** evergreen, in
bundles of 2, needlelike, 3–6 in. long, bluish or dark
green, straight to curved, sheath base persistent, tips
pointed. **CONES** pollen cones oval, 0.2 in. long, orange.
Seed cones whorled, egg-shaped, asymmetrical, 2–3.5
in. long, reddish brown, eventually gray, cone scale tips
with curved claw. Mature cones remain closed and persist on the tree. Seeds oval, 0.3 in. long, dark brown,
wing >2 times longer than seed. **ECOLOGY** grows along
the coast, usually within 10 miles of the ocean, in even-
aged pure stands in mixed conifer forests, coastal sage
scrub, and chaparral. Soils are often shallow and poorly
drained. Moderately shade tolerant and fairly fire resistant thanks to its thick bark; however, it grows in fire-
prone areas, often in dense stands, which increases fire
mortality. Cones open due to fire or on very hot days,
allowing seed dispersal to occur. It is a short-lived species, often dying from disease by the century mark and
rarely reaching 200 years of age.

Pinus ponderosa
PINACEAE
PONDEROSA PINE, YELLOW PINE
Native, common, seed cones mature in 2 years,
90–200 ft. East-side forest, low to high elevation
Tree, crown open, oval to flat-topped, branches
whorled, spreading, lower branches self-pruning as
tree grows. Trunk usually straight, bark thick, deeply
furrowed and yellow to dark reddish brown on younger
trees, becoming orange-brown and platelike, layers flake off. **LEAVES** evergreen, in bundles of 3(2–5),
needlelike, 4–10 in. long, yellowish green, tips pointed.
CONES pollen cones clustered, oval to oblong, to 1.5
in. long, yellow to reddish purple. Seed cones located
at branch tips, egg-shaped, 3–5.5 in. long, reddish
brown or green when immature, brown at maturity,
cone scale tip pointed, sometimes with a straight, outward-facing prickle. Seeds about 0.3 in. long, winged,
brownish purple. **ECOLOGY** shade intolerant, grows on
dry slopes, in draws within shrub-steppe and other dry
habitats, on ridgetops and in flats. Historically ponderosa pine largely grew in widely spaced, even-aged
stands with a mostly herbaceous understory, maintained principally by frequent, low-intensity fires.
Seed germinated after fire, resulting in trees of a similar age, and the wide spacing and low understory
decreased risk of an intense crown fire. Very drought
tolerant, allowing it to grow where precipitation is too
low for most other tree species. In the absence of fire
or other disturbances, Douglas-fir and other species
with greater shade tolerance outcompete it on more
moderate sites. Var. *washoensis*, sometimes given specific rank, is mostly found above 6600 ft. elevation.
Identify it by its cones, 3–4 in. long, prickle on scale tip
inward-facing, which are similar to but smaller than *P.
jeffreyi* cones.

Pinus radiata

PINACEAE
MONTEREY PINE
Native and non-native, locally common,
seed cones mature in 2 years, 50–117 ft.
Coastal, west-side forest, low elevation

Tree, crown cone-shaped to flattened, bark gray, furrowed, trunk straight to crooked, twigs reddish brown to gray. **LEAVES** evergreen, in bundles of 3 (rarely 2), needlelike, 3.5–6 in. long, sheath persistent at base of needles, surfaces dark yellowish green, edges minutely toothed, tips pointed. **CONES** pollen cones cylindric, orangish brown, to 0.5 in. long. Seed cones single or clustered, egg-shaped, curved and asymmetrical, 3–5.5 in. long, reddish brown, cone scale tips knoblike, <1 in. long, with small prickle. Some cones shed seeds soon after maturity, but many remain closed and persist for years on the tree. Seeds oval, dark brown, with a wing about 1 in. long. **ECOLOGY** grows near the coast within the fog zone in conifer forests and oak woodlands on sandy, well-drained soils with a clay layer beneath. Cones open with higher temperatures and lower humidity and close when temperatures drop or humidity increases. Fires and hot weather trigger seed dispersal. Mature trees are often killed by fire, but the post-fire seed rain speeds recovery. Native populations are few, endemic to and rare in California, all south of the range covered here, but the species has been planted well outside its native range and is now naturalized in places along the coast and has become a major timber tree in New Zealand and elsewhere. Common associates in our region are bishop pine and cypress. The similar *P. attenuata* has knoblike tips of cone scales that are longer than 1 in. with a stout prickle.

Pinus sabiniana

PINACEAE

GRAY PINE, GHOST PINE, FOOTHILLS PINE
Native, common, seed cones mature in
2 years, 40–80 ft. Rocky sites, chaparral,
west-side forest, low to mid elevation

Tree, crown open and spreading, sparse, trunks often
divided close to the base, straight to leaning, bark dark
gray to blackish, furrowed, forming irregular plates
that flake off revealing orangish underbark, branches
point upward, twigs light purplish brown. **LEAVES** evergreen, in bundles of 3, needlelike, 6–13 in. long, grayish green, flexible, drooping. **CONES** pollen cones oval,
0.5 in. long, yellow. Seed cones dangling, stalks to 2 in.
long, egg-shaped, 6–10 in. long, dull brown and resinous, scale tip with curved, clawlike tip. Cones persist
on the tree, open or closed, for periods of time after
maturity. Seeds winged, dark brown, egg-shaped, 1 in.
long, wing shorter than seed. **ECOLOGY** grows on open,
rocky slopes in oak woodlands, chaparral, and mixed
conifer forests, most commonly in mountain foothills.
Mature trees are shade intolerant; younger trees tolerate partial shade. Cones are among the most massive of
pine species, sometimes 2 pounds or more; their scales
open slowly over several months to release the seeds,
which are dispersed by water, gravity, and animals,
especially scrub jays and acorn woodpeckers. Fire was
a natural component of gray pine ecosystems; its suppression causes the species to decline where it occurs
with other conifers and to increase in oak woodland
communities. Mature trees have thick, fire-resistant
bark and few branches near the ground, features that
aid in fire survival. Seedling establishment is high in
burned-over areas, due to heat-mediated seed scarifica-
tion and a preference for bare mineral soil.

Pseudotsuga menziesii
PINACEAE
DOUGLAS-FIR
Native, common, seed cones mature in 1
year, to 300 ft. Coastal, west-side forest,
east-side forest, low to mid elevation

Tree, crown triangular, rounded, or flattened, trunk straight, bark dark brown, smooth with resin blisters when young, thick and deeply furrowed with age, branches spreading to drooping, twigs hairy. Buds sharp-pointed, scales overlapping. **LEAVES** evergreen, single, needlelike, 0.5–1 in. long, yellowish green to dark green, spreading at all angles from twig or turned upward, tip pointed, not notched. **CONES** pollen cones on branch undersides, yellowish red, 0.2–0.5 in. long. Seed cones dangling, immature cones green, becoming reddish brown to gray, oval, 2.5–4 in. long, scales with three-pronged "mousetail" bract. Cones open at maturity then fall intact to the ground. Seeds winged, 0.2 in. long, wing longer than seed. **ECOLOGY** a generalist, fairly tolerant of both drought and shade, and therefore grows in many habitats. Fire was an important component in many Douglas-fir ecosystems. In denser, moist forests, fires were stand-replacing, with trees killed and replaced by Douglas-fir seedlings. In drier, more open forests, fire killed young Douglas-firs, while mature trees sometimes survived. Without fire, Douglas-fir is increasing on many drier sites, such as in Garry oak or ponderosa pine forests, and decreasing on wetter sites, replaced by western hemlock and other trees with greater shade tolerance. Named for botanists Archibald Menzies and David Douglas, Douglas-fir is not a true fir (*Abies* spp.). True firs have erect seed cones that fall apart at maturity, and rounded buds. State tree of Oregon.

Tsuga heterophylla
PINACEAE
WESTERN HEMLOCK
Native, common, seed cones mature in
1 year, 100–167 ft. West-side forest, east-
side forest, low to mid elevation

Tree, crown narrow and triangular, tip drooping,
branch tips tilted downward, canopy appears lacy from
below. Trunk straight, bark grayish to reddish brown,
thin, furrowed and scaly with age. Buds egg-shaped,
grayish brown, twigs hairy, yellowish brown.
LEAVES evergreen, single, stalked, needlelike, 0.2–1 in.
long, length variable, green above, white stomatal band
beneath, tip rounded. Leaf stalk remains attached to
branch when needle is shed. Needles protrude out to
the side of branches, creating a flat appearance.
CONES pollen cones yellow, oval, 0.1 in. long. Seed
cones egg-shaped, 0.5–1 in. long, tan, scales egg-
shaped. Seeds and wing to about 0.2 in. long.
ECOLOGY slow growing and shade tolerant, often establishing on moist sites under the canopy of other tree
species and creating a shady environment in which its
seedlings can outcompete Douglas-fir and other rivals.
Seed is mostly wind-dispersed and germinates on a variety of substrates. Given
long intervals between disturbance
events, western hemlock can become
the dominant tree, living a millen-
nium or more, but often succumbing to
insects or disease by 300 years of age.
State tree of Washington.

Tsuga mertensiana
PINACEAE
MOUNTAIN HEMLOCK
Native, common, seed cones mature in 1
year, 75–130 ft. West-side forest, east-side
forest, subalpine, mid to high elevation

Tree, crown narrowly triangular to flattened and irregular, tip erect to slightly droopy, branch ends often tilted upward. Bark rough when young, becoming thick and furrowed with age, blackish gray to reddish brown. **LEAVES** evergreen, single, needlelike, 0.4–0.8 in. long, yellowish to bluish green, whitish stomatal bands on both surfaces. Leaf stalk remains attached to branch when needle is shed. Needles of equal lengths, protruding at many angles from branch, creating a brushy appearance. **CONES** pollen cones bluish green, 0.2 in. long. Seed cones dangling, elliptic, 1–3 in. long, green to brownish purple when immature, becoming dark brown, cone scales fan-shaped. Seeds winged, dark brown, 0.2 in. long, wing slightly longer than seed. **ECOLOGY** grows with a variety of other conifers on cool mountain slopes, often in areas with a deep winter snowpack, forming dense, shady stands with straight trunks at lower elevations, displacing many species with less shade tolerance. Becomes shorter and crooked to shrubby near and above timberline. Common associates are subalpine fir and silver fir. Long-lived, often 400 years or more, and slow to recover from fire and other disturbances. *Abies amabilis*, which has greater shade tolerance, can replace it over time, under certain conditions.

Callitropsis nootkatensis
(*Cupressus nootkatensis, Chamaecyparis nootkatensis*)
CUPRESSACEAE
ALASKA YELLOW-CEDAR, ALASKA CEDAR
Native, locally common, seed cones mature
in 1–2 years, 67–133 ft. West-side forest, east-
side forest, subalpine, low to high elevation

Tree, sometimes shrubby, crown pyramidal when
young, becoming narrow, tip drooping, bark grayish brown, in vertical strips, inner bark yellowish,
branches mostly drooping. **LEAVES** evergreen, opposite, overlapping, scalelike, 0.06–0.1 in. long, bluish green, tips spreading and sharp-pointed, prickly.
CONES pollen cones grayish brown, to 0.2 in. long. Seed
cones round, 0.5 in. long, light green when immature, becoming dark reddish brown, cone scales with
short horn near tip. **ECOLOGY** grows in cool, wet places,
mostly in the mountains, often in avalanche chutes,
on ridgetops, near bogs, and on moist forest slopes, but
also near sea level on the Olympic Peninsula, Vancouver Island, and elsewhere. Its narrow crown and drooping branches effectively limit snow loads. Assumes a
shrubby form above timberline and spreads, creating
patches as much as 50 ft. across. Long-lived, often over
1000 years, and fairly shade tolerant
but less so than some conifers, such as
Pacific silver fir and mountain hemlock. Much of the seed produced is not
viable. Also reproduces vegetatively
from branches near ground level that
root. Leaves give off an unpleasant odor
when crushed.

Calocedrus decurrens (*Libocedrus decurrens*)
CUPRESSACEAE
INCENSE CEDAR
Native, common, seed cones mature in 1
year, 67–230 ft. Serpentine, west-side forest,
east-side forest, low to high elevation

Tree, crown cone-shaped, tip erect, trunk tapered
from wide base, bark reddish or orangish brown, furrowed with long ridges between, shed as fibrous strips,
branches dip downward, foliage has a fan-shaped
appearance. **LEAVES** evergreen, scalelike, in appar-
ent whorl of 4, overlapping, 0.1–0.5 in. long, curved,
shiny green, tips curved inward, pointed. **CONES** pollen cones light to reddish brown. Seed cones dangling
at branch tips, tulip- or duckbill-shaped, some scales
bent back at maturity, 0.7–1.5 in. long, reddish or
golden brown. Cones eventually deciduous but often
fragment the following spring. Seeds winged, light
brown, 0.3 in. **ECOLOGY** grows on moist to dry sites,
often in forests with Pacific madrone and a variety of
conifers and oaks. Usually remains shorter than other
tree species on moister, cool sites, growing scattered
among them. It can grow in serpentine soils, competes
well on hot, dry sites, and is rarely found in limestone.
Relatively slow growing and long-lived, typically 500
years or more. Moderately shade tolerant and extremely
drought tolerant. Mature trees can survive low-intensity fires, thanks to their thick bark, but scarring
caused by fire can provide entry to pocket dry rot fungi.
Seeds are wind-dispersed, aided by the long (about 1
in.) wing.

Chamaecyparis lawsoniana
(Cupressus lawsoniana)
CUPRESSACEAE
PORT ORFORD CEDAR

Native, scattered, seed cones mature in 1 year, 67–133 ft. Coastal, streambanks, west-side forest, low to mid elevation

Tree, crown cone-shaped, tip erect, bark thick, silvery brown, furrows and ridges uneven, branches droop only at the tips, foliage has a lacy, feathery appearance. **LEAVES** evergreen, scalelike, opposite, overlapping, 0.1 in. long, bright green, tips curved inward, pointed. **CONES** pollen cones dark brown, to 0.2 in. long. Seed cones round, 0.2–0.4 in. long, whitish green when immature, becoming reddish brown. Seeds to 0.2 in. long, wing same length as seed or slightly longer. **ECOLOGY** grows in a variety of habitats and soils, from sand dunes and streambanks to forest slopes, forming communities with many tree species. Long-lived, often more than 600 years, and shade tolerant, it grows on cool, moist sites, often near the coast where humidity is high. Port Orford cedar grows best on deep soils on slopes and terraces near the ocean; many of the large trees in these areas have been logged, leaving a few remnant individuals and young groves. In other parts of its range, it grows in small, scattered populations, often near water. It is resistant to fire damage but is susceptible to an introduced phytophthora root rot fungus, among other pests.

Hesperocyparis bakeri
(*Cupressus bakeri, Callitropsis bakeri*)
CUPRESSACEAE
MODOC CYPRESS, BAKER'S CYPRESS
Native, rare, seed cones mature in 2 years,
23–100 ft. Rocky sites, serpentine, chaparral,
east-side forest, mid to high elevation

Tree, crown rounded, narrow, sparse, bark thin, smooth and cherry-red when young, becoming plate-like and grayish brown with age, branches oppo-site with adjacent pairs at right angles to each other. **LEAVES** evergreen, opposite, scalelike, dark green to grayish green, pitlike resin gland present on lower (outward-facing) surface. **CONES** pollen cones round, yellowish, to 0.1 in. long. Seed cones round, 0.5–1 in. long, silvery to dull brown, surface warty. Mature cones remain closed and persist on the tree. Seeds brown, to 0.2 in. long. **ECOLOGY** shade intolerant, often growing in a transitional area between commu-nities, as between ponderosa pine forest and juniper woodlands. On dry sites it is often found in chaparral and associated with knobcone pine; on more moder-ate sites, it grows in mixed conifer forests. Stands tend be open and stunted, and soils well drained, derived from either serpentine or igneous rocks such as basalt. Often found on north- to northeast-facing slopes. Seed cones open only sporadically without fire. With fire, cones open (heat causes the resin sealing the cone scales to melt), and the seed falls on exposed soil. Seed-lings are usually abundant following fire. Trees have little fire resistance and are easily killed by fire.

Hesperocyparis macnabiana
(*Cupressus macnabiana*)
CUPRESSACEAE
MACNAB CYPRESS
Native, locally common, seed cones mature
in 2 years, 10–40 ft. Serpentine, chaparral,
east-side forest, low to mid elevation

Shrub or tree, aromatic, crown cone-shaped, dense,
bark grayish brown, furrowed, fibrous, smallest twigs
with comblike branching pattern. **LEAVES** evergreen,
opposite, scalelike, bluish or grayish green, pitlike
resin gland present on lower (outward-facing) surface,
resin abundant. **CONES** pollen cones round, yellowish,
to 0.1 in. long. Seed cones round, 0.5–1 in. long, gray
to reddish brown, cone scale with hornlike projection.
Cones remain closed and persist on the tree. Seeds
brown, to 0.2 in. long. **ECOLOGY** shade intolerant, often
grows in a transitional area between community types,
mostly in even-aged stands. On dry sites, it is often
associated with chaparral and pine-oak woodlands; on
more moderate sites, it grows in mixed conifer forests.
Often found on serpentine but also grows in alluvial or
igneous-derived soils. Prefers north- to northeast-
facing slopes. Seed cones open only sporadically without fire. When a fire sweeps through a MacNab cypress
population, the tree's crown usually burns, heating the
cones, which then open; and the seed falls on exposed
soil. Seed is abundant after fire, but seedlings less so,
possibly due to low seed germination rates. In some
cases, seeds are released when cones stop receiving
nutrients (due to branch or tree death) and dry out.
Thus some seedlings can establish in openings without fire.

Hesperocyparis macrocarpa
(*Cupressus macrocarpa*)
CUPRESSACEAE
MONTEREY CYPRESS
Native and non-native, rare, seed cones mature in 2 years, 60–83 ft. Coastal, west-side forest, low elevation
Tree, crown narrow in protected spots, otherwise irregular, flattened and spreading, bark thick, fibrous, furrowed, brown to gray, branches opposite with adjacent pairs at right angles to each other, twigs round. **LEAVES** evergreen, opposite, scalelike, bright to dark green, pitlike resin gland absent or shallow on lower (outward-facing) surface, resinless. **CONES** pollen cones round, yellowish, to 0.2 in. long. Seed cones oval to round, 1–1.5 in. long, grayish brown, cone scales smooth. Cones remain closed and persist on the tree. Seeds dark brown, to 0.2 in. long. **ECOLOGY** native to a coastal bluff near Monterey, California, growing in thin, granitic soils, but now naturalized along other parts of the California and Oregon coasts. It is not considered native to Oregon. Flattened, irregularly spreading crowns form as a response to high winds and salt spray; when grown in protected areas, crowns are

much narrower and erect. Heating from fire causes cones to open and release the seeds. Cones also occasionally open without fire. Seedlings grow best in mineral soils and are shade intolerant. Monterey cypress lives 200–300 years. Fossils indicate the species once had a greater range. Rare in California.

Juniperus californica
CUPRESSACEAE
CALIFORNIA JUNIPER
Native, common, seed cones mature in 1
year, 3–13(33) ft. Rocky sites, chaparral,
east-side forest, low to mid elevation

Shrub or tree, multi-stemmed, crown rounded, bark
thin, gray, shed in strips, branches spreading to
ascending. **LEAVES** evergreen, in whorls of 3, needlelike on young plants, scalelike otherwise, rarely overlapping, to 0.1 in. long, light green, flattened, gland
on lower (outward-facing) surface visible, tip rounded
to pointed. **CONES** pollen and seed
cones mostly on separate plants. Seed
cone round, dry, 0.3–0.5 in. long, bluish brown becoming reddish brown,
stalked. Seeds brown, to 0.3 in. long.
ECOLOGY grows in chaparral and forests
in thin, rocky soils. Seedlings are shade
dependent, shade intolerant otherwise.

Juniperus communis
CUPRESSACEAE
COMMON JUNIPER, DWARF JUNIPER
Native, common, seed cones mature in 2 years,
1.7–10 ft. Rocky sites, west-side forest, east-side
forest, alpine, subalpine, low to high elevation
Shrub or small tree, multi-stemmed, bark thin, reddish brown, scaly and peeling, branches erect to trailing, sometimes mat-forming. **LEAVES** evergreen, in
whorls of 3, needlelike, awl-like to lance-shaped, 0.3–
0.5 in. long, whitish above, dark green below, tip some-

times rounded, mostly sharply pointed.
CONES pollen and seed cones on separate plants. Seed cone berrylike, fleshy,
round to oval, 0.2–0.5 in. long, green
becoming bright blue to blackish with
whitish bloom, in leaf axil, stalkless.
Seeds 1–3. **ECOLOGY** grows in open forests, rocky slopes, chaparral.

Juniperus horizontalis
CUPRESSACEAE
CREEPING JUNIPER
Native, scattered, seed cones mature in 1–2 years, 6–12
in. Rocky sites, east-side forest, low to mid elevation
Shrub, bark brown, fibrous, shed in thin strips, stems
creeping, twigs erect, smooth, mat-forming.
LEAVES evergreen, opposite, scalelike, to 0.1 in. long,
overlapping, green, gland oval, dry, on lower (outward-

facing) surface, tips spreading, rounded
or pointed. **CONES** pollen and seed cones
on separate plants, seed cones berrylike,
fleshy, round to oval, 0.3 in. long, bluish
black to brownish with whitish bloom,
stalks curved. Seeds 2–6.
ECOLOGY grows in rocky or sandy soils,
in dunes, rock outcrops, streambanks.
Leaves turn reddish purple in winter.

Juniperus maritima
CUPRESSACEAE
SEASIDE JUNIPER
Native, scattered, seed cones mature in 1–2 years,
3–50 ft. Coastal, west-side forest, low elevation
Tree or shrub, crown cone-shaped to rounded, bark
brown, scaly to stringy, shed in strips, twigs reddish
brown, non-hairy. **LEAVES** evergreen, opposite, awl-like
on young plants, scalelike otherwise, rarely overlapping, to 0.1 in. long, dark green, rounded, gland on
lower (outward-facing) surface visible, tips rounded.
CONES pollen and seed cones on separate plants. Seed
cones mostly kidney-shaped, berrylike, fleshy, 0.2–0.3
in. long, light blue or tan when immature, becoming blackish blue, stalks mostly straight, seeds visible,
extending beyond cone scales. Seeds 1(2).
ECOLOGY grows in forests, forest edges, coastal bluffs,
and rock outcrops in sandy or granitic soils. Formerly
considered part of *J. scopulorum*; scientists think seaside juniper was isolated during the Pleistocene, lead-
ing to DNA and chemical differences. Distinguish seaside juniper by seed cones that mature faster (in 14–16
months), dark green leaves with rounded tips, and visible seeds. Rare in British Columbia.

Juniperus occidentalis
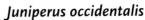
CUPRESSACEAE
WESTERN JUNIPER, SIERRA JUNIPER
Native, locally common, seed cones mature in 2 years, 17–67 ft. Rocky sites, west-side forest, east-side forest, subalpine, mid to high elevation

Tree, crown cone-shaped to rounded, trunk single, bark reddish brown to brown, furrowed, stringy, branches spreading to ascending. **LEAVES** evergreen, in whorls of 3 or opposite, awl-like on young plants, scalelike otherwise, rarely overlapping, to 0.1 in. long, green, flattened, gland on lower (outward-facing) surface visible, tip rounded to pointed. **CONES** pollen and seed cones sometimes on separate plants. Seed cones egg-shaped, berrylike, fleshy, 0.3–0.5 in. long, bluish green when immature, becoming blackish blue, stalked. Seeds 1–3. **ECOLOGY** western juniper grows primarily in sagebrush steppe and open conifer forest communities, in sandy or rocky soils. Drought tolerant, it can grow with as little as 8 in. of rain per year, thanks in part to its deep root system. Susceptible to

fire damage, rarely surviving severe fire. It does not resprout, recovering instead through seed germination. Seeds are dispersed by birds and mammals. Historically, in fire-prone habitats it was restricted to protected areas such as rocky sites. Suppression of fire has resulted in the expansion of its habitat.

Juniperus osteosperma
CUPRESSACEAE
UTAH JUNIPER
Native, common, seed cones mature in
1–2 years, 15–27 ft. Rocky sites, east-
side forest, mid to high elevation

Tree or shrub, crown rounded, trunk single or multi-
stemmed, bark thin, grayish brown to whitish gray,
peeling in strips. **LEAVES** evergreen, opposite, awl-like
on young plants, scalelike otherwise, rarely overlapping, to 0.1 in. long, light yellowish green, curved,
gland on lower (outward-facing) surface indistinct, tip
rounded. **CONES** pollen and seed cones on the same
plant. Seed cones round, berrylike, leathery, 0.2–0.5
in. long, bluish brown when immature, becoming reddish brown, stalks straight. Seeds 1–2. **ECOLOGY** grows
on rocky sites, often in association with pines or other
junipers, its deep roots allowing it to slowly form open
stands in areas that are too dry for other tree species.
Has allelopathic effect on many native grass species.
More abundant since European settle-
ment, possibly due to fire suppression,
climate change, and grazing, which
reduces fire fuels. The similar *J. californica* has an easily seen leaf gland,
and pollen and seed cones on separate
plants; *J. occidentalis* has bluish black
seed cones.

Juniperus scopulorum
CUPRESSACEAE
**ROCKY MOUNTAIN JUNIPER, ROCKY
MOUNTAIN REDCEDAR**

Native, common, seed cones mature in 2
years, 3–30 ft. Rocky sites, west-side forest,
east-side forest, low to mid elevation

Tree or shrub, crown cone-shaped to narrow, bark reddish brown, scaly to stringy, branches often extend
down to ground level, twigs bright reddish brown, non-
hairy. **LEAVES** evergreen, opposite, awl-like on young
plants, scalelike otherwise, rarely overlapping, to 0.1
in. long, bluish gray, rounded, gland on lower (outward-facing) surface visible, sometimes spreading, tips
pointed or rounded. **CONES** pollen and seed cones on
separate plants. Seed cones round, berrylike, fleshy,
0.2–0.4 in. long, light blue or tan when immature,
becoming blackish blue, stalks mostly straight, seeds
not visible, within cone scales. Seeds 2(1).
ECOLOGY grows in a variety of open, dry forests, grasslands, and shrubby areas. Shade intolerant, slow growing, and long-lived, 300 years or more. The fleshy cones
stay on the plant over winter and are consumed in great
quantities by various bird species; they and other animals act as dispersal agents, spreading the seed far and
wide. Seed requires a resting period of 12–18 months
between maturity and germination. Seedlings grow
best in partial shade on moist sites; however, damage
from frost is common.

Sequoia sempervirens

CUPRESSACEAE

COAST REDWOOD

Native, locally common, seed cones
mature in 1 year, 200–367 ft. Coastal, west-
side forest, low to mid elevation

Tree, crown cone-shaped, becoming open and irregular with age, trunk flared at the base, bark thick, reddish brown, ridged and furrowed, branches spreading to sweeping downward with upward-facing tips, twigs dark green. **LEAVES** evergreen, alternate, needlelike, to 1 in. long, dark green above, 2 whitish stomatal bands below, tips pointed. Leaves near cones and at branch tips may be shorter, triangular to lance-shaped and grow against the stem. **CONES** pollen cones round to egg-shaped, 0.1–0.2 in. long, single at branch tips or on side branchlets. Seed cones oval, woody, 0.5–1.5 in. long, reddish brown and open at maturity, dangling at branch tips. Seeds to 0.2 in. long, wings 2, narrow. **ECOLOGY** grows near the coast, not directly adjacent to but usually within 35 miles of the ocean, where fog is common, humidity is high, and frost and drought are rare. Intolerant of salt-laden spray and breezes. Coast redwood forests occur along streams, on slopes, and in valleys. Adapted to survive fire, having thick, fire-resistant bark; trees resprout from the base and along the trunk when the crown is damaged or killed. Many specimens live over 2000 years. Coast redwood and giant sequoia are the state trees of California. *Taxus brevifolia* has similar leaf shape, but it and all yews lack the whitish stomatal bands below and have fleshy red arils.

Thuja plicata
CUPRESSACEAE
WESTERN REDCEDAR

Native, common, seed cones mature in 1 year, 70–233 ft. Coastal, bog/fen/wetland, streambanks, west-side forest, east-side forest, low to mid elevation

Tree, crown cone-shaped, tip drooping, trunk straight, often flared at the base, bark thin, reddish to grayish brown, with long, shallow furrows. Branches point upward at the tip, twigs sweep downward, the foliage has a lacy, flattened look. **LEAVES** evergreen, opposite, scalelike, overlapping and braidlike, 0.1–0.2 in. long, surfaces shiny yellowish green, tips flat against stem, pointed. **CONES** pollen cones reddish, 0.1 in. long. Seed cones rosebud-shaped, 0.5–0.6 in. long, bluish when immature, becoming brown. Seeds winged, reddish brown, to 0.3 in. wings included. **ECOLOGY** shade tolerant and long-lived (800–1000 years), rarely dominating plant communities but scattered instead into a mix of species, including western hemlock, red alder, and Douglas-fir. Very wet places are an exception, and here western redcedar often rules. Seed is produced copiously and wind-dispersed, germinating best on disturbed or open sites; in shady places, reproduction is primarily vegetative. Often found in places where fire is infrequent but can survive low-intensity fire for, despite its thin bark, it has a remarkable resistance to decay and can persevere even if nearly girdled. Extensively utilized by First Nations and Native Americans, its wood made into a variety of objects, the bark peeled for baskets and other items, and the foliage used as kindling. Provincial tree of British Columbia.

Taxus brevifolia
TAXACEAE
PACIFIC YEW, WESTERN YEW

Native, scattered, seeds mature in 1 year, 20–40 ft.

West-side forest, east-side forest, low to mid elevation
Tree or shrub, crown open, often irregular, trunk
straight to contorted, bark thin, scaly, outer bark purplish brown, inner bark reddish purple, branches
spreading to drooping. Leaves in 2 rows along
branches, forming flat sprays. **LEAVES** evergreen, alternate, linear, 0.5–1 in. long, flexible, surfaces yellowish
green (paler beneath), narrowed to a short stalk at the
base, tips pointed. **CONES** pollen cones and arils on separate plants. Pollen cones round, 0.1 in. across, yellowish. Seeds not in a cone, rather the seed coat becomes
enlarged and fleshy, a bright red aril, cup-shaped, edible. Seeds to 0.25 in. long, poisonous. **ECOLOGY** grows
in shady, mixed conifer or occasionally hardwood forests along streams, on slopes, and in draws, usually in
areas where fire is rare. Reproduces through rooting
branches or by seed. Seeds are dispersed mainly by
birds. Can resprout from the base but not after fire, due
to heat damage. First Nations and Native Americans
used the strong, dense wood of this slow-growing species to make implements. Its thin bark is the source of
the cancer drug taxol; most taxol is now made syntheti-
cally rather than harvested from the wild.

Torreya californica
TAXACEAE
CALIFORNIA NUTMEG

Native, scattered, seed cones mature in 2 years, 15–90 ft. Streambanks, east-side forest, low to high elevation Tree, crown rounded, bark thin, brown, orange-tinged, smooth to scaly, branches spreading to drooping, twigs reddish brown. Leaves in 2 rows along branches, forming flat sprays. **LEAVES** evergreen, alternate, linear, 1–3 in. long, rigid, dark green above, 2 grooved lighter stomatal bands below, narrowed to a short stalk at base, tips sharp-pointed. **CONES** pollen cones and arils on separate plants. Pollen cones whitish, egg-shaped. Seed 1, not in a cone, rather the seed coat becomes enlarged and somewhat fleshy, an aril, leathery, light green with purple streaks, olive-like, 1–1.5 in. long, inedible unless properly prepared. **ECOLOGY** grows in conifer forests and woodlands, on moist slopes, streambanks, canyons, and sheltered areas, occasionally in chaparral, and often scattered in the understory beneath larger trees. Slow growing and shade tolerant. Easily killed by fire but resprouts afterward. Seeds are eaten and dispersed by birds. Native Americans processed and ate the seeds, and used the wood to make bows. Leaves emit a foul odor when crushed. Endemic to California.

Atriplex canescens
AMARANTHACEAE (CHENOPODIACEAE)
FOURWING SALTBUSH
Native, common, blooms all summer, 1.5–7
ft. Shrub-steppe, low to mid elevation
Shrub, erect, crown rounded, twigs whitish, scaly, becoming smooth, spines absent. **LEAVES** deciduous or not, alternate, linear to oval, 0.5–2 in. long, surfaces grayish, scaly, edges smooth, tips rounded or pointed. **FLOWERS** male and female flowers on separate plants, male flowers in leafy clusters, tepals 5, scaly, sometimes reddish, female flowers enclosed by bracts, clusters leafy or not. **FRUIT** 1-seeded capsule, to 0.5 in. long, 4-winged, wings wavy or toothed. **ECOLOGY** grows in coastal sage scrub, shrub-steppe communities, juniper woodlands, and other arid places, often in salty soils. A variable species, hybridizes readily.

Atriplex confertifolia
AMARANTHACEAE (CHENOPODIACEAE)
SHADSCALE SALTBUSH
Native, locally common, blooms all summer, 12–32 in. Shrub-steppe, low to mid elevation
Shrub, erect, crown rounded, many-branched, branches and twigs spiny, scaly, gray, or whitish. **LEAVES** evergreen to semi-deciduous, alternate, oval to round, 0.5–1 in. long, surfaces grayish scaly, edges smooth, tips rounded. **FLOWERS** male and female flowers on separate plants, clusters in leaf axils, male flowers yellow, tepals 5, female flowers partially enclosed by bracts joined <½ their length. **FRUIT** 1-seeded capsule, oval to round. **ECOLOGY** grows in sagebrush steppe, pinyon-juniper woodlands, and other arid places, on flats, ridges, and slopes. Prefers well-drained, somewhat salty soils.

Atriplex gardneri var. *falcata*
(*Atriplex falcata*)
AMARANTHACEAE (CHENOPODIACEAE)
SICKLE SALTBUSH, JONES SALTBUSH
Native, locally common, blooms all summer,
6–24 in. Shrub-steppe, mid elevation

Shrub, trailing to erect, clump-forming, stems grayish, scaly, branch tips not spiny. **LEAVES** deciduous,
alternate, linear to spatula-shaped, 0.5–2 in. long, 5–10
times longer than wide, surfaces grayish green, scaly.
FLOWERS male and female flowers mostly on separate plants, in clusters, in leaf axils and at stem ends,
male flowers brown, bracts of female flowers fused to
near the tips. **FRUIT** fruiting bracts lance-shaped, tip
toothed, teeth joined ½
of length. **ECOLOGY** grows
in sagebrush steppe or
scrub communities, in
saline soils, often with
greasewood.

Atriplex lentiformis
AMARANTHACEAE (CHENOPODIACEAE)
BIG SALTBUSH
Native, locally common, blooms mid summer–
autumn, 2.5–13 ft. Bog/fen/wetland, disturbed,
shrub-steppe, low to mid elevation

Shrub, erect, often as wide as it is tall, branches not
spine-tipped, twigs often hairy. **LEAVES** persistent,
alternate, triangular to egg-shaped, 0.2–2 in. long, surfaces grayish green, edges smooth to wavy, tips pointed
or rounded. **FLOWERS** in branched clusters, unisexual,
usually on separate plants, petals and sepals absent,
male flowers yellow, female flowers with egg-shaped
to round fused bracts below, bract edges wavy or not.
FRUIT dry, reddish, 1-seeded.
ECOLOGY grows in salt marshes, riparian areas, shrub-steppe, and disturbed
areas.

Atriplex leucophylla
AMARANTHACEAE (CHENOPODIACEAE)
BEACH SALTBUSH

Native, locally common, blooms early spring–autumn, 4–12 in. Coastal, bog/fen/wetland, low elevation

Subshrub, stems mostly trailing. **LEAVES** evergreen, alternate but can seem opposite, oval to egg-shaped, 0.5–1.5 in. long, surfaces grayish green, scaly-hairy, edges smooth, tips rounded or pointed. **FLOWERS** unisexual or bisexual, both types on the same plant, male and bisexual flowers in clusters at branch tips, female clusters in leaf axils. Female flowers lack tepals, are enclosed by 2 round bracts that are fused ⅔ of their length, scaly-hairy, texture spongy. **FRUIT** 1-seeded capsule.

ECOLOGY grows in sand dunes and sandy soils along beaches and salt marshes, rarely inland, usually within range of salt spray.

Grayia spinosa (Atriplex spinosa)
AMARANTHACEAE (CHENOPODIACEAE)
SPINY HOPSAGE

Native, scattered, blooms all spring, 1–5 ft. Shrub-steppe, low to mid elevation

Shrub, erect, crown rounded and much-branched, bark gray, twigs reddish brown with star-shaped hairs, tips spiny. **LEAVES** deciduous or not, alternate, lance- to spoon-shaped, 0.5–1 in. long, green with whitish pointed tip, edges smooth. **FLOWERS** male and female flowers on separate plants, male flowers have 4 tepals with clusters in leaf axils, female flowers are enclosed by 2 roundish, whitish to rosy red bracts, clusters at branch tips. **FRUIT** 1-seeded capsule, round to heart-shaped, brown.

ECOLOGY grows in valleys, flat areas, and slopes in sagebrush steppe, juniper woodlands, and other arid communities, often in alkaline or salty soils.

Krascheninnikovia lanata (*Eurotia lanata*)
AMARANTHACEAE (CHENOPODIACEAE)
WINTERFAT

Native, common, blooms late spring–early summer,
1–2 ft. Shrub-steppe, low to mid elevation
Subshrub, stems erect, grayish turning reddish brown,
densely hairy, hairs often star-shaped. **LEAVES** deciduous, often falling when new leaves emerge, alternate, linear, 0.5–1.5 in. long, grayish green, hairy,
edges rolled under, leaf axils often have clusters of
smaller leaves within. **FLOWERS** clusters in upper stem
leaf axils, flowers unisexual, male flowers shed soon
after blooming, female flowers enclosed by 2 partially
fused, long-hairy bracts. **FRUIT** 1-seeded capsule, hairy.
ECOLOGY grows in arid shrub communi-
ties and pine-juniper woodlands, often
in salty soils.

Salsola tragus (*Salsola kali*)
AMARANTHACEAE (CHENOPODIACEAE)
RUSSIAN THISTLE, TUMBLEWEED

Non-native, common, blooms late summer, 0.3–3
ft. Disturbed, shrub-steppe, low to mid elevation
Shrublike annual with rigid stems and a rounded
shape, branches hairy or not, purplish when young.
LEAVES alternate, linear, 0.5–1 in. long, lowest leaves
longer, to 2.5 in., edges smooth, tips spiny.
FLOWERS solitary or in small clusters in leaf axils, with
spiny bracts, tepals white to purplish, 5, joined at the
base, becoming winged. **FRUIT** 1-seeded capsule, cup-
shaped, winged, purplish. **ECOLOGY** grows on disturbed areas in the shrub-steppe and other arid lands,
along roadsides, and field edges from
low to montane elevation. Stem often
detaches at ground level in autumn,
forming a tumbleweed.

Sarcobatus vermiculatus
AMARANTHACEAE (CHENOPODIACEAE)
GREASEWOOD

Native, locally common, blooms late spring–mid summer, 3–7 ft. Shrub-steppe, low to mid elevation
Shrub, spreading, bark whitish, branches rigid, often spine-tipped. **LEAVES** deciduous, alternate, fleshy, linear, 0.5–1.5 in. long, surfaces green, hairy or not, edges smooth, tips rounded. **FLOWERS** unisexual, both on same plant, male flowers in catkinlike clusters, stamens covered by diamond-shaped scales, female flowers with cup-shaped tepal around the pistil, solitary in leaf axils. **FRUIT** 1-seeded capsule, oval, winged around the middle. **ECOLOGY** grows in arid shrub communities, roadsides, pine-juniper woodlands, and dry streambeds, often in alkaline or salty soils.

Suaeda nigra (*Suaeda moquinii*)
AMARANTHACEAE (CHENOPODIACEAE)
BUSH SEEPWEED

Native, locally common, blooms late spring–autumn, 0.7–5 ft. Vernal-wet, shrub-steppe, low to mid elevation
Subshrub or shrub, sometimes annual, erect to spreading, much-branched, stems shiny, green to reddish, non-hairy. **LEAVES** deciduous, alternate, linear or lance-shaped, 0.2–1 in. long, fleshy, surfaces green to reddish, abruptly narrowed at the base, tips rounded, bracts shorter than leaves. **FLOWERS** single or in small clusters in leaf axils, bisexual, sepals 5, fleshy, stamens 5, petals absent. **FRUIT** seeds erect, black, wrapped inside sepals. **ECOLOGY** grows in saline or alkaline soils, often in seasonally moist habitats such as salt flats, seeps, streambanks, and slopes.

Rhus ovata
ANACARDIACEAE
SUGAR SUMAC, SUGAR BUSH
Native, uncommon, blooms all spring, 7–33
ft. Chaparral, low to mid elevation

Shrub or tree, erect, crown rounded, twigs reddish.
LEAVES evergreen, alternate, oval to egg-shaped, 1–3 in.
long, surfaces shiny green, smooth, folded at midrib,
edges smooth, toothed, or lobed, tips pointed.
FLOWERS in dense, pyramid-shaped clusters at stem
ends, flowers bell-shaped, petals and sepals 5, sepals
red, petals white to pinkish. **FRUIT** berrylike, flattened
globe with sugary coating, red, glandular-hairy, edible.
ECOLOGY grows in chaparral slopes and canyons, also
planted to curtail erosion. Primarily a
southern California species.

See Anacardiaceae with compound
leaves, page 370; see *Rhus* with compound leaves, page 370

Ilex aquifolium
AQUIFOLIACEAE
ENGLISH HOLLY
Non-native, scattered, blooms mid–late spring,
7–17 ft. Disturbed, west-side forest, low elevation

Shrub or tree, erect, many-branched, twigs hairy.
LEAVES evergreen, alternate, egg-shaped, 1–2.5 in.
long, shiny dark green above, edges smooth, toothed,
or lobed, teeth and lobes often with sharp, spiny
tips. **FLOWERS** in clusters in leaf axils, mostly male
or female, on separate or the same plant, small, petals and sepals 4, whitish, sweet-scented. **FRUIT** berry,
round, red, inedible, toxic to humans in quantity.
ECOLOGY invasive escapee from cultivation, grows in
sun or shade, in disturbed areas and forests. Seeds spread by birds. Can be con-
fused with *Berberis* spp. that have compound leaves, yellow flowers, and dusky
blue berries.

Hedera helix
ARALIACEAE
ENGLISH IVY

Non-native, common, blooms spring–autumn, 0.3–100 ft. Disturbed, west-side forest, low to mid elevation

Woody vine, stems trailing or climbing. **LEAVES** evergreen, alternate, triangular to egg-shaped, 1.5–4 in. long, surfaces glossy, dark green, edges smooth to 3- to 5-lobed, tips pointed. **FLOWERS** small, greenish yellow, in ball-like clusters. **FRUIT** berry, bluish black, eaten by wildlife, often spread by birds, inedible and toxic to humans. **ECOLOGY** invasive escapee from wide cultivation, grows in forests and disturbed areas, choking out native species. Can cover tree trunks and crown.

See Araliaceae with basal leaves, page 419

Oplopanax horridus
ARALIACEAE
DEVIL'S CLUB

Native, common, blooms mid spring–mid summer, 3–10 ft. Bog/fen/wetland, west-side forest, east-side forest, low to high elevation

Shrub, stems mostly unbranched, densely spiny.

LEAVES deciduous, alternate, maple-leaf-shaped, 4–14 in. long, surfaces dark green, prickly below, edges 7- to 9-lobed, toothed, tips pointed. **FLOWERS** small, white, petals and sepals 5, in a long, narrow cluster at stem ends. **FRUIT** berry, red, seeds several, relished by wildlife, especially bears, inedible for humans. **ECOLOGY** drought intolerant, grows along streambanks, seeps, in moist forests, and avalanche chutes. Important medicinal species for Native Americans. Spines on all parts of the plant cause irritation when touched.

Aristolochia californica
ARISTOLOCHIACEAE
CALIFORNIA PIPEVINE, CALIFORNIA
DUTCHMAN'S PIPE

Native, locally common, blooms winter–early
spring, to 17 ft. Streambanks, chaparral,
west-side forest, low elevation

Vine, often climbing, stems hairy when young.
LEAVES deciduous, alternate, arrowhead- to egg-shaped,
1.5–6 in. long, green above, hairy below, edges smooth,
tips rounded. **FLOWERS** single in leaf axils, tubular,
U-shaped, odor foul, sepals brownish purple, petals
absent, grows larger with age. **FRUIT** capsule, cylindric
to egg-shaped, wings 6, 1–2.5 in. long. **ECOLOGY** grows
along streambanks in forests and chap-
arral, pollinated by fungus gnats, hosts
larvae of the pipevine swallowtail but-
terfly. Endemic to California.

Antennaria suffrutescens
ASTERACEAE
EVERGREEN EVERLASTING, SHRUBBY
EVERLASTING

Native, uncommon, blooms mid summer,
2–5 in. Serpentine, mid elevation

Subshrub, erect, multi-stemmed, basal leaves
absent by bloom time. **LEAVES** evergreen, alternate,
spatula-shaped, 0.2–0.5 in. long, green above, densely
white-hairy below, edges smooth, tips notched.
FLOWERS aggregated into heads, single at stem ends,
male and female flowers on separate plants, bracts
woolly-hairy, glandular, all disk flowers, petals yellow.
FRUIT achene, bumpy. **ECOLOGY** grows exclusively on
serpentine substrates, on open slopes or
forests. Rare in California.

See Asteraceae with basal leaves, page
350; compound leaves, page 374

Artemisia arbuscula
ASTERACEAE
LOW SAGEBRUSH
Native, common, blooms mid–late summer, 4–16 in. East-side forest, shrub-steppe, mid elevation
Aromatic shrub, stems grayish green to brown, many-branched, form rounded. **LEAVES** evergreen except deciduous on flower stalks, alternate, wedge-shaped, 0.1–0.5 in. long, surfaces grayish green, densely hairy, tips 3-lobed, lobes to ⅓ of total leaf length.
FLOWERS aggregated into heads, inflorescence unbranched, heads single or in small clusters along leafy flowering stalk, bracts egg-shaped, grayish green, hairy, all disk flowers, bisexual, petals yellow.

FRUIT achene, brown, glandular.
ECOLOGY grows on hills, ridges, and slopes in dry forest or shrub-steppe communities, soils usually eroded or shallow, rocky or clayey. The similar *A. tridentata* is usually taller with larger leaves and has a branched inflorescence.

See *Artemisia* with compound leaves, page 374

Artemisia cana
ASTERACEAE
SILVER SAGEBRUSH, BOLANDER SAGEBRUSH
Native, common, blooms late summer–autumn, 20–32 in. Vernal-wet, streambanks, meadows, mid to high elevation
Shrub, rounded, much-branched, rhizomatous, stems white with velvety hair. **LEAVES** deciduous, alternate, linear to lance-shaped, 1–1.5 in. long, surfaces densely hairy to non-hairy, grayish green to bright green, edges mostly smooth, rarely lobed, tips pointed.
FLOWERS aggregated into heads, 2–3 heads in upper leaf axils, all disk flowers, bisexual, fertile, petals yellow. **FRUIT** achene, glandular, sticky. **ECOLOGY** grows

near vernal ponds, along streambanks, in meadows, and on gravelly soils, tolerates some flooding, from mid to high elevation. Ours is ssp. *bolanderi*.

Artemisia dracunculus
ASTERACEAE
TARRAGON, DRAGON SAGEWORT
Native, common, blooms mid summer–autumn,
1.7–5 ft. Disturbed, meadows, low to mid elevation
Subshrub or herbaceous, erect, stems several, green
to reddish brown, non-hairy. **LEAVES** alternate, linear,
0.5–3 in. long, surfaces mostly bright green and non-
hairy, sometimes grayish green and sparsely hairy,
edges mostly smooth but can be lobed, tips pointed.
FLOWERS aggregated into heads, heads ball-shaped and
nodding, in many-branched clusters, all disk flowers, outer female only and fertile, inner flowers bisexual but sterile, petals yellow. **FRUIT** achene, non-hairy.
ECOLOGY grows in
open, dry places,
disturbed sites,
meadows, and open
forests from low to
mid elevation.

Artemisia nova (*Artemisia arbuscula* ssp. *nova*)
ASTERACEAE
BLACK SAGEBRUSH
Native, locally common, blooms late summer–autumn,
4–20 in. Rocky sites, shrub-steppe, mid elevation
Shrub, stems similar in length, bark dark gray, shed
in strips. **LEAVES** persistent, alternate, wedge-shaped,
0.2–1 in. long, surfaces dark green to grayish, with
glandular, black-tipped hairs, 3-lobed at tip, not lobed
on flower stalks. **FLOWERS** aggregated into heads, heads
on short stalks in narrow clusters, all disk flowers,
bracts greenish yellow, edges and tips translucent.
FRUIT achene, ridged, smooth or glandular.
ECOLOGY highly drought tolerant, grows in shallow,
rocky soils on valley floors to mountain
slopes, in dwarf shrub communities,
pinyon-juniper woodlands, and other
shrub-steppe communities. The similar
A. arbuscula has lighter-colored leaves,
lacks glandular-tipped hairs, and has
lobed leaves on flowers stalks.

Artemisia rigida
ASTERACEAE
STIFF SAGEBRUSH, SCABLAND SAGEBRUSH, RIGID SAGEBRUSH

Native, locally common, blooms late summer–autumn, 8–16 in. Rocky sites, shrub-steppe, low to mid elevation Aromatic shrub, stems brittle, many-branched, grayish brown. **LEAVES** deciduous, alternate, pitchfork-shaped, sometimes linear, 0.5–1.5 in. long, surfaces silvery green and hairy, usually 3-lobed (sometimes 5 or 0), lobes > ⅓ total leaf length. **FLOWERS** aggregated in heads, heads in leaf axils, single or clustered, bracts oval, densely hairy, all disk flowers, bisexual, petals yellowish red to red. **FRUIT** achene, non-hairy.

ECOLOGY grows on basalt-derived shallow soils and rock outcrops, plains to montane. The similar *A. tripartita* has flowers in branched clusters and evergreen leaves.

Artemisia rothrockii

ASTERACEAE

TIMBERLINE SAGEBRUSH

Native, locally common, blooms mid–
late summer, 8–20 in. Meadows, shrub-
steppe, subalpine, high elevation

Aromatic shrub, trunk narrow, bark gray to grayish brown, fibrous, twigs densely hairy. **LEAVES** evergreen, alternate, lance- to wedge-shaped, 0.5–1 in.
long, surfaces glandular, sticky, hairy to non-hairy,
edges 3-lobed, lobes ⅓ total blade length, tips rounded.
FLOWERS aggregated into heads, heads in narrow, long
clusters, leaves on flowering stems unlobed, bracts
egg-shaped, hairy, all disk flowers, 12–20 per
head, all bisexual, fertile, petals yellow.
FRUIT achene, glandular.
ECOLOGY grows in meadows
and meadow-forest ecotones in
well-drained soils with a clay
component at higher elevations.
Endemic to California.

Artemisia suksdorfii
ASTERACEAE
COASTAL WORMWOOD, COASTAL MUGWORT, SUKSDORF'S SAGEWORT

Native, common, blooms all summer, 1.7–5 ft.
Coastal, streambanks, disturbed, low elevation
Subshrub or herbaceous, fragrant, erect, stems light brown, mostly non-hairy. **LEAVES** deciduous, alternate, lance-shaped, 3–6 in. long, dark green and non-hairy above, densely white-hairy beneath, edges smooth, toothed or lobed, tips pointed. **FLOWERS** aggregated into heads, in dense, branched clusters at stem ends, bracts lance-shaped, green and shiny, discoid, petals yellow, outer flowers female only, inner flowers bisexual, all fertile, hairs absent between flowers. **FRUIT** achene, non-hairy.
ECOLOGY grows on beaches, roadsides, and coastal bluffs at lower elevations.

Artemisia tilesii
ASTERACEAE
TILESIUS' WORMWOOD, CASCADE WORMWOOD, ALEUTIAN MUGWORT

Native, locally common, blooms mid–late summer, 8–24 in. Streambanks, meadows, east-side forest, low to high elevation
Subshrub, erect, rhizomatous, stems whitish, hairy or not. **LEAVES** deciduous, alternate, lance- to egg-shaped, 2–6 in. long, hairy or not above, white-woolly hairy below, edges smooth, or more often 1–2 times lobed, lobe and leaf tips pointed. **FLOWERS** aggregated into heads, in narrow clusters, heads wider than long, bracts lance- to egg-shaped, all disk flowers, outer ring of flowers female only, the inner bisexual, all fertile, petals yellow.
FRUIT achene, non-hairy.
ECOLOGY grows in rocky or sandy soils, on shorelines, streambanks, slopes, meadows, and open forests. The similar *A. ludoviciana* tends to be hairier and has heads taller than wide.

Artemisia tridentata
ASTERACEAE
BIG SAGEBRUSH
Native, common, blooms late summer–autumn, 1.3–10 ft. East-side forest, shrub-steppe, low to high elevation
Shrub, erect, aromatic, bark gray to light brown, shreddy when older, twigs usually densely white-hairy. **LEAVES** evergreen, alternate, wedge-shaped, 0.5–1 in. long, surfaces grayish green, densely hairy, tips 3-lobed, lobes to ⅓ total leaf length. Produces smaller, deciduous, smooth-edged leaves in winter; they are shed in the summer. **FLOWERS** aggregated into heads, clusters branched, dense, 2–12 in. long, bracts lance- to egg-shaped, grayish green, densely hairy, all disk flowers, bisexual, petals yellow. **FRUIT** achene, glandular, sparsely hairy to non-hairy. **ECOLOGY** grows in arid places, in shrub-steppe, open forest, on talus slopes, and ridges from lowland to subalpine elevation. Prefers deep, well-drained soils, commonly lives 40–50 years, can live more than 100 years. Heavy grazing increases abundance. Intolerant of fire, it does not resprout after a burn. Provides forage, nesting sites, cover, and other benefits to many wildlife species.

Artemisia tripartita
ASTERACEAE
THREETIP SAGEBRUSH
Native, locally common, blooms mid–late summer, 0.7–3 ft. Shrub-steppe, low to mid elevation
Aromatic shrub, bark gray to brown, stems branched or not, twigs hairy. **LEAVES** evergreen, alternate, pitch-fork-shaped, sometimes linear, 0.5–1.5 in. long, surfaces grayish green, edges 3-lobed, lobes > ⅓ total leaf length. **FLOWERS** aggregated into heads, heads in leafy, branched clusters, bracts lance-shaped, grayish white-hairy, all disk flowers, bisexual, petals yellow. **FRUIT** achene, 1-seeded, glandular or not. **ECOLOGY** grows in deeper soils, on drainages and slopes in places with cold winters in shrub-grass communities. Has declined in abundance, much of its habitat lost to agriculture.

Artemisia vulgaris
ASTERACEAE
COMMON WORMWOOD, LOBED WORMWOOD, MUGWORT

Non-native, locally common, blooms late summer–autumn, 1.7–5 ft. Coastal, streambanks, disturbed, low elevation

Subshrub or herbaceous, rhizomatous, stems brown to reddish brown, sparsely hairy or smooth. **LEAVES** deciduous, alternate, 2–4 in. long, lance- to egg-shaped, green and non-hairy above, usually densely white-hairy beneath, edges deeply divided into unequal lobes, tips pointed, stalks with small leaflets at base.
FLOWERS aggregated into heads, in leafy branched clusters at stem ends, bracts lance-shaped and hairy, discoid, outer flowers female only, inner flowers bisexual, all fertile, petals yellow, hair absent between flowers. **FRUIT** achene, non-hairy.
ECOLOGY grows along roadsides, intertidal riverbanks, and disturbed places.

Baccharis pilularis
ASTERACEAE
COYOTE BRUSH, CHAPARRAL BROOM

Native, common, blooms mid summer–autumn, 0.3–13 ft. Coastal, west-side forest, low to mid elevation

Shrub, mat-forming or erect, stems many-branched, dark brown, non-hairy, shiny and sticky (glandular).
LEAVES evergreen, alternate, lance- to egg-shaped, 0.2–1.5 in. long, surfaces green, non-hairy, glandular, edges smooth or toothed, tips rounded or pointed.
FLOWERS plants male or female, flowers aggregated into heads, heads in leafy branched clusters at stem ends, all disk flowers, petals cream to yellow.
FRUIT achene, 1-seeded, non-hairy. **ECOLOGY** forms mats with trailing stems near the coast in dunes and beaches; farther inland, in grasslands, oak woodlands, and elsewhere, it is erect with a dense, rounded form.

Baccharis salicifolia
ASTERACEAE
MULE FAT

Native, locally common, blooms early spring–autumn,
1–13 ft. Bog/fen/wetland, streambanks, low elevation
Shrub, erect to spreading, nonrhizomatous, stems
green or tan, non-hairy, sticky (glandular). **LEAVES** evergreen, alternate, oval to lance-shaped, 1–6 in. long, surfaces green, non-hairy, glandular, shiny above, paler
beneath, edges mostly toothed, tips pointed.
FLOWERS plants male or female, flowers aggregated
into heads, heads in branched clusters, all disk flowers,
petals white, bracts sometimes red-tipped.
FRUIT achene, 1-seeded, non-hairy. **ECOLOGY** grows
in riparian communi-
ties, along streambanks,
seeps, and canyon bot-
toms, often forming
thickets.

Brickellia californica
ASTERACEAE
CALIFORNIA BRICKELLBUSH

Native, common, blooms mid summer–autumn, 2–5
ft. Rocky sites, west-side forest, low to mid elevation
Shrub, erect, stems many, hairy, glandular.
LEAVES deciduous, alternate, triangular to egg-shaped,
0.5–4 in. long, surfaces green, hairy to non-hairy, often
glandular, edges toothed, tips pointed or rounded.
FLOWERS in leafy, branched clusters, aggregated into
heads, 8–12 flowers per head, all disk flowers, bisexual, pale yellowish green. **FRUIT** achene, 1-seeded,
hairy. **ECOLOGY** grows on dry rocky slopes in chaparral,
coastal sage scrub, and pine forests, as well as on rock
outcrops from low to mid elevation.

Brickellia grandiflora
ASTERACEAE
LARGE-FLOWERED BRICKELLIA,
LARGE-FLOWERED THOROUGHWORT,
LARGE-FLOWERED TASSELFLOWER

Native, common, blooms late summer–
autumn, 12–28 in. Rocky sites, east-side forest,
shrub-steppe, mid to high elevation

Subshrub or herbaceous, stems one to several, short-hairy. **LEAVES** deciduous, alternate (mostly), heart- to egg-shaped, 1–4.5 in. long, surfaces hairy and glandular, edges toothed, tips pointed. **FLOWERS** aggregated into heads, clusters flat-topped, heads often nodding, bracts with shingled arrangement, all disk flowers, bisexual, petals yellowish green to cream. **FRUIT** achene tipped by tuft of hair.

ECOLOGY grows on rocky slopes, shady forests, mid to high elevation. Rare in British Columbia.

Brickellia greenei
ASTERACEAE
GREENE'S BRICKELLBUSH

Native, locally common, blooms all summer, 8–20 in. Rocky sites, serpentine, mid to high elevation

Subshrub, stems many, branched, glandular-hairy. **LEAVES** deciduous, alternate, stalks to 0.1 in. long, egg-shaped, 0.5–1 in. long, surfaces sticky-glandular, edges toothed, tips pointed. **FLOWERS** aggregated into heads, heads single or in small clusters, bracts shingled, all disk flowers, bisexual, petals pale yellowish green to purplish. **FRUIT** achene, non- to short-hairy, tipped by tuft of hair. **ECOLOGY** grows on open, rocky slopes and in riparian areas, often on serpentine substrates, montane.

Brickellia microphylla
ASTERACEAE
LITTLELEAF BRICKELLBUSH

Native, locally common, blooms mid summer–
autumn, 12–28 in. Vernal-wet, rocky sites,
east-side forest, mid to high elevation

Subshrub or shrub, much-branched, stems sticky,
hairy, hairs glandular and not. **LEAVES** deciduous,
alternate, roundish to egg-shaped, 0.2–1 in. long, surfaces glandular-hairy or simply hairy, edges smooth to
toothed, tips rounded or pointed. **FLOWERS** aggregated
into heads, heads in branched clusters, bracts shingled, tips spreading, all disk flowers, bisexual, petals
white. **FRUIT** achene, hairy or not, tipped by tuft of
hair. **ECOLOGY** grows in rocky or sandy
areas, in dry open forests, plains,
washes, and draws.

Brickellia oblongifolia
ASTERACEAE
NARROW-LEAVED BRICKELLIA,
MOJAVE BRICKELLBUSH

Native, locally common, blooms late
spring–mid summer, 4–24 in. Rocky sites,
shrub-steppe, mid to high elevation

Subshrub or herbaceous, stems many, branched,
glandular-hairy. **LEAVES** deciduous, alternate, stalks to
0.1 in. long, oblong to linear, 0.5–1.5 in. long, surfaces
short-hairy, hairs often glandular, edges smooth, tips
pointed or rounded. **FLOWERS** aggregated into heads
of 25–50 flowers, heads single or in small, flat-topped
clusters, all disk flowers, bisexual, petals cream or pale
yellowish green, often purplish.
FRUIT achene, ribbed, glandular or
glandular-hairy. **ECOLOGY** grows on dry
rocky slopes and cliffs within shrub-
steppe, grassland, or dry forest plant
communities. Rare in British Columbia.

Chrysothamnus humilis

(*Ericameria humilis, Chrysothamnus viscidiflorus* var. *humilis*)
ASTERACEAE
TRUCKEE RABBITBRUSH, TRUCKEE GREEN RABBITBRUSH

Native, locally common, blooms mid summer–autumn, 4–12 in. Shrub-steppe, subalpine, mid to high elevation
Shrub, erect, bark dark gray, stems green, densely to sparsely hairy, sparingly glandular. **LEAVES** alternate, oval to lance-shaped, 0.5–1 in. long, surfaces grayish green, hairy and sparsely glandular, edges smooth, tips pointed. **FLOWERS** aggregated into heads, arranged in flat-topped clusters, leaves usually longer than the heads, all disk flowers, petals yellow, bracts leafy, 2–4

flowers per head. **FRUIT** achene, densely hairy, reddish brown. **ECOLOGY** grows in sagebrush communities and open desert slopes, tolerates alkaline conditions, mid to high elevation.

Chrysothamnus viscidiflorus

(*Ericameria viscidiflora*)
ASTERACEAE
GREEN RABBITBRUSH, LACELEAF GREEN RABBITBRUSH

Native, common, blooms mid summer–autumn, 0.7–4 ft. East-side forest, shrub-steppe, low to high elevation
Shrub, erect, much-branched, stems green to tan, sparsely hairy to smooth. **LEAVES** deciduous, alternate, linear to lance-shaped, 0.5–3 in. long, flat to twisted, surfaces green, sticky-glandular, edges wavy, sometimes fringed with hair, tips pointed. **FLOWERS** aggregated into heads, in rounded clusters at stem ends, all disk flowers, petals yellow, style protruding, mostly

3–13 flowers per head. **FRUIT** achene, densely hairy, reddish brown. **ECOLOGY** prefers sandy and alkaline soils on slopes and ridges in shrub-steppe and open forests, often colonizing disturbed sites. A variable species, lives 12–13 years on average, resprouts following fire.

Columbiadoria hallii (*Haplopappus hallii*)
ASTERACEAE
HALL'S GOLDENWEED, COLUMBIA RIVER DAISY
Native, locally common, blooms late
summer–autumn, 1–2 ft. Meadows, rocky
sites, east-side forest, mid elevation

Subshrub, erect, branched at base, stems straight.
LEAVES deciduous, alternate, oval to lance-shaped,
1–2 in. long, lowermost ephemeral, surfaces green,
sparsely hairy, edges smooth, tips pointed.
FLOWERS aggregated into heads, heads clustered at
stem ends, petals yellow, ray and disk flowers, rays
few, typically 5 or 8, bracts shingled, shiny with green
tips. **FRUIT** achene, 1-seeded. **ECOLOGY** grows on rocky
places on slopes,
ridges, meadows,
open forests, and
crevices.

Ericameria arborescens
ASTERACEAE
GOLDENFLEECE
Native, locally common, blooms late
summer–autumn, 0.3–17 ft. Chaparral,
west-side forest, low to mid elevation

Shrub, erect to spreading, crown rounded, stems
sparsely hairy or smooth, glandular, resinous.
LEAVES deciduous, alternate, linear to needle-shaped,
1–3.5 in. long, surfaces pitted with glands, resinous,
hairy or not, tips pointed. **FLOWERS** aggregated into
heads, in flat-topped clusters at stem ends, bracts shingled, all disk flowers, bisexual, petals yellow.
FRUIT achene, densely short-hairy, tipped by tuft of
hair. **ECOLOGY** grows on dry slopes, in
open forests, woodlands, and chaparral.

Ericameria bloomeri (Haplopappus bloomeri)
ASTERACEAE
RABBITBRUSH GOLDENWEED
Native, locally common, blooms late summer–autumn, 8–24 in. Rocky sites, east-side forest, mid to high elevation

Shrub, stems branched, hairy or not, often glandular, twigs brittle. **LEAVES** deciduous, alternate, linear to lance-shaped, 1–3 in. long, surfaces glandular or not, sparsely to woolly hairy, edges smooth, tips pointed. **FLOWERS** aggregated into heads, in clusters at stem tips, petals yellow, both ray and disk flowers, rays 1–5, bracts in several loose rows. **FRUIT** achene, tan to reddish brown. **ECOLOGY** grows in rocky openings of conifer forests in mountainous areas. Rare, possibly extirpated, in British Columbia.

Ericameria discoidea
(Haplopappus macronema)
ASTERACEAE
WHITESTEM GOLDENBUSH, DISCOID GOLDENWEED, SHARP-SCALE GOLDENWEED
Native, locally common, blooms mid summer–autumn, 4–16 in. Rocky sites, alpine, subalpine, high elevation

Shrub, stems erect to spreading, branched, twigs densely white-hairy. **LEAVES** deciduous, alternate, oval to lance-shaped, 0.5–1.5 in. long, surfaces glandular, edges often wavy, tips rounded or pointed. **FLOWERS** aggregated into heads, heads single or in small clusters at stem tips, petals yellow, all disk flowers, bracts glandular, of similar length or lower row longer. **FRUIT** achene, brownish, hairy. **ECOLOGY** grows on rocky slopes, talus, or open forest in subalpine to alpine areas.

Ericameria greenei (*Haplopappus greenei*)
ASTERACEAE
GREENE'S GOLDENWEED, GOLDENBUSH,
COLUMBIA GOLDENWEED

Native, locally common, blooms mid summer–
autumn, 4–12 in. Rocky sites, west-side forest,
east-side forest, mid to high elevation

Shrub, erect, stems green to reddish brown, branched,
hairy, glandular-hairy, or smooth. **LEAVES** deciduous,
alternate, lance- to spoon-shaped, 0.5–1.5 in. long, surfaces hairy, glandular-hairy, or smooth, edges smooth,
tips rounded. **FLOWERS** aggregated into heads, heads in
leafy clusters at stem ends, bracts somewhat equal in
length, both ray and disk flowers present, disk flowers
7–20, petals yellow. **FRUIT** 1-seeded achene, tan to reddish, hairy or not. **ECOLOGY** grows on rocky slopes in
open conifer forests, at mid to high elevation.

Ericameria linearifolia
ASTERACEAE
NARROWLEAF GOLDENBUSH

Native, common, blooms all spring, 1–5 ft.
Rocky sites, chaparral, low to mid elevation

Shrub, erect to spreading, bark reddish to grayish
brown, stems hairy or not, resinous. **LEAVES** deciduous,
alternate, linear, 0.5–2 in. long, surfaces grayish green,
hairy or not, sticky-glandular, edges smooth, tips
pointed, with smaller bundles of leaves in the axils.
FLOWERS aggregated into heads, heads single at stem
tips, bracts linear to lance-shaped, glandular, nearly of
equal length in 2–3 rows, ray and disk flowers, petals
yellow. **FRUIT** achene, 1-seeded, brown, hairy.
ECOLOGY grows in rocky or sandy soils
on slopes and in valleys of chaparral,
scrub, and forest communities.

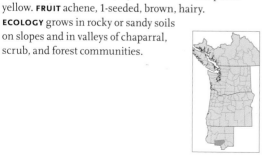

Ericameria nauseosa

(*Chrysothamnus nauseosus*)
ASTERACEAE
GRAY RABBITBRUSH, RUBBER RABBITBRUSH
Native, common, blooms late summer–
autumn, 0.3–8.3 ft. West-side forest, east-side
forest, shrub-steppe, low to mid elevation

Shrub, erect to spreading, sweet fragrance, stems branched, twigs velvety hairy. **LEAVES** deciduous, alternate, linear to lance-shaped, 0.5–3 in. long, surfaces grayish green or green, hairy or not, often glandular, edges smooth, tips pointed. **FLOWERS** aggregated in heads, heads in flat-topped to rounded clusters, bracts oval to lance-shaped, 3–5 rows, shingle-like, all disk flowers, petals yellow. **FRUIT** achene, tan, smooth or hairy. **ECOLOGY** grows in shrub-steppe, open, dry forest, and disturbed sites, often in rocky or sandy soils, low to mid elevation. Recovers from fire by resprouting from the root crown and seed germination. Poor browse for mammals but provides good nesting cover for birds. Tested during World War II as a source of rubber; it and other compounds found in this plant are attracting renewed interest.

Ericameria ophitidis (*Haplopappus ophitidis*)

ASTERACEAE
SERPENTINE GOLDENBUSH, SERPENTINE
MACRONEMA
Native, rare, blooms late summer, 4–12 in.
Serpentine, chaparral, high elevation

Shrub, erect to spreading, stems green to reddish brown, hairy or not, sometimes glandular. **LEAVES** deciduous, alternate, linear, 0.2–0.5 in. long, surfaces glandular, not pitted, hairy or not, tips pointed, often with bundles of smaller leaves in leaf axils. **FLOWERS** aggregated into heads, single or in flat-topped clusters, bracts shingled, glandular, tips bent back, all disk flowers, 5–6 per head, bisexual, petals pale yellow. **FRUIT** achene, short-hairy, tipped by tuft of hair. **ECOLOGY** a serpentine endemic of open forests and chaparral. Endemic to California.

Ericameria parryi
ASTERACEAE
PARRY'S GOLDENBUSH, PARRY'S RABBITBRUSH
Native, locally common, blooms mid
summer–autumn, 0.3–3 ft. Rocky sites,
alpine, subalpine, mid to high elevation

Shrub, erect, stems green becoming gray, densely
hairy. **LEAVES** deciduous, alternate, linear to spoon-
shaped, 0.5–3 in. long, surfaces greenish or gray, hairy
or not, glandular, edges smooth, tips pointed.
FLOWERS aggregated into heads, heads single or in
clusters, bracts in several rows with pointed tips, all
disk flowers, petals yellow. **FRUIT** achene, tan, hairy.
ECOLOGY grows in open forests, rocky slopes, and stony
alpine areas. Populations
are often small and scat-
tered, increase with overgrazing or disturbance.

Ericameria resinosa (*Haplopappus resinosus*)
ASTERACEAE
COLUMBIA GOLDENWEED
Native, uncommon, blooms late summer, 12–20 in.
Rocky sites, shrub-steppe, low to mid elevation

Shrub, broomlike habit, stems glandular, resinous.
LEAVES deciduous, alternate, linear, 0.5–1 in. long, surfaces non-hairy, glandular, tips pointed.
FLOWERS aggregated into heads, heads solitary or in
small clusters at stem tips, ray flowers 3–7, about 0.25
in. long, disk flowers 10–15, petals pale yellow to white,
bracts linear, shingled, smooth, resinous, tips pointed.
FRUIT achene, tan to brown, hairy. **ECOLOGY** grows on
cliffs, rocky slopes, and in crevices, often in basalt.

Eriophyllum lanatum
ASTERACEAE
OREGON SUNSHINE, WOOLLY YELLOW DAISY
Native, common, blooms spring–summer,
4–24 in. Coastal, meadows, rocky sites,
shrub-steppe, low to high elevation
Subshrub or herbaceous, erect to trailing, stems woolly hairy. **LEAVES** deciduous, alternate, sometimes opposite, lance-shaped, 0.4–3.2 in. long, surfaces usually woolly hairy, sometimes smooth, edges smooth to 1–3 times divided into lobes, lobes sometimes toothed, tips rounded or pointed. **FLOWERS** aggregated into heads, heads single or in small clusters at stem tips, petals yellow, both ray and disk flowers, bracts oval to lance-shaped, hair absent in receptacle. **FRUIT** achene, hairy, non-hairy, or glandular, hair tuft present or absent. **ECOLOGY** variable species (10 recognized varieties) with various habitats, including drier meadows, rocky slopes, and coastal areas.

Eriophyllum staechadifolium
(*Eriophyllum stoechadifolium*)
ASTERACEAE
SEASIDE WOOLLY SUNFLOWER
Native, locally common, blooms mid spring–
late summer, 1–5 ft. Coastal, low elevation
Subshrub, stems erect, much-branched, hairy to non-hairy. **LEAVES** deciduous, alternate, linear, lance-, or egg-shaped, 1–3 in. long, green above, white woolly-hairy below, edges lobed, lobes often again lobed, lobe edges smooth to toothed. **FLOWERS** aggregated into heads, heads in dense clusters, bracts similar lengths, hairy, ray and disk flowers, rays 0.1–0.2 in. long, yellow. **FRUIT** achene, glandular and hairy, tipped by tuft of hair. **ECOLOGY** grows near the coast in coastal sage scrub and on sand dunes and bluffs.

Grindelia hirsutula
ASTERACEAE
HAIRY GUMWEED

Native, common, blooms mid spring–late summer, 0.7–5 ft. Coastal, streambanks, disturbed, low to mid elevation

Subshrub, erect, stems sparsely branched, glandular, usually hairy. **LEAVES** deciduous, alternate, oval to lance-shaped, 0.5–3 in. long, surfaces either hairy with few glands, or non-hairy and densely glandular, edges mostly toothed, tips rounded or pointed.
FLOWERS aggregated in heads, heads in (mostly) dense clusters, bract tips bent back or straight, usually glandular, ray and disk flowers, petals yellow. **FRUIT** achene, 1-seeded, yellow or reddish brown, top knobby with tuft of hair.
ECOLOGY grows on beaches, along streambanks and roadsides, in forest openings. Rare in British Columbia.

Grindelia integrifolia
ASTERACEAE
PUGET SOUND GUMWEED, WILLAMETTE VALLEY GUMWEED

Native, common, blooms summer–autumn, 8–32 in. Coastal, meadows, low elevation

Subshrub or herbaceous, stems several, branched, usually hairy, sometimes glandular. **LEAVES** deciduous, stem leaves alternate, lance-shaped, 1.5–3 in. long, often clasping stem, surfaces glandular-hairy, edges smooth or toothed, tips pointed. **FLOWERS** aggregated into heads, heads single or in flat-topped clusters, petals yellow, both ray and disk flowers, bracts curved, sticky-glandular, tips sharply pointed. **FRUIT** achene, smooth to ridged. **ECOLOGY** grows along beaches, on coastal bluffs, meadows, salt marshes, and elsewhere at lower elevations west of the Cascades.

Gutierrezia sarothrae
ASTERACEAE
MATCH BRUSH, SNAKEWEED
Native, locally common, blooms mid–late summer,
4–24 in. Meadows, shrub-steppe, low to mid elevation
Shrub or subshrub, erect, stems many, brown, short-
hairy, twigs green to tan. **LEAVES** alternate, linear to
lance-shaped, 1–1.5 in. long, surfaces pitted, edges
smooth, tips pointed. **FLOWERS** aggregated into heads,
heads small, in dense, flat-topped clusters, petals yellow, both ray and disk flowers, rays short, female only,
3–8, bracts shingled, sticky-glandular.
FRUIT achene, hairy, hair tuft at tip short.
ECOLOGY grows in open, rocky places, in shrub-steppe
and grasslands, abundance
increases with overgrazing.

Luina hypoleuca
ASTERACEAE
SILVERBACK LUINA, LITTLELEAF LUINA
Native, locally common, blooms mid summer–
autumn, 6–16 in. Rocky sites, serpentine,
subalpine, low to high elevation
Subshrub or herbaceous, erect to spreading, stems
white woolly-hairy. **LEAVES** deciduous, alternate, oval to
egg-shaped, 1–2.5 in. long, 1.5–3.5 times longer than
wide, shiny, green and non-hairy above, densely white-
hairy below, edges smooth, tips pointed.
FLOWERS aggregated into heads, heads in flat-topped
clusters, all disk flowers, petals creamy yellow, bracts
lance-shaped, densely hairy, sometimes glandular, tuft
of hair at bract tip. **FRUIT** achene, non-
hairy to sparsely long-hairy.
ECOLOGY grows on moist to dry rocky
slopes, cliffs, talus, sometimes on
serpentine.

Nestotus stenophyllus
(*Stenotus stenophyllus, Haplopappus stenophyllus*)
ASTERACEAE
NARROWLEAF GOLDENWEED
Native, locally common, blooms mid
spring–mid summer, 1–5 in. Rocky sites,
shrub-steppe, mid to high elevation

Subshrub, tufted, taprooted. **LEAVES** deciduous, alternate, linear, 0.2–1 in. long, rigid, surfaces green, glandular-hairy, edges fringed with hairs, tips pointed. **FLOWERS** aggregated into heads, heads solitary on stalk, both ray and disk flowers, rays showy, petals yellow, bracts green, oval to lance-shaped, densely short glandular-hairy, tips pointed. **FRUIT** achene, hairy, hair tuft white. **ECOLOGY** grows in shrub-steppe communities, on basaltic or granitic soils, often in lithosol.

Pleiacanthus spinosus
(*Lygodesmia spinosa, Stephanomeria spinosa*)
ASTERACEAE
THORN SKELETONWEED
Native, locally common, blooms all summer, 4–24
in. Rocky sites, shrub-steppe, mid to high elevation
Subshrub, erect, stems several and slender, woolly
hairy between bud scales at plant base, stems and
branches spine-tipped. LEAVES deciduous, alternate,
linear below, 1–3 in. long, scalelike above, surfaces
green, non-hairy, edges smooth, tips pointed.
FLOWERS single along branches, aggregated into heads
of 3–5 flowers, all ray flowers, petals pink to reddish
purple, bracts in 2 rows, lance-shaped. FRUIT achene,
1-seeded, tuft of hair present, of two
lengths. ECOLOGY grows in dry, open,
rocky places at mid to high elevation.

Stephanomeria tenuifolia
(*Stephanomeria minor*)
ASTERACEAE
NARROWLEAVED SKELETONWEED, BUSH
WIRELETTUCE, NARROWLEAF STEPHANOMERIA
Native, locally common, blooms late summer,
8–28 in. Rocky sites, east-side forest,
shrub-steppe, low to high elevation
Subshrub or herbaceous, stems slender, many-
branched, non-hairy. LEAVES deciduous, alternate, linear to threadlike, 2–3 in. long, lower leaves withered
by bloom time, upper leaves reduced, non-hairy, edges
smooth or toothed. FLOWERS aggregated into heads,
heads solitary at branch ends, all ray flowers, bisexual, 4–5 per head, petals pink to white,
bracts lance-shaped, outer row much
shorter than inner. FRUIT achene, tan,
non-hairy, ridged. ECOLOGY grows on
open, rocky slopes and ridges, in crevices and at bases of cliffs in shrub-
steppe and open, dry forest communities from low to high elevation.

Tetradymia canescens
ASTERACEAE
SPINELESS HORSEBRUSH, GRAY HORSEBRUSH
Native, common, blooms all summer, 4–24 in. East-side forest, shrub-steppe, low to mid elevation
Shrub, erect, stems much-branched, velvety hairy with sparsely hairy streaks, spines absent. **LEAVES** deciduous, alternate, lance- to spoon-shaped, 0.2–1.5 in. long, surfaces densely hairy, edges smooth, tips mostly rounded. **FLOWERS** in clusters at branch ends, aggregated into heads, all disk flowers, 4 per head, petals cream to bright yellow, bracts 4–5, oval to egg-shaped. **FRUIT** achene, 1-seeded, hairy or not. **ECOLOGY** grows in shrub-steppe, open forests, and other dry, open places from low to mid elevation.

Tetradymia glabrata
ASTERACEAE
LITTLELEAF HORSEBRUSH
Native, scattered, blooms late spring–mid summer,
1–4 ft. Shrub-steppe, mid to high elevation
Shrub, erect, stems several, velvety hairy with non-hairy streaks, branches many. **LEAVES** deciduous, alternate, linear, 0.2–1 in. long, surfaces green, sparsely hairy to non-hairy, edges smooth, ends sometimes spine-tipped, clusters of smaller leaves in the axils. **FLOWERS** in clusters at stem ends, flowers aggregated into heads, all disk flowers, petals cream to yellow, bracts and flowers 4 per head. **FRUIT** achene, 1-seeded, densely hairy, glandular on ridges, tuft of hair present. **ECOLOGY** grows in shrub-steppe, juniper woodlands, and other dry, open places from mid to high elevation. Tolerant of saline and alkaline soils. Contains toxins that are poisonous to sheep.

Tetradymia spinosa
ASTERACEAE
SPINY HORSEBRUSH
Native, common, blooms mid spring–mid summer,
0.3–3 ft. East-side forest, shrub-steppe, mid elevation
Shrub, erect, rhizomatous, stems spiny, densely white-hairy. **LEAVES** alternate, hardening into curved spines, 0.2–1 in. long, with smaller clusters of green, non-hairy leaves in the axils. **FLOWERS** aggregated into heads, heads 1–2 in spine axils, all disk flowers, petals yellow, bracts densely hairy. **FRUIT** achene, 1-seeded, densely long-hairy, obscuring the tufts of hair at the tip. **ECOLOGY** grows in areas with high levels of bare ground, shrub-steppe and dry forest communities, often in sandy or salty soils, mid elevation.

Alnus incana ssp. *tenuifolia*
BETULACEAE
THINLEAF ALDER, MOUNTAIN ALDER

Native, locally common, blooms early spring, 7–40 ft. Lake/pond, streambanks, mid to high elevation Shrub or tree, thicket-forming, bark yellowish or grayish brown, smooth, twigs hairy. **LEAVES** deciduous, alternate, oval to egg-shaped, 1.5–4 in. long, lower surface hairy or not, edges doubly toothed, sometimes wavy, tips mostly rounded. **FLOWERS** in catkins, blooms on previous year's growth before the leaves unfold, flowers unisexual, male and female catkins on same plant, stamens usually 4. **FRUIT** nutlets, edges thin but not winged, female catkins conelike, persistent on plant, egg-shaped, to 0.5 in. long. **ECOLOGY** grows mostly in wet places such as streambanks, lakeshores, meadow and bog edges, usually in mountainous areas.

Alnus rhombifolia

BETULACEAE

WHITE ALDER

Native, locally common, blooms late winter–early spring, 17–80 ft. Streambanks, low to mid elevation Tree, trunks often several, bark light gray to whitish, becoming reddish brown and scaly with age, twigs hairy. **LEAVES** deciduous, alternate, oval to diamond-shaped, 1.5–3 in. long, dark green above, paler and hairy beneath, edges singly or doubly toothed with pointed tips, not wavy or rolled under, leaf tips rounded. **FLOWERS** clustered in unisexual catkins on same plant, blooms on the previous year's twigs before the leaves unfold, stamens usually 1–3. **FRUIT** nutlet,

thin but not winged, female catkins conelike, persistent on plant, oval to egg-shaped, to 1 in. long. **ECOLOGY** grows on sandy or rocky banks of year-round streams and rivers, from low to montane elevation, often in warm, dry areas. The similar *A. rubra* always has non-scaly bark, doubly toothed leaf edges that are rolled under, and winged nutlets.

Alnus rubra
BETULACEAE
RED ALDER

Native, common, blooms early spring, to 83
ft. Bog/fen/wetland, streambanks, disturbed,
west-side forest, low to mid elevation

Tree, bark gray, smooth, crown rounded, twigs reddish. Bark on older trees may split into rectangular plates and appear lighter in color due to extensive
lichen patches. **LEAVES** deciduous, alternate, oval, 2–6
in. long, green above, grayish green below, often rusty
hairy, edges rolled under, doubly toothed, leaf tips
pointed. **FLOWERS** clustered in unisexual catkins on the
same plant, blooms on the previous year's twigs before
the leaves unfold. **FRUIT** nutlet, edges winged, wing to
½ as wide as nutlet, female catkins conelike, persistent
on plant, oval to egg-shaped, to 1 in. long.

ECOLOGY pioneer species, grows in moist forests,
streambanks, floodplains, clearcuts, and burned areas,
lowland to montane. Shade intolerant,
relatively short-lived, and fast growing,
often germinating and resprouting in
profusion on disturbed sites. Its root
nodules contain bacteria that can trans-
form atmospheric nitrogen into a form
usable by plants; this nitrogen is added
to the soil through decomposition of
fallen leaves and decaying roots.

Alnus viridis ssp. *fruticosa*

BETULACEAE

SIBERIAN ALDER

Native, locally common, blooms all spring, 3–10(20) ft. Coastal, streambanks, low to mid elevation

Sprawling shrub, bark grayish brown. **LEAVES** deciduous, alternate, widely egg-shaped, 2–3 in. long, shiny dark green above, often hairy on the veins below, edges with double set of small, sharp teeth, tips pointed. **FLOWERS** clustered in unisexual catkins on same plant, blooms on the current year's twigs as the leaves unfold. **FRUIT** winged nutlet, wing at least ½ as wide as nutlet, female catkins conelike, persist on plant. **ECOLOGY** grows mainly along sandy or rocky coastlines as well as on streambanks, lakeshores, and other moist, open areas from sea level to the mountain foothills.

Alnus viridis ssp. *sinuata* (Alnus sinuata)

BETULACEAE

SITKA ALDER, SLIDE ALDER, MOUNTAIN ALDER

Native, common, blooms mid spring–mid summer, 3–30 ft. Streambanks, rocky sites, west-side forest, east-side forest, subalpine, low to high elevation

Shrub or small tree, thicket-forming, bark reddish brown to gray, twigs glandular. **LEAVES** deciduous, alternate, egg-shaped, 1.5–4 in. long, papery thin, shiny yellowish green and non-hairy above, paler with hair on veins below, edges wavy, coarsely double-toothed, tips pointed. **FLOWERS** clustered in unisexual catkins, male and female on same plant, blooms on the current year's twigs as the leaves unfold. **FRUIT** winged nutlet, wing at least ½ as wide as nutlet, female catkins conelike, persist on plant. **ECOLOGY** grows on open moist slopes, rocky streambanks, avalanche chutes, glacial moraines, and other habitats, usually montane to subalpine. Ssp. *fruticosa* has firmer, dark green leaves with edges that are finely doubly toothed, grows mainly near the coast.

Betula glandulosa (*Betula nana*)
BETULACEAE
RESIN BIRCH, SCRUB BIRCH, BOG BIRCH
Native, locally common, blooms late spring–mid summer, 3–10 ft. Bog/fen/wetland, streambanks, alpine, subalpine, low to high elevation
Shrub, erect to spreading, rhizomatous, bark smooth, dark brown to blackish, twigs mostly non-hairy, covered with large, resinous, wartlike glands.
LEAVES deciduous, alternate, round to egg-shaped, 0.2–1 in. long, leathery, glandular and hairy or not below, margins scalloped, tips rounded. **FLOWERS** in catkins, blooming as the leaves unfold, flowers unisexual, male and female flowers on the same plant, catkins 0.5–1 in. long, catkin bracts non-hairy.
FRUIT samara, wings < ½ as wide as the nutlet. **ECOLOGY** grows in bogs, streambanks, arctic and alpine tundra and rocky slopes, both wet and drier habitats. Hybridizes with other *Betula* spp. where ranges overlap. The similar *B. pumila* has larger leaves and only scattered glands on twigs. Rare in California.

Betula occidentalis
BETULACEAE
WATER BIRCH

Native, common, blooms mid–late spring, 10–33 ft. Lake/pond, streambanks, low to high elevation Shrub or tree, bark smooth, black when young becoming reddish brown to coppery with age, twigs with many resinous, reddish glands. **LEAVES** deciduous, alternate, round to egg-shaped, 1–3 in. long, surfaces yellowish green, glandular and hairy below, edges usually doubly toothed, tips rounded or pointed.
FLOWERS in catkins, blooms before or as the leaves unfold, flowers unisexual, male and female flowers on the same plant, catkins 1–1.5 in. long, catkin bracts

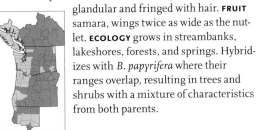

glandular and fringed with hair. **FRUIT** samara, wings twice as wide as the nutlet. **ECOLOGY** grows in streambanks, lakeshores, forests, and springs. Hybridizes with *B. papyrifera* where their ranges overlap, resulting in trees and shrubs with a mixture of characteristics from both parents.

Betula papyrifera
BETULACEAE
PAPER BIRCH

Native, common, blooms mid–late spring,
50–67(100) ft. West-side forest, east-
side forest, low to mid elevation

Tree, often with 2–3 main trunks, bark white, gray, or
pale brown, shed in paper-thin strips, crown rounded,
branches, twigs, and bark of young trees reddish
brown, twigs hairy. **LEAVES** deciduous, alternate, egg-
shaped, 2–3.5 in. long, shiny green, hairy or not above,
hairy with tufts of hair in vein axils below, edges singly or doubly toothed, tips taper to a point. **FLOWERS** in
catkins, blooms before or as the leaves emerge, flowers unisexual, male and female flowers on the same
plant, male catkins long and drooping, female catkins
erect, 1–2 in. long. **FRUIT** samara, wings as broad as
the nutlet. **ECOLOGY** grows in open to dense forests,
preferring open, well-drained sites, often with rocky
soil, usually moist. Shade intolerant, often establishing
after fire, timber harvest, farming, or like disturbance;
seeds readily germinate on bare mineral soil or on tree
stumps. Bark's high oil content makes it waterproof
and durable.

Betula pumila
BETULACEAE
BOG BIRCH
Native, locally common, blooms all spring,
1–10 ft. Bog/fen/wetland, lake/pond, east-
side forest, low to mid elevation

Shrub, erect to spreading, bark dark reddish brown,
smooth, twigs with scattered, small resinous glands,
hairy or not. **LEAVES** deciduous, alternate, oval to
roundish, 1–3 in. long, green above, paler, glandular,
and hairy or not below, edges scalloped, tips rounded.
FLOWERS in catkins, flowers unisexual, male and
female flowers on the same plant, catkins 0.5–1 in.
long, catkin scales hairy or not. **FRUIT** samara, wings
slightly narrower than the
nutlet. **ECOLOGY** grows in
bogs, swamps, and lake-
shores, prefers alkaline
soils. The similar *B. glan-
dulosa* has smaller leaves
and large resinous glands
on its twigs.

Corylus avellana
BETULACEAE
COMMON FILBERT, EUROPEAN HAZELNUT
Non-native, locally common, blooms
winter–early spring, 3–17(27) ft. Disturbed,
west-side forest, low elevation

Shrub or tree, erect, crown spreading, bark smooth,
dark brown, twigs yellowish to pale brown, glandular-hairy. **LEAVES** deciduous, alternate, oval, 2–5 in.
long, surfaces green, hairy, edges doubly toothed,
tips pointed. **FLOWERS** in catkins, flowers unisexual,
male and female flowers on the same plant, male catkins pendent, in clusters of 2–4. **FRUIT** nut, hairy, surrounded by stiff hairy bracts about as long as the nut,
bracts deeply divided, nut clearly visible.
ECOLOGY escapee from cultivation, grows
in open to shady forests, along streams, and
near human settlements. Shade tolerant.
Blooms slightly earlier than our native *C.
cornuta*.

Corylus cornuta

BETULACEAE

BEAKED HAZELNUT

Native, common, blooms winter–early spring,
3–17(50) ft. Streambanks, west-side forest,
east-side forest, low to mid elevation

Shrub or tree, erect, crown spreading, bark smooth,
light to dark brown, twigs yellowish to orange-brown,
hairy (sometimes glandular) when young, buds hairy,
oval to round. **LEAVES** deciduous, alternate, oval to
heart-shaped, 2–4 in. long, surfaces green, hairy, edges
doubly toothed, tips pointed. **FLOWERS** in catkins, flowers unisexual, male and female flowers on the same
plant, male catkins pendent, usually in clusters of 1–2,
female catkins short with red stigmas. **FRUIT** nut, in
clusters of 2–3, enclosed by stiff, hairy bracts extending beyond the nut, forming a beak. **ECOLOGY** grows in
open to shady forests, along streams, and in meadows.
The straight species, var. *cornuta*, has velvety-hairy
nuts and beaks 2 times longer than the nut; var. *californica* has non-hairy nuts and beaks as long as the nut.
The similar *C. avellana* has divided bracts that expose
the nut, beak absent.

Eriodictyon californicum
BORAGINACEAE
YERBA SANTA

Native, common, blooms mid spring–mid summer, 3–10 ft. Disturbed, chaparral, low to mid elevation

Shrub, erect, rhizomatous, stems black, twigs sticky-glandular, sparsely hairy. **LEAVES** evergreen, alternate, oval to lance-shaped, 1.5–6 in. long, surfaces dark green, glandular and mostly non-hairy above, lighter green and hairy below, edges smooth or toothed, rolled under, tips pointed. **FLOWERS** in clusters at stem ends, buds not grayish-hairy, flowers funnel-shaped, 0.3–0.7 in. long, sepals sparsely hairy or not, petals white, blue, or purple, styles 2. **FRUIT** capsule. **ECOLOGY** grows on forest slopes, in chaparral, ridges, and other places. Leaves used medicinally in teas and other applications.

Nama lobbii (*Eriodictyon lobbii*)
BORAGINACEAE
LOBB'S FIDDLELEAF, LOBB'S NAMA, WOOLLY NAMA

Native, locally common, blooms mid spring–late summer, 8–24 in. Disturbed, west-side forest, east-side forest, mid elevation

Subshrub or herbaceous, rhizomatous, mat-forming, woolly to glandular-hairy. **LEAVES** deciduous, alternate, lance- to egg-shaped, about 1 in. long on vegetative branches, and 1.5–2.5 in. long on flowering branches, edges rolled under, clusters of smaller leaves in leaf axils. **FLOWERS** clusters in upper leaf axils, funnel- to bell-shaped, petals pink to purple, sepal lobes linear. **FRUIT** capsule, seeds dark brown, 10–12 seeds per fruit. **ECOLOGY** grows in sandy or rocky soils in open, dry forests and ridges, in montane areas.

Comandra umbellata
COMANDRACEAE (SANTALACEAE)
BASTARD TOADFLAX
Native, locally common, blooms mid spring–
mid summer, 4–12 in. Disturbed, meadows,
shrub-steppe, low to high elevation
Subshrub or herbaceous, erect, rhizomatous, stems
clustered. **LEAVES** deciduous, alternate, lance- to egg-
shaped, 0.2–2 in. long, surfaces greenish to whitish
waxy, edges smooth, tips pointed or not. **FLOWERS** in
rounded to flat-topped clusters at stem ends, flowers
bell-shaped, petals absent, sepal lobes lance- to egg-
shaped, erect to spreading, white to purplish.
FRUIT berrylike, blue, purplish, or brown, fleshy to
dry, edible. **ECOLOGY** parasitic on
roots of other plants, grows on rocky
slopes, ridges, or sandy, well-drained
soils in shrub-steppe from low to high
elevation.

Calystegia malacophylla
CONVOLVULACEAE
**SIERRA FALSE BINDWEED, SIERRA MORNING
GLORY**
Native, common, blooms all summer, 0.3–3 ft.
Chaparral, east-side forest, mid to high elevation
Vine, stems trailing or weakly climbing, densely
brownish- to grayish-hairy, basal rosette of leaves
absent. **LEAVES** deciduous, alternate, arrowhead-shaped, <2.5 in. long, surfaces densely hairy,
edges unevenly toothed, tips pointed or notched.
FLOWERS single in leaf axils, bracts lance- to egg-
shaped, tips pointed, >0.2 in. wide, covering or partially covering sepals, flowers trumpet-shaped, petals
white with pink, 1–2 in. long, sepals
hairy. **FRUIT** capsule, round.
ECOLOGY grows in chaparral and on forest slopes. Endemic to California.

Calystegia occidentalis
(*Convolvulus polymorphus*)
CONVOLVULACEAE
WESTERN MORNING GLORY

Native, common, blooms late spring–mid summer, to >3 ft. Serpentine, chaparral, east-side forest, shrub-steppe, low to high elevation
Vine, stems trailing to climbing, light green, hairy. **LEAVES** deciduous, alternate, mostly arrowhead-shaped, 0.5–1.5 in. long, surfaces green and hairy, edges somewhat lobed, tips rounded or pointed. **FLOWERS** 1–4 in leaf axils, bracts linear to oblong, to 0.2 in. wide, not covering sepals, flowers trumpet-shaped, petals white, pinkish, or light yellow, 1–2 in. long, sepals unequal in size. **FRUIT** capsule, round.

ECOLOGY grows in chaparral and pine forest slopes, often on serpentine outcrops, shade tolerant.

Calystegia purpurata
CONVOLVULACEAE
PACIFIC FALSE BINDWEED

Native, locally common, blooms late spring–early summer, to 23 ft. Coastal, chaparral, low elevation
Vine, base woody, rhizomatous, stems climbing or trailing, non-hairy. **LEAVES** deciduous, alternate, arrowhead-shaped, 0.5–2 in. long, surfaces green, edges wavy or not, tips pointed or rounded. **FLOWERS** single or few in leaf axils, bracts linear, not covering the sepals, flowers trumpet-shaped, petals white, cream to purplish, or purple-striped, 1–2 in. long. **FRUIT** capsule, roundish, somewhat inflated. **ECOLOGY** grows in chaparral and coastal scrub, often in rocky soils. Endemic to California.

Calystegia sepium (*Convolvulus sepium*)
CONVOLVULACEAE
HEDGE MORNING GLORY, LADY'S-NIGHTCAP, HEDGE BINDWEED

Non-native, common, blooms mid spring–late summer, 7–10 ft. Coastal, bog/fen/wetland, streambanks, low elevation

Vine, stems trailing or climbing, often forms hedge-like structure over other plants, rhizomatous, hairy or not. **LEAVES** deciduous, alternate, arrowhead-shaped, 2–5 in. long, surfaces hairy or not, tips pointed. **FLOWERS** mostly single in leaf axils, bracts egg- to heart-shaped, covering the sepals, flowers trumpet-shaped, petals white to deep pink, 1–2.5 in. long. **FRUIT** capsule, round to egg-shaped, 0.5 in. long. **ECOLOGY** grows on streambanks, shorelines, marshes, and other moist places.

Calystegia silvatica
CONVOLVULACEAE
SHORTSTALK FALSE BINDWEED

Non-native, scattered, blooms mid summer–autumn, to 20 ft. Bog/fen/wetland, disturbed, low elevation

Vine, stems trailing or climbing, rhizomatous, non-hairy. **LEAVES** deciduous, alternate, arrowhead-shaped, 2–5 in. long, surfaces green, non-hairy, tips pointed. **FLOWERS** single in leaf axils, bracts egg-shaped with sac-like base, covering the sepals, flowers trumpet-shaped, petals white, 2–3 in. long. **FRUIT** capsule, roundish, somewhat inflated. **ECOLOGY** grows in disturbed areas, marsh edges, fields, often in moist ground. The similar *C. sepium* has smaller flowers and bracts not sac-like at the base.

Glossopetalon spinescens
(*Glossopetalon nevadense*)
CROSSOSOMATACEAE
SPINY GREASEBUSH, NEVADA GREASEWOOD
Native, locally common, blooms all spring, 3–10 ft.
Rocky sites, shrub-steppe, low to high elevation
Shrub, erect to spreading, many-branched, branches grooved, spine-tipped. **LEAVES** deciduous, alternate, oblong to lance-shaped, 0.2–0.7 in. long, surfaces grayish green, edges smooth, tips rounded or pointed, 2 bristles near leaf base. **FLOWERS** single to few in leaf axils, mostly male or female, both types on one plant, sepals and petals 4–6, petals white, oval. **FRUIT** capsule, egg-shaped, seeds 1–2. **ECOLOGY** grows in arid areas, on rocky slopes, in crevices, and on ridgetops, in shrub-steppe and woodlands, low to high elevation.

Elaeagnus angustifolia
ELAEAGNACEAE
RUSSIAN OLIVE

Non-native, locally common, blooms late
spring–early summer, 10–33 ft. Streambanks,
disturbed, low to mid elevation

Tree or shrub, erect, crown rounded, bark gray,
smooth, becoming furrowed with age, stems and
branches thorny or not, twigs silvery white, often
scaly. **LEAVES** deciduous, alternate, lance-shaped,
1.5–3 in. long, green or silvery and scaly above, silvery
scaly below, edges smooth, tips pointed or rounded.
FLOWERS 1–3 in leaf axils, fragrant, flowers funnel-shaped, silvery, petals absent, sepal lobes 4, bright
yellow within, stamens 4. **FRUIT** berrylike, oval, yellowish brown, sparsely scaly when mature, palatable,
sweet but dry. **ECOLOGY** invasive escapee from cultivation, grows in riparian areas, lakeshores, springs, and
disturbed areas, mostly in arid climates, lowland to
montane. Often planted as windbreaks or for erosion
control. The similar *Shepherdia argentea* has opposite leaves, separate male and female plants, and 8
stamens.

Elaeagnus commutata
ELAEAGNACEAE
SILVERBERRY
Native, scattered, blooms early summer,
3–13 ft. Streambanks, disturbed,
meadows, low to mid elevation

Shrub, erect, rhizomatous, thicket-forming, thorns absent, stems silvery or brownish, scaly, twigs brown or green. **LEAVES** deciduous, alternate, oval to lance-shaped, 1–3 in. long, both surfaces silvery scaly, can have brown spots below, edges wavy, tips pointed or rounded. **FLOWERS** 1–3 in leaf axils, fragrant, functionally male or female, flowers funnel-shaped, silvery outside, petals absent, sepal lobes 4, yellow inside, stamens 4. **FRUIT** berrylike, egg-shaped, silvery, edible, dry. **ECOLOGY** grows on sand or gravel bars, wet meadows, forest edges, shrubfields, and disturbed places, from steppe to montane areas.

Elaeagnus umbellata
ELAEAGNACEAE
AUTUMN OLIVE

Non-native, scattered, blooms mid spring, 10–17 ft. Streambanks, disturbed, low elevation

Shrub or tree, erect, crown rounded, bark gray, smooth, becoming furrowed with age, stems and branches thorny or not, twigs golden brown, scaly. **LEAVES** deciduous, alternate, oval to egg-shaped, 2–4 in. long, dark green above, silvery scaly below, edges wavy, tips pointed. **FLOWERS** clusters of 5–10 flowers in leaf axils, fragrant, flowers funnel-shaped, white to cream-colored, petals absent, sepal lobes 4, stamens 4. **FRUIT** berrylike, oval, pink to red, sparsely scaly, palatable, sweet and juicy. **ECOLOGY** invasive escapee from cultivation, grows in fields, forest edges, lakeshores, and disturbed places, rarely in wet soils. The similar *E. angustifolia* has silvery twigs, narrower leaves, sepals bright yellow within, yellowish brown fruit, and grows in wet soils.

Andromeda polifolia
ERICACEAE
BOG ROSEMARY
Native, scattered, blooms late spring–mid summer,
2–32 in. Bog/fen/wetland, low to mid elevation
Shrub, stems spreading, non-hairy, rhizomatous.
LEAVES evergreen, alternate, leathery, linear to oval,
0.5–1.5 in. long, to 0.25 in. wide, non-hairy and green
above, waxy white below, edges smooth and rolled
under, tips pointed. **FLOWERS** in few-flowered clusters
or single at stem tips, flower stalks 0.5–0.8 in. long,
flowers nodding, urn-shaped, 0.2–0.3 in. long, petals
pinkish, anthers tipped by 2 slender bristles.
FRUIT capsule, round, non-hairy, 0.16–0.25 in. wide.
ECOLOGY shade intolerant, grows in sphagnum bogs,
peat, acidic wetlands, and pool edges. Ours is var.
polifolia.

See Ericaceae with opposite leaves, page 317; whorled
leaves, page 351

Arbutus menziesii

ERICACEAE

PACIFIC MADRONE, ARBUTUS, MADRONA

Native, common, blooms late winter–spring, 20–80 ft. Coastal, west-side forest, low to mid elevation

Tree or shrub, trunks single to multiple, often curving, bark brownish red, peeling, inner bark light green, becoming reddish. **LEAVES** evergreen, alternate, oval to egg-shaped, 3–6 in. long, surfaces mostly non-hairy, dark green above, whitish green below, edges smooth to finely toothed, tips pointed or rounded. **FLOWERS** in clusters at branch ends, fragrant, flowers urn-shaped, petals creamy white to pinkish, 0.2–0.3 in. long, anthers tipped by 2 slender bristles. **FRUIT** berry, round, to 1 in. across, orange to red, surface bumpy. **ECOLOGY** grows along shorelines, in open forests, on coastal bluffs, and rocky slopes, coastal lowlands to montane. Tolerant of salt water and drought. Intolerant of root disturbance, transplantation, shade, and pollution, it is declining in abundance in many urban areas. Resprouts following fire, and its seed readily germinates in burned-over areas. Relatively long-lived, to 300 years or more.

Arctostaphylos bakeri
ERICACEAE
BAKER'S MANZANITA
Native, rare, blooms late winter–early spring,
3–10 ft. Serpentine, chaparral, low elevation
Shrub, erect, twigs glandular-hairy, or hairy with
glands on twig surface. **LEAVES** evergreen, alternate,
egg-shaped, 1.2 in. long, surfaces dull, dark green,
bumpy, glandular-hairy, edges smooth, tips pointed.
FLOWERS in clusters at stem tips, stalks hairy or
glandular-hairy, bracts scalelike, 0.1–0.2 in. long, flowers urn-shaped, white to pinkish. **FRUIT** berry, round,
brownish orange. **ECOLOGY** grows in chaparral and
associated dry forests on serpentine outcrops. Endemic
to California.

Arctostaphylos canescens
ERICACEAE
HOARY MANZANITA
Native, common, blooms winter–mid spring, 1–10
ft. Chaparral, west-side forest, low to mid elevation
Shrub, erect, twigs densely short-hairy. **LEAVES** evergreen, alternate, roundish, oval, or egg-shaped, 1–2
in. long, waxy, hairs velvety and gray, edges smooth,
tips pointed. **FLOWERS** branched clusters, drooping
when young, bracts leaflike, lance-shaped, 0.2–1 in.
long, velvety white- to grayish-hairy, flowers urn-
shaped, white to pink. **FRUIT** berry, round, hairy or
glandular-hairy, less hairy with age. **ECOLOGY** grows
on ridges and slopes in chaparral and forests, lowland to montane. Ssp. *sonomensis*, with
glandular-hairy ovaries and young fruit,
found in chaparral and pine forests, is
rare in California.

Arctostaphylos columbiana
ERICACEAE
HAIRY MANZANITA, BRISTLY MANZANITA
Native, common, blooms winter–early
spring, 3–17 ft. Rocky sites, chaparral, west-
side forest, low to mid elevation

Shrub or small tree, twigs densely hairy, hairs long and
short, sometimes glandular. **LEAVES** evergreen, alternate, non-overlapping, lance- to egg-shaped, 1.5–2.5
in. long, dark green, dull, surface sometimes bumpy,
finely hairy, sometimes non-hairy, sparsely glandular, edges smooth, tips pointed. **FLOWERS** in branched
clusters, drooping when young, bracts leaflike, oval to
lance-shaped, 0.5–0.7 in. long, finely glandular-hairy,
flowers urn-shaped, petals white. **FRUIT** berry, round,
sparsely hairy. **ECOLOGY** grows in chaparral, in gaps
and edges of conifer forests, on rock outcrops, lowland to mid-montane.

Arctostaphylos glandulosa
ERICACEAE
EASTWOOD'S MANZANITA

Native, common, blooms winter–early spring, 3–10
ft. Rocky sites, chaparral, low to high elevation
Shrub, erect, bark reddish, stems hairy, hairs glandular or not, burl present. **LEAVES** evergreen, alternate,
oval to egg-shaped, 1–2 in. long, upper and lower surfaces same color, green to grayish, hairiness varies,
edges smooth or toothed, tips pointed. **FLOWERS** in
clusters at stem tips, stalks hairy, glandular or not,
bracts scale or leaflike, 0.1–0.5 in. long, flowers urn-
shaped, white to pink, ovary densely hairy, sometimes glandular. **FRUIT** berry, roundish, smooth or
glandular-hairy, edible.
ECOLOGY grows on dry
rocky slopes in chapar-
ral and forests, resprouts
from the burl after fire, has
allelopathic effect on pine
seedlings.

Arctostaphylos hispidula
(*Arctostaphylos stanfordiana* ssp. *hispidula*)
ERICACEAE
GASQUET MANZANITA, HOWELL'S MANZANITA

Native, rare, blooms late winter–early spring, 3–10
ft. Serpentine, chaparral, low to mid elevation
Shrub, erect, twigs glandular-hairy. **LEAVES** evergreen,
alternate, oval to lance-shaped, 0.5–1 in. long, surfaces dull, dark green, bumpy, glandular-hairy, edges
smooth, tips pointed. **FLOWERS** in clusters at stem tips,
stalks hairy or glandular-hairy, bracts scalelike, 0.1–0.2
in. long, flowers urn-shaped, white to pinkish. **FRUIT**
berry, round, non-hairy. **ECOLOGY** grows on serpentine
outcrops in chaparral, and open forests in sandstone.

Arctostaphylos hookeri
ERICACEAE
HOOKER'S MANZANITA

Native, uncommon, blooms late winter–spring, 0.3–5
ft. Coastal, meadows, chaparral, low elevation
Shrub, erect to trailing, bark smooth, dark red, twigs
sparsely short-hairy. **LEAVES** evergreen, alternate, oval,
0.5–1 in. long, surfaces shiny, green, hairy or not,
edges smooth, tips pointed. **FLOWERS** in clusters at
stem tips, stalks short-hairy, bracts scalelike, 0.1–0.2
in. long, flowers urn-shaped, white. **FRUIT** berry, round,
non-hairy. **ECOLOGY** grows near the coast in prairies,
sandy chaparral, or conifer forests in the lowlands.
Endemic to California.

Arctostaphylos klamathensis
ERICACEAE
KLAMATH MANZANITA

Native, rare, blooms mid spring–early
summer, 4–20 in. Rocky sites, serpentine,
subalpine, mid to high elevation
Shrub, trailing, twigs sparsely glandular-hairy.
LEAVES evergreen, alternate, oval to egg-shaped, 0.5–1.5
in. long, surfaces bumpy, sparsely hairy, edges smooth,
tips rounded. **FLOWERS** in clusters, stalks glandular-
hairy, bracts scalelike, 0.1–0.2 in. long, flowers urn-
shaped, white, ovary glandular-hairy. **FRUIT** berry,
round, non-hairy. **ECOLOGY** grows on rock outcrops
and forest slopes in subalpine areas, often on serpentine. Endemic
to, and rare in,
California.

Arctostaphylos malloryi
ERICACEAE
MALLORY'S MANZANITA

Native, rare, blooms late winter–early spring, 3–10 ft. Chaparral, west-side forest, mid elevation

Shrub, erect, twigs short-hairy and glandular-hairy, sticky. **LEAVES** evergreen, alternate, roundish to egg-shaped, 1 in. long, surfaces dull, whitish bloom present, densely white- or grayish-hairy, becoming non-hairy with age, edges smooth, tips pointed. **FLOWERS** in clusters at stem tips, stalks glandular-hairy, bracts scalelike, 0.1–0.2 in. long, densely hairy, flowers urn-shaped, white, ovary densely hairy. **FRUIT** berry, roundish, hairy or not. **ECOLOGY** grows in chaparral and conifer forests with soils of volcanic origin. Endemic to, and rare in, California.

Arctostaphylos manzanita
ERICACEAE
WHITELEAF MANZANITA
Native, common, blooms late winter–early spring, 5–27
ft. Chaparral, east-side forest, low to mid elevation
Shrub or small tree, erect, twigs hairy, glandular-hairy,
or neither. **LEAVES** evergreen, alternate, egg-shaped,
1–2 in. long, surfaces green, whitish bloom present or
not, short-hairy, edges smooth, tips pointed.
FLOWERS in clusters at stem tips, stalks not sticky, hairy
or not, bracts scalelike, 0.1–0.2 in. long, flowers urn-
shaped, white, ovary glandular-hairy or not.
FRUIT berry, roundish, hairy or not. **ECOLOGY** grows
in chaparral, oak woodlands, or open conifer forests,
low to montane
elevation.

Arctostaphylos ×*media*
ERICACEAE
MEDIA MANZANITA, HYBRID MANZANITA
Native, scattered, blooms all spring, 1–2 ft. Rocky
sites, chaparral, west-side forest, low to mid elevation
Low shrub, trailing with branch tips turned upward,
twigs sparsely short-hairy to long-hairy, or glandular. **LEAVES** evergreen, alternate, lance- to egg-shaped,
about 1 in. long, green, shiny, sparsely hairy below,
edges smooth, tips rounded or pointed. **FLOWERS** in
small clusters at branch tips, bracts sometimes leaflike, mostly >0.2 in. long, flowers urn-shaped, white
to pink, ovary sparsely hairy. **FRUIT** berry, roundish,
red, hairy or not. **ECOLOGY** grows in chaparral, rock
outcrops, or forest openings, lowland to
montane. Hybrid of *A. uva-ursi* and *A.
columbiana*, often found in the horticul-
tural trade.

Arctostaphylos mewukka
ERICACEAE
INDIAN MANZANITA
Native, locally common, blooms early–mid spring,
3–10 ft. Chaparral, east-side forest, mid elevation
Shrub, erect, twigs smooth or sparsely glandular and
hairy. **LEAVES** evergreen, alternate, roundish or egg-
shaped, 1–3 in. long, surfaces dull, with whitish or
grayish bloom, edges smooth, tips pointed or rounded.
FLOWERS in clusters at stem tips, stalks hairy or not,
bracts scalelike, 0.1–0.2 in. long, flowers urn-shaped,
white, ovary smooth. **FRUIT** berry, round, dark brown,
non-hairy. **ECOLOGY** grows on montane slopes in
chaparral or in forest edges. Endemic to California.
The rare ssp. *truei* has
leaves >1.5 in. wide with
rounded tips.

Arctostaphylos nevadensis
ERICACEAE
PINEMAT MANZANITA
Native, common, blooms mid spring–early
summer, 4–20 in. West-side forest, east-side
forest, subalpine, mid to high elevation
Shrub, trailing or mat-forming, twigs sparsely short-
hairy. **LEAVES** evergreen, alternate, lance- or egg-
shaped, 0.5–1 in. long, bright green, shiny, edges
smooth, mostly non-hairy, glandular, tips pointed.
FLOWERS in small clusters at branch tips, bracts mostly
0.08–0.12 in. long, linear to lance-shaped, those at base
sometimes 0.2–0.4 in. long, flowers urn-shaped, white,
ovary non-hairy. **FRUIT** berry, brownish red, non-hairy.
ECOLOGY grows on rocky soils, in coni-
fer forests and other places, montane
to alpine. The similar *A. uva-ursi* has
rounded leaf tips and red berries, and is
often at lower elevations.

Arctostaphylos nortensis
ERICACEAE
DEL NORTE MANZANITA
Native, rare, blooms late winter–spring, 5–17
ft. Serpentine, chaparral, mid elevation
Shrub, erect, twigs glandular-hairy. **LEAVES** evergreen,
alternate, egg-shaped, 1–1.5 in. long, surfaces grayish-
hairy with whitish bloom, turning dark green, dull,
edges smooth, sometimes hairy, tips pointed.
FLOWERS in clusters at stem tips, stalks glandular-
hairy, bracts leaflike, 0.2–0.4 in. long, flowers urn-
shaped, white, ovary densely hairy. **FRUIT** berry, round,
sparsely white-hairy. **ECOLOGY** grows in chaparral
and conifer forests, often on serpentine. Endemic to
California.

Arctostaphylos patula
ERICACEAE
GREEN MANZANITA
Native, common, blooms late spring–
early summer, 3–10 ft. Chaparral, east-side
forest, subalpine, low to high elevation
Shrub, erect to spreading, thicket-forming, twigs
densely hairy, hairs usually tipped with golden glands.
LEAVES evergreen, alternate, roundish to egg-shaped,
1–2.5 in. long, bright yellowish green, shiny, mostly
non-hairy, edges smooth, tips pointed. **FLOWERS** in
clusters at stem tips, bracts scalelike, about 0.2 in. long,
densely hairy, usually glandular, flowers urn-shaped,
pink. **FRUIT** berry, dark chestnut-brown, non-hairy.
ECOLOGY grows in chap-
arral and forest openings,
from steppe to montane
areas.

Arctostaphylos stanfordiana
ERICACEAE
STANFORD'S MANZANITA
Native, locally common, blooms late
winter–early spring, 0.3–10 ft. Serpentine,
chaparral, low to mid elevation

Shrub, erect or trailing, twigs smooth, hairy or glandular-hairy. **LEAVES** evergreen, alternate, oval to lance-shaped, 1–2 in. long, surfaces green, shiny or with whitish bloom, glandular-hairy or not, edges smooth, tips pointed. **FLOWERS** in clusters at stem tips, stalks glandular-hairy, bracts scalelike, to 0.1 in. long, flowers urn-shaped, white to pink, ovary non-hairy. **FRUIT** berry, round, non-hairy. **ECOLOGY** grows in chaparral or forest openings, can be on serpentine. The type is common, erect, and with mostly smooth twigs; plants that are either erect and glandular-hairy, or trailing and simply hairy, belong to one of two rare California subspecies.

Arctostaphylos uva-ursi
ERICACEAE
KINNIKINNICK, BEARBERRY
Native, common, blooms winter–early summer, 4–20
in. Coastal, rocky sites, west-side forest, east-side
forest, alpine, subalpine, low to high elevation
Shrub, trailing or mat-forming, twigs sparsely short-
to long-hairy or glandular. **LEAVES** evergreen, alternate,
spoon- to egg-shaped, 0.5–1 in. long, dark green, shiny,
hairy or not, edges smooth, tips rounded. **FLOWERS** in
small clusters at branch tips, bracts scalelike, mostly
0.1–0.2 in. long, non-hairy, flowers urn-shaped, white
to pink, ovary non-hairy. **FRUIT** berry, roundish, bright
red, edible, insipid. **ECOLOGY** grows in sandy or rocky
soils, in coastal
dunes, conifer for-
ests, rock outcrops,
and dry, exposed
sites from low-lying
to alpine areas. Tends
to occur at higher ele-
vations away from the
coast. Circumboreal.

Arctostaphylos viscida
ERICACEAE
STICKY WHITELEAF MANZANITA
Native, locally common, blooms winter–
mid spring, 3–17 ft. Rocky sites, chaparral,
west-side forest, low to mid elevation
Shrub or tree, erect, twigs non-hairy to densely hairy,
glandular or not. **LEAVES** evergreen, alternate, round
to egg-shaped, 1–2 in. long, waxy, whitish green, dull,
non-hairy to sparsely glandular-hairy, edges smooth or
fringed with hair, tips pointed. **FLOWERS** in branched,
open clusters, cluster branches densely glandular
when young, bracts scalelike, mostly to 0.2 in. long,
glandular-hairy, flowers urn-shaped, petals white.
FRUIT berry, flattened sphere, reddish
brown, glandular-hairy or not.
ECOLOGY grows on rocky slopes, in
chaparral and forest openings, lowland
to montane.

Elliottia pyroliflora
(*Cladothamnus pyroliflorus*)
ERICACEAE
COPPERBUSH

Native, uncommon, blooms mid summer,
1.7–10 ft. Bog/fen/wetland, streambanks, west-
side forest, subalpine, mid to high elevation
Shrub, erect, bark copper-colored, shreddy, branches
and twigs non-hairy to sparsely short-hairy.
LEAVES deciduous, alternate but seemingly whorled,
oval to lance-shaped, 1–2 in. long, shiny green and
non-hairy above, paler with a waxy coating below,
edges smooth, tips pointed or rounded. **FLOWERS** single or in small clusters at branch tips, flowers saucer-shaped, petals 5, oval, 0.4–0.6 in. long, salmon to
copper-colored, stamens 8–10, the style curved, persistent in fruit, 0.4 in. long. **FRUIT** capsule, roundish, 0.2–0.3 in. across, seeds many and very small.
ECOLOGY grows along streambanks and in moist conifer forests, also in bogs and subalpine forests. Common in British Columbia.

Gaultheria hispidula
ERICACEAE
CREEPING SNOWBERRY
Native, rare, blooms mid–late spring, to 1 in. Bog/
fen/wetland, east-side forest, mid to high elevation
Shrub, vinelike, mat-forming, stems creeping, slender, to 16 in. long, densely short brownish-hairy,
hairs appressed. **LEAVES** evergreen, alternate, oval to
egg-shaped, 0.2–0.4 in. long, green above, appressed
short-hairy below, edges rolled under, tips rounded
or pointed. **FLOWERS** mostly single in leaf axils, flowers nodding, sepals and petals 4, bell-shaped, white
to pinkish, sepals red-hairy, anthers tipped by short
bristles. **FRUIT** berrylike, white, to 0.2 in. across, edible, spicy and aromatic. **ECOLOGY** grows
in sphagnum bogs, fens, and mossy
conifer forests, often on downed logs.
Locally common in British Columbia.

Gaultheria humifusa
ERICACEAE
ALPINE WINTERGREEN
Native, locally common, blooms mid summer,
4–12 in. Alpine, subalpine, high elevation
Shrub, stems trailing, hairy or not. **LEAVES** evergreen,
alternate, oval to egg-shaped, 0.5–1 in. long, surfaces green, non-hairy, edges toothed and hairy, tips
pointed or rounded. **FLOWERS** single in leaf axils, stalks
short, flowers bell-shaped, pinkish, lobes spreading, sepals pinkish red to red, non-hairy, anthers not
bristle-tipped. **FRUIT** berrylike, reddish, round, 0.2–0.3
in. across. **ECOLOGY** grows in wet meadows, moist forests, streambanks, rocky slopes, subalpine to alpine.
Hybridizes with *G. ovatifolia*,
which has hairy sepals and prefers drier habitats.

Gaultheria ovatifolia
ERICACEAE
OREGON WINTERGREEN, SLENDER TEABERRY, WESTERN TEABERRY

Native, locally common, blooms mid spring–early summer, to 2 in. Bog/fen/wetland, west-side forest, subalpine, mid to high elevation
Shrub, stems trailing, woolly to sparsely hairy, mat-forming. **LEAVES** evergreen, alternate, egg- to heart-shaped, 1–1.5 in. long, surfaces green, non-hairy, edges wavy or toothed, tips pointed. **FLOWERS** single in leaf axils, stalks short, flowers bell-shaped, white to pinkish, sepals reddish brown, woolly hairy, anthers not bristle-tipped. **FRUIT** berrylike, bright red, round, 0.2–0.3 in. across, edible. **ECOLOGY** grows in moist to dry forests, streambanks, rocky slopes, bogs, and shrubfields. Hybridizes with *G. humifusa*, which has non-hairy sepals and prefers wetter habitats.

Gaultheria shallon
ERICACEAE
SALAL

Native, common, blooms mid spring–mid summer, 1.5–7 ft. Coastal, bog/fen/wetland, west-side forest, low to mid elevation
Shrub, erect, spreading or trailing, thicket-forming. **LEAVES** evergreen, alternate, oval to egg-shaped, 1–3.5 in. long, surfaces dark green, leathery, non-hairy, edges finely toothed, tips pointed. **FLOWERS** in narrow loose clusters in leaf axils, stalks densely glandular-hairy, flowers nodding, urn-shaped, densely glandular-hairy, petals white to pink, sepals glandular-hairy, anthers tipped by slender bristles. **FRUIT** berrylike, purplish black, round, 0.2–0.4 in. across, glandular, edible. **ECOLOGY** grows on well-drained forest slopes, coastal bluffs, and bogs, often an abundant understory plant in Douglas-fir communities. Used extensively by the floral industry; makes a good groundcover or hedge in the garden but spreads aggressively. Fruit prized by First Nations and Native Americans and relished by wildlife.

Harrimanella stelleriana
(*Cassiope stelleriana*)
ERICACEAE
ALASKA BELLHEATHER, ALASKAN MOUNTAIN-
HEATHER, ALASKAN MOSS-HEATHER
Native, uncommon, blooms mid summer,
1–4 in. Alpine, subalpine, high elevation
Shrub, creeping, mat-forming, stems hairy.
LEAVES evergreen, alternate, linear to lance-shaped,
0.1–0.2 in. long, spreading (not covering stem), green,
non-hairy above, groove absent below, tips pointed or
rounded. **FLOWERS** single at stem tips, bell-shaped,
0.1–0.4 in. long, petals white to pinkish, lobes about ½
total length, sepals reddish, flower stalks hairy, anthers
bristle-tipped. **FRUIT** capsule, round, 0.2
in. across. **ECOLOGY** grows in wet meadows, boggy areas, and on rocky slopes,
often near seeps, subalpine to alpine.

Kalmiopsis fragrans
ERICACEAE
UMPQUA KALMIOPSIS
Native, rare, blooms late spring–early summer,
8–16 in. Rocky sites, low to mid elevation
Shrub, erect to trailing, twigs red to purplish, glandular-hairy, becoming gray and sparsely hairy with age.
LEAVES evergreen, alternate, fragrant, oblong to oval,
0.5–1 in. long, pale green, moderately glandular above,
darker and sparsely glandular below, edges smooth,
tips rounded or pointed. **FLOWERS** in flat-topped clusters at stem ends, flowers saucer-shaped, petals deep
pink to purplish, joined ⅓ total length, mostly non-
hairy within, style longer or shorter than stamens, stamens 0.3–0.6 in. long.
FRUIT capsule, round.
ECOLOGY grows on rock outcrops and at the base of cliffs
and boulders, often in soils
derived from volcanic ash.
Endemic to Oregon.

Kalmiopsis leachiana
ERICACEAE
SISKIYOU KALMIOPSIS, OREGON KALMIOPSIS
Native, rare, blooms late spring–early summer,
8–16 in. Rocky sites, mid to high elevation

Shrub, erect, twigs pale red to purplish, glandular-hairy, becoming gray and sparsely hairy with age. **LEAVES** evergreen, alternate, fragrant, oblong to oval, 0.5–1 in. long, dark green and densely glandular above, paler below, edges smooth, tips rounded. **FLOWERS** in flat-topped clusters at stem ends, flowers saucer-shaped, petals reddish pink, joined ½ total length, hairy within, style either longer or shorter than the stamens, stamens 0.1–0.3 in. long. **FRUIT** capsule, round. **ECOLOGY** grows on rocky slopes and sunny ridges in shrub or open forest communities. The similar *K. fragrans*, also rare, is trailing, has petals joined ⅓ their length, inner surface mostly non-hairy, stamens mostly 0.3–0.6 in. long, on rock outcrops. Endemic to Oregon.

Leucothoe davisiae
ERICACEAE
SIERRA LAUREL, BLACK LAUREL

Native, uncommon, blooms late spring–mid summer, 1–5 ft. Bog/fen/wetland, west-side forest, east-side forest, mid to high elevation

Shrub, erect, colony-forming, twigs brown, non-hairy. **LEAVES** evergreen, alternate, oval, 0.5–2.5 in. long, surfaces non-hairy, glossy green above, edges toothed, tips pointed or rounded. **FLOWERS** in narrow clusters at stem tips and upper leaf axils, flowers urn-shaped, petals and sepals white. **FRUIT** capsule, rounded, brown. **ECOLOGY** grows in bogs, meadow edges, and in wet forests. Plant poisonous to livestock and people if eaten. Rare in Oregon.

Menziesia ferruginea
ERICACEAE
FOOL'S HUCKLEBERRY, RUSTY MENZIESIA, MOCK AZALEA

Native, common, blooms mid spring–early summer, 3–8 ft. Streambanks, west-side forest, east-side forest, subalpine, low to high elevation

Shrub, erect, thicket-forming, twigs finely hairy, older branches often non-hairy. **LEAVES** deciduous, alternate, oval to egg-shaped, 0.5–2.5 in. long, surfaces green, glandular-hairy, edges hairy and toothed, midvein extends beyond tip, tips pointed. **FLOWERS** in small clusters at stem tips, flowers urn-shaped, petals greenish red to yellowish bronze, sepals green, glandular-hairy. **FRUIT** capsule, oval. **ECOLOGY** grows in shady forests and streambanks. Similar in appearance to the true huckleberries of *Vaccinium*, which have fleshy berries and leaves with midveins not extended beyond leaf tip.

Phyllodoce breweri
ERICACEAE
PURPLE MOUNTAIN-HEATHER
Native, locally common, blooms mid
summer, 4–16 in. Meadows, east-side forest,
alpine, subalpine, high elevation
Shrub, stems trailing with erect tips, twigs densely
glandular. **LEAVES** evergreen, alternate, linear, 0.2–1 in.
long, surfaces green, non-hairy, edges smooth to finely
toothed, rolled under, tips blunt. **FLOWERS** in small
clusters at stem ends, flowers nodding, bell-shaped,
petals pinkish purple, sepals fringed with hair near
base, stamens not bristle-tipped, hairy, extend beyond
petals. **FRUIT** capsule, round, glandular-hairy.

ECOLOGY grows in
open subalpine for-
ests and meadows,
higher elevations to
alpine areas.

Phyllodoce empetriformis
ERICACEAE
PINK MOUNTAIN-HEATHER
Native, common, blooms mid summer, 2–20 in.
Meadows, alpine, subalpine, mid to high elevation
Shrub, erect, mat-forming, glandular and hairy when
young. **LEAVES** evergreen, alternate, somewhat spreading, linear to oblong, 0.2–0.5 in. long, surfaces non-
hairy, edges sometimes glandular and toothed, tips
pointed or not. **FLOWERS** in flat-topped clusters at stem
ends, flowers nodding, bell-shaped, petals deep pink,
smooth, sepals reddish and fringed with hair, stamens
not bristle-tipped, non-hairy, shorter than petals.
FRUIT capsule, round, glandular-hairy. **ECOLOGY** grows
in montane to alpine meadows, heaths,
and slopes.

Phyllodoce glanduliflora
ERICACEAE
YELLOW MOUNTAIN-HEATHER
Native, locally common, blooms mid summer, 4–16
in. Meadows, alpine, subalpine, high elevation
Shrub, erect, mat-forming, glandular-hairy.
LEAVES evergreen, alternate, somewhat spreading,
linear to oblong, 0.2–0.5 in. long, surfaces often
glandular-hairy, edges densely glandular and toothed,
tips pointed or not. **FLOWERS** in flat-topped clusters at
stem ends, flowers nodding, urn-shaped, petals yellowish to greenish white, glandular, sepals greenish, not fringed with hair, glandular, stamens hairy,
not bristle-tipped. **FRUIT** capsule, round, densely
glandular-hairy. **ECOLOGY** grows in
meadows and open forests, upper montane to alpine, often in wetter or colder
habitats than *P. empetriformis*.

Phyllodoce ×*intermedia*
ERICACEAE
INTERMEDIATE MOUNTAIN-HEATHER
Native, uncommon, blooms mid summer, 2–20
in. Meadows, alpine, subalpine, high elevation
Shrub, erect, mat-forming. **LEAVES** evergreen, alternate, somewhat spreading, linear to oblong, 0.2–0.5 in.
long, surfaces glandular-hairy or not, edges glandular
and toothed, tips pointed or not. **FLOWERS** in flat-topped
clusters at stem ends, flowers nodding, tubular, petals
pinkish, sepals glandular, not fringed with hair, stamens not bristle-tipped. **FRUIT** capsule, round,
glandular-hairy. **ECOLOGY** grows in meadows and
heaths, upper montane to alpine areas. Hybrid of *P.
empetriformis* and *P. glanduliflora*, found
when the parent species grow adjacent
to each other.

Rhododendron albiflorum
ERICACEAE
WHITE RHODODENDRON
Native, common, blooms late spring–mid summer,
3–8 ft. Streambanks, west-side forest, east-
side forest, subalpine, mid to high elevation
Shrub, erect, rhizomatous, twigs with reddish hairs.
LEAVES deciduous, alternate, oval to lance-shaped,
1.5–3.5 in. long, surfaces bright green, sparsely hairy
to non-hairy, edges toothed to smooth, tips pointed or
rounded. **FLOWERS** in few-flowered clusters in leaf axils
of previous year's growth, flowers cup-shaped, fragrant, petals white with spreading lobes, sepals glandular with reddish hairs, stamens
10, flower stalks glandular-hairy.
FRUIT capsule, egg-shaped, hairy
and glandular. **ECOLOGY** grows in
moist conifer forests, subalpine
parklands, and streambanks.

Rhododendron columbianum
(*Ledum glandulosum, Rhododendron neoglandulosum*)
ERICACEAE
TRAPPER'S TEA, WESTERN LABRADOR TEA
Native, common, blooms late spring–mid
summer, 1.7–7 ft. Bog/fen/wetland, streambanks,
alpine, subalpine, low to high elevation
Fragrant shrub, erect, rhizomatous, stems bumpy,
glandular, and hairy. **LEAVES** evergreen, alternate,
leathery, oval to egg-shaped, 1–3 in. long, dark green
above, glandular and densely white-hairy below,
edges smooth, sometimes rolled under, tips rounded.
FLOWERS in rounded clusters at stem ends, bracts scaly
and fringed with hair, flowers saucer-shaped, petals
creamy white and hairy inside, sepals
hairy and glandular, stamens much longer than the style. **FRUIT** capsule, egg-
shaped, non-hairy, nodding.
ECOLOGY grows in bogs, swamps, and
streambanks. Leaves used to make tea
but can be toxic in excess.

Rhododendron groenlandicum
(*Ledum groenlandicum*)
ERICACEAE
LABRADOR TEA

Native, common, blooms mid spring–mid summer, 0.7–5 ft. Bog/fen/wetland, west-side forest, low to high elevation

Aromatic shrub, erect, rhizomatous, stems with dense, rust-colored hairs. **LEAVES** evergreen, alternate, leathery, oblong to oval, 1–2 in. long, dark green above, glandular with long rusty hairs below, edges smooth and rolled under, tips rounded. **FLOWERS** in rounded clusters at stem ends, bracts scaly, sometimes hairy, flowers saucer-shaped, petals creamy white and hairy inside, sepals hairy, stamens only slightly longer than the style. **FRUIT** capsule, egg-shaped, hairy, nodding. **ECOLOGY** grows in bogs and moist forest habitats, lowland to montane. Leaves often brewed to make a fragrant tea.

Rhododendron macrophyllum
ERICACEAE
PACIFIC RHODODENDRON, CALIFORNIA ROSE BAY, COAST RHODODENDRON
Native, locally common, blooms mid spring–early summer, 3–17 ft. Coastal, west-side forest, low to mid elevation

Shrub or tree, erect to spreading, bark smooth to furrowed, sometimes peeling, twigs hairy, becoming non-hairy with age. **LEAVES** evergreen, alternate, leathery, oval to egg-shaped, 3–5.5(8) in. long, dark green above, paler below, surfaces with some branched hairs but mostly non-hairy, edges smooth, tips pointed or rounded. **FLOWERS** in 10- to 20-flowered clusters at stem tips, flowers fragrant, bell-shaped, showy, 1–1.5 in. long, petals pale to purplish pink, lobes spreading with wavy edges, sepals short, stamens 10. **FRUIT** capsule, glandular with rusty-red hairs. **ECOLOGY** grows in forest openings and edges, also in deep shade, and in ridgetop shrub thickets. State flower of Washington.

Rhododendron occidentale
ERICACEAE
WESTERN AZALEA
Native, locally common, blooms mid spring–early summer, 3–17 ft. Coastal, bog/fen/wetland, west-side forest, low to high elevation

Shrub or small tree, erect to spreading, bark smooth to furrowed, sometimes peeling, twigs slender, hairy, glandular, or smooth. **LEAVES** deciduous, alternate, oval to egg-shaped, 1–3.5 in. long, surfaces light green, hairy, glandular or smooth, edges fringed with hair, tips pointed or rounded. **FLOWERS** in clusters at stem tips, flowers funnel-shaped, 1–2.5 in. long, showy, petals white to pink, often with contrasting yellow or orange blotch on upper lobe, stamens 5. **FRUIT** capsule, glandular-hairy. **ECOLOGY** grows in streambanks, seeps, bogs, and other moist areas in conifer forests and ocean bluffs, often in shrub thickets, preferring open to partial shade conditions. A favorite in the native plant garden.

Vaccinium alaskaense

ERICACEAE

ALASKA HUCKLEBERRY

Native, common, blooms mid–late spring,
1.6–5 ft. West-side forest, east-side forest,
subalpine, low to high elevation

Shrub, erect, bark grayish, twigs yellowish green,
somewhat angled, finely hairy or not. **LEAVES** deciduous, alternate, oval to egg-shaped, 1–2.5 in. long,
green above, paler, waxy with midvein glandular-hairy
below, edges usually smooth, tips pointed to rounded.
FLOWERS single in leaf axils, blooms after leaves fully
open, flowers nodding, urn-shaped, pinkish green to
bronze, usually wider than long. **FRUIT** berry, bluish to
purplish black, waxy or not, 0.3–0.4
in. across, edible. **ECOLOGY** grows
in conifer forests, forest openings,
and shrubfields. The similar *V.
ovalifolium* has smooth leaf midveins and flowers longer than wide.

Vaccinium caespitosum

(*Vaccinium cespitosum*)

ERICACEAE

DWARF BILBERRY, DWARF HUCKLEBERRY

Native, common, blooms late spring–early summer,
4–12 in. Coastal, bog/fen/wetland, meadows,
alpine, subalpine, low to high elevation

Shrub, erect to spreading, rhizomatous, mat-forming, twigs somewhat angled, yellowish green to reddish, mostly hairy. **LEAVES** deciduous, alternate, lance-
shaped, 0.5–1 in. long, light green above, paler and
glandular below, edges with glandular-tipped teeth
from tip to midleaf, tips pointed or rounded.
FLOWERS single in leaf axils, flowers narrowly urn-
shaped, white to pink, 2 times longer
than wide. **FRUIT** berry, light blue to
blackish blue with a grayish waxy coating, 0.2–0.3 in. across, edible. **ECOLOGY**
grows in bogs, forest openings, heaths,
meadows, dry or wet habitats. The similar *V. deliciosum* has widely urn-shaped
pink flowers, not twice as long as wide,
and non-hairy twigs.

Vaccinium deliciosum
ERICACEAE
CASCADE BILBERRY, BLUE HUCKLEBERRY
Native, common, blooms late spring–early
summer, 6–12 in. Meadows, west-side forest,
alpine, subalpine, mid to high elevation
Shrub, erect, mat-forming, rhizomatous, twigs
rounded, greenish brown, mostly non-hairy.
LEAVES deciduous, alternate, egg-shaped, 0.5–1.5
in. long, dull green above, paler, waxy with midvein
glandular-hairy below, edges toothed except near leaf
base, tips pointed or rounded. **FLOWERS** single in leaf
axils, widely urn-shaped, pinkish, slightly longer than
wide. **FRUIT** berry, blue with a waxy coating, 0.2–0.3
in. across, edible, sweet. **ECOLOGY** grows in conifer forests, meadows, heaths, and talus slopes.
Berries are a favored and important
late-season food for bears.

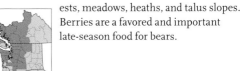

Vaccinium macrocarpon

(*Oxycoccus macrocarpus*)
ERICACEAE
CRANBERRY

Non-native, locally common, blooms late
spring–early summer, 1.5–6 in. Bog/fen/
wetland, disturbed, low to mid elevation
Vine, stems trailing to climbing, rhizomatous, twigs
round, brown. **LEAVES** evergreen, alternate, oval, 0.3–
0.7 in. long, green above, paler, waxy below, edges
smooth, rolled under, tips rounded. **FLOWERS** single in
leaf axils, nodding, petals 4, joined at base, pink, bent
back, anthers not bristle-tipped. **FRUIT** berry, red to
pink, round to egg-shaped, 0.4–0.6 in. across, edible.
ECOLOGY native to eastern North America, grows in
shorelines, forests, roadsides, and other disturbed
places. This is the cultivated commercial cranberry.

Vaccinium membranaceum

ERICACEAE
BLACK HUCKLEBERRY, THINLEAF
HUCKLEBERRY, MOUNTAIN HUCKLEBERRY

Native, common, blooms mid–late spring, 1.7–5
ft. Vernal-wet, meadows, west-side forest, east-
side forest, subalpine, mid to high elevation
Shrub, erect, not rhizomatous, bark grayish, twigs yellowish green, somewhat angled, hairy or not.
LEAVES deciduous, alternate, oval to egg-shaped, 1–2
in. long, green above, paler and glandular below, edges
finely toothed, tips pointed. **FLOWERS** single in leaf
axils, nodding, urn-shaped, yellowish pink, longer
than wide. **FRUIT** berry, black to dark purplish red, not
waxy, 0.35–0.5 in. across, edible. **ECOLOGY** grows in
conifer forests, forest openings, shrub thickets, alpine
heaths, and wet meadows. Berries were used extensively by First Nations and Native Americans, who
often set fires to create and maintain berry patches.
Fire caused the shrubs to resprout from the roots,
renewing the bush, and opened patches for better
shrub growth.

Vaccinium myrtilloides
ERICACEAE
VELVETLEAF HUCKLEBERRY

Native, rare, blooms mid spring–early summer, 4–20 in. Bog/fen/wetland, west-side forest, low to mid elevation Shrub, erect, rhizomatous, twigs round, greenish brown, velvety-hairy. **LEAVES** deciduous, alternate, oval, 0.5–1.5 in. long, green above, usually densely hairy below, edges smooth, tips pointed. **FLOWERS** solitary or in small clusters at stem tips, opening before leaves are fully unfurled, flowers bell-shaped, petals greenish white to pinkish, sepals green, anthers not bristle-tipped. **FRUIT** berry, blue with pale waxy coating, 0.2–0.3 in. across, edible, very sweet. **ECOLOGY** grows in open conifer forests, forest openings, meadows, and bogs. Locally common in British Columbia.

Vaccinium myrtillus
ERICACEAE
WHORTLEBERRY, DWARF BILBERRY

Native, locally common, blooms late spring–mid summer, 4–12 in. East-side forest, subalpine, mid to high elevation Shrub, erect, loosely broom-shaped, rhizomatous, twigs greenish and angled, short-hairy. **LEAVES** deciduous, alternate, oval to egg-shaped, 0.5–1 in. long, veins raised below, edges toothed, tips pointed or rounded. **FLOWERS** single in leaf axils, nodding, urn-shaped, white to pink. **FRUIT** berry, dark red, reddish blue, or bluish black, sometimes all three colors on same bush, 0.2–0.3 in. across, edible. **ECOLOGY** grows in conifer forests and forest openings, shrub thickets, and subalpine parklands. The similar *V. scoparium* has non-hairy twigs, leaves mostly <0.5 in., and smaller, bright red berries.

Vaccinium ovalifolium
ERICACEAE
OVAL-LEAF HUCKLEBERRY, OVAL-LEAF
BLUEBERRY

Native, common, blooms mid–late spring,
1.3–6.7 ft. Bog/fen/wetland, meadows, west-
side forest, subalpine, low to high elevation
Shrub, erect, not rhizomatous, bark grayish, twigs yellowish green, somewhat angled, non-hairy.
LEAVES deciduous, alternate, oval to egg-shaped, 1–1.5
in. long, green above, paler and waxy below, edges
usually smooth, tips rounded. **FLOWERS** single in leaf
axils, blooms before leaves fully opened, flowers nodding, urn-shaped, pinkish, usually longer than wide.
FRUIT berry, bluish to purplish black,
usually waxy, 0.2–0.4 in. across, edible.
ECOLOGY grows in conifer forests, forest
openings, bogs, and shrubfields.

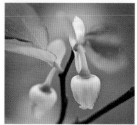

Vaccinium ovatum
ERICACEAE
EVERGREEN HUCKLEBERRY, CALIFORNIA
HUCKLEBERRY

Native, common, blooms early spring–mid summer,
1.7–10 ft. Coastal, west-side forest, low elevation
Shrub, erect to spreading, twigs round, hairy when
young, leaves in 2 rows, forming flat sprays.
LEAVES evergreen, alternate, lance- to egg-shaped, 1–2
in. long, leathery, shiny green above, paler, sparsely
glandular-hairy below, edges sharply toothed, tips
pointed. **FLOWERS** in small clusters in leaf axils, flowers bell-shaped, white to bright pink, longer than wide,
sepals red. **FRUIT** berry, purplish black, sometimes
reddish brown, waxy or not, 0.2–0.3
in. across, edible. **ECOLOGY** grows in
open conifer forests, in forest edges,
often within the reach of salt spray, also
epiphytic on coast redwood trunks.
Desirable ornamental, can act as a
groundcover.

Vaccinium oxycoccos (Oxycoccus oxycoccos)
ERICACEAE
BOG CRANBERRY, WILD CRANBERRY

Native, locally common, blooms mid
spring–early summer, to 16 in. Coastal, bog/
fen/wetland, low to mid elevation

Shrub, vinelike, stems slender, trailing, hairy or not.
LEAVES evergreen, alternate, lance- to egg-shaped, 0.1–
0.5 in. long, leathery, shiny green above, grayish below,
edges smooth and rolled under, tips pointed.
FLOWERS single to few at stem ends and leaf axils, flowers nodding on slender stems, petals 4, pink, separate and curled back. **FRUIT** berry, pale pink to ruby
red, 0.2–0.5 in. long, edible, tart. **ECOLOGY** grows in
bogs and fens, mostly with sphagnum
moss. The similar *V. vitis-idaea* is mat-
forming, with bell-shaped flowers.

Vaccinium parvifolium
ERICACEAE
RED HUCKLEBERRY

Native, common, blooms all spring, 3–10 ft.
West-side forest, low to mid elevation

Shrub, erect, not rhizomatous, twigs slender, bright
green and angled. **LEAVES** deciduous, alternate, oval
to egg-shaped, 0.5–1 in. long, veins prominent below,
edges mostly smooth (young leaves can be toothed),
tips rounded. **FLOWERS** single in leaf axils, nodding,
sometimes hidden beneath leaves, urn-shaped, pink,
bronze, or yellowish. **FRUIT** berry, bright red, 0.2–0.4
in. across, edible, tart. **ECOLOGY** grows in shady conifer
forests, often on stumps or other rotting wood.

Vaccinium scoparium
ERICACEAE
GROUSEBERRY
Native, common, blooms early–mid summer,
4–10 in. Meadows, west-side forest, east-side
forest, alpine, subalpine, mid to high elevation
Shrub, erect, broom-shaped, rhizomatous, twigs
greenish and angled, non-hairy. **LEAVES** deciduous,
alternate, lance- to egg-shaped, 0.3–0.5 in. long, veins
raised below, edges toothed, tips pointed.
FLOWERS single in leaf axils, nodding, urn-shaped,
pink. **FRUIT** berry, bright red, 0.1–0.2 in. across, edible.
ECOLOGY grows in conifer forests, shrubfields, meadows, and talus slopes. Similar to *V. myrtillus*, which has
leaves mostly longer than 0.5 in., hairy
twigs, and larger, often bluish berries.
Rare in California.

Vaccinium uliginosum
(*Vaccinium occidentale*)
ERICACEAE
BOG BLUEBERRY, BOG BILBERRY
Native, scattered, blooms mid spring–
early summer, 4–12 in. Bog/fen/wetland,
meadows, low to high elevation
Shrub, mat-forming, twigs round, yellowish green and
short-hairy, older branches grayish red. **LEAVES** deciduous, alternate, oval to egg-shaped, 0.5–1 in. long, green
above, veins prominent below, both surfaces usually
hairy, edges smooth, tips rounded. **FLOWERS** single to
few in leaf axils, flowers urn-shaped, longer than wide,
pink, often with white stripes. **FRUIT** berry, blue with
waxy coating, 0.2–0.3 in. across, edible,
sweet. **ECOLOGY** grows in bogs, swamps,
wet meadows, rocky tundra, and shrub
thickets.

Vaccinium vitis-idaea
ERICACEAE
LINGONBERRY, MOUNTAIN CRANBERRY, ROCK
CRANBERRY

Native, scattered, blooms mid summer, 0.5–14
in. Bog/fen/wetland, low to high elevation

Shrub, erect to trailing, rhizomatous, mat-forming, twigs round or angled, short-hairy. **LEAVES** evergreen, alternate, oval to egg-shaped, 0.2–0.5 in. long, bright green above, brown to black glandular-hairy below, edges rolled under, tips notched. **FLOWERS** single to several at stem tips, flowers bell-shaped, 4-lobed, pinkish. **FRUIT** berry, round, bright red, 0.2–0.4 in. across, edible, acidic. **ECOLOGY** grows in forests, bogs, and heaths. The simi-

lar *V. oxycoccos* has flowers with separate petals that are bent back.

Alhagi maurorum (*Alhagi pseudalhagi*)
FABACEAE
CAMELTHORN

Non-native, locally common, blooms late spring–mid
summer, 1–3 ft. Streambanks, disturbed, low elevation

Shrub, erect, rhizomatous, stems green, branches spine-tipped. **LEAVES** deciduous, alternate, oval to egg-shaped, 0.3–1 in. long, edges smooth, tips rounded or pointed. **FLOWERS** in clusters in leaf axils, flowers pea-shaped, 0.4 in. long, reddish purple. **FRUIT** pod, 0.5–1 in. long, constricted between seeds, non-hairy. **ECOLOGY** invasive Asian import, grows in arid agricultural areas and streambanks.

See Fabaceae with compound leaves, page 381

Cercis orbiculata (*Cercis occidentalis*)
FABACEAE
WESTERN REDBUD, CALIFORNIA REDBUD
Native, locally common, blooms mid spring,
7–23 ft. Chaparral, west-side forest, east-
side forest, low to mid elevation

Shrub or tree, crown rounded, twigs reddish.
LEAVES deciduous, alternate, roundish to kidney-
shaped, 1–4 in. long, green, shiny, edges smooth,
tips rounded. **FLOWERS** in small clusters along the
branches, flowers pea-like, about 0.5 in. long, pink to
reddish purple, flowers before the leaves unfold.
FRUIT pod, 2–4 in. long, flat, brown, seeds per pod
about 7. **ECOLOGY** grows on dry slopes, in canyons, and
along streambanks in chaparral, woodlands, and conifer forests, low to mid elevation.

Spartium junceum
FABACEAE
SPANISH BROOM

Non-native, common, blooms all spring,
5–15 ft. Disturbed, low to mid elevation

Shrub or small tree, erect, stems green but turning
brown with age, round with few branches, rushlike.
LEAVES ephemeral, alternate, oval to lance-shaped,
0.5–1 in. long, hairy below, edges smooth. **FLOWERS** in
clusters at stem ends, flowers pea-like, bright yellow,
about 1 in. long, fragrant, sepals lobed, style bent near
the tip. **FRUIT** pod, 2–4 in. long, brown, hairy.
ECOLOGY grows in disturbed areas, roadsides, oak
woodlands, and grasslands from the lowlands to the
foothills. Differs from other brooms, *Cytisus scoparius*

and *Genista monspessulana*, by its round
stems, simple, short-lived leaves, and
flowers in clusters at stem ends.

Chrysolepis chrysophylla
FAGACEAE
GOLDEN CHINQUAPIN, GIANT CHINQUAPIN
Native, locally common, blooms spring–
summer, 17–100 ft. Chaparral, west-side forest,
east-side forest, low to mid elevation

Tree or shrub, branches spreading, crown cone-
shaped, bark thin and dark gray when young, becoming thick, furrowed, and reddish brown with age,
twigs scaly, hairy. **LEAVES** evergreen, alternate, oval to
lance-shaped, 1–6 in. long, dark green and sparsely to
non-hairy above, golden to yellowish green, scaly and
densely hairy below, edges smooth, sometimes rolled
up, tips pointed. **FLOWERS** plants male and female,
flowers small, petals absent, arranged in catkins in leaf
axils. Catkins erect or spreading, unisexual, or bisexual with male flowers above the female. **FRUIT** spiny
bur, about 1 in. long, containing 1–3 nuts, matures in
2nd season. **ECOLOGY** grows as a tree on sites with deep
soils, winter precipitation, and summer fog, among
conifers and evergreen hardwood species. Found in
shrubby form on dry, open sites with poor soils, at
higher elevations in cold, snowy places, and in chaparral. Somewhat shade tolerant and often lives 400–500
years. Resprouts readily if topkilled; older plants can
survive low-intensity fire. Rare in Washington.

Chrysolepis sempervirens
FAGACEAE
BUSH CHINQUAPIN
Native, common, blooms mid summer, to 7 ft. Chaparral, west-side forest, east-side forest, low to high elevation

Shrub, rhizomatous, branches spreading, crown rounded, bark gray or brown, thin and smooth, twigs scaly hairy. **LEAVES** evergreen, alternate, oval to lance-shaped, 1–3 in. long, dull green above, golden or rusty red and hairy below, sometimes non-hairy with age, edges smooth, tips rounded. **FLOWERS** plants male and female, flowers small, petals lacking, arranged in catkins in leaf axils. Catkins erect or spreading, unisexual, or bisexual with male flowers above the female. **FRUIT** spiny bur, about 1–2.5 in. long, containing 1–3 nuts. **ECOLOGY** grows in the understory of conifer forests, in montane chaparral, ridges, and other habitats. Resprouts after fire; can be shaded out eventually in some communities without fire. The similar *C. chrysophylla* has dark green leaves with pointed tips.

Notholithocarpus densiflorus
(Lithocarpus densiflorus)
FAGACEAE
TANOAK

Native, locally common, blooms late spring–
late summer, 10–100 ft. West-side forest,
east-side forest, low to mid elevation

Tree or shrub, bark gray or brown, smooth to furrowed, twigs densely hairy, yellowish. **LEAVES** evergreen, alternate, oval to egg-shaped, 1–5.5 in. long,
rounded and shiny green above, woolly hairy becoming
sparsely hairy below, exposing the bluish gray surface,
edges rolled under, sometimes toothed, tips rounded.
FLOWERS male and female, flowers small, lacking petals, arranged in catkins in leaf axils. Catkins erect,
cream in color, unisexual, or bisexual with male flowers above the 1 female flower. **FRUIT** acorn, round to
oval, 0.5–1.5 in. long, cap scales spiny, matures in 2nd
year, edible but bitter. **ECOLOGY** grows in mixed evergreen forests, including Douglas-fir, oaks, pines, and
Pacific madrone. Shade tolerant but benefits from disturbances that open up the canopy. Resprouts after
fire; some older trees survive less intense fires. Most
specimens produce an abundance of acorns every
other year, providing high-quality forage for wildlife
and in the past to Native Americans. Seeds germinate
in shade or sun, and in many types of soil; however,
they are so highly prized, relatively few become established. The similar *Chrysolepis chrysophylla* has scaly
leaf undersides, pointed leaf tips, and spiny burr fruits.

Quercus berberidifolia
FAGACEAE
SCRUB OAK
Native, locally common, blooms early spring,
3–13 ft. Chaparral, low to mid elevation

Shrub, sometimes small tree, bark gray, scaly, twigs gray, yellowish or reddish brown. **LEAVES** evergreen, alternate, oval to egg-shaped, 0.5–1 in. long, glandular-hairy below, also with tiny star-shaped hairs against the leaf surface, glossy or dull green above, sparsely to non-hairy, edges spiny-toothed, tips rounded. **FLOWERS** arranged in catkins, catkins male or female, on the same plant, blooming as the leaves unfold. **FRUIT** acorn, oval or egg-shaped, 0.5–1 in. long, light to dark brown, cap bowl-shaped, scales warty, hairy, matures in 1 season, edible. **ECOLOGY** grows in chaparral and in coastal sage scrub, from low to montane areas.

Quercus chrysolepis
FAGACEAE
CANYON LIVE OAK

Native, common, blooms mid spring, to 83 ft. Rocky sites, chaparral, west-side forest, low to mid elevation

Tree or shrub, trees can be tall and slender or short and crooked, depending on habitat. Bark thin, pale grayish brown, scaly and furrowed. Twigs golden brown, hairy, less so with age. **LEAVES** evergreen, alternate, oblong to egg-shaped, 1–3.5 in. long, dark green above, bluish with whitish bloom and yellow, glandular-hairy below, both sides with hair tufts, edges sharp-toothed or smooth, leaf tip pointed. **FLOWERS** male flowers in drooping catkins, female flowers (usually 1) in leaf axil, both types on the same plant. **FRUIT** acorn, matures in 2 years, egg-shaped, 0.5–1.5 in. long, tip rounded, cap saucer-shaped, cap hairy inside, scales hairy, edible. **ECOLOGY** grows in canyons, on slopes, ridges, and valleys in mixed conifer forests and chaparral, from low to montane areas. Variable species, relatively intolerant of shade and very tolerant of drought, persisting on drier and rocky sites. On sites with better soil and more moisture, it is replaced over time by other plant species without disturbance. Produces abundant acorn crops, prized by wildlife and in the past by Native Americans.

Quercus douglasii
FAGACEAE
BLUE OAK

Native, locally common, blooms mid spring, 20–67 ft. Meadows, east-side forest, low to mid elevation Tree, crown rounded, bark gray, scaly, twigs reddish or yellowish brown, hairy, less so with age. **LEAVES** deciduous, alternate, oval, lance- or egg-shaped, 1–2.5 in. long, green or bluish green below, with whitish bloom, dull blue-green or grayish above, both surfaces with star-shaped hairs, edges lobed, toothed, or smooth, tips rounded. **FLOWERS** male flowers in drooping catkins, female flowers (usually 1) in leaf axil, both on the same plant. **FRUIT** acorn, egg- or spindle-shaped, 1–1.5 in. long, cap cup-shaped, non-hairy within, scales warty, matures in 1 year, edible. **ECOLOGY** grows on open, dry slopes, forming oak savannas with an herbaceous understory, or in dense forests or woodlands. Highly resistant to drought but drops leaves in such times. Bark is thin, making trees susceptible to fire damage, and the ability to resprout after fire declines with age. Historically fires, most likely started by humans, were frequent in oak communities; fire suppression

results in increased density of oaks and invasion of other trees into oak savannas. Abundant seed crops occur every 2–3 years. Acorns are dispersed and consumed by rodents, scrub jays, and magpies; some animals store acorns in caches, uneaten portions of which later germinate and grow. Endemic to California.

Quercus durata
FAGACEAE
LEATHER OAK

Native, locally common, blooms mid spring,
3–10 ft. Rocky sites, serpentine, chaparral,
east-side forest, low to mid elevation

Shrub, erect, crown rounded, bark scaly, branches tangled, twigs gray or yellowish, hairy, often some hair
spreading and yellowish. **LEAVES** evergreen, alternate,
lobed, oblong to oval, 0.5–1.5 in. long, rounded rather
than flat, surfaces grayish green, hairy, edges rolled
under, spiny-toothed, tips pointed or not.
FLOWERS male flowers in drooping catkins, female
flowers 1–2 in leaf axils, both types on the same plant.
FRUIT acorn, matures in 1 year, roundish to egg-
shaped, 0.5–1 in. long, tip rounded, cap cup-shaped,
scales reddish or yellowish, warty, often glandular, edible. **ECOLOGY** grows in chaparral and
in conifer forests, shade intolerant. Var.
durata is found only on serpentine; the
rare var. *gabrielensis* grows in granitic
soils, leaves greenish above. Endemic to
California.

Quercus garryana
FAGACEAE
GARRY OAK, OREGON WHITE OAK
Native, common, blooms mid–late spring,
3–83 ft. Rocky sites, west-side forest,
east-side forest, low elevation

Tree or shrub, bark light gray to grayish brown, scaly and furrowed. Twigs reddish brown, initially hairy, becoming smooth with age. **LEAVES** deciduous, alternate, oval to egg-shaped, 2–5 in. long, shiny and dark green above, paler and hairy beneath, edges deeply lobed, lobes and leaf tip rounded. **FLOWERS** male flowers in drooping catkins, female flowers in clusters of 2–4 in leaf axils, both on the same plant. **FRUIT** acorn, matures in 1 year, oblong to roundish, about 1 in. long, cap cup- or saucer-shaped, non-hairy inside, scales warty, hairy or not, edible. **ECOLOGY** grows on rocky outcrops, in drier meadows, forest edges, also in floodplains; mostly at lower elevations west of the Cascades and the Sierras, although sometimes extending east along river valleys. Slow growing and long-lived, 200–500 years, withstanding flooding and drought and thriving in poor soils or exposed sites. Garry oak communities are diverse and important habitat for many wildlife species. Oak habitat had been maintained in part through burning by Native Americans; fire suppression and human development has meant sharp habitat reduction. Var. *breweri* is a colony-forming shrub, 6.5–10 ft. tall, leaves velvety hairy below, endemic to the Siskiyou region.

Quercus kelloggii
FAGACEAE
CALIFORNIA BLACK OAK, KELLOGG'S OAK
Native, common, blooms late spring,
33–83 ft. Meadows, west-side forest, east-
side forest, low to mid elevation

Tall, sturdy tree, bark dark brown to black, becoming
checkered and furrowed with age. Twigs brown or reddish brown, non-hairy. **LEAVES** deciduous, alternate,
oval to egg-shaped, 3.5–8 in. long, bright yellow-green
and non-hairy above, pale green and usually hairy
beneath, edges deeply lobed, each lobe with several
bristle-pointed teeth. **FLOWERS** male flowers in drooping, hairy catkins, female flowers solitary or in clusters
of 2–7 in leaf axils, both on the same plant.
FRUIT acorn, matures in 2 years, oval, 1–1.5 in. long,
nut hairy, cap cup- to saucer-shaped, hairy inside,
scales mostly smooth, edible. **ECOLOGY** grows in valleys and slopes in conifer forests or oak woodlands,
often on rocky substrates. Grows with *Q. douglasii*,
Q. wislizeni, and other oaks among the conifers, most
often with ponderosa pine. Shade intolerant but tolerant of drought and fire, often surviving low-intensity
fires. Fire also opens up habitat for the oak, removing seedlings and saplings of competing species. Oak
communities provide important nesting and foraging
habitat for wildlife, some of which, like the acorn woodpecker, depend on acorns for much of their food sup-
ply. Hybridizes with *Q. wislizeni*; the resulting crosses
can be identified by their sparse canopy of evergreen
leaves in winter.

Quercus lobata
FAGACEAE
VALLEY OAK
Native, locally common, blooms early
spring, 33–100 ft. Streambanks, meadows,
east-side forest, low to mid elevation

Tree, bark gray, scaly, twigs yellowish gray, hairy.
LEAVES deciduous, alternate, oval to egg-shaped, 2–4
in. long, light green below, shiny dark green or grayish
above, both sides with star-shaped hairs, edges deeply
lobed, lobe tips rounded, leaf tip rounded.
FLOWERS male flowers in drooping catkins, female
flowers (usually 1) in leaf axil, both on the same plant.
FRUIT acorn, matures in 1 year, oval or spindle-shaped,
1–2.5 in. long, tip pointed, cap cup-shaped, non-hairy
inside, scales grayish or cream, warty, edible.
ECOLOGY grows in valleys and slopes, trees widely
spaced with an herbaceous understory, as well as in

riparian areas, where it forms open to
dense forests with a shrubby understory. Rodents, deer, and acorn woodpeckers, scrub jays, and other birds eat
the acorns and utilize other parts of the
tree. Thick bark helped valley oak survive fires, which were frequent historically. Endemic to California.

Quercus sadleriana
FAGACEAE
SADLER'S OAK, DEER OAK

Native, locally common, blooms mid spring, 3–10 ft.
Rocky sites, west-side forest, mid to high elevation
Shrub, rhizomatous, bark gray, smooth, twigs reddish
or brown, with whitish bloom, non-hairy. **LEAVES** evergreen, alternate, oval to egg-shaped, 3–5.5 in. long,
side veins straight, light green with whitish bloom and
few star-shaped hairs below, dark green and non-hairy
above, edges sharp-toothed, tips pointed.
FLOWERS male flowers in drooping catkins, female
flowers (usually 1) in leaf axil, both on the same plant.
FRUIT acorn, matures in 1 year, oval to round, to 1
in. long, cap cup- or
funnel-shaped, non-
hairy inside, scales gray
with reddish tips, warty,
edible. **ECOLOGY** grows
on open slopes and
ridges in conifer forests.

Quercus vacciniifolia (*Quercus vaccinifolia*)
FAGACEAE
HUCKLEBERRY OAK

Native, locally common, blooms early–mid
summer, to 5 ft. West-side forest, east-side
forest, subalpine, mid to high elevation
Shrub, twigs reddish brown, sparsely to non-hairy.
LEAVES evergreen, alternate, oblong, 0.5–1.5 in. long,
green with whitish bloom below, dull green above,
both sides sparsely star-shaped hairy to non-hairy,
edges smooth or irregularly sharp-toothed, tips
pointed. **FLOWERS** male flowers in drooping catkins,
female flowers (usually 1) in leaf axil, both on the same
plant. **FRUIT** acorn, matures in 2 years, egg-shaped,
0.3–0.7 in. long, tip pointed,
cap saucer-shaped, hairy
inside, scales silvery brown,
hairy, edible. **ECOLOGY** grows
on steep slopes, ridges, and
rocky areas in conifer forests.
The similar *Q. chrysolepis* has
yellow glandular hairs on its
leaves.

Quercus wislizeni
FAGACEAE
INTERIOR LIVE OAK

Native, common, blooms mid–late spring, 7–67 ft.
Chaparral, east-side forest, low to mid elevation
Tree or shrub, canopy with many short branches,
bark blackish gray, furrowed, twigs brown or reddish
brown, hairy or not. **LEAVES** evergreen, alternate, oval
to egg-shaped, 1–3 in. long, surfaces non-hairy, shiny
dark green above, edges smooth or with spine-tipped
teeth, tips mostly pointed. **FLOWERS** male flowers in
drooping catkins, female flowers in clusters of 2–4 in
leaf axils, both on the same plant. **FRUIT** acorn, matures
in 2 years, oval to egg-shaped, 1–2 in. long, cap cup-
shaped, hairy inside, scales not warty, hairy or not,
edible. **ECOLOGY** grows in valleys and slopes in moister
areas of arid ecoregions within chaparral, oak woodlands, and conifer-oak communities, frequently with
gray pine, California buckeye, ceanothus, chamise,

and scrub oak. Lives to about 200 years
of age and has a low tolerance of flooding, snow, and cold. Fire often topkills
interior live oak but is a key factor in its
persistence, as it resprouts readily following fire, giving it an advantage over
non-sprouting species in post-fire recovery. Oak communities provide wildlife
with cover, nesting sites, and forage.

Ribes acerifolium (*Ribes howellii*)
GROSSULARIACEAE
MAPLELEAF CURRANT
Native, scattered, blooms mid summer, 2–3 ft.
West-side forest, subalpine, mid to high elevation
Shrub, erect to spreading, prickles absent, branches
and twigs hairy and glandular, glands stalked or
not. **LEAVES** deciduous, alternate, mapleleaf-shaped,
1–3 in. wide, hairy and glandular below, non-hairy
above, edges 5-lobed, lobe edges toothed, tips pointed.
FLOWERS in drooping, 7- to 15-flowered clusters, flowers saucer-shaped, greenish white with pink tinge,
hairy and glandular, sepals pinkish, petals red.
FRUIT berry, black with whitish bloom, glandular-hairy,
edibility unknown. **ECOLOGY** grows on
streambanks, meadow thickets, open
ridges, and rock slides, from montane to
alpine areas.

Ribes aureum
GROSSULARIACEAE
GOLDEN CURRANT
Native, locally common, blooms all spring,
3–10 ft. Streambanks, east-side forest,
shrub-steppe, low to mid elevation
Shrub, erect, prickles absent, twigs reddish, hairy or
not, becoming dark gray. **LEAVES** deciduous, alternate,
mapleleaf-shaped, 0.5–1.5 in. long, surfaces green,
sparsely hairy, edges 3-lobed, lobes few-toothed or
shallowly lobed, tips rounded. **FLOWERS** in branched
loose clusters with 5–18 flowers, flowers bell-shaped,
sepals golden yellow, smooth, about 0.3 in. long, lobes
spreading, petals small, erect, yellow, orange, or reddish. **FRUIT** berry, round, 0.3 in. long,
orange to burgundy, palatable.
ECOLOGY streambanks and floodplains
in grassland, sagebrush steppe, and in
woodland or forest communities from
low to montane elevation.

Ribes binominatum
GROSSULARIACEAE
GROUND GOOSEBERRY, SISKIYOU
GOOSEBERRY, TRAILING GOOSEBERRY
Native, locally common, blooms late spring–
early summer, 0.3–3 ft. West-side forest,
subalpine, mid to high elevation

Shrub, spreading to trailing, spines at nodes, prickles
otherwise absent, rooting at the nodes. **LEAVES** deciduous, alternate, roundish, 1–2 in. wide, surfaces hairy,
edges 3- to 5-lobed, lobe edges toothed, tips rounded.
FLOWERS single or in drooping 2- to 3-flowered clusters, flowers bell-shaped, green, sepals greenish white
or green with red edges, petals shorter, white to pink,
stamens longer than petals, ovary spiny.
FRUIT berry, yellowish green, spines
yellow, glandular-hairy or simply hairy,
edibility unknown. **ECOLOGY** grows in
montane and subalpine forests, also
found in meadows.

Ribes bracteosum
GROSSULARIACEAE
STINK CURRANT
Native, locally common, blooms late winter–
spring, 3–10 ft. Streambanks, west-side
forest, subalpine, low to high elevation

Shrub, erect to straggly, prickles absent, stems brownish, sparsely hairy, with round, yellowish, crystalline
glands and a sweet skunky odor, particularly when
leaves are crushed. **LEAVES** deciduous, alternate, mapleleaf-shaped, 1–9 in. long, sparsely hairy below, shiny
green and non-hairy above, both surfaces with yellowish glands, edges 5- to 7-lobed, lobe edges toothed, tips
pointed. **FLOWERS** in long, narrow, erect clusters, flowers saucer-shaped, sepals brownish pur-
ple, greenish or white, glandular, petals
small, white. **FRUIT** berry, bluish black
with a whitish bloom, glandular, edible, unpleasant-tasting. **ECOLOGY** grows
on streambanks, shorelines, moist forests, floodplains, and avalanche chutes,
from low to subalpine elevation. Prefers
shade.

Ribes californicum
GROSSULARIACEAE
HILLSIDE GOOSEBERRY, CALIFORNIA GOOSEBERRY
Native, locally common, blooms late winter–early spring, 2–4.5 ft. Chaparral, west-side forest, low to mid elevation

Shrub, erect, spines 3 at stem nodes, prickles otherwise absent. **LEAVES** deciduous, alternate, roundish, 0.5–1 in. wide, surfaces hairy or not, edges 3- to 5-lobed, lobe edges with few blunt teeth, tips rounded. **FLOWERS** single or in 2- to 3-flowered clusters along the branches, drooping, sepals dark red, can be green-tinged, bent back, petals white, stamens and pistil longer than petals. **FRUIT** berry, red, hairs glandular and not, palatable. **ECOLOGY** grows in chaparral and forest communities, including mixed evergreen, oak woodlands, and the redwoods.

Ribes cereum
GROSSULARIACEAE
WAX CURRANT, SQUAW CURRANT
Native, common, blooms early spring–early summer, 2–5 ft. Rocky sites, east-side forest, shrub-steppe, subalpine, low to high elevation

Shrub, erect to spreading, prickles absent, twigs hairy, some hairs glandular, grayish or reddish brown. **LEAVES** deciduous, alternate, kidney- or fan-shaped, 0.5–1 in. long, top glossy green, surfaces smooth to glandular-hairy, edges toothed and 3- to 5-lobed, lobes shallow, tips rounded. **FLOWERS** dense clusters of 2–8 flowers or solitary, flowers bell-shaped, sepals greenish white, white, or pinkish, smooth or glandular-hairy, about 0.3 in. long, lobes spreading, petals erect, short, white to pink, anther with cup-shaped gland at tip. **FRUIT** berry, red, smooth or somewhat glandular, bitter, inedible. **ECOLOGY** grows on dry rocky slopes, draws, shrubfields, open forests, from the steppe to alpine areas.

Ribes divaricatum
GROSSULARIACEAE
COAST BLACK GOOSEBERRY, STRAGGLY
GOOSEBERRY, WILD BLACK GOOSEBERRY

Native, common, blooms all spring, 3–10 ft. Coastal, meadows, west-side forest, low to mid elevation
Shrub, erect to spreading, prickles 3 at nodes, stout, prickles otherwise absent, branches and twigs gray to brownish, hairy. **LEAVES** deciduous, alternate, maple-leaf-shaped, 1–2.5 in. wide, hairy below, smooth or sparsely hairy above, edges 3- to 5-lobed, lobe edges blunt-toothed, tips rounded. **FLOWERS** single or in 2- to 4-flowered drooping clusters, flowers bell-shaped, sepals red to purplish green, bent back, petals white, stamens longer than petals, styles hairy at base. **FRUIT** berry, purplish black, smooth, palatable. **ECOLOGY** grows on streambanks, shorelines, forest edges, bluffs, from low to montane elevation.

Ribes erythrocarpum
GROSSULARIACEAE
CRATER LAKE CURRANT

Native, locally common, blooms mid summer, 4–8 in. West-side forest, subalpine, mid to high elevation
Shrub, trailing, stems rooting, spines and prickles absent. **LEAVES** deciduous, alternate, roundish, 1–2 in. wide, surfaces short glandular-hairy, edges 3- to 5-lobed, lobes rounded, edges toothed, tips rounded. **FLOWERS** in upright 6- to 20-flowered clusters, flowers saucer-shaped, sepals and petals yellow to copper-colored. **FRUIT** berry, red, glandular-hairy, edibility unknown. **ECOLOGY** grows on rocky slopes and in conifer forests, forming carpets in subalpine mountain hemlock forests. *Ribes* spp. are hosts of white pine blister rust, an exotic fungal pathogen, and efforts to limit damage to white pines have included removal of currants and gooseberries. Endemic to Oregon. The similar *R. laxiflorum* has stalked glands on lower side of leaf, purplish green flowers with red petals.

Ribes glandulosum
GROSSULARIACEAE
SKUNK CURRANT
Native, locally common, blooms late spring, 2–3 ft.
Rocky sites, east-side forest, low to high elevation
Shrub, stems trailing or spreading, prickles absent, twigs sparsely hairy and glandular. **LEAVES** deciduous, alternate, mapleleaf-shaped, 1–3 in. wide, surfaces green, non-hairy except sometimes along veins below, 5- to 7-lobed, lobe edges toothed, tips pointed. **FLOWERS** in 6- to 15-flowered clusters, narrow and erect, flowers bowl-shaped, petals white to pink, sepals white to rose, to 0.1 in. long. **FRUIT** berry, dark red, glandular-hairy, palatable or not. **ECOLOGY** grows on rocky slopes, in moist forests, shrub thickets, roadsides, and clearings.

Ribes hudsonianum
GROSSULARIACEAE
NORTHERN BLACK CURRANT
Native, common, blooms late spring–mid summer, 2–7 ft. Bog/fen/wetland, streambanks, east-side forest, mid to high elevation
Shrub, erect, prickles absent, stems with round, yellowish, crystalline glands, with a sweet, unpleasant odor. **LEAVES** deciduous, alternate, mapleleaf-shaped, 1–5 in. long, surfaces variably hairy, yellowish glands few to many, edges 5-lobed, bottom 2 lobes smaller, lobe edges toothed, tips pointed. **FLOWERS** in long, narrow clusters, upright to spreading, flowers saucer-shaped, green or white, yellow glands absent to many, hairy, sepals and petals white, sepals larger, spreading, petals mostly erect. **FRUIT** berry, black with whitish bloom, glands present or not, unpalatable, bitter. **ECOLOGY** grows on streambanks, moist forests, meadow edges, bogs, swamps, and rocky slopes, montane to subalpine, occasionally lowland. Rare in California.

Ribes inerme
GROSSULARIACEAE
WHITESTEM GOOSEBERRY

Native, scattered, blooms late spring, 3–10
ft. Streambanks, meadows, east-side forest,
subalpine, low to high elevation

Shrub, erect to spreading, spines at the nodes, prickles
otherwise absent, branches gray. **LEAVES** deciduous,
alternate, mapleleaf-shaped, 1–3 in. wide, surfaces
hairy or not, edges 3- to 5-lobed, lobe edges toothed,
tips rounded or pointed. **FLOWERS** in drooping, 2-
to 4-flowered clusters, flowers bell-shaped, hairy
or not, sepals greenish, purplish, or reddish, petals
small, white or pinkish, stamens longer than petals.
FRUIT berry, reddish purple, palatable. **ECOLOGY** grows on streambanks,
meadow edges, forested ridges and
slopes, from low to subalpine elevation. Var. *klamathense* has densely hairy
leaf surfaces, hairy sepals, and black
berries, grows in southwest Oregon
and northern California, and is rare in
Oregon.

Ribes lacustre
GROSSULARIACEAE
BLACK SWAMP GOOSEBERRY, PRICKLY
CURRANT

Native, common, blooms mid spring–mid summer, 2–7
ft. Coastal, bog/fen/wetland, streambanks, west-side
forest, east-side forest, subalpine, low to high elevation

Shrub, erect to spreading, spines at nodes, with prickles in between, branches and twigs hairy.
LEAVES deciduous, alternate, mapleleaf-shaped, 1–2
in. wide, surfaces smooth to sparsely hairy, shiny
above, rarely glandular, edges 5-lobed, lobe edges
blunt-toothed, tips pointed. **FLOWERS** in drooping 7- to
15-flowered clusters, flowers saucer-shaped, sepals yellowish green or reddish brown, spread-
ing, petals shorter, pinkish, ovary with
reddish purple glandular hairs.
FRUIT berry, dark purple to black,
glandular-hairy, palatable, bland.
ECOLOGY grows on moist to dry forest slopes, streambanks, swamps, and
ridges, from lowland to subalpine areas.

Ribes laxiflorum
GROSSULARIACEAE
TRAILING BLACK CURRANT
Native, common, blooms early spring–mid
summer, 2–3 ft. Coastal, rocky sites, west-
side forest, low to mid elevation

Shrub, stems trailing or spreading, rarely vinelike and
tall, prickles absent, twigs reddish brown, hairy and
sparsely glandular. **LEAVES** deciduous, alternate, mapleleaf-shaped, 1.5–4 in. wide, dark green and non-hairy
above, paler, hairy and glandular-hairy below, 5- to
7-lobed, lobe edges toothed, tips rounded or pointed.
FLOWERS in 8- to 18-flowered, narrow, erect clusters,
flowers bowl-shaped, reddish glandular-hairy, sepals
greenish white, deep red, or purplish,
0.1–0.15 in. long, petals red to purplish,
shorter than sepals. **FRUIT** berry, purplish black with whitish bloom,
glandular-hairy, unpalatable.
ECOLOGY grows on cliffs, rocky slopes,
moist forests, avalanche chutes,
and clearings. Rare in Oregon and
California.

Ribes lobbii
GROSSULARIACEAE
**FUCHSIA-FLOWERED GOOSEBERRY, GUMMY
GOOSEBERRY, LOBB'S GOOSEBERRY**
Native, scattered, blooms mid spring–early
summer, 2–5 ft. Meadows, west-side forest, east-
side forest, subalpine, low to high elevation

Shrub, erect to spreading, stems and twigs brownish to
grayish red, hairy, spines 3 at nodes, prickles otherwise
absent. **LEAVES** deciduous, alternate, roundish to egg-
shaped, 0.5–1 in. wide, sparsely hairy to smooth above,
mostly hairy and glandular below, edges 3- to 5-lobed,
lobe edges with few blunt teeth, tips rounded.
FLOWERS single or double along the branches, drooping, sepals bright red, bent back, pet-
als white to pinkish, stamens and pistil
longer than petals. **FRUIT** berry, reddish,
sticky with glandular hairs, unpalatable.
ECOLOGY grows on streambanks, rock
outcrops, shady to open forest slopes,
mostly montane to subalpine, sometimes lowland.

Ribes malvaceum
GROSSULARIACEAE
CHAPARRAL CURRANT
Native, locally common, blooms autumn–spring,
to 7 ft. Chaparral, low to mid elevation

Shrub, erect, spines and prickles absent, with stiff
glandular hairs. **LEAVES** deciduous, alternate, roundish, 1–2 in. wide, surfaces glandular-hairy, edges 3- to
5-lobed, lobe edges toothed, tips rounded.
FLOWERS in drooping, 10- to 25-flowered clusters, urn-
shaped, glandular-hairy, sepals pink to purple, spreading, petals white to pink, erect. **FRUIT** berry, purple
with whitish bloom, glandular-hairy, palatable, bland.
ECOLOGY grows in chaparral or oak woodlands, from
low to montane eleva-
tion. Loses its leaves in
hot, dry summers; new
leaves unfold in autumn.
Endemic to California.

Ribes marshallii
GROSSULARIACEAE
HUPA GOOSEBERRY, MARSHALL'S GOOSEBERRY
Native, locally common, blooms mid
spring–mid summer, 3–7 ft. West-side
forest, subalpine, mid to high elevation

Shrub, stems arching, spines 3 at nodes, prickles
otherwise absent, hairy. **LEAVES** deciduous, alternate, roundish, 1–1.5 in. wide, surfaces hairy and
glandular-hairy, edges 3- to 5-lobed, lobe edges blunt-
toothed, tips mostly rounded. **FLOWERS** single or in
clusters of 2–3, drooping, flowers bell-shaped, hairy,
sepals purple or brownish red, bent back, petals bright
yellow, stamens and pistil longer than petals.
FRUIT berry, dark red, spiny,
sparsely hairy, edibility
unknown. **ECOLOGY** grows in
montane to subalpine conifer
forests. Rare in California.

Ribes menziesii
GROSSULARIACEAE
CANYON GOOSEBERRY

Native, scattered, blooms late winter–spring, 3–7 ft.
Chaparral, west-side forest, low to mid elevation
Shrub, erect, spines 3 at nodes, prickles numerous in
between, glandular-hairy or simply hairy.
LEAVES deciduous, alternate, egg-shaped, 0.5–1.5 in.
wide, sparsely hairy to smooth above, mostly hairy and
glandular below, edges 3- to 5-lobed, lobe edges with
few blunt teeth, tips rounded. **FLOWERS** single or in
2-flowered clusters, drooping, sepals purplish red, bent
back, petals white, pinkish, or yellow, stamens and
pistil longer than petals. **FRUIT** berry, reddish purple,
hairs glandular and not, spiny, unpalat-
able. **ECOLOGY** grows in ravines and canyon slopes within chaparral and mixed
evergreen and coast redwood forests,
low to montane elevation.

Ribes montigenum
GROSSULARIACEAE
MOUNTAIN GOOSEBERRY

Native, locally common, blooms mid summer,
0.7–3 ft. Alpine, subalpine, high elevation
Shrub, spreading, spines at nodes, with prickles in
between, branches and twigs hairy and glandular-
hairy. **LEAVES** deciduous, alternate, mapleleaf-shaped,
0.5–1 in. wide, grayish green and hairy above, glandular-hairy below, edges 5-lobed, lobe edges blunt-
toothed, tips pointed. **FLOWERS** in drooping 4- to
10-flowered clusters, flowers saucer-shaped, glandular-
hairy, sepals yellowish green to pinkish, spreading,
petals shorter, pinkish or purplish, filaments purplish
red. **FRUIT** berry, bright orangy red,
glandular-hairy, palatable.
ECOLOGY subalpine to alpine talus
slopes, ridges, and open forests. The
similar *R. lacustre* has dark purple berries and mostly nonglandular leaves.

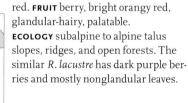

Ribes nevadense
GROSSULARIACEAE
SIERRA CURRANT, MOUNTAIN PINK CURRANT
Native, scattered, blooms late spring–early
summer, 3–7 ft. Streambanks, west-side
forest, east-side forest, mid elevation

Shrub, erect, spines and prickles absent.
LEAVES deciduous, alternate, roundish, 1–3 in. wide,
surfaces glandular, hairy below, non-hairy above,
edges 3- to 5-lobed, lobe edges blunt-toothed, tips
rounded. **FLOWERS** in upright or drooping 8- to 20-
flowered clusters, flowers bell-shaped, sepals bright
pink to reddish, petals white. **FRUIT** berry, bluish
black with whitish bloom, glandular-hairy, edibility
unknown. **ECOLOGY** grows
on streambanks and in forest
edges in montane regions.

Ribes niveum
GROSSULARIACEAE
SNAKE RIVER GOOSEBERRY, SNOW
GOOSEBERRY, SNOW CURRANT
Native, scattered, blooms mid spring, 3–10 ft.
Streambanks, east-side forest, mid elevation

Shrub, erect to arching, stems root at the tips, 1–3
spines at the nodes, prickles otherwise present or not.
LEAVES deciduous, alternate, fan-shaped, 1–2 in. wide,
hairy or not above, hairy below, edges 3- to 5-lobed,
lobe edges toothed, tips pointed. **FLOWERS** single or in
clusters of 2–5, dangling, flowers bell-shaped, sepals
white to pinkish, bent back, petals erect, white to pinkish, stamens and pistil hairy, longer than petals.
FRUIT berry, purple to bluish black,
smooth, palatable, sour. **ECOLOGY** grows
in thickets, on streambanks, in open
forest, and shrubfields, from the foothills up into the mountains.

Ribes oxyacanthoides
GROSSULARIACEAE
NORTHERN GOOSEBERRY
Native, common, blooms late spring–early summer,
1–7 ft. Rocky sites, east-side forest, low to mid elevation
Shrub, erect to spreading, bark yellowish to grayish
brown, branches with 1–3 spines at the nodes, spines
to 0.5 in. long, prickles present between nodes, twigs
hairy, sometimes glandular. **LEAVES** deciduous, alternate, mapleleaf-shaped, 0.5–1.5 in. wide, surfaces
glandular-hairy to smooth, 3- to 5-lobed, lobe edges
rounded and toothed, tips mostly rounded. **FLOWERS** in
drooping to spreading 1- to 3-flowered clusters, flowers
bell-shaped, sepals greenish white to purplish, spreading to bent back, petals erect, white
or pinkish, stamens as long as petals,
styles hairy at base. **FRUIT** berry, round,
reddish to bluish purple, non-hairy,
palatable. **ECOLOGY** a variable species
with several varieties, growing in shrub
thickets, forest openings, rocky slopes,
and rock outcrops.

Ribes roezlii
GROSSULARIACEAE
SIERRA GOOSEBERRY
Native, locally common, blooms all spring, 2–4 ft.
West-side forest, east-side forest, low to mid elevation
Shrub, erect, spines 1–3 at the nodes, twigs hairy.
LEAVES deciduous, alternate, roundish, 0.5–1 in.
wide, surfaces nonglandular, hairy or not, edges 3- to
5-lobed, lobe edges toothed, tips rounded.
FLOWERS single or in pairs, dangling, sepals purplish
to brownish red, bent back, petals mostly white, stamens and pistil longer than petals, ovary glandular-
hairy and prickly. **FRUIT** berry, purplish red, prickly
and glandular-hairy, palatable. **ECOLOGY** grows on
fairly moist, often shady forest slopes,
also in oak woodlands. Var. *amictum*,
with gland-tipped prickles and densely
grayish white hairs on leaf undersides
and sepals, is rare in California.

Ribes sanguineum
GROSSULARIACEAE
RED-FLOWERING CURRANT

Native, common, blooms early spring, 3–10 ft. Coastal, west-side forest, east-side forest, low to mid elevation Shrub, erect, prickles absent, stems reddish brown, hairy, twigs hairy. **LEAVES** deciduous, alternate, maple-leaf-shaped, 1–3 in. wide, dark green above, lighter below, both surfaces hairy, sometimes glandular, edges 5-lobed, lobe edges toothed, tips pointed. **FLOWERS** in drooping, spreading, or erect 5- to 40-flowered clusters, flowers bell-shaped, hairy and glandular-hairy, sepals pale pink to deep red, sometimes white, petals small, white to pale pink. **FRUIT** berry, bluish black with whitish bloom, glandular-hairy, edible but tasteless. **ECOLOGY** grows on open forest slopes, forest edges, and rock outcrops, lowland to montane. Prefers sunny sites and well-drained soils.

Ribes triste
GROSSULARIACEAE
RED SWAMP CURRANT, NORTHERN RED CURRANT

Native, scattered, blooms mid spring–early summer, 1–3 ft. Bog/fen/wetland, streambanks, west-side forest, east-side forest, low to mid elevation Shrub, spreading to trailing, stems root at the nodes, prickles absent, twigs glandular-hairy. **LEAVES** deciduous, alternate, mapleleaf-shaped, 1–4 in. wide, non-hairy above, hairy beneath, 3- to 5-lobed, lobe edges toothed, tips pointed. **FLOWERS** in drooping 6- to 13-flowered clusters, flowers saucer-shaped, dark reddish purple or greenish white with purplish tinge, sepals greenish purple, spreading, petals shorter, erect, reddish purple. **FRUIT** berry, bright red, edible, sour. **ECOLOGY** grows on streambanks, in moist forests, near springs, and rock slides, lowland to montane.

Ribes velutinum
GROSSULARIACEAE
DESERT GOOSEBERRY

Native, locally common, blooms all spring, 2–7 ft.
East-side forest, shrub-steppe, low to mid elevation
Shrub, spreading, crown rounded, spines mostly 1(2–
3) at the nodes, prickles absent elsewhere.
LEAVES deciduous, alternate, leathery, roundish, 0.2–1
in. wide, surfaces hairy or not, edges 3- to 5-lobed, lobe
edges smooth or few-toothed, tips rounded.
FLOWERS single or in clusters of 2–3, bell-shaped, outer
surface hairy, sepals and petals 5, whitish to yellow,
sometimes pink-tinged. **FRUIT** berry, dark red or purplish, dry, unpalatable, utilized by Native Americans.
ECOLOGY grows in sagebrush steppe or
scrub, and on slopes of ponderosa pine
or juniper communities, lowland to
montane.

Ribes viscosissimum
GROSSULARIACEAE
STICKY CURRANT

Native, locally common, blooms late spring–early
summer, 3–7 ft. Streambanks, west-side forest,
east-side forest, subalpine, mid to high elevation
Shrub, erect, often straggly, prickles absent, branches
reddish brown, twigs hairy and glandular-hairy.
LEAVES deciduous, alternate, mapleleaf-shaped, 1–4
in. wide, grayish green, surfaces glandular-hairy, nonglandular hairs present or not, 3- to 5-lobed, lobe edges
toothed, tips rounded or pointed. **FLOWERS** in erect
to drooping 6- to 17-flowered clusters, flowers bell-
shaped, greenish white or creamy with pink tinges,
sepals whitish green, sometimes pink-
tinged, spreading, petals shorter than
sepals, white or cream, anthers with
cup-like gland at the tip. **FRUIT** berry,
bluish black, smooth or glandular-hairy,
unpalatable. **ECOLOGY** grows in open to
dense forests, streambanks, montane to
subalpine.

Ribes watsonianum
GROSSULARIACEAE
SPINY GOOSEBERRY, WATSON'S GOOSEBERRY
Native, locally common, blooms mid spring–
mid summer, 3–7 ft. Meadows, east-side
forest, subalpine, mid to high elevation
Shrub, erect, spines 1–3 at the nodes, prickles otherwise absent, branches grayish-hairy and glandular.
LEAVES deciduous, alternate, roundish, 1–2 in. wide,
surfaces hairy, often glandular, usually more densely
hairy below, edges 3- to 5-lobed, lobes rounded, edges
toothed, tips rounded. **FLOWERS** single or in clusters of
2–3, dangling, flowers bell-shaped, hairy and sparsely
glandular, sepals greenish white, sometimes pink-
tinged, petals white to pinkish, ovary
bristly. **FRUIT** berry, yellowish green
to reddish, with gland-tipped bristles,
dry, unpalatable, desired by wildlife.
ECOLOGY grows at meadow edges and
in forests, on slopes, ridges, and in canyons, shade tolerant, montane.

Ribes wolfii
GROSSULARIACEAE
WOLF'S CURRANT, ROTHROCK CURRANT
Native, locally common, blooms late spring–
early summer, 3–17 ft. Bog/fen/wetland,
east-side forest, mid to high elevation
Shrub, erect to spreading, spines and prickles absent,
bark whitish, twigs glandular-hairy, also with sessile
glands. **LEAVES** deciduous, alternate, pentagonal to
roundish, 1–3 in. wide, hairy or not above, usually
hairy and/or glandular-hairy below, 3- to 5-lobed, lobes
rather shallow with rounded edges, tips rounded.
FLOWERS in narrow, erect to spreading clusters, flowers
evenly spaced, flowers saucer-shaped, glandular-hairy,
sepals spreading, greenish to pinkish,
petals erect, cream, greenish, or pinkish, stamens as long as petals, style non-
hairy. **FRUIT** berry, egg-shaped, black,
glandular-hairy, edible. **ECOLOGY** grows
in wet meadows and moist montane forests. Rare in Oregon.

Umbellularia californica
LAURACEAE
CALIFORNIA LAUREL, OREGON MYRTLE
Native, common, blooms autumn–
spring, 30–80 ft. Coastal, chaparral, west-
side forest, low to mid elevation

Tree or shrub, crown rounded, trunks single to multiple, bark dark brown, scaly, twigs 3-angled.
LEAVES evergreen, alternate, oblong to lance-shaped, 1–4 in. long, surfaces gland-dotted, yellowish green, non-hairy above, hairy or not below, edges smooth, tips pointed. **FLOWERS** in clusters in upper leaf axils, bisexual, flowers small, greenish, tepals 6, stamens 9. **FRUIT** olive-like, egg-shaped, green to dark purple, seed 1, edible when roasted. **ECOLOGY** grows in a variety of habitats, forest slopes, valley bottoms, ridgetops, floodplains, chaparral, coastal bluffs, adapting from a tall tree on moist sites with rich soils to a shrub in poor soils and harsh sites. Has a spicy scent (especially if the

leaves or bark are bruised or crushed) that triggers headaches in some people. Shade tolerant, vulnerable to fire damage but resprouts readily. Its wood, often referred to as myrtlewood, is made into bowls, cabinets, and decorative objects. Native Americans used its leaves to treat colds and ate the fruit.

Fremontodendron californicum
MALVACEAE (STERCULIACEAE)
CALIFORNIA FLANNELBUSH

Native, common, blooms mid spring–mid summer,
1–30 ft. Chaparral, east-side forest, low to mid elevation
Shrub or small tree, erect, crown rounded, bark dark
gray, ridged, inner bark gelatinous, branches long,
twigs hairy when young. **LEAVES** evergreen, alternate, leathery, roundish to egg-shaped, 0.5–2 in.
long, dark green and hairy above, paler and densely
hairy beneath, edges usually 3-lobed, tips rounded or
pointed. **FLOWERS** single in twig axils, stalked, tulip-
shaped, to 1.5 in. across, sepals 5, yellow, petals absent.
FRUIT egg-shaped capsule, to 1.5 in. long, densely hairy,
seeds many. **ECOLOGY** grows in chapar-
ral, pinyon-juniper woodlands, and ponderosa pine communities. Often used as
an ornamental and for erosion control, a
delicacy for deer.

Iliamna rivularis
MALVACEAE
STREAMBANK GLOBEMALLOW

Native, locally common, blooms all summer,
2–7 ft. Streambanks, meadows, east-
side forest, low to mid elevation
Subshrub, stems many, green, hairy. **LEAVES** deciduous, alternate, mapleleaf-shaped, 2–6 in. long, green,
star-shaped hairy, lobes 5–7, lobe edges toothed, tips
pointed. **FLOWERS** one to several in leaf axils with
bracts about 0.2 in. long, flowers bowl-shaped, petals
5, about 1 in. long, pink to purplish, sepal lobes 0.2
in. long, tips rounded. **FRUIT** capsule, splits into 2- to
4-seeded segments at maturity, segments
hairy, kidney-shaped.
ECOLOGY grows along
streambanks, meadows,
and roadsides. The similar
I. longisepala has pointed
sepal lobes >0.5 in. long;
I. latibracteata has bracts
>0.5 in. long; and *I. bakeri*
has 3-lobed upper leaves.

Sphaeralcea grossulariifolia
MALVACEAE
CURRANT-LEAVED GLOBEMALLOW
Native, locally common, blooms late spring–mid summer, 1–3 ft. Shrub-steppe, low to mid elevation
Subshrub, erect, stems many, grayish. **LEAVES** deciduous, alternate, round to heart-shaped, 1–2 in. long, green to grayish green, star-shaped hairy, edges 3- to 5-lobed, lobes toothed, tips rounded. **FLOWERS** single or clustered in leaf axils and at stem tips, flowers bowl-shaped, petals 5, reddish, 0.5–1 in. long, sepals star-shaped hairy, with 3 linear bracts beneath, stamens gathered in central tube. **FRUIT** capsule, splits into about 12 mostly 2-seeded segments at maturity, segments kidney-shaped. **ECOLOGY** grows in the shrub-steppe and dry forests, short-lived, populations fluctuate.

Sphaeralcea munroana
MALVACEAE
ORANGE GLOBEMALLOW
Native, scattered, blooms late spring–mid summer, 8–32 in. Disturbed, shrub-steppe, low to mid elevation
Subshrub, erect or spreading, stems several, grayish-hairy to green. **LEAVES** deciduous, alternate, triangular to kidney-shaped, 1–2.5 in. long, grayish green to green, hairy, edges 3- to 5-lobed or with rounded teeth, tips rounded. **FLOWERS** in leaf axils and at stem ends, single or clustered, flowers bowl-shaped, petals 5, 0.5–1 in. long, apricot to reddish, sepals with 3 linear bracts beneath, stamens gathered in central tube. **FRUIT** capsule, splits into 3 1-seeded segments at maturity, segments kidney-shaped. **ECOLOGY** grows in the shrub-steppe, forest openings, and disturbed areas, low to mid elevation. Rare in British Columbia.

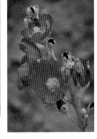

Morus alba
MORACEAE
WHITE MULBERRY

Non-native, scattered, blooms all spring, 10–50 ft.
Streambanks, disturbed, low to mid elevation

Shrub or small tree, spreading, bark grayish brown, thorns absent, with milky sap. **LEAVES** deciduous, alternate, egg-shaped, 2–5 in. long, surfaces hairy or not, edges toothed to somewhat lobed, tips pointed. **FLOWERS** mostly unisexual, small, on same plant or not, male flowers in drooping catkins, female clusters shorter and wider, sepals 4, petals absent. **FRUIT** achene in blackberrylike coating, fleshy, blackish, purple, red, white, or pink, palatable, sweet. **ECOLOGY** Eurasian import, found along streams, in moist soils, and in disturbed areas, low to mid elevation. Often cultivated for its fruit. Leaves are consumed by silkworms in its native habitat.

Morella californica (Myrica californica)
MYRICACEAE
CALIFORNIA WAX-MYRTLE, PACIFIC WAX-MYRTLE, PACIFIC BAYBERRY
Native, common, blooms all spring, 6.5–33 ft. Coastal, bog/fen/wetland, streambanks, west-side forest, low elevation

Shrub or tree, bark light gray to yellowish brown, twigs green to reddish brown with numerous glands. **LEAVES** evergreen, alternate, lance-shaped, 1.5–5 in. long, shiny dark green above, dotted with black glands below, edges smooth or coarsely toothed, tips pointed. **FLOWERS** in catkins, blooms on previous year's growth, flowers mostly unisexual, plants both male and female, catkins usually all male or female but can be

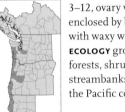

both. Catkins 0.5–1 in. long, stamens 3–12, ovary with waxy glands and partly enclosed by bract. **FRUIT** nut-like, round, with waxy wart-like bumps, grayish. **ECOLOGY** grows in conifer-dominated forests, shrub thickets, sand dunes, streambanks, and other habitats along the Pacific coast, shade tolerant.

Myrica gale
MYRICACEAE
SWEET GALE
Native, locally common, blooms mid
spring, 2–7 ft. Bog/fen/wetland, lake/pond,
streambanks, low to mid elevation

Fragrant shrub, sometimes thicket-forming, bark
reddish brown to black, twigs dotted with yellowish
glands. **LEAVES** deciduous, alternate, lance-shaped,
1–2.5 in. long, surfaces grayish green with yellow
glands, edges few-toothed near tip end, tips rounded.
FLOWERS in catkins, blooms before the leaves unfold
on previous year's growth, flowers unisexual, male
and female flowers mostly on separate plants. Catkins
0.5–1 in. long, female catkins cone-
like, persistent, stamens 3–5. **FRUIT** nut,
glandular, bract attached, forming short
wings. **ECOLOGY** grows in swamps,
bogs, streambanks, and lakeshores,
shade intolerant. Spongy mini-bracts
allow fruit to float, aiding seed dispersal; roots fix nitrogen through mycorrhi-
zal associations.

Eucalyptus globulus
MYRTACEAE
TASMANIAN BLUE GUM
Non-native, common, blooms winter–early
spring, 100–200 ft. Disturbed, low elevation

Tree, crown rounded, narrow, trunks single, sheds its
bark, exposing tan or bluish gray inner bark. **LEAVES**
aromatic, evergreen, alternate except opposite on seedlings and sprouts, crescent- or lance-shaped, 4–12 in.
long, edges smooth, tips pointed. **FLOWERS** single in
axils of upper leaves, flowers with numerous white stamens, the sepals and petals form a cap over the flower
and are shed as it opens. **FRUIT** capsule, woody, warty
with whitish waxy coating, 0.25–1 in. across. **ECOLOGY**
Australian import, moderately
invasive, grows in fields, roadsides, and other disturbed areas.
Fast growing, fire-adapted, and
very flammable. Often planted
as an ornamental and grown
commerically for its oil, which is
used medicinally, as a flavoring,
and in cosmetics.

Dendromecon rigida
PAPAVERACEAE
TREE POPPY, BUSH POPPY
Native, common, blooms all spring, 3–10 ft.
Disturbed, chaparral, low to mid elevation
Shrub, erect, crown irregular, bark grayish brown,
shreddy, twigs yellowish green to reddish, slender.
LEAVES evergreen, alternate, lance-shaped, 1–4 in.
long, surfaces grayish green, edges finely toothed, tips
pointed. **FLOWERS** single at branch tips, saucer-shaped,
petals 4, bright yellow, 1–2.5 in. across, stamens many,
orange. **FRUIT** capsule, long and narrow, podlike, seeds
many, black. **ECOLOGY** grows in washes and slopes
in chaparral and woodland communities, often in
recently burned sites.

Platanus racemosa
PLATANACEAE
CALIFORNIA SYCAMORE

Native, locally common, blooms early–mid spring,
30–80 ft. Streambanks, low to mid elevation
Tree, trunks erect or leaning, often forked, older bark
dark brown, furrowed near the ground and mottled tan
or gray, with white above due to peeling. **LEAVES** deciduous, alternate, roundish, 4–10 in. long, 3- to 5-lobed,
main lobes of similar length, dark green above, paler
and densely hairy below, lobe edges smooth or toothed,
tips pointed. **FLOWERS** unisexual, in ball-like clusters, several on a dangling stalk, male clusters on new
twigs, female clusters on branches of past years, male
flowers greenish yellow, female brown-
ish red. **FRUIT** hairy achenes in ball-like
cluster, about 1 in. across.

ECOLOGY grows along streambanks
and in moist canyons in various plant
communities. Fast growing, often lives
200 years or more. Seeds are wind-
disseminated and eaten by birds.

Linanthus pungens (*Leptodactylon pungens*)
POLEMONIACEAE
GRANITE GILIA, PRICKLY PHLOX

Native, locally common, blooms mid spring–mid summer, 4–24 in. Rocky sites, east-side forest, shrub-steppe, subalpine, low to high elevation
Shrub, erect to straggly, much-branched, hairy or not, aromatic. **LEAVES** deciduous, alternate (sometimes lowermost opposite), rigid, deeply lobed into 3–7 linear segments, appearing compound, lobes linear, to 0.5 in. long, lobe edges smooth, tips spiny, often containing bundles of smaller leaves in the axil. **FLOWERS** solitary in leaf axils, opening at night, sweet-scented, trumpet-shaped, lobes to 0.5 in. long, petals white to white marked with lavender, rarely yellowish white to coppery, sepal lobe length unequal. **FRUIT** capsule, egg-shaped. **ECOLOGY** grows in sandy or rocky areas in shrub-steppe, woodlands, and forests.

See Polemoniaceae with opposite leaves, page 335

Polygala subspinosa
POLYGALACEAE
SPINY MILKWORT

Native, rare, blooms early–mid summer, 5–10 in. Rocky sites, shrub-steppe, mid to high elevation
Subshrub, stems hairy or not, becoming spiny with age. **LEAVES** deciduous, alternate, oval to egg-shaped, 0.2–1 in. long, surfaces green, hairy or not, edges smooth, tips pointed. **FLOWERS** in thorn-tipped clusters, pea-like, pink to purplish with inner yellow petal. **FRUIT** capsule, stalked, to 0.5 in. long. **ECOLOGY** grows in open, rocky or sandy areas in desert scrub and juniper woodlands.

Aconogonon davisiae (*Polygonum davisiae*)
POLYGONACEAE
DAVIS' KNOTWEED
Native, locally common, blooms all summer, 6–16 in.
Rocky sites, alpine, subalpine, mid to high elevation
Subshrub, stems erect, with white, waxy coating,
sparsely hairy to non-hairy. **LEAVES** deciduous, alternate, lance- to egg-shaped, 1–2 in. long, surfaces
yellowish green, hairy or not, tips pointed, stipules
reddish brown, to 1 in. long. **FLOWERS** in few-flowered
clusters in leaf axils, flowers bell-shaped, to 0.2 in.
long, tepals greenish yellow to pinkish white.
FRUIT achene, shiny, yellowish brown. **ECOLOGY** grows
on rocky or sandy slopes of conifer forests in the
mountains.

See Polygonaceae
with basal leaves,
page 352

Eriogonum microthecum
POLYGONACEAE
SLENDER BUCKWHEAT, SLENDERBUSH
BUCKWHEAT
Native, locally common, blooms all summer,
0.3–4.3 ft. Shrub-steppe, low to high elevation
Subshrub or shrub, erect to spreading, stems hairy
or not. **LEAVES** deciduous, alternate, linear, oval, or
egg-shaped, 0.5–1 in. long, greenish, usually hairy
above, grayish-hairy beneath, tips rounded or pointed.
FLOWERS in open, branched, flat-topped clusters, flowers top-shaped, to 0.1 in. long, stalk absent, white,
pink, or yellow, tepal outer surface non-hairy.
FRUIT achene, brown, non-hairy. **ECOLOGY** grows in
rocky, sandy, or gravelly soils, in shrub-
steppe and open forests or woodlands.

See *Eriogonum* with basal leaves, page
352

Polygonum bolanderi
POLYGONACEAE
BOLANDER'S KNOTWEED
Native, locally common, blooms mid
summer–autumn, 8–24 in. Chaparral, east-
side forest, low to mid elevation

Subshrub, bark brown, stems wiry, erect, gnarled with age. **LEAVES** persistent, alternate, crowded at stem tips, linear, 0.1–0.5 in. long, edges smooth, tips pointed, stipules 0.5 in. long, fringed. **FLOWERS** single to paired in leaf axils, flowers bell-shaped, 0.1 in. long, tepals white to pink. **FRUIT** achene, light brown, shiny. **ECOLOGY** grows in dry rocky or gravelly areas within oak woodlands, ponderosa pine forest, and chaparral. Endemic to California.

Polygonum paronychia
POLYGONACEAE
BEACH KNOTWEED
Native, locally common, blooms spring–
summer, 0.3–3 ft. Coastal, low elevation

Subshrub, stems not wiry, erect to trailing, rooting at the nodes, stipules persistent. **LEAVES** deciduous, alternate, crowded at stem tips, linear to lance-shaped, 0.5–1 in. long, midrib hairy below, edges rolled under, tips pointed, stipules 1 in. long, ragged. **FLOWERS** in few-flowered clusters in leaf axils, flowers bell-shaped, 0.2–0.4 in. long, tepals white to pink, lobes unequal. **FRUIT** achene, black, shiny. **ECOLOGY** grows along the coast in sand dunes and shrubby areas. Rare in British Columbia.

Polygonum shastense
POLYGONACEAE
SHASTA KNOTWEED

Native, locally common, blooms mid summer,
2–16 in. Rocky sites, subalpine, high elevation
Subshrub, stems trailing to erect, not wiry, stipules
deciduous. **LEAVES** deciduous, alternate, oval to lance-
shaped, 0.2–1 in. long, midrib on lower surface non-
hairy, edges rolled under, tip pointed, stipules 0.2 in.
long. **FLOWERS** in few-flowered clusters in leaf axils,
flowers bell-shaped, 0.2–0.4 in. long, tepals white to
pink. **FRUIT** achene, brown, shiny. **ECOLOGY** grows in
rocky or gravelly areas within lodgepole pine or subalpine forests.

Ceanothus cordulatus
RHAMNACEAE
MOUNTAIN WHITETHORN, WHITETHORN
CEANOTHUS, SNOW BUSH

Native, locally common, blooms mid
spring–early summer, 2–5 ft. West-side
forest, east-side forest, mid elevation
Shrub, branches spreading or bending toward the
ground, twigs rigid, thornlike, grayish green. **LEAVES**
evergreen, alternate, oval to egg-shaped, 0.5–1 in.
long, dull green above, paler below, surfaces hairy or
not, edges smooth or finely toothed, tips rounded.
FLOWERS small, in dense egg-shaped clusters, 0.5–
1.5 in. long, petals and sepals cream-colored,
sweet-scented. **FRUIT** capsule, round, 3-lobed,
ridged, hornless. **ECOLOGY** grows on open
slopes, rocky ridges, under oaks or in conifer
forests. Increases in abundance after fire; few
seedlings are seen in unburned areas. The similar *C. incanus* has leaves 1–2 in. long, flowers in
clusters 1–6 in. long, and wrinkled capsules.

See *Ceanothus* with opposite leaves, page 340

Ceanothus diversifolius
RHAMNACEAE
PINEMAT
Native, locally common, blooms mid spring,
to 1 ft. East-side forest, mid elevation
Shrub, trailing, rooting at the nodes, twigs flexible,
green, sometimes reddish, hairy. LEAVES evergreen,
alternate, oval to egg-shaped, 0.5–1.5 in. long, dull
bluish green above, paler beneath, both sides hairy,
hairs wavy, edges with glandular-tipped teeth, tips
rounded. FLOWERS in small clusters, 0.5–1 in. long, at
tip of short, erect branches, sepals and petals grayish
blue, purplish, or white. FRUIT capsule, ridged, hornless. ECOLOGY grows on open slopes and flat areas
within conifer-oak and conifer-only
forests. Stems can reach 6 ft. long and
form loose mats, making this an effec-
tive groundcover and slope stabilizer.
Endemic to California.

Ceanothus foliosus
RHAMNACEAE
WAVYLEAF CEANOTHUS
Native, locally common, blooms all spring, 2–12 ft.
Chaparral, west-side forest, low to mid elevation
Shrub, erect to spreading, stems reddish brown, twigs
flexible, green or reddish green. LEAVES evergreen,
alternate, oval to egg-shaped, 0.2–1 in. long, wavy, fragrant, shiny dark green above, paler beneath, both
sides hairy or not, edges toothed or not, tips rounded or
pointed. FLOWERS small, in rounded clusters, 0.5–1.5
in. long, petals and sepals blue to purplish. FRUIT capsule, roundish, ridged, hornless. ECOLOGY grows on
hill slopes and flats in chaparral, oak woodlands, and
mixed evergreen for-
ests. Endemic to Cal-
ifornia. Var. *vineatus*,
short, mound-form-
ing, leaves hairy only
on veins below, edges
mostly smooth, is
rare in California.

Ceanothus incanus
RHAMNACEAE
COAST WHITETHORN

Native, common, blooms all spring, 5–13 ft. Coastal, chaparral, west-side forest, low to mid elevation
Shrub, erect, crown broad and rounded, bark light gray, twigs bluish gray, waxy, hairy, often thorny. **LEAVES** evergreen, alternate, egg-shaped, 1–2 in. long, mostly >0.5 in. wide, 3-veined from base, green and hairy or not above, bluish green with appressed hairs below, edges mostly smooth, tips rounded. **FLOWERS** in dense clusters in upper leaf axils, 1–6 in. long, flowers small, petals and sepals 5, cream to white, strongly sweet-scented. **FRUIT** capsule, sticky-glandular when young, becoming wrinkled and dark brown when mature. **ECOLOGY** grows on ridges, slopes, and flats in chaparral and forest openings, shade tolerant, resprouts after fire. Endemic to California.

Ceanothus integerrimus
RHAMNACEAE
DEER BRUSH

Native, common, blooms late spring–early summer, 3–13 ft. Chaparral, west-side forest, east-side forest, low to mid elevation
Shrub, erect, branches straight, slender, twigs flexible, greenish, hairy. **LEAVES** deciduous, sometimes persistent, alternate, thin, lance- to egg-shaped, 0.5–2.5 in. long, dull green above, pale green and usually hairy below, edges smooth, tips pointed. **FLOWERS** small, in dense clusters, 1.5–8 in. long, petals and sepals blue to white, sometimes pink, blue flowers more common in the northern part of range, white in southern. **FRUIT** capsule, round, usually ridged, sticky, hornless. **ECOLOGY** grows in conifer and oak forests and chaparral. Increases in abundance after fire, due to heat-mediated seed germination.

Ceanothus lemmonii
RHAMNACEAE
LEMMON'S CEANOTHUS
Native, locally common, blooms mid spring, 1.7–3 ft. Chaparral, west-side forest, mid elevation
Erect to spreading shrub, mounded, twigs pale or grayish green, flexible. **LEAVES** evergreen, alternate, oval to oblong, 0.5–1 in. long, shiny green above, hairy or not, paler and densely hairy below, edges finely toothed, tips glandular, leaf tips rounded or pointed. **FLOWERS** small, in dense, oblong clusters, petals and sepals blue to purplish. **FRUIT** capsule, round, lobes ridged, hornless. **ECOLOGY** grows in forest openings and rocky slopes in chaparral, conifer forests, and pine-oak woodlands, where summers are hot and winters cold. Endemic to California.

Ceanothus leucodermis
RHAMNACEAE
CHAPARRAL WHITETHORN
Native, common, blooms all spring, 5–13 ft. Chaparral, east-side forest, low to mid elevation
Shrub, erect to spreading, bark light gray, twigs rigid, gray, waxy, hairy, spiny. **LEAVES** evergreen, alternate, oval to egg-shaped, 0.5–1 in. long, mostly <0.5 in. wide, 3-veined from base, grayish green and dull above, hairy below, edges toothed or not, tips pointed or rounded. **FLOWERS** dense clusters in upper leaf axils, 1–6 in. long, flowers small, petals and sepals 5, pale blue, sometimes white, fragrant. **FRUIT** capsule, sticky-glandular when young, brown and smooth to lightly wrinkled when mature. **ECOLOGY** grows on dry rocky slopes in chaparral and openings of oak woodlands and conifer forests, shade tolerant. The similar *C. incanus* has leaves mostly wider than 0.5 in., wrinkled capsules, and white flowers.

Ceanothus parryi
RHAMNACEAE
PARRY'S CEANOTHUS, LADY-BLOOM
Native, common, blooms mid spring, 7–17 ft.
Chaparral, west-side forest, low elevation

Shrub, erect, bark dark brown, branches slender, twigs sometimes drooping, grayish green to brown, becoming smooth with age. **LEAVES** evergreen, alternate, oblong to oval, 0.5–1.5 in. long, mostly >2 times longer than wide, shiny dark green and non-hairy above, paler and hairy below, edges rolled under, tips rounded. **FLOWERS** in clusters at stem ends and upper leaf axils, 2.5–5.5 in. long, flowers small, petals and sepals 5, deep blue. **FRUIT** capsule, lobed, smooth, brown, hornless. **ECOLOGY** grows on rocky slopes and flats in chaparral and openings in coast redwood or mixed evergreen forests, often on northerly aspects. Non-native in Oregon.

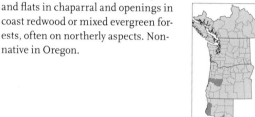

Ceanothus sanguineus
RHAMNACEAE
REDSTEM CEANOTHUS, OREGON TEA TREE
Native, locally common, blooms mid spring–
mid summer, 3–10 ft. West-side forest,
east-side forest, low to mid elevation

Shrub, erect, stems becoming reddish purple, non-hairy, twigs flexible. **LEAVES** deciduous, alternate, oval to egg-shaped, 1–4 in. long, green and non-hairy above, hairy below, edges finely toothed with glandular tips, leaf tips rounded. **FLOWERS** small, in dense, oval clusters on short branches, 1–3 in. long, sepals and petals 5, white, sepal lobes deciduous. **FRUIT** capsule, round, 3-lobed, hornless, sticky, explosive. **ECOLOGY** grows on relatively moist rocky or sandy slopes, forests, and shrubby areas, lowland to montane. Fixes nitrogen and is a favored browse of deer and elk. Seed germinates after fire.

Ceanothus sorediatus
(*Ceanothus oliganthus* var. *sorediatus*)
RHAMNACEAE
JIM BRUSH

Native, common, blooms winter–mid spring, 5–12 ft. Chaparral, west-side forest, low to mid elevation Shrub, sometimes treelike, erect, crown rounded, twigs reddish brown, flexible, mostly non-hairy, spines absent. **LEAVES** evergreen, alternate, oval to egg-shaped, 0.5–1 in. long, 3-veined from the base, leathery, dark green, hairy or not above, paler and hairy below, edges toothed, gland-tipped, tips rounded or pointed. **FLOWERS** in clusters at stem ends and upper leaf axils, to 1.5 in. long, flowers small, petals and sepals 5, blue, purple, or whitish, ovary smooth.

FRUIT capsule, lobed, somewhat sticky when young, smooth and brown with age, hornless. **ECOLOGY** grows on rocky slopes, ridges, and flats in chaparral and openings of oak woodlands, pine and mixed evergreen forests.

Ceanothus thyrsiflorus
RHAMNACEAE
BLUEBLOSSOM CEANOTHUS

Native, locally common, blooms all spring, 3–10 ft. Coastal, west-side forest, low to mid elevation Shrub, erect to spreading, twigs green, flexible. **LEAVES** evergreen, alternate, oval to egg-shaped, 0.5–1.5 in., shiny dark green and non-hairy above, paler, hairy or not, veins dark and raised below, edges with glandular-tipped teeth, leaf tip rounded. **FLOWERS** small, in dense, oval clusters, 0.5–3 in. long, sepals and petals 5, light to dark blue, sepal lobes deciduous. **FRUIT** capsule, round, 3-lobed, hornless, blackish, explosive. **ECOLOGY** habit variable, shorter where exposed to

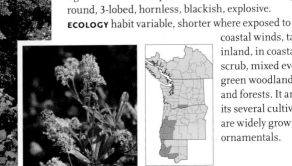

coastal winds, taller inland, in coastal scrub, mixed evergreen woodlands, and forests. It and its several cultivars are widely grown as ornamentals.

Ceanothus tomentosus
RHAMNACEAE
WOOLLYLEAF CEANOTHUS
Native, common, blooms winter–mid spring, 3–12 ft. Chaparral, east-side forest, low to mid elevation
Shrub, sometimes treelike, erect, crown open, rounded, twigs hairy when young, becoming non-hairy and grayish brown with age, thorns absent. **LEAVES** evergreen, alternate, oval to egg-shaped, 0.5–1 in. long, 3-veined from base, dark green and short-hairy above, mostly densely hairy below, edges with gland-tipped teeth, tips rounded. **FLOWERS** in clusters at stem ends and upper leaf axils, 0.5–2 in. long, flowers small, petals and sepals 5, dark purplish blue, pale blue, or white. **FRUIT** capsule, lobed, sticky-glandular, brown, hornless. **ECOLOGY** grows in chaparral, woodlands, and pine forests, foothills to montane. Prefers rocky soils.

Ceanothus velutinus
RHAMNACEAE
SNOWBRUSH, TOBACCO BRUSH, VARNISH-LEAF
Native, common, blooms mid spring–mid summer, 2–10 ft. West-side forest, east-side forest, low to mid elevation
Aromatic shrub, erect to spreading, twigs green to reddish brown, hairy or not. **LEAVES** evergreen, alternate, oval to egg-shaped, 2–4 in. long, shiny green, non-hairy and sticky above, grayish, hairy or not below, edges finely toothed with glandular tips, leaf tips rounded. **FLOWERS** small, in dense, oval clusters, 1–3 in. long, sepals and petals 5, white to cream. **FRUIT** capsule, 3-lobed, hornless, sticky, explosive. **ECOLOGY** grows on rocky slopes, open forests, and shrubby areas, montane, sometimes lowland. Seeds are long-lived, 200 years or more, and readily germinate after fire, as heat cracks the hard seed coat.

Frangula californica (*Rhamnus californica*)
RHAMNACEAE
CALIFORNIA COFFEEBERRY, CALIFORNIA
BUCKTHORN
Native, common, blooms mid spring–early
summer, 5–17 ft. Chaparral, west-side forest,
east-side forest, low to mid elevation

Shrub, bark and twigs gray, brown, or reddish, twigs
hairy or not. **LEAVES** usually evergreen, alternate, oval
to egg-shaped, 1–4 in. long, surfaces hairy or not,
edges smooth or toothed, sometimes rolled under, tips
pointed or rounded. **FLOWERS** stalked, rounded clusters
with >5 flowers in leaf axils, petals and sepals greenish, petals smaller than sepals. **FRUIT** stone fruit, red to
black, seeds mostly 2, edible.
ECOLOGY grows in a variety of habitats,
including coastal scrub, chaparral, oak
woodlands, and conifer forests from low
to montane elevation. Resprouts after
fire.

Frangula purshiana (*Rhamnus purshiana*)
RHAMNACEAE
CASCARA BUCKTHORN
Native, scattered, blooms all spring, 3–33
ft. Streambanks, west-side forest, east-
side forest, low to mid elevation

Shrub or tree, bark silvery gray, twigs various colors,
smooth or yellowish brown hairy. **LEAVES** deciduous,
alternate, oblong to egg-shaped, 2.5–6 in. long, surfaces hairy or not, side veins 10–12 and parallel, edges
finely toothed, tips pointed or rounded.
FLOWERS stalked, rounded clusters with >8 flowers
in leaf axils, unisexual and bisexual flowers on same
plant, petals and sepals greenish, sepals hairy, petals smaller than sepals. **FRUIT** stone
fruit, purplish black, edible but toxic if
eaten in quantity. **ECOLOGY** shade tolerant, grows on streambanks, in hardwood and conifer forests. Bark and fruit
have laxative properties. Ssp. *ultrama-
fica*, endemic to and rare in California,
has blue or grayish green leaves with
rounded tips, and is <7 ft. tall.

Frangula rubra (*Rhamnus rubra*)
RHAMNACEAE
RED BUCKTHORN, SIERRA COFFEEBERRY
Native, common, blooms mid spring–early
summer, to 7 ft. Chaparral, west-side forest,
east-side forest, mid to high elevation
Shrub, bark and twigs reddish to gray. **LEAVES** deciduous, alternate, oval to egg-shaped, 0.5–2.5 in. long,
green or grayish, surfaces hairy or not, edges smooth
to toothed, tips rounded or pointed. **FLOWERS** stalked,
rounded clusters in leaf axils, flowers 4–15, petals and
sepals greenish, petals smaller than sepals.
FRUIT stone fruit, reddish purple to black, inedible,
possibly has laxative properties. **ECOLOGY** grows on forest slopes, in sage-
brush scrub, chap-
arral, and juniper
woodlands. Leaf
characters vary by
habitat.

Rhamnus alnifolia
RHAMNACEAE
ALDERLEAF COFFEEBERRY, BUCKTHORN
Native, locally common, blooms late spring–
early summer, 2–5 ft. Bog/fen/wetland,
streambanks, east-side forest, mid elevation
Shrub, erect to spreading, bark gray, twigs brown.
LEAVES deciduous, alternate, oval to egg-shaped, 2.5–
4.5 in. long, surfaces hairy or not, edges with glandular-tipped teeth, tips pointed. **FLOWERS** male and
female flowers on separate plants, flowers 1–5, in leaf
axils, sepals 5, yellowish green, petals absent.
FRUIT berry, bluish black, nutlets 3, inedible.
ECOLOGY grows in streambanks, edges of wet meadows
or seeps from the steppe zone
into the mountains. Rare in
California.

Rhamnus crocea
RHAMNACEAE
REDBERRY BUCKTHORN, SPINY REDBERRY
Native, locally common, blooms late winter–spring, to 7 ft. Coastal, chaparral, west-side forest, low to mid elevation
Shrub, bark gray, smooth to ridged, branches spreading, rigid, twigs red to reddish purple, tips spinelike. **LEAVES** evergreen, alternate, oval to egg-shaped, about 0.5 in. long, shiny green above, paler below, surfaces non-hairy, edges smooth or toothed, tips rounded. **FLOWERS** male and female flowers on separate plants, flowers in leaf axils, solitary or in small flat-topped clusters, sepals 4, yellowish green, petals absent. **FRUIT** berry, bright red, nutlets 2, edible. **ECOLOGY** grows in coastal sage scrub, chaparral, oak woodlands, and conifer forests, low to montane elevation.

Rhamnus ilicifolia
RHAMNACEAE
HOLLYLEAF REDBERRY, EVERGREEN BUCKTHORN
Native, locally common, blooms early–mid spring, 3–13 ft. Chaparral, west-side forest, low to mid elevation
Shrub, erect, bark gray, twigs dark red, hairy or not. **LEAVES** evergreen, alternate, round to egg-shaped, 1–1.5 in. long, dark green and non-hairy above, bright green and mostly hairy below, edges smooth or sharp-toothed, tips rounded. **FLOWERS** male and female flowers on separate plants, flowers in leaf axils, solitary or in small flat-topped clusters, sepals 4, yellowish green, petals absent. **FRUIT** berry, bright red, nutlets 2, edible. **ECOLOGY** grows in chaparral and oak woodland communities from low to montane elevation. Rare in Oregon.

Adenostoma fasciculatum
ROSACEAE
CHAMISE

Native, common, blooms late spring–early
summer, 2–12 ft. Chaparral, low to mid elevation
Shrub, erect to spreading, resinous, branches many,
rigid, bark grayish brown, peeling in strips, twigs reddish. **LEAVES** evergreen, clustered, needlelike, 0.2–0.4
in. long, straight to curved, glandular, sticky.
FLOWERS in showy, pyramid-shaped clusters at stem
ends, 1.5–5 in. long, flowers small, saucer-shaped, petals white, round to egg-shaped, stamens 15.
FRUIT achene, oval. **ECOLOGY** shade intolerant, grows
on ridges and slopes in chaparral, coastal scrub, forest,
and woodland habitats. Shrub crown
appears white when in bloom, turns reddish brown as fruit matures. Fire stimulates seed germination; plants often
resprout following a burn.

See Rosaceae with compound leaves,
page 389

Amelanchier alnifolia
ROSACEAE
WESTERN SERVICEBERRY, SASKATOON

Native, common, blooms mid spring–mid summer,
3–20 ft. Streambanks, west-side forest, east-side
forest, shrub-steppe, low to high elevation
Shrub or tree, erect, sometimes thicket-forming, bark
grayish, twigs reddish brown. **LEAVES** deciduous, alternate, oval to roundish, 1–2 in. long, surfaces hairy,
becoming mostly smooth with age, edges toothed
near tip end, leaf tips rounded. **FLOWERS** in clusters at
branch ends, flower stalks hairy, petals 5, white, oval
to lance-shaped, 0.5–1 in. long, sepals triangular, stamens 20, styles mostly 5. **FRUIT** pome, round to egg-
shaped, to 0.5 in. long, purplish black,
non-hairy, edible, sweet.
ECOLOGY grows in forests, forest edges,
drainages in shrub-steppe communities, and on rocky slopes.

Amelanchier alnifolia var. *pumila*
(*Amelanchier pumila*)
ROSACEAE
DWARF SERVICEBERRY
Native, locally common, blooms mid–late spring,
3–10 ft. East-side forest, mid to high elevation
Shrub, stems one to several, bark grayish, twigs
reddish brown. **LEAVES** deciduous, alternate, leathery, oval to roundish, 0.5–2 in. long, top half of edge
toothed. **FLOWERS** in clusters at branch ends, flower
stalks smooth, petals 5, white, lance-shaped, 0.3–0.5
in. long, sepals triangular, stamens 15, styles 4–5,
ovary smooth. **FRUIT** pome, round to egg-shaped, to
0.4 in. long, dark purple with a whitish waxy coating,
non-hairy, edible,
sweet.
ECOLOGY grows in
shrubby areas and
forests in moun-
tainous regions.

Amelanchier utahensis
ROSACEAE
UTAH SERVICEBERRY
Native, locally common, blooms mid spring, 1.5–10
ft. Streambanks, meadows, rocky sites, west-side
forest, east-side forest, low to high elevation
Shrub, erect to spreading, sometimes thicket-forming,
bark grayish, twigs mostly hairy. **LEAVES** deciduous,
alternate, oval to egg-shaped, 0.5–1 in. long, surfaces
grayish green, somewhat leathery, hairy or not above,
densely hairy below, edges toothed from the tip ½ or
closer to base, tips rounded. **FLOWERS** in clusters at
branch ends, flower stalks hairy, petals 5, white, lance-
shaped, to 0.3 in. long, sepals lance-shaped, stamens
10–15, styles 2–4. **FRUIT** pome, round
to egg-shaped, to 0.5 in. long, reddish
to dark purple, mostly hairy, edible but
insipid, not tasty. **ECOLOGY** grows on
rocky slopes, streambanks, in valleys,
and conifer forests. The similar *A. alni-
folia* has longer petals, smooth fruit,
styles 4–5, and leaves smooth below by
fruiting stage.

Cercocarpus betuloides

(*Cercocarpus montanus, Cercocarpus montanus* var. *glaber*)
ROSACEAE
BIRCHLEAF MOUNTAIN MAHOGANY,
ALDERLEAF MOUNTAIN MAHOGANY

Native, common, blooms early spring–mid summer, 3–23 ft. Rocky sites, west-side forest, east-side forest, shrub-steppe, subalpine, low to high elevation

Shrub or small tree, erect, bark gray or brown, smooth. **LEAVES** evergreen, alternate, leathery, roundish to lance-shaped, 0.5–1 in. long, dark green and smooth above, paler and mostly hairy beneath, edges toothed, tips pointed. **FLOWERS** solitary to small clusters in leaf axils, flowers bell-shaped, greenish, petals absent, sepals hairy, lobes egg-shaped, bent back, stamens 25–40, anthers hairy.

FRUIT achene, hairy, tipped by twisted, feathery style, 1–4 in. long.
ECOLOGY grows on rocky slopes, in shrub-steppe, and forest openings in mountainous areas, a long-lived species.

Cercocarpus ledifolius

ROSACEAE
CURLLEAF MOUNTAIN MAHOGANY, DESERT MOUNTAIN MAHOGANY

Native, common, blooms all spring, 3–33 ft. West-side forest, east-side forest, subalpine, mid to high elevation

Shrub or small tree, erect, bark reddish or gray, furrowed with age, twigs reddish to gray, hairy.
LEAVES evergreen, alternate, leathery, linear to lance-shaped, 0.5–1 in. long, dark green and glandular above, white-hairy below, edges smooth, rolled under, tips pointed. **FLOWERS** solitary to small clusters in leaf axils, flowers bell-shaped, greenish, petals absent, sepals hairy, lobes egg-shaped, bent back, stamens 20–30, anthers non-hairy.
FRUIT achene tipped by feathery style, 2–3 in. long.
ECOLOGY grows on rocky slopes, in shrub-steppe, and forests in mountainous areas.

Cotoneaster lacteus
ROSACEAE
MILKFLOWER COTONEASTER, PARNEY'S COTONEASTER, LATE COTONEASTER

Non-native, locally common, blooms late spring–mid summer, 3–30 ft. Coastal, disturbed, low elevation
Shrub, many-branched, stems arching, fountain-like. **LEAVES** evergreen, alternate, oval to egg-shaped, 1.5–4 in. long, dark green above, veins often sunken, hairy below, tips pointed or rounded. **FLOWERS** in many-flowered clusters at branch tips, flowers saucer-shaped, to 0.4 in. across, petals white, stamens 20, anthers purple, styles 2. **FRUIT** berrylike, bright red, round, 0.3 in. across. **ECOLOGY** invasive, escaped ornamental, grows in disturbed areas, shrub thickets, open forest, meadows, and other places close to human settlements, mostly at lower elevations.

Crataegus castlegarensis
ROSACEAE
CASTLEGAR HAWTHORN

Native, locally common, blooms late spring, 8–17 ft. Streambanks, low to mid elevation
Shrub, erect, stems several, thorns about 1 in. long, straight or curved, reddish brown, thorns often branched on twigs. **LEAVES** deciduous, alternate, lance- to diamond-shaped, 1.5–2.5 in. long, variably hairy above and below, somewhat leathery, edges toothed, often 3- to 4-lobed, tips pointed, main veins extending to leaf edge. **FLOWERS** in clusters, flower stalks hairy, flowers saucer-shaped, petals roundish, white, sepal lobes triangular, edges toothed, stamens 10, anthers pink. **FRUIT** pome, roundish, blackish purple, 0.5 in. long, sparsely hairy. **ECOLOGY** grows on streambanks, shrubby slopes, marsh edges, roadsides.

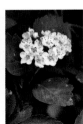

Crataegus chrysocarpa var. *piperi*
(*Crataegus columbiana* var. *piperi*)
ROSACEAE
PIPER'S HAWTHORN
Native, locally common, blooms mid spring,
7–12 ft. Streambanks, mid elevation
Shrub, sometimes colony-forming, bark reddish, twigs
light brown, thorns 1–2.5 in. long, mostly straight.
LEAVES deciduous, alternate, diamond-shaped, 1–2.5
in. long, glossy green in late summer, turning yellow
in autumn, hairy below, hairy or not above, edges with
short, angular lobes and teeth, teeth gland-tipped,
main veins not extending to leaf edge between lobes.
FLOWERS clusters in leaf axils or at stem ends, flower
stalks hairy, flowers saucer-shaped,
petals white, to 0.3 in. long, sepal
lobes lance-shaped, stamens 10, ivory.
FRUIT pome, round, pinkish orange
when immature, becoming bright red,
hairy, 0.5 in. long. ECOLOGY grows
along streams, draws, and forest edges,
montane.

Crataegus douglasii
ROSACEAE
BLACK HAWTHORN, DOUGLAS' HAWTHORN
Native, common, blooms mid–late spring,
13–20 ft. Streambanks, meadows, west-side
forest, east-side forest, low to mid elevation
Shrub, erect, branches gray, twigs tan to dark brown,
thorns 0.5–1.5 in. long, single, mostly straight, dark
brown. LEAVES deciduous, alternate, oval to egg-
shaped, 1.5–3 in. long, dark green and densely short-
hairy above, paler beneath, hairy only on veins, edges
sharp-toothed, several short lobes near tip, main veins
extend to leaf edge. FLOWERS clusters in leaf axils or at
stem ends, flowers saucer-shaped, petals white, roundish, to 0.3 in. long, sepal lobes triangular, stamens 10, ovary non-hairy.
FRUIT pome, blackish purple, oval
to egg-shaped, 0.5 in. long, edible.
ECOLOGY grows along streams, in shrub
thickets, and forests from low to mid
elevation.

Crataegus macracantha var. *occidentalis* (*Crataegus succulenta*)
ROSACEAE
FLESHY HAWTHORN, LARGE-THORNED HAWTHORN, WESTERN LARGE-THORNED HAWTHORN

Native, locally common, blooms late spring–early summer, 8–20 ft. Streambanks, meadows, low elevation
Shrub, erect, twigs purplish black, thorns many, dark brown, 1–2 in. long. LEAVES deciduous, alternate, oval to egg-shaped, 1–2 in. long, surfaces dark green, leathery, hairy when young, edges with short angular lobes and teeth, teeth not gland-tipped, main veins not extending to leaf edge between lobes, fall color variable, bronze to orange with some yellow and deep red. FLOWERS clusters in leaf axils or at stem ends, flower stalks hairy, flowers saucer-shaped, petals white, sepal lobes triangular, stamens 10, mostly ivory. FRUIT pome, round, orange when immature, becoming bright red, hairy, 0.5 in. long, seeds pitted. ECOLOGY grows on streambanks, shorelines, wetland edges, and fields at lower elevations.

Crataegus monogyna
ROSACEAE
ONE-SEEDED HAWTHORN, ENGLISH HAWTHORN, COMMON HAWTHORN

Non-native, scattered, blooms mid spring–mid summer, 7–33 ft. Disturbed, low elevation
Shrub or tree, bark grayish brown, scaly, twigs gray to reddish brown, thorns 0.5 in. long. LEAVES deciduous, alternate, egg-shaped, 0.5–1.5 in. long, veins extend to leaf edge between lobes, edges deeply 5- to 7-lobed and toothed, tips pointed. FLOWERS in many-flowered clusters in leaf axils or stem ends, flower stalks smooth, flowers saucer-shaped, petals white to pink, sepal lobes triangular, stamens 20. FRUIT pome, dark red, round to egg-shaped, 0.5 in. long, 1-seeded, edible. ECOLOGY Eurasian import, escapee from cultivation, grows in disturbed places or forest edges in low-lying areas.

Crataegus okanaganensis
ROSACEAE
OKANAGAN VALLEY HAWTHORN
Native, locally common, blooms late spring, to
20 ft. Streambanks, low to mid elevation

Shrub, erect, stems often multiple, twigs dark reddish
brown, thorns curved, stout, 1–2 in. long.
LEAVES deciduous, alternate, oval to egg-shaped, 1.5–2
in. long, leathery, medium green, hairy above, non-
hairy except on veins below, edges sharp-toothed,
sometimes lobed, main side veins extend to leaf edge,
tips pointed, fall color crimson to coppery. **FLOWERS** in
clusters, flowers saucer-shaped, petals white, roundish, sepal lobes triangular, glandular, stamens 10–12
(rarely 5), anthers mostly ivory, ovary
non-hairy. **FRUIT** pome, roundish, 0.5
in. across, hairy, dark red when immature, becoming deep purple, sepals bent
back. **ECOLOGY** grows in shrub thickets, streambanks, hillsides, ditches, and
other moist places.

Crataegus phippsii
ROSACEAE
PHIPPS' HAWTHORN
Native, rare, blooms late spring, 17–23 ft.
Streambanks, low to mid elevation

Tree or shrub, erect, branches dark gray, twigs purplish brown, hairy, thorns sparse, somewhat thin,
1–1.5 in. long, slightly curved. **LEAVES** deciduous, alternate, egg-shaped, 1.5–3 in. long, surfaces hairy, especially on veins below, leathery, edges sharp-toothed,
lobes rounded, shallow. **FLOWERS** in clusters, flower
stalks hairy, flowers saucer-shaped, petals roundish, white, sepal lobes triangular, hairy, stamens 10,
anthers pink. **FRUIT** pome, round to flask-shaped, 0.5
in. across, hairy, reddish to
purplish when immature,
becoming purplish black at
maturity, sepals persistent,
bent back. **ECOLOGY** grows
in shrub thickets, on slopes,
floodplains, streambanks, and
shorelines.

Crataegus suksdorfii
(*Crataegus douglasii* var. *suksdorfii*)
ROSACEAE
SUKSDORF'S HAWTHORN
Native, locally common, blooms late spring, 10–17 ft.
Coastal, streambanks, west-side forest, low elevation
Shrub, erect, branches grayish, twigs tan, thorns 0.5–1 in. long, dark brown, straight or curved.
LEAVES deciduous, alternate, oval to diamond-shaped, 1–2.5 in. long, dark green above, paler beneath, sometimes hairy, edges singly or doubly toothed, sometimes lobed, main veins mostly not extending to leaf edge.
FLOWERS clusters in leaf axils or at stem ends, flowers saucer-shaped, petals white, roundish, to 0.3 in. long,

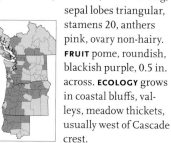

sepal lobes triangular, stamens 20, anthers pink, ovary non-hairy. FRUIT pome, roundish, blackish purple, 0.5 in. across. ECOLOGY grows in coastal bluffs, valleys, meadow thickets, usually west of Cascade crest.

Dryas drummondii
ROSACEAE
YELLOW MOUNTAIN-AVENS, DRUMMOND'S MOUNTAIN-AVENS, YELLOW DRYAS
Native, rare, blooms late spring, 2–10 in. Streambanks, rocky sites, alpine, subalpine, low to high elevation
Dwarf shrub, stems trailing, often rooting, forming large patches. LEAVES evergreen, alternate, oval to egg-shaped, 0.5–1.5 in. long, dark green above, white woolly-hairy beneath, edges toothed and often rolled under, tips rounded. FLOWERS solitary, nodding, flower stalk with a few small leaves, flowers bowl-shaped, petals yellow, 8–10, oval to egg-shaped, 0.3–0.5 in. long, sepals egg-shaped, hairy, often glandular-hairy.

FRUIT achene topped by a feathery, yellow style. ECOLOGY grows in cliff crevices, rocky slopes, and in gravelly areas along streams. Locally common in British Columbia.

Dryas octopetala
ROSACEAE
EIGHTPETAL MOUNTAIN-AVENS, WHITE
MOUNTAIN-AVENS
Native, locally common, blooms late spring–
mid summer, 2–8 in. Meadows, rocky sites,
alpine, subalpine, mid to high elevation

Dwarf shrub, stems trailing, stems root, forming large
patches. **LEAVES** evergreen, alternate, egg- to lance-
shaped, 0.5–1.5 in. long, dark green above, glands on
midvein and white woolly-hairy below, edges toothed
and often rolled under, tips rounded. **FLOWERS** solitary,
nodding, flower stalk with 0–1 small leaves, flowers
saucer-shaped, petals white to cream, 8–10, oval, 0.3–
0.7 in. long, sepals lance-shaped, hairy,
some hairs black and glandular.
FRUIT achene topped by long, feathery
style. **ECOLOGY** grows on rocky slopes,
meadows, gravel bars, and ridgetops
from montane to alpine areas.

Heteromeles arbutifolia
ROSACEAE
TOYON, CHRISTMAS BERRY
Native, locally common, blooms late
spring–mid summer, 3–10 ft. Chaparral,
east-side forest, low to mid elevation

Shrub or tree, bark gray, twigs gray and hairy.
LEAVES evergreen, alternate, oval, 2–4 in. long, glossy
dark green above, edges finely toothed, tips pointed.
FLOWERS in rounded clusters at stem ends, flowers
small, petals 5, roundish, white, to 0.15 in. long, sepals
urn-shaped with short triangular lobes. **FRUIT** pome,
oval, 0.2–0.5 in. long, bright red, sometimes yellowish, lingering through winter, edible, spicy-sweet.
ECOLOGY grows in
chaparral and oak
woodlands. Shade
tolerant and consid-
ered a good orna-
mental. Resprouts
following fire.

Holodiscus discolor
ROSACEAE
OCEANSPRAY, CREAMBUSH, IRONWOOD

Native, common, blooms late spring–mid summer, 3–13 ft. Coastal, west-side forest, east-side forest, low to mid elevation

Shrub, erect to arching, stems slender, bark reddish gray. **LEAVES** deciduous, alternate, egg-shaped, 0.5–3 in. long, hairy or not above, hairy beneath, edges lobed and toothed, tips rounded. **FLOWERS** tiny, in nodding, many-branched, pyramid-shaped clusters, 2–10 in.

long, resembles a foamy spray of ocean water, petals white, 0.1 in. long, slightly longer than the sepals. **FRUIT** achene, light brown, hairy, 0.1 in. long. **ECOLOGY** grows in both moist and dry forests, streambanks, rocky slopes, and coastal bluffs.

Holodiscus discolor var. *microphyllus*
(*Holodiscus microphyllus, Holodiscus dumosus*)
ROSACEAE
ROCK-SPIREA
Native, common, blooms mid summer,
1–3 ft. Rocky sites, east-side forest, alpine,
subalpine, mid to high elevation

Shrub, erect to spreading, bark shedding, twigs reddish gray, hairy. **LEAVES** deciduous, alternate, round to wedge-shaped, 0.5–1.5 in. long, surfaces dull, one or both long-hairy, glands absent or covered by hairs, edges singly toothed at tip end, tips rounded.
FLOWERS in non- to few-branched clusters at stem ends, 1–3 in. long, flow-ers tiny, petals white to cream.
FRUIT achene, brown.
ECOLOGY grows in forest and wood-land openings, in rock outcrops, and in dry rocky alpine habitats.

Malus fusca (*Pyrus fusca*)
ROSACEAE
PACIFIC CRABAPPLE, OREGON CRABAPPLE,
WESTERN CRABAPPLE
Native, scattered, blooms early spring–mid
summer, 10–40 ft. Coastal, bog/fen/wetland,
streambanks, west-side forest, low elevation

Shrub or tree, sometimes thicket-forming, crown rounded, spreading, bark furrowed with age, twigs sometimes thorny. **LEAVES** deciduous, alternate, lance- to egg-shaped, 1–3.5 in. long, hairy or not above, hairy below, edges toothed, often lobed, tips pointed.
FLOWERS in flat-topped clusters, flowers fragrant, showy, petals 5, egg-shaped, to 0.5 in. long, white to pink, sepals bent back.
FRUIT apple, oval to egg-shaped, to 0.5 in. long, yellow to purplish red, edible, sour. **ECOLOGY** grows in bogs, estuary edges, sand dunes, and other coastal habitats; also in conifer forests. Provides good cover for wildlife, fruit a desirable edible, often made into jams or jellies.

Malus pumila
(*Malus ×domestica, Malus sylvestris*)
ROSACEAE
PARADISE APPLE, CULTIVATED APPLE
Non-native, uncommon, blooms mid spring, 13–40
ft. Disturbed, meadows, low to mid elevation
Tree, many-branched, twigs hairy. **LEAVES** deciduous,
alternate, oval to egg-shaped, 2–4 in. long, surfaces
hairy or smooth, edges toothed, tips pointed.
FLOWERS in flat-topped clusters, few-flowered, flowers
fragrant, showy, petals 5, egg-shaped, 0.5–1 in. long,
white to pink, sepals persistent. **FRUIT** apple, egg- to
cone-shaped, >1 in. long, sepals present, color various,
edible, tart to sweet. **ECOLOGY** escapee from cultivation, grows in disturbed areas,
forest edges, roadsides, often
near human settlements, our
common orchard apple.

Neviusia cliftonii
ROSACEAE
SHASTA SNOW-WREATH
Native, rare, blooms mid spring, 1.5–8 ft.
Streambanks, east-side forest, low elevation
Shrub, erect, bark brown, branches slender.
LEAVES deciduous, alternate, egg- to heart-shaped,
1–2.5 in. long, surfaces with stiff appressed hairs,
edges toothed and with short lobes, tips pointed.
FLOWERS in few-flowered, flat-topped clusters, flowers
saucer-shaped, sepals 5–6, green, edges toothed, egg-
shaped, to 0.2 in. long, petals 0–2, lance-shaped, white,
to 0.2 in. long, stamens numerous, white and showy.
FRUIT achene, to 0.15 in. long. **ECOLOGY** grows on forested slopes, often north-facing, stream-
banks, limestone or volcanic substrates.
Looks similar to *Holodiscus discolor*
and *Physocarpus capitatus* when not in
flower. Endemic to California, discovered in 1992 near Lake Shasta.

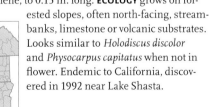

Oemleria cerasiformis
(*Osmaronia cerasiformis*)
ROSACEAE
INDIAN PLUM, OSO BERRY

Native, common, blooms late winter–early spring, 3–17 ft. Streambanks, west-side forest, low to mid elevation Shrub or small tree, erect, bark purplish brown, twigs green becoming reddish brown. **LEAVES** deciduous, alternate, oval to egg-shaped, 2–5 in. long, sometimes hairy beneath, edges smooth, tips pointed. **FLOWERS** in nodding clusters on side branches and in leaf axils, flowers mostly unisexual, male and female flowers on separate plants, blooms before leafing out, flowers saucer- to cup-shaped, petals 5, greenish white, 0.1–0.25 in. long. **FRUIT** small plums, to 0.5 in. long, peach-colored when immature, bluish black when ripe, edible but bitter. **ECOLOGY** grows in open forests, canyons, chaparral, and along streams, an early-flowering shrub and one of the very first to leaf out in spring.

Peraphyllum ramosissimum

ROSACEAE

WILD CRABAPPLE

Native, locally common, blooms mid–late spring, 3–10 ft. East-side forest, shrub-steppe, mid to high elevation Shrub, erect, branches spreading, many, bark dark gray. **LEAVES** deciduous, alternate, closely spaced, appearing clustered, linear to lance-shaped, 0.5–1.5 in. long, hairy below, edges smooth or with glandular-tipped teeth, leaf tips pointed. **FLOWERS** solitary or in small clusters, flowers saucer- to disk-shaped, sweet-scented, petals 5, oval to egg-shaped, to 0.3 in. long, white to reddish pink, sepal lobes triangular, hairy. **FRUIT** pome, yellowish to purplish red, round, to 0.5 in.

long, edible, somewhat sweet when ripe but with bitter aftertaste.

ECOLOGY shade intolerant, grows in sagebrush and bitterbrush communities, pinyon-juniper woodlands or pine forests in arid plains to mountainous areas.

Petrophytum cinerascens

(*Petrophyton cinerascens*)

ROSACEAE

CHELAN ROCKMAT, HALFSHRUB ROCKMAT

Native, rare, blooms mid summer, 2–6 in. Rocky sites, low elevation

Subshrub, forming matted clumps. **LEAVES** deciduous, alternate, spatula- to lance-shaped, 0.5–1 in. long, surfaces grayish green, hairy, edges smooth, 3-nerved. **FLOWERS** in densely flowered, nodding clusters, 1–2.5 in. long, narrow, cluster stalks with small leaves, flowers brushlike, stamens 20–25, about 2 times longer than petals and sepals, petals 5, white, sepals 5, lance-shaped and erect, grayish-hairy, 0.05 in. long.

FRUIT podlike capsule, 0.1 in. long.

ECOLOGY a narrow endemic, grows on basalt cliffs, rock outcrops, and ledges in the border zone between the foothills of the Wenatchee Mountains and the Columbia Plateau in Washington.

Petrophytum hendersonii
(*Petrophyton hendersonii*)
ROSACEAE
OLYMPIC ROCKMAT, ROCK SPIRAEA, OLYMPIC
MOUNTAIN ROCKMAT

Native, locally common, blooms mid summer, 0.5–2.5
in. Rocky sites, alpine, subalpine, mid to high elevation
Subshrub, mat-forming. **LEAVES** deciduous, alternate, closely spaced so appearing clustered, spatula-
to lance-shaped, 0.5–1 in. long, surfaces green, hairy,
edges smooth, 3-nerved. **FLOWERS** in densely flowered,
nodding clusters, 1–1.5 in. long, narrow, flowering
stalks with small leaves, flowers brushlike, stamens
35–40, equal to or slightly longer than petals, petals 5,
oval, to 0.1 in. long, white, sepals 5, oval,
bent back, hairy. **FRUIT** podlike capsule,
0.1 in. long. **ECOLOGY** grows on cliffs,
crevices, and rocky slopes. Endemic to
Washington's Olympic Mountains.

Physocarpus capitatus
ROSACEAE
PACIFIC NINEBARK

Native, common, blooms late spring, 3–13
ft. Coastal, streambanks, west-side forest,
east-side forest, low to mid elevation
Shrub, erect to arching, bark brown, shredding, twigs
smooth to star-shaped hairy. **LEAVES** deciduous, alternate, egg- to heart-shaped, 1–4 in. long, dark green
above, star-shaped hairy beneath, edges 3- to 5-lobed
and doubly-toothed, tips pointed. **FLOWERS** in densely
flowered, flat-topped clusters at stem ends, flowers
saucer-shaped, petals 5, roundish, mostly 0.2 in. long,
white, sepals 5, star-shaped hairy, pistils 3–5, non-hairy
to sparsely star-shaped hairy. **FRUIT** podlike capsule, reddish, non-hairy, to 0.4
in. long. **ECOLOGY** grows along streams
and lakes, in forest edges and clearings,
from low to montane elevation.

Physocarpus malvaceus
ROSACEAE
MALLOW NINEBARK

Native, common, blooms late spring–early summer, 1.5–7 ft. Meadows, east-side forest, mid elevation Shrub, erect to arching branches, bark grayish brown, papery, shredding, twigs smooth to star-shaped hairy. **LEAVES** deciduous, alternate, egg- to heart-shaped, 1–2 in. long, dark green above, star-shaped hairy beneath, edges 3- to 5-lobed and doubly toothed, tips pointed. **FLOWERS** in rounded clusters at stem ends, flowers saucer-shaped, petals 5, roundish, mostly 0.1 in. long, white, sepals 5, star-shaped hairy, pistils usually 2, can be 3–5, densely star-shaped hairy. **FRUIT** podlike capsule, reddish, star-shaped hairy, to 0.4 in. long. **ECOLOGY** grows in dry forests, draws, wetland edges, streambanks, and on rocky slopes.

Prunus andersonii
ROSACEAE
DESERT PEACH

Native, locally common, blooms early–mid spring, 7–10 ft. Disturbed, shrub-steppe, mid to high elevation Shrub, erect, rhizomatous, thicket-forming, stems short-lived, twigs rigid, thorns numerous. **LEAVES** deciduous, alternate, oval to lance-shaped, 0.5–1 in. long, edges toothed, tips pointed. **FLOWERS** solitary or in small clusters in leaf axils, flowers star-shaped, petals 5, egg-shaped, to 0.4 in. long, white to pink, sepals with gland-tipped teeth. **FRUIT** stone fruit, fuzzy, round, about 0.5 in. across, greenish yellow to dark red, fleshy layer dry, edible. **ECOLOGY** grows in shrub-steppe, pinyon-juniper woodlands, rocky slopes, and disturbed sites in arid ecoregions. Resprouts from the root system after fire.

Prunus avium
ROSACEAE
SWEET CHERRY

Non-native, scattered, blooms early–mid spring,
17–83 ft. Disturbed, west-side forest, low elevation
Tree, erect, crown rounded, bark reddish brown, shiny,
smooth, ringed by lenticels, peels in horizontal strips,
twigs grayish brown. **LEAVES** deciduous, alternate,
oval to egg-shaped, 3–6 in. long, pairs of veins mostly
more than 8, often hairy beneath, edges toothed, tips
pointed, leaf stalks with 1–2 glands near leaf base.
FLOWERS in small flat-topped clusters, flowers bowl-
shaped, petals 5, white, egg-shaped with notched
tip, 0.3–0.5 in. long. **FRUIT** stone fruit,
smooth, round, 0.5–1 in. across, bright
to dark red, edible, tasty.
ECOLOGY escapee from cultivation,
found in fields and forest edges. The
similar *P. cerasus* is generally shorter,
with non-hairy leaves, mostly 2–3 in.
long, vein pairs fewer than 8.

Prunus cerasifera
ROSACEAE
CHERRY PLUM, MYROBALAN PLUM
Non-native, scattered, blooms late winter–spring,
13–27 ft. Streambanks, disturbed, low elevation

Tree, erect, crown rounded, bark reddish brown to
dark gray, furrowed with age, twigs reddish brown.
LEAVES deciduous, alternate, oval to egg-shaped, 1–3
in. long, surfaces green to purplish, edges toothed,
tip pointed or rounded. **FLOWERS** solitary or in small
clusters, blooms before the leaves emerge, flowers saucer-shaped, petals 5, oval to egg-shaped, white to reddish pink, 0.3–0.5 in. long, sepals non-hairy.
FRUIT stone fruit, smooth, round, 0.5–1 in. across, yellow to red, edible, sweet.

ECOLOGY potentially invasive escapee
from cultivation, grows along roadsides,
trails, streambanks, and other places
in low-lying areas, mostly near human
settlements.

Prunus emarginata
ROSACEAE
BITTER CHERRY
Native, common, blooms mid–late spring,
7–50 ft. Coastal, streambanks, west-side forest,
east-side forest, low to mid elevation

Shrub or tree, often thicket-forming, bark reddish
brown to gray, smooth, ringed with lenticels, twigs reddish purple. **LEAVES** deciduous, alternate, stalk with
1–2 glands at leaf base, oval, lance-, or egg-shaped,
0.5–3 in. long, edges toothed, tips mostly rounded.
FLOWERS in few-flowered, usually flat-topped clusters, not leafy at base, flowers saucer-shaped, petals 5,
egg-shaped, 0.1–0.3 in. long, white. **FRUIT** stone fruit,
smooth, round to egg-shaped, 0.3–
0.5 in. long, bright red to dark purple,
inedible, bitter. **ECOLOGY** grows along
streambanks, in open forests, on rocky
slopes, from the lowlands to montane
elevation. Twigs are desired wildlife
browse; birds and other animals consume the fruit.

Prunus subcordata
ROSACEAE
KLAMATH PLUM, SIERRA PLUM
Native, locally common, blooms mid–late spring,
3–20 ft. Streambanks, meadows, west-side
forest, east-side forest, low to mid elevation
Shrub or tree, spreading, stout, often thicket-forming,
bark grayish purple, stems branched, often thorny,
hairy. **LEAVES** deciduous, alternate, one to several
glands often present near leaf base, egg-shaped, 1–2.5
in. long, edges toothed, tips rounded or pointed.
FLOWERS solitary or in few-flowered clusters, sepals
bell-shaped with spreading lobes, petals 5, egg-shaped,
0.2–0.4 in. long, white. **FRUIT** stone fruit, smooth, oval
to round, about 1 in. long, dark red to
reddish purple, rarely yellow, edible,
tart. **ECOLOGY** grows along streambanks, in open forests, and in shrub
thickets from low to montane elevation.

Prunus virginiana
ROSACEAE
CHOKECHERRY
Native, common, blooms late spring–mid
summer, 13–27 ft. Streambanks, west-side
forest, east-side forest, low to mid elevation
Shrub or tree, often thicket-forming, bark reddish
to gray-brown, smooth or scaly, twigs mostly hairy.
LEAVES deciduous, alternate, stalk with 1–2 glands at
the stem end, widely oval to egg-shaped, 1–4 in. long,
smooth above, hairy or not beneath, edges toothed,
tips mostly pointed. **FLOWERS** in many-flowered, narrow clusters, 2–6 in. long, flowers saucer-shaped, petals 5, roundish, to 0.3 in. long, white, sepals non-hairy.
FRUIT stone fruit, smooth, round to egg-shaped, to 0.5
in. long, red, purple, or black, edible but tart, astrin-
gent, producing a choking sensation after being eaten.
ECOLOGY grows along streams and other sources of
water, in open forests, forest edges, and rocky slopes
from low to montane elevation. Twigs are desired wildlife browse; birds and other animals consume the fruit,
which is often used to make jelly or wine.

Purshia tridentata
ROSACEAE
BITTERBRUSH, ANTELOPE-BRUSH, ANTELOPE
BITTERBRUSH

Native, common, blooms all spring, 3–8 ft. East-side forest, shrub-steppe, low to high elevation
Shrub, erect to spreading, much-branched, twigs sturdy, hairy. **LEAVES** deciduous, alternate, wedge-shaped, 0.5–1 in. long, greenish and hairy above, woolly hairy below, 3-lobed near the tip, lobe tips rounded. **FLOWERS** solitary on short shoots, flowers disk-shaped, petals 5, spoon- to egg-shaped, 0.2–0.4 in. long, cream to yellow, sepals bell-shaped, glandular and hairy. **FRUIT** achene, spindle-shaped, to 0.5 in.

long, reddish brown, hairy, glandular, bitter-tasting. **ECOLOGY** grows in shrub-steppe, dry forests, rocky slopes, and ridgetops. Foliage provides forage for wildlife; fruit are often cached and eaten by birds and small mammals through the winter.

Rubus bartonianus
ROSACEAE
BARTONBERRY, BARTON'S RASPBERRY

Native, rare, blooms mid spring, 3–10 ft.
Streambanks, rocky sites, low to mid elevation
Shrub, erect, bark yellowish, shreddy, branches reddish brown, prickles absent, twigs hairy or not.
LEAVES deciduous, alternate, mapleleaf-shaped, 1–2 in. long, 3- to 5-lobed, surfaces non-hairy above, hairy beneath, edges doubly toothed, tips pointed.
FLOWERS single at branch ends, flowers saucer-shaped, petals 5, white, egg-shaped, 1 in. long, styles hairy from base to tip. **FRUIT** raspberrylike, round, deep red, edible. **ECOLOGY** grows on rocky basalt slopes and streambanks. Prefers partial shade, resprouts after fire. A narrow endemic to the Hells Canyon area of the Snake River and its tributaries.

See *Rubus* with compound leaves, page 399

Rubus chamaemorus
ROSACEAE
CLOUDBERRY

Native, locally common, blooms late spring–early summer, 2–12 in. Bog/fen/ wetland, meadows, low to mid elevation

Subshrub, rhizomatous, stems sparsely to densely hairy, prickles absent. **LEAVES** deciduous, alternate, mapleleaf-shaped, 5- to 7-lobed, 1–5 in. wide, hairy below, edges toothed, tips mostly rounded. **FLOWERS** solitary, stalked, unisexual, male and female flowers on separate plants, flowers saucer-shaped, petals 5, white, 0.3–0.5 in. long, sepals hairy or not. **FRUIT** raspberrylike, at first reddish, then golden yellow, tart, a highly desired edible. **ECOLOGY** grows in bogs, boggy areas within forests, and wet meadows, lowland to montane.

Rubus lasiococcus
ROSACEAE
DWARF BRAMBLE, CREEPING RASPBERRY, ROUGHFRUIT BERRY

Native, locally common, blooms late spring– mid summer, 4 in. West-side forest, east-side forest, subalpine, mid to high elevation

Subshrub, stems trailing, sometimes rooting at the nodes, prickles absent. **LEAVES** deciduous, alternate, heart-shaped, 1–2.5 in. wide, 3-lobed, sparsely hairy above and below, edges doubly toothed, tips rounded. **FLOWERS** single or paired, stalked, flowers saucer-shaped, white, petals 5, 0.2–0.3 in. long, sepals hairy. **FRUIT** berry, red, about 0.5 in. across, hairy, edible, tasty. **ECOLOGY** grows along forest floors and in shrub thickets, montane to subalpine. Rare in British Columbia. Can act as a groundcover.

Rubus nivalis
ROSACEAE
SNOW DWARF BRAMBLE, SNOW DEWBERRY, SNOW BRAMBLE

Native, locally common, blooms late spring–mid summer, to 1 ft. West-side forest, low to mid elevation Subshrub, stems trailing, rooting at the nodes, prickles slender, curved. **LEAVES** evergreen, alternate, egg-shaped, can be unlobed, 3-lobed, to occasionally divided into 3 leaflets, 1–2.5 in. long, shiny and non-hairy above, prickly hairy on veins below, edges toothed. **FLOWERS** single to paired, stalked flowers in leaf axils, petals 5, narrowly oval-shaped, pink to purplish red, sepals hairy, purplish red, bent back. **FRUIT** berry, round, red, short-hairy, to 0.2 in. wide, edible. **ECOLOGY** grows in open to shady areas in moist forests. Rare in British Columbia and California.

Rubus parviflorus
ROSACEAE
THIMBLEBERRY

Native, common, blooms spring–summer, 1.5–7 ft. Coastal, streambanks, west-side forest, east-side forest, subalpine, low to high elevation Shrub, erect, rhizomatous, often thicket-forming, prickles absent, stems glandular-hairy when young, non-hairy with gray, shreddy bark with age. **LEAVES** deciduous, alternate, mapleleaf-shaped, 3- to 7-lobed, 2–6 in. long, surfaces light green, soft-hairy, edges toothed, tips pointed, fall color yellow. **FLOWERS** in flat-topped clusters at stem ends, flowers saucer-shaped, petals 5, egg-shaped, white to pinkish, 0.5–1 in. long. **FRUIT** raspberrylike, resembles a thimble when separated from the receptacle, red, hairy, to 0.5 in. across, edible, delicious. **ECOLOGY** shade tolerant, grows in forests, along streambanks, roadsides, and shorelines from low to subalpine elevation.

Spiraea douglasii
ROSACEAE
HARDHACK, DOUGLAS'S SPIRAEA, PINK SPIRAEA
Native, common, blooms all summer, 2–7 ft.
Bog/fen/wetland, streambanks, meadows,
subalpine, low to high elevation

Shrub, erect, rhizomatous, often thicket-forming, bark brown, stems hairy when young. **LEAVES** deciduous, alternate, oval to egg-shaped, 1–4 in. long, dark green above, paler beneath, hairy or not, edges toothed from tip to about midleaf, tips pointed or rounded. **FLOWERS** in oval, many-flowered clusters, much longer than wide, 2–8 in. long, flowers very small, petals 5, light pink to pinkish red, 0.1 in. long, sepals hairy. **FRUIT** podlike capsule, brown, to 0.1 in. long. **ECOLOGY** grows in bogs, swamps, wet meadows, and streambanks from low to subalpine elevation.

Spiraea lucida
(*Spiraea betulifolia* var. *lucida*)
ROSACEAE
WHITE SPIRAEA, BIRCH-LEAVED SPIRAEA
Native, common, blooms late spring–mid
summer, 10–24 in. Meadows, west-side forest,
east-side forest, low to mid elevation

Shrub, erect, rhizomatous, stems non-hairy, sparingly branched. **LEAVES** deciduous, alternate, oval to egg-shaped, 1–3 in. long, dark green above, paler beneath, edges toothed from tip to about midleaf, tips rounded or pointed. **FLOWERS** in flat-topped clusters at stem ends, flowers very small, petals 5, round, white to pinkish, 0.1 in. long, sepals non-hairy. **FRUIT** podlike capsule, brown, 0.1 in. long. **ECOLOGY** grows in open forests, rocky slopes, streambanks, and clearings from low to montane elevation.

Spiraea ×pyramidata
ROSACEAE
PYRAMIDAL SPIRAEA
Native, locally common, blooms late spring–
mid summer, 1–3 ft. Meadows, west-side
forest, east-side forest, low to mid elevation

Shrub, erect, rhizomatous, stems hairy, especially
upper portion. **LEAVES** deciduous, alternate, lance- to
egg-shaped, 1–3 in. long, surfaces usually hairy but
can be smooth, edges toothed from tip to about midleaf, tips mostly rounded. **FLOWERS** in dense, pyramid-shaped clusters, flowers very small, petals 5, light
pink, occasionally cream or bright pink, rounded, to
0.1 in. long, sepals hairy. **FRUIT** podlike capsule, brown,
about 0.1 in. long. **ECOLOGY** a fertile hybrid, grows in
habitats intermediate to those of the par-
ent species, *S. lucida* and *S. douglasii*, in
forest openings, wetland edges, clearings, and roadsides.

Spiraea splendens
(*Spiraea densiflora*)
ROSACEAE
ROSY SPIRAEA, MOUNTAIN MEADOW-SWEET
Native, common, blooms all summer,
0.7–3 ft. Bog/fen/wetland, streambanks,
subalpine, mid to high elevation

Shrub, rhizomatous, bark reddish brown, stems non-
hairy. **LEAVES** deciduous, alternate, oval to egg-shaped,
0.5–3 in. long, dark green above, paler and often hairy
beneath, edges toothed from tip to about midleaf, tips
rounded. **FLOWERS** in flat-topped clusters, flower stalks
hairy, flowers small, petals 5, egg-shaped, reddish
pink, to 0.1 in. long, sepals non-hairy. **FRUIT** capsule,
cigar-shaped, reddish
brown, 0.1 in. long.
ECOLOGY grows in wet
meadows, shrub thick-
ets, along streams and
lakes, and on rocky
slopes from mid eleva-
tion to subalpine areas.

Populus alba
SALICACEAE
WHITE POPLAR, SILVER POPLAR
Non-native, scattered, blooms early spring,
60–120 ft. Disturbed, low to mid elevation

Tree, colony-forming, crown narrow or spreading, oval, bark light gray, smooth when young, becoming furrowed with age, twigs gray or reddish brown, densely white-hairy. LEAVES deciduous, alternate, roundish or egg-shaped, 2.5–4 in. long, dark green, hairy or not above, densely white-hairy below, edges toothed to lobed, lobes 3–5 if present, tips pointed. FLOWERS plants male or female, flowers in drooping catkins, blooming before the leaves unfold. Catkins 1–3 in. long, catkin scales densely hairy. FRUIT capsule, brown. ECOLOGY potentially invasive escapee from cultivation, often found near homes and in disturbed areas. Female plants tend to have spreading crowns, male crowns are narrower. Hybridizes with *P. tremuloides*; hybrids have shallowly 3-lobed leaves.

Populus fremontii
SALICACEAE
FREMONT COTTONWOOD
Native, scattered, blooms early spring, 66–100 ft.
Bog/fen/wetland, streambanks, low to mid elevation

Tree, crown spreading, bark tan and deeply furrowed, twigs tan to brown, hairy or not, hairs whitish if present. LEAVES deciduous, alternate, diamond- to triangularly egg-shaped, 1.5–3 in. long, both sides yellowish green and hairy or not, edges hairy and coarsely toothed, tips taper to a point. FLOWERS plants male or female, flowers in drooping catkins, blooming before the leaves unfold. Catkins 2–4 in. long, catkin scales non-hairy, stamens 40–60, ovary round. FRUIT capsule, round, non-hairy. ECOLOGY grows in streambanks, floodplains, near springs and other wet places in arid areas, from low to montane elevation, forming riparian communities with willows and other plants and providing rich habitat for nesting birds, including golden eagles, and other wildlife. Shade intolerant, resprouts following fire.

Populus nigra
SALICACEAE
LOMBARDY POPLAR

Non-native, scattered, blooms all spring, to
60 ft. Disturbed, low to mid elevation

Tree, columnar, bark black, furrowed, branches erect,
twigs yellowish brown. **LEAVES** deciduous, alternate,
triangular to diamond-shaped, 1–2 in. long, surfaces non-hairy, bright green above, edges scalloped
to toothed, tips pointed. **FLOWERS** separate male and
female plants, seemingly only male plants present in
U.S., flowers in catkins, blooming before the leaves
unfold, male catkins reddish, 1–2 in. long.
FRUIT absent. **ECOLOGY** often planted as windbreaks,
found in disturbed areas near original plantings,
thought to spread vegetatively.

Populus tremuloides
SALICACEAE
QUAKING ASPEN
Native, common, blooms mid spring, 50–60(117) ft. Streambanks, west-side forest, east-side forest, subalpine, low to high elevation

Tree, often thicket-forming, bark typically greenish white, becoming gray and fissured with age, branches and twigs greenish white. **LEAVES** deciduous, alternate, leaf stalk flattened, round to egg-shaped, 1–3 in. long, about as long as wide, surfaces non-hairy, green above, whitish waxy coating below, edges scalloped, tips pointed. **FLOWERS** in catkins, flowers unisexual, male and female flowers on separate plants. Catkins 1.5–4 in. long, stamens 6–14, stigmas 2, catkin scales persistent, hairy. **FRUIT** capsule, non-hairy.

ECOLOGY grows along streams, floodplains, wetlands, on talus slopes, in a wide range of habitats and elevations and providing forage and nesting cover for an equally wide variety of animals. The common name refers to the tendency of the leaves to quiver with the slightest wind: the flattened leaf stalk allows the leaf to twist easily. Individual trees are relatively short-lived (80–100 years), but they resprout readily from the root system, and a clonal grove can live for centuries. Fires historically eliminated competing trees and renewed such groves; fire suppression policies have led to decreased abundance of this species.

Populus trichocarpa
(Populus balsamifera ssp. *trichocarpa)*
SALICACEAE
BLACK COTTONWOOD
Native, common, blooms early spring, 133–200(250) ft. Streambanks, west-side forest, east-side forest, subalpine, low to high elevation

Tree, bark grayish brown, furrowed, crown spreading, branches gray, twigs reddish brown, often hairy. **LEAVES** deciduous, alternate, triangularly egg-shaped, 2–3.5 in. long, green above, waxy and whitish beneath, edges finely toothed, tips pointed. **FLOWERS** in catkins, flowers unisexual, male and female flowers on separate plants. Catkins 3–4 in. long, stamens 30–50, stigmas 2–4, ovary hairy, catkin scales not persistent, hairy. **FRUIT** capsule, hairy or not. **ECOLOGY** grows on streambanks, floodplains, lakeshores, and other moist habitats from the lowlands to subalpine areas. Does not form thickets but can resprout if damaged. Buds and leaves resinous, lending the spring air a spicy-sweet fragrance. Common name refers to the tuft of cottony hair on the seeds, a dispersal mechanism that allows them to float through the air. Provides high-value habitat for nesting birds and foraging animals. Shade intolerant, fast growing, and relatively short-lived, but communities often persist in areas with either frequent flooding or periods of standing water.

Salix alba
SALICACEAE
WHITE WILLOW

Non-native, scattered, blooms mid spring, 50–80 ft.
Lake/pond, streambanks, disturbed, low elevation
Tree, crown narrow to rounded, bark yellowish brown,
twigs grayish green to yellow, hairy, becoming non-
hairy with age. **LEAVES** deciduous, alternate, lance-
shaped, stalk with glands, 2–4 in. long, 5–8 times longer than wide, surfaces grayish green, hairy, hair long
and silky below, edges toothed, tips pointed.
FLOWERS separate male and female plants, flowers in
catkins, blooming as the leaves unfold,
catkin bracts yellow, hairy, male catkins
1–2 in. long, stamens 2, female catkins
to 2.5 in. long, ovary non-hairy.
FRUIT pear-shaped, non-hairy, stalk
grows as fruit matures. **ECOLOGY** grows
in moist soils in disturbed places, shorelines, and streambanks, sun to part
shade.

Salix amygdaloides
SALICACEAE
PEACHLEAF WILLOW
Native, common, blooms mid spring, 13–40 ft.
Streambanks, shrub-steppe, low to mid elevation
Tree or shrub, bark yellowish brown, scaly, branches
and twigs non-hairy, branches flexible at the base,
twigs mostly yellowish or reddish brown.
LEAVES deciduous, alternate, stalks without glands,
blade oval to lance-shaped, 2–5 in. long, 3–6 times longer than wide, non-hairy, with whitish bloom beneath,
green above, margins finely toothed, tips pointed.
FLOWERS plants male or female, flowers in catkins,
blooming as the leaves unfold. Male catkins 1–3 in.
long, stamens mostly 5(3–7), hairy, female catkins
1.5–4.5 in. long, ovary smooth, styles to 0.02 in. long,
catkin scales yellow, hairy. **FRUIT** capsule, pear-shaped,
smooth. **ECOLOGY** streambanks, floodplains, and lakeshores, often in shrub-steppe, lowland to montane.
Shade intolerant. The similar *S. lasiandra* var. *caudata*
has leaves lacking a whitish bloom beneath. Rare in
British Columbia.

Salix arctica
SALICACEAE
ARCTIC WILLOW
Native, common, blooms mid summer, 1–10 in.
Meadows, alpine, subalpine, high elevation
Dwarf shrub, stems trailing, mat-forming, branches
erect or trailing, twigs yellowish brown to purplish.
LEAVES deciduous, alternate, blade oval to egg-shaped,
0.5–3 in. long, 1–3 times longer than wide, grayish
green, non-hairy, with whitish bloom beneath, tips
pointed or rounded. **FLOWERS** plants male or female,
flowers in catkins, blooming as the leaves unfold. Catkins often longer than 1 in., stamens 2, ovary hairy,
styles to 0.08 in. long, reddish to purple, catkin scales
brown to black, long-hairy. **FRUIT** cap-
sule, club- or pear-shaped, hairy.
ECOLOGY grows in meadows, open
slopes, and ridges, subalpine to alpine
areas, circumpolar. The similar *S. casca-
densis* has smaller, narrower leaves and
catkins mostly shorter than 1 in.

Salix barclayi
SALICACEAE
BARCLAY'S WILLOW

Native, common, blooms late spring–
mid summer, 3–10 ft. Bog/fen/wetland,
streambanks, meadows, west-side forest,
alpine, subalpine, mid to high elevation

Shrub, branches erect, twigs yellowish green to reddish brown, hairy or not. **LEAVES** deciduous, alternate,
blade oval to egg-shaped, 1–3 in. long, 1.5–3 times
longer than wide, with whitish bloom below, shiny
green with hairy midrib above, otherwise hairy or not,
edges toothed, tips pointed. **FLOWERS** plants male or
female, flowers in catkins, blooming as or after the
leaves unfold. Catkins 0.5–3 in. long, stamens 2, non-
hairy, ovary smooth, style to 0.1 in. long,
catkin scales dark brown or blackish,
long-hairy. **FRUIT** capsule, club- or pear-
shaped, non-hairy. **ECOLOGY** grows
along streams and lakes, in wet meadows and fens, slopes, and forest openings, montane to alpine areas.

Salix bebbiana
SALICACEAE
BEBB WILLOW
Native, common, blooms mid spring, 2–33 ft. Bog/fen/wetland, streambanks, east-side forest, low to mid elevation

Shrub or small tree, bark grayish brown, furrowed, twigs yellowish green or reddish brown, hairy, lacks whitish bloom. **LEAVES** deciduous, alternate, blade lance- to egg-shaped, 1.5–3 in. long, 2–3 times longer than wide, with whitish bloom beneath, dull green above, both surfaces hairy or not, edges smooth, wavy or toothed, tips mostly pointed. **FLOWERS** plants male or female, flowers in catkins, blooming before or as the leaves unfold. Catkins 0.5–2 in. long, stamens 2, ovary hairy, style to 0.02 in. long, catkin scales yellowish to brown, hairy. **FRUIT** capsule, pear-shaped, short-hairy. **ECOLOGY** grows in moist forests, shrub thickets, swamps, and along streams and lakes. Rare in California.

Salix boothii
SALICACEAE
BOOTH'S WILLOW
Native, scattered, blooms mid spring–mid
summer, 1–20 ft. Bog/fen/wetland, lake/pond,
meadows, subalpine, mid to high elevation

Shrub, erect, not colony-forming, twigs yellowish,
grayish, or reddish brown, hairy or not. **LEAVES** deciduous, alternate, stipules leaflike, blade oval, 1–4 in.
long, 2.5–5 times longer than wide, green beneath,
glossy green above, both surfaces hairy or not, edges
smooth, wavy, or toothed, tips pointed. **FLOWERS** plants
male or female, flowers in catkins, blooming right
before or as leaves unfold. Catkins 0.5–2.5 in. long,
stamens 2, hairy, ovary smooth, style to
0.06 in. long, catkin scales brown, hairy.
FRUIT capsule, pear-shaped, non-hairy.
ECOLOGY grows in meadows, seepages
and along streams and lakes in montane to subalpine areas. Rare in British
Columbia. Some authorities include *S.
myrtillifolia* within Booth's willow.

Salix brachycarpa
SALICACEAE
SHORTFRUIT WILLOW
Native, locally common, blooms mid summer,
0.7–5 ft. Bog/fen/wetland, streambanks,
meadows, subalpine, mid to high elevation
Shrub, erect, twigs reddish to dark brown, hairy.
LEAVES deciduous, alternate, stalk to 0.1 in. long, blade
oval to egg-shaped, 0.5–1 in. long, about 3 times longer than wide, with whitish bloom and hairy beneath,
shiny above, hairy or not, edges smooth, tips rounded
or pointed. **FLOWERS** plants male or female, flowers
in catkins, blooming as the leaves unfold. Catkins
0.2–1 in. long, stamens 2, ovary hairy, style longer
than stigmas, to 0.06 in. long, catkin
scales brown, hairy. **FRUIT** capsule, pear-
shaped, hairy. **ECOLOGY** grows in forests, meadows, rocky slopes, and floodplains in montane to subalpine areas.
Salt tolerant. The similar *S. glauca* has
longer leaf stalks, to 0.5 in., and longer
catkins. Rare in Oregon.

Salix breweri
SALICACEAE
BREWER'S WILLOW
Native, locally common, blooms early spring, 3–13
ft. Streambanks, serpentine, mid elevation
Shrub, branches reddish or yellowish brown, lacking a
whitish bloom, twigs yellowish, densely hairy.
LEAVES deciduous, alternate, blade oval to lance-
shaped, 2.5–5.5 in. long, 3–7 times longer than wide,
whitish and hairy beneath, hairs tangled, hairy above,
edges smooth, toothed, or wavy, somewhat rolled
under, tips mostly pointed. **FLOWERS** plants male or
female, flowers in catkins, blooming before the leaves
unfold. Catkins 0.5–2.5 in. long, stamens 2, non-hairy,
ovary hairy, style to 0.03 in. long, catkin
scales tan to pinkish, hairy.
FRUIT capsule, pear-shaped, hairy.
ECOLOGY grows only on serpentine,
in rocky areas and along streambanks
in mountainous areas. The similar *S.
delnortensis* has leaves 1–3 times longer than wide and brown catkin scales.
Endemic to California.

Salix candida
SALICACEAE
SAGELEAF WILLOW
Native, locally common, blooms late spring–
early summer, 1–3 ft. Bog/fen/wetland,
streambanks, meadows, low to high elevation
Shrub, erect, sometimes forming thickets by layer-
ing, branches grayish or yellowish brown, variably
hairy, twigs densely woolly-hairy. **LEAVES** deciduous,
alternate, lance-shaped, 2–4 in. long, 3.5–10 times longer than wide, dark green and somewhat hairy above,
densely woolly-hairy below, edges smooth, rolled
under, tips pointed. **FLOWERS** plants male or female,
flowers in catkins, blooming as the leaves unfold. Catkins 1–2.5 in. long, stamens 2, ovary
hairy, styles to 0.08 in. long, catkin
scales brown or tan, long-hairy.
FRUIT capsule, pear-shaped, hairy.
ECOLOGY grows in floodplains, bogs,
shorelines, shrub thickets, and meadows, restricted to calcium-rich soils.
Rare in Washington.

Salix cascadensis
SALICACEAE
CASCADE WILLOW

Native, locally common, blooms mid summer, 0.5–4
in. Meadows, alpine, subalpine, high elevation
Dwarf shrub, rhizomatous, mat-forming, stems erect
or trailing, twigs yellowish brown to grayish brown,
hairy or not. **LEAVES** mostly deciduous, some persisting >1 year, alternate, blade oval, 0.5–1 in. long,
3–5 times longer than wide, hairy becoming mostly
non-hairy, usually with whitish bloom beneath, tips
pointed. **FLOWERS** plants male or female, flowers in
catkins, blooming as the leaves emerge. Catkins 0.5–1
in. long, stamens 2, ovary hairy, styles to 0.04 in. long,
catkin scales brown,
long-hairy. **FRUIT** capsule, stalked, pear-
shaped, mostly densely
hairy, rarely non-hairy.
ECOLOGY grows in
meadows, on rocky
slopes, and ridges, sub-
alpine to alpine areas.

Salix columbiana
(*Salix exigua* var. *columbiana*, *Salix fluviatilis*)
SALICACEAE
COLUMBIA RIVER WILLOW

Native, locally common, blooms late spring–mid
summer, 7–22 ft. Streambanks, low elevation
Shrub, erect, colony-forming, branches reddish brown
with a whitish bloom, twigs yellow or reddish brown,
hairy or not. **LEAVES** deciduous, alternate, blade linear,
oval, or lance-shaped, 2–4.5 in. long, 6–13 times longer than wide, young leaves silvery hairy, becoming
greenish and sparsely hairy, whitish beneath, edges
toothed or wavy, sometimes rolled under, tips pointed.
FLOWERS plants male or female, flowers in catkins,
blooming after the leaves unfold. Cat-
kins 1–3.5 in. long, stamens 2, hairy,
ovary hairy, style minute, catkin scales
yellow, hairy. **FRUIT** capsule, pear-
shaped, hairy. **ECOLOGY** grows along
streams, on sand dunes, and gravelly
floodplains along the Columbia and
some of its tributaries.

Salix commutata

SALICACEAE

UNDERGREEN WILLOW, VARIABLE WILLOW

Native, common, blooms late spring,
0.7–10 ft. Lake/pond, streambanks, alpine,
subalpine, mid to high elevation

Shrub, erect, twigs yellowish to reddish brown, densely hairy. **LEAVES** deciduous, alternate, stipules leafy, blade oval, 0.5–4 in. long, 1.5–3.5 times longer than wide, densely hairy, less so with age, lacks whitish bloom beneath, edges smooth or toothed, tips pointed to rounded. **FLOWERS** plants male or female, flowers in catkins, blooming as or after the leaves unfold. Catkins 0.5–2.5 in. long, stamens 2, non-hairy, ovary non-hairy, styles to 0.06 in. long, catkin scales tan or brown, hairy. **FRUIT** capsule, club- or pear-shaped, sparsely hairy or smooth, often reddish. **ECOLOGY** grows on gravelly streambanks, floodplains, lakeshores, wetlands, and rocky slopes, montane to alpine areas. The similar *S. barclayi* has leaves with a whitish bloom beneath.

Salix delnortensis

SALICACEAE

DEL NORTE WILLOW

Native, uncommon, blooms early–mid spring,
3–7 ft. Streambanks, serpentine, low elevation

Shrub, sometimes forming thickets by rooting stems, branches reddish brown, lacking a whitish bloom, twigs yellowish to reddish brown, velvety hairy. **LEAVES** deciduous, alternate, blade oval to egg-shaped, 2–4 in. long, 1–3 times longer than wide, whitish and tangled hairy beneath, hairy above, edges smooth or wavy, somewhat rolled under, tips rounded or pointed. **FLOWERS** plants male or female, flowers in catkins, blooming before the leaves unfold. Catkins 0.5–2 in. long, stamens 2, non-hairy, anthers purple becoming yellow, ovary hairy, style longer than stigmas, catkin scales brown. **FRUIT** capsule, top-shaped, hairy. **ECOLOGY** grows only in rocky, serpentine streambanks. The similar *S. breweri* has leaves 3–7 times longer than wide, yellow anthers, and tan to pinkish catkin scales. Rare in Oregon.

Salix discolor

SALICACEAE

PUSSY WILLOW

Native, common, blooms early spring, 7–20 ft. Bog/fen/wetland, streambanks, east-side forest, low to mid elevation

Shrub or tree, erect, usually not clump-forming, bark furrowed, twigs yellowish to reddish brown, hairy or not. **LEAVES** deciduous, alternate, oval to egg-shaped, 1–5.5 in. long, 2–5 times longer than wide, surfaces hairy or not, sometimes whitish waxy below, edges smooth or toothed, tips pointed. **FLOWERS** plants male or female, flowers in catkins, blooming before the leaves unfold. Catkins 1–4.5 in. long, stamens 2, ovary hairy, style to 0.04 in. long, catkin scales brown to black, sometimes both colors, long-hairy. **FRUIT** capsule, pear-shaped with long neck, hairy. **ECOLOGY** shade intolerant, grows in peaty, poorly drained soils in bogs, streambanks, marsh edges, swamps, moist forests, and disturbed habitats. Bracts covering catkin buds are densely covered with long silky hairs, hence the common name.

Salix drummondiana

SALICACEAE

DRUMMOND'S WILLOW

Native, common, blooms mid spring–mid summer, 3–17 ft. Lake/pond, streambanks, meadows, subalpine, mid to high elevation

Shrub, erect, not colony-forming, branches with whitish bloom, twigs hairy or not, with whitish bloom. **LEAVES** deciduous, alternate, blade oval to lance-shaped, 1.5–3.5 in. long, 3–6 times longer than wide, densely hairy and whitish beneath, dark green and sparsely hairy above, edges rolled under, tips pointed. **FLOWERS** plants male or female, flowers in catkins, blooming before the leaves unfold. Catkins 1–3.5 in. long, stamens 2, ovary hairy, styles to 0.06 in. long, catkin scales brown or black. **FRUIT** capsule, pear-shaped, hairy. **ECOLOGY** grows along streams and lakes, meadows, forests, and open slopes in montane to subalpine areas. The similar *S. geyeriana* has leaves that are densely hairy above with flat edges; *S. sitchensis* branches lack a whitish bloom, stamen 1. Rare in Oregon.

Salix eastwoodiae
SALICACEAE
MOUNTAIN WILLOW, SIERRA WILLOW
Native, common, blooms mid spring–mid summer, 2–13 ft. Bog/fen/wetland, lake/pond, streambanks, meadows, alpine, subalpine, high elevation
Shrub, branches and twigs yellowish, reddish or purplish brown, long-hairy, whitish bloom present or not. **LEAVES** deciduous, alternate, blade oval to lance-shaped, 1–2.5 in. long, 2–3 times longer than wide, both sides greenish and wavy-hairy, without whitish bloom beneath, edges rolled under or not, toothed or not, tips mostly pointed. **FLOWERS** plants male or female, flowers in catkins, blooming as the leaves unfold. Catkins 0.5–2 in. long, stamens 2, hairy or not, ovary hairy, styles to 0.06 in. long, catkin scales brown or black, hairy. **FRUIT** capsule, pear-shaped, hairy, less so with age. **ECOLOGY** grows in bogs, along streams and lakes, meadows, and rocky slopes in subalpine to alpine areas.

Salix exigua
SALICACEAE
COYOTE WILLOW, NARROW-LEAF WILLOW
Native, common, blooms mid spring, 2–17 ft. Streambanks, low to mid elevation
Shrub, rarely small tree, rhizomatous, thicket-forming, stems slender, erect, twigs yellowish to reddish brown, hairy, less so with age. **LEAVES** deciduous, alternate, blade linear to strap-shaped, 1.2–6 in. long, 5–20 times longer than wide, grayish green, densely hairy with whitish bloom beneath, glossy and hairy or not above, edges smooth, tips pointed. **FLOWERS** plants male or female, flowers in catkins, blooming as or after leaves unfold. Catkins 0.3–3 in. long, stamens 2, hairy, ovary hairy or not, styles absent or very short, catkin scales yellowish, hairy. **FRUIT** capsule, pear- or club-shaped, hairy or not. **ECOLOGY** shade intolerant, grows along streambanks and in floodplains, often where sandy or gravelly.

Salix farriae
SALICACEAE
FARR'S WILLOW

Native, scattered, blooms late spring–early summer,
1–3 ft. Bog/fen/wetland, lake/pond, streambanks,
meadows, subalpine, mid to high elevation

Shrub, erect, not colony-forming, twigs yellowish to
reddish brown, sparsely or non-hairy. **LEAVES** deciduous, alternate, oval to egg-shaped, 1–2.5 in. long, 2–4
times longer than wide, surfaces mostly non-hairy
with some tiny, rust-colored hairs, a white waxy coating below, edges smooth to toothed, tips pointed or
rounded. **FLOWERS** plants male or female, flowers in
catkins, blooming as or after the leaves unfold. Catkins 1–1.5 in. long, stamens 2, ovary
smooth, style to 0.05 in. long, catkin
scales brown to blackish, non-hairy to
long-hairy. **FRUIT** capsule, pear-shaped,
non-hairy. **ECOLOGY** grows in streambanks, wet meadows, and lakeshores in
montane to subalpine areas. The similar *S. barclayi* lacks rust-colored hairs on
the leaves and has leaf edges uniformly
toothed. Rare in Oregon.

Salix ×fragilis
SALICACEAE
CRACK WILLOW

Non-native, scattered, blooms mid spring–
mid summer, 30–60 ft. Streambanks,
disturbed, low to mid elevation

Tree, crown rounded, bark dark gray, with network of
ridges, branches ascending, twigs greenish brown,
brittle at the base, becoming non-hairy with age.
LEAVES deciduous, alternate, stalks with glands, lance-
shaped, 3–7 in. long, shiny dark green above, paler
grayish green below, non-hairy, edges toothed, tips
pointed. **FLOWERS** plants male or female, flowers in
catkins. Male catkins 1–2 in. long, stamens 2, anthers
yellow, filaments hairy or not, catkin
scales yellow, hairy, female catkins to
4 in. long, catkin scales green, hairy.
FRUIT capsule, slenderly pear-shaped,
white woolly-hairy. **ECOLOGY** European
import, grows along streambanks and
in moist, disturbed areas. Shade intolerant, fast growing, often planted for erosion control.

Salix geyeriana
SALICACEAE
GEYER WILLOW

Native, common, blooms mid spring, 2–17 ft.
Bog/fen/wetland, lake/pond, streambanks,
meadows, subalpine, low to high elevation

Shrub, erect, not colony-forming, branches yellow-ish, grayish brown, or purplish, with whitish bloom, twigs slender, hairy or not. **LEAVES** deciduous, alternate, blade oval to lance-shaped, 1.5–3.5 in. long, 4–7 times longer than wide, whitish beneath, glossy green above, both sides hairy, edges smooth or toothed, tips pointed. **FLOWERS** plants male or female, flowers in catkins, blooming as the leaves unfold. Catkins 0.3–1 in. long, stamens 2, hairy, ovary hairy, styles to 0.01 in. long, catkin scales yellowish or brown. **FRUIT** capsule, hairy. **ECOLOGY** grows along streams and lakes, in wet meadows and swamps, from lowland to subalpine areas. The similar *S. drummondiana* has rolled-under leaf margins, longer catkins, and blooms before the leaves emerge.

Salix glauca
SALICACEAE
GRAYLEAF WILLOW

Native, rare, blooms mid summer, 1–7 ft.
Bog/fen/wetland, streambanks, meadows,
alpine, subalpine, mid to high elevation

Shrub, not colony-forming, stems erect or trailing, twigs mostly reddish or grayish brown, hairy, whitish bloom absent. **LEAVES** deciduous, alternate, blade oval, egg-, or lance-shaped, 1–3 in. long, 2–4 times longer than wide, whitish beneath, both sides hairy, less so with age, edges rolled under or not, smooth, tips pointed or rounded. **FLOWERS** plants male or female, flowers in catkins, blooming as the leaves emerge. Catkins 0.5–3 in. long, stamens 2, hairy or not, ovary hairy, styles to 0.06 in. long, catkin scales mostly brown, hairy. **FRUIT** capsule, stalked, club- or pear-shaped, hairy. **ECOLOGY** grows in shrub thickets, along streams, in swamps and fens, as well as on open slopes from montane to alpine areas. Common in British Columbia.

Salix gooddingii
SALICACEAE
GOODDING'S WILLOW, GOODDING'S BLACK
WILLOW

Native, common, blooms early–mid
spring, 20–60 ft. Bog/fen/wetland,
streambanks, meadows, low elevation

Tree, crown spreading, bark dark grayish brown to
blackish, scaly and ridged, twigs yellowish to reddish
brown, hairy, becoming non-hairy with age.

LEAVES deciduous, alternate, stalks with glands, linear
to oval, 2.5–5 in. long, many times longer than wide,
white-hairy when young becoming short-hairy below
with age, green above, lacks waxy coating below, edges
finely toothed, tips pointed.

FLOWERS plants male or female, flowers in catkins, blooming as the leaves
unfold. Male catkins 1–3 in. long, stamens 4–6, female catkins 1.5–3 in.
long, ovary hairy or not, stalked, catkin
scales tan. **FRUIT** capsule, pear-shaped.
ECOLOGY grows in streambanks, seeps,
marshes, meadows, and other moist
places, tolerates alkaline soils.

Salix hookeriana
SALICACEAE
COAST WILLOW, HOOKER'S WILLOW, DUNE
WILLOW

Native, common, blooms mid spring, 2–27 ft.
Coastal, bog/fen/wetland, low elevation

Shrub or tree, branches erect, twigs densely hairy,
less so with age. **LEAVES** deciduous, alternate, blade
oval to egg-shaped, 1.5–5 in. long, 1.5–4 times longer than wide, shiny green, hairy or not above, hairy
with whitish bloom beneath, edges mostly smooth but
sometimes wavy or toothed, tips rounded or pointed.

FLOWERS plants male or female, flowers in catkins, blooming before leaves
unfold. Catkins 1–3.5 in. long, stamens
2, styles to 0.1 in. long, longer than stigmas, catkin scales brown to blackish.
FRUIT capsule, pear- or club-shaped,
hairy or not. **ECOLOGY** shade intolerant, primarily coastal, in interdunal wet
areas, beach edges, along bluffs.

Salix jepsonii
SALICACEAE
JEPSON'S WILLOW

Native, locally common, blooms late spring–early summer, 3–10 ft. Bog/fen/wetland, lake/pond, meadows, subalpine, mid to high elevation Shrub, erect, sometimes thicket-forming, branches yellowish to reddish brown, twigs gray to reddish brown, velvety hairy. **LEAVES** deciduous, alternate, lance-shaped, 2–4 in. long, 3–8 times longer than wide, dark green and sparsely hairy above, densely short-hairy below, edges mostly smooth, tips rounded. **FLOWERS** plants male or female, flowers in catkins, blooming as the leaves unfold. Catkins 0.5–2 in. long, stamen 1, ovary hairy, style to 0.02 in. long, catkin scales brown to tan, hairy. **FRUIT** capsule, pear-shaped, hairy. **ECOLOGY** grows in streambanks, lakeshores, and wet meadows.

Salix laevigata
SALICACEAE
RED WILLOW, POLISHED WILLOW

Native, common, blooms late winter–spring, 7–50 ft. Lake/pond, streambanks, low to mid elevation Tree, branches flexible or brittle at the base, twigs mostly reddish or yellowish brown, hairy or not. **LEAVES** deciduous, alternate, stalked, stipules leaf-like or absent, blade oval, egg-, or lance-shaped, 2–7.5 in. long, 3–9 times longer than wide, usually white-hairy below, glossy green and hairy or not above, edges smooth, wavy, or toothed, tips pointed or rounded. **FLOWERS** plants male or female, flowers in catkins, blooming before, as, or after the leaves unfold. Catkins 1–3 in. long, stamens 3–7, hairy, ovary smooth, style to 0.01 in. long, catkin scales tan, hairy. **FRUIT** capsule, stalked, club- or pear-shaped, to 0.2 in. long, smooth. **ECOLOGY** grows along streams and lakeshores, in seepage areas, and canyons, lowland to montane. Rare in Oregon.

Salix lasiandra (*Salix lucida* ssp. *lasiandra*)
SALICACEAE
PACIFIC WILLOW, CAUDATE WILLOW

Native, common, blooms mid spring, 3–40 ft. Bog/
fen/wetland, streambanks, low to mid elevation
Tree or shrub, erect, not clump-forming, bark dark
gray to dark brown, ridged when older, twigs brownish, hairy or not. **LEAVES** deciduous, alternate, lance-
shaped, 2–7 in. long, 3–10 times longer than wide,
glossy above, hairy or not, whitish bloom beneath, stomates only on underside, edges toothed, tips pointed.
FLOWERS plants male or female, flowers in catkins,
blooming as the leaves unfold. Catkins 1–4 in. long,
stamens 3–6, hairy, ovary non-hairy, styles to 0.03 in.
long, catkin scales yellow-
ish, hairy. **FRUIT** capsule,
stalked, pear-shaped, 0.2–
0.4 in. long, non-hairy.
ECOLOGY shade intolerant,
grows in streambanks,
shorelines, floodplains,
lowland to montane.

Salix lasiandra var. *caudata*
(*Salix lucida* ssp. *caudata*)
SALICACEAE
GREENLEAF WILLOW, WHIPLASH WILLOW

Native, common, blooms mid spring, 3–37 ft. Bog/
fen/wetland, streambanks, low to mid elevation
Tree or shrub, erect, not clump-forming, bark dark
gray to dark brown, ridged when older, twigs brownish, hairy or not. **LEAVES** deciduous, alternate, lance-
shaped, 2–7 in. long, 3–10 times longer than wide,
glossy above, hairy or not, whitish bloom absent below,
stomates on both surfaces, edges toothed, tips pointed.
FLOWERS plants male or female, flowers in catkins,
blooming as the leaves unfold. Catkins 1–4 in. long,
stamens 3–6, hairy, ovary non-hairy,
styles to 0.03 in. long, catkin scales yellowish, hairy. **FRUIT** capsule, stalked,
pear-shaped, 0.2–0.4 in. long, non-hairy.
ECOLOGY shade intolerant, grows in
streambanks, shorelines, floodplains,
lowland to montane.

Salix lasiolepis
SALICACEAE
ARROYO WILLOW

Native, common, blooms winter–mid spring, 5–33
ft. Coastal, streambanks, low to mid elevation
Shrub or small tree, twigs yellowish to reddish brown,
velvety hairy to nearly smooth. **LEAVES** firm to leathery,
alternate, stalked, stipules leafy or not, blade oblong
to lance-shaped, 1.4–5 in. long, 3–7 times longer than
wide, densely hairy to non-hairy, dark green above,
with whitish bloom below, tips pointed or rounded.
FLOWERS plants male or female, flowers in catkins,
blooming before the leaves unfold. Catkins 1–3.5 in.
long, stamens 2, styles to 0.02 in. long, catkin scales
blackish, hairy.

FRUIT capsule, pear-
shaped, 0.1–0.2
in. long, smooth.
ECOLOGY grows
along stream-
banks, coastal head-
lands, sand dunes,
low elevation to
mid-montane.

Salix lemmonii
SALICACEAE
LEMMON'S WILLOW

Native, common, blooms all spring, 3–13 ft.
Bog/fen/wetland, lake/pond, streambanks,
meadows, subalpine, mid to high elevation
Shrub, twigs reddish or yellowish brown, hairy or not,
with whitish bloom. **LEAVES** deciduous, alternate, blade
oval or strap-shaped, 1.5–4.5 in. long, 3.5–10 times
longer than wide, hairy with whitish bloom below,
glossy and sparsely hairy above, edges rolled under or
not, toothed or not, tips pointed. **FLOWERS** plants male
or female, flowers in catkins, blooming before or as the
leaves unfold. Catkins 0.5–2 in. long, stamens 2, hairy
or not, ovary hairy, styles to 0.04 in.
long, catkin scales brown, hairy.
FRUIT capsule, pear-shaped, hairy.
ECOLOGY grows along streams and
lakeshores, burned-over areas, and
wet meadows from montane to subalpine areas. The similar *S. geyeriana* has
shorter catkins and very short styles, to
0.01 in. long.

Salix ligulifolia
SALICACEAE
STRAPLEAF WILLOW
Native, locally common, blooms all spring,
3–27 ft. Streambanks, mid elevation
Shrub, twigs mostly yellowish green or brown, long-
hairy or not, lacks whitish bloom. **LEAVES** deciduous,
alternate, stipules leaflike, blade oval or strap-shaped,
2.5–5 in. long, 3–6 times longer than wide, hairy or
not with whitish bloom below, dull and sparsely hairy
or smooth above, edges finely toothed, tips pointed.
FLOWERS plants male or female, flowers in catkins,
blooming before or as the leaves emerge. Catkins 1–2
in. long, stamens 2, hairy or not, ovary smooth, styles
to 0.02 in. long, catkin scales brown,
hairy. **FRUIT** capsule, pear-shaped, non-
hairy. **ECOLOGY** grows along streams
and in floodplains in montane areas.
Hybridizes with *S. geyeriana*. Rare in
Oregon.

Salix lutea
(*Salix rigida* var. *watsonii*, *Salix eriocephala* var. *watsonii*)
SALICACEAE
YELLOW WILLOW
Native, locally common, blooms all spring, 10–23 ft.
Bog/fen/wetland, streambanks, mid to high elevation
Shrub or tree, branches and twigs mostly yellowish,
twigs sometimes hairy or with sparkling wax crystals.
LEAVES deciduous, alternate, stalked, stipules leafy or
not, blade lance-shaped, 1.5–3.5 in. long, 3–5.5 times
longer than wide, with whitish bloom below, both
sides hairy or not, edges smooth, toothed, or wavy, tips
pointed. **FLOWERS** plants male or female, flowers in
catkins, blooming as the leaves unfold. Catkins 0.5–2
in. long, stamens 2, non-hairy, styles
to 0.02 in. long, ovary smooth, catkin
scales brown. **FRUIT** capsule, egg- or
pear-shaped, non-hairy.
ECOLOGY streambanks, wet meadows,
slopes, and draws, lowland to montane.
The similar *S. prolixa* has tan to reddish
brown twigs with peeling bark.

Salix maccalliana
SALICACEAE
MACCALLA'S WILLOW
Native, locally common, blooms late spring–
mid summer, 3–17 ft. Bog/fen/wetland, lake/
pond, streambanks, mid elevation
Shrub, erect, not colony-forming, branches reddish
brown, twigs yellowish or reddish brown, hairy but
becoming non-hairy with age. **LEAVES** deciduous, alternate, leathery, stalks without glands, oblong to lance-
shaped, 1.5–3.5 in. long, glossy bright green above,
midrib yellowish, paler and hairy or not below, edges
mostly toothed, tips pointed. **FLOWERS** plants male
or female, flowers in catkins, blooming as the leaves
unfold. Male catkins 0.5–1.5 in. long, stamens 2,
anthers purple turning yellow, filaments hairy, female
catkins 1–2 in. long, ovary hairy, stalked, catkin scales
yellow to pale brown. **FRUIT** capsule, pear-shaped,
hairy. **ECOLOGY** grows in fens, bogs, lakeshores,
streambanks, and other wet places, often in peaty soils.
The similar *S. boothii* has thin leaves and non-hairy
ovaries and capsules. Rare in Washington.

Salix melanopsis
SALICACEAE
DUSKY WILLOW
Native, common, blooms mid spring–mid
summer, 3–13 ft. Streambanks, meadows,
subalpine, mid to high elevation
Shrub, erect, colony-forming, twigs mostly grayish or
reddish brown, hairy, less so with age. **LEAVES** deciduous, alternate, blade oval to lance-shaped, 1–5 in. long,
3.5–8 times longer than wide, whitish bloom present
or not below, glossy above, both sides hairy to almost
smooth, edges smooth or sharply toothed, tips pointed
or rounded. **FLOWERS** plants male or female, flowers in
catkins, blooming as or after the leaves unfold. Catkins
1–2.5 in. long, stamens 2, styles to 0.02
in. long, catkin scales tan. **FRUIT** capsule, club- or pear-shaped, non-hairy.
ECOLOGY pioneer species, grows in gravelly or rocky streambanks, floodplains,
and meadows, mostly montane to subalpine. Uncommon in British Columbia.

Salix monochroma
SALICACEAE
ONECOLOR WILLOW, ONE-COLORED WILLOW
Native, locally common, blooms all spring,
7–13 ft. Streambanks, low to mid elevation
Shrub, branches lacking whitish bloom, twigs mostly
dark reddish or yellowish brown, shiny, sparsely hairy
or smooth, sometimes with sparkling wax crystals.
LEAVES deciduous, alternate, stipules leaflike, blade
oval, 2.5–4 in. long, 2–3.5 times longer than wide, both
sides dark green, smooth below, dull and sometimes
hairy above, edges toothed, tips pointed.
FLOWERS plants male or female, flowers in catkins,
blooming before or as the leaves emerge. Catkins 1–3
in. long, stamens 2, non-hairy, ovary smooth, styles
to 0.02 in. long, catkin scales brown. **FRUIT** capsule,
stalked, pear-shaped, smooth. **ECOLOGY** grows along
streams on moist slopes, lowland to montane.

Salix myrtillifolia
SALICACEAE
BLUEBERRY WILLOW

Native, scattered, blooms mid spring–mid summer, 4–24 in. Bog/fen/wetland, lake/pond, streambanks, low to mid elevation

Shrub, erect to trailing, clump-forming, twigs yellowish, grayish, or reddish brown, sparsely hairy. **LEAVES** deciduous, alternate, oval to egg-shaped, 1–3 in. long, 1–4.5 times longer than wide, glossy green above, both surfaces non-hairy, edges scalloped, wavy or not, tips pointed or rounded. **FLOWERS** plants male or female, flowers in catkins, blooming as the leaves unfold. Catkins 0.5–2 in. long, stamens 2, ovary non-hairy, styles to 0.03 in. long, catkin scales tan, brown, or black, hairy or not. **FRUIT** capsule, pear-shaped, non-hairy. **ECOLOGY** grows on mossy streambanks, lakeshores, bogs, and forests. Some authorities include blueberry willow within *S. boothii*.

Salix nivalis
SALICACEAE
SNOW WILLOW

Native, rare, blooms mid summer, 0.4–1.5 in. Meadows, rocky sites, alpine, subalpine, high elevation

Dwarf shrub, mat-forming, twigs erect or trailing, yellowish to reddish brown, hairy or not. **LEAVES** deciduous, alternate, stalk sometimes glandular, stipules absent, oval to egg-shaped, 0.2–1 in. long, 1–3 times longer than wide, with whitish bloom beneath, hairy or not, glossy dark green and non-hairy above, edges rolled under, gland-dotted, tips rounded or pointed. **FLOWERS** plants male or female, flowers in catkins, blooming after the leaves unfold. Catkins 0.5–1 in. long, stamens 2, hairy or not, ovary hairy, styles to 0.02 in. long, catkin bracts tan or reddish, short-hairy. **FRUIT** capsule, top-shaped, hairy. **ECOLOGY** rocky slopes, ledges, and meadows in alpine areas. Locally common in British Columbia.

Salix pedicellaris
SALICACEAE
BOG WILLOW
Native, locally common, blooms mid
spring–mid summer, 0.7–5 ft. Bog/fen/
wetland, low to mid elevation

Shrub, colony-forming via rooting stems, stems erect
or trailing, sparingly branched, twigs yellowish brown
or reddish yellow, hairy or not. **LEAVES** deciduous,
alternate, blade oval to lance-shaped, 1–2.5 in. long,
2–5 times longer than wide, pale with whitish bloom
below, dull green above, both sides mostly smooth,
edges sometimes rolled under, smooth, tips pointed
or rounded. **FLOWERS** plants male or female, flowers in
catkins, blooming as the leaves emerge.
Catkins 0.5–1.5 in. long, stamens 2,
ovary smooth, reddish, styles to 0.01 in.
long, catkin scales yellowish to pinkish.
FRUIT capsule, club-shaped, smooth,
sometimes reddish, often with whitish bloom. **ECOLOGY** grows in bogs and
fens, lowland to montane.

Salix petrophila
SALICACEAE
ALPINE WILLOW
Native, locally common, blooms mid summer, 1–4
in. Meadows, alpine, subalpine, high elevation

Dwarf shrub, stems trailing, mat-forming, twigs yellowish, hairy or not. **LEAVES** deciduous, alternate, oval,
lance-, or egg-shaped, 1–2 in. long, 1.5–4.5 times longer than wide, surfaces variably hairy, edges smooth,
tips pointed or rounded. **FLOWERS** plants male or
female, flowers in catkins, blooming as the leaves
unfold. Catkins 1–3 in. long, stamens 2, ovary hairy,
style to 0.06 in. long, catkin scales tan to light brown,
hairy. **FRUIT** capsule, pear-shaped, hairy.
ECOLOGY grows on rocky slopes and
meadows in subalpine spruce-fir forests
to alpine areas.

Salix planifolia (*Salix phylicifolia* var. *planifolia*)
SALICACEAE
DIAMONDLEAF WILLOW, PLANE-LEAVED
WILLOW, TEA-LEAVED WILLOW
Native, common, blooms late spring, 0.3–13
ft. Bog/fen/wetland, lake/pond, streambanks,
meadows, subalpine, mid to high elevation

Shrub, stems erect or trailing, twigs mostly purplish, hairy or not, with whitish bloom or not. LEAVES deciduous, alternate, blade oval to lance-shaped, 1–2.5 in. long, 2–5 times longer than wide, whitish bloom below, glossy green above, both sides hairy or not, edges toothed or smooth, tips pointed or rounded. FLOWERS plants male or female, flowers in catkins, blooming before the leaves unfold. Catkins 0.5–3 in. long, stamens 2, non-hairy, ovary hairy, styles to 0.08 in. long, catkin scales brown to black. FRUIT capsule, pear-shaped, hairy. ECOLOGY grows in meadows, forest openings, swamps, along streams, lakes, and other moist places, from montane to subalpine areas.

Salix prolixa (*Salix rigida* var. *mackenzieana*)
SALICACEAE
MACKENZIE'S WILLOW
Native, common, blooms early spring, 3–17 ft. Bog/
fen/wetland, streambanks, low to mid elevation

Shrub or small tree, branches gray to reddish brown, twigs yellowish green to reddish brown, hairy or not. LEAVES deciduous, alternate, stipules leafy, blade oval, lance-, or egg-shaped, 2–6 in. long, 2.5–5 times longer than wide, with whitish bloom and non-hairy below, dull above, hairy or not, edges toothed, tips pointed. FLOWERS plants male or female, flowers in catkins, blooming as the leaves unfold. Catkins 0.5–2.5 in. long, stamens 2, ovary smooth, styles to 0.03

in. long, catkin scales brown. FRUIT capsule, pear-shaped, non-hairy. ECOLOGY riverbanks, lakeshores, wetland margins, and forest openings, lowland to montane. Prefers sandy or gravelly substrates.

Salix pseudomonticola
SALICACEAE
FALSE MOUNTAIN WILLOW
Native, scattered, blooms early–mid spring, 3–20 ft.
Bog/fen/wetland, subalpine, mid to high elevation
Shrub, erect, not clump-forming, branches lack waxy
coating, twigs yellowish green to reddish brown, hairy
or not. **LEAVES** deciduous, alternate, oval to egg-shaped,
1–4 in. long, 1.5–3 times longer than wide, hairy on
midvein above, surfaces otherwise hairy or not, edges
toothed or not, tips pointed. **FLOWERS** plants male or
female, flowers in catkins, blooms before the leaves
unfold. Catkins 0.5–3 in. long, stamens 2, ovary non-
hairy, style to 0.07 in. long, catkin scales brown to
blackish, long-hairy.
FRUIT capsule, pear-shaped,
non-hairy. **ECOLOGY** grows
in bogs, fens, shrub thickets,
and spruce-fir forest openings and edges, montane to
subalpine elevation. Rare in
Washington.

Salix pseudomyrsinites
SALICACEAE
TALL BLUEBERRY WILLOW, FIRMLEAF WILLOW
Native, scattered, blooms mid spring–mid
summer, 3–23 ft. Bog/fen/wetland, lake/
pond, streambanks, low to mid elevation
Shrub, erect, not clump-forming, twigs yellowish to
reddish brown, hairy. **LEAVES** deciduous, alternate,
oblong, oval, or egg-shaped, 1–4.5 in. long, 2–5 times
longer than wide, surfaces usually hairy, edges toothed
or not, tips pointed or rounded. **FLOWERS** plants male
or female, flowers in catkins, blooming as the leaves
unfold. Catkins 1–3 in. long, stamens 2, ovary non-
hairy, styles to 0.06 in. long, catkin scales tan, brown,
or black, hairy or not. **FRUIT** capsule,
pear-shaped, non-hairy. **ECOLOGY** grows
in forests, lakeshores, streambanks, and
shrub thickets. The similar *S. myrtillifolia* is shorter, with non-hairy leaves
and shorter styles, and can grow in drier
habitats.

Salix scouleriana
SALICACEAE
SCOULER'S WILLOW
Native, common, blooms winter–early spring, 3–40 ft. Lake/pond, streambanks, west-side forest, east-side forest, low to mid elevation

Shrub or tree, bark brown, twigs hairy, yellowish when young. **LEAVES** deciduous, alternate, blade oval, lance-, or reverse egg-shaped, 1.2–4 in. long, 2–4 times longer than wide, with whitish bloom below, glossy with hairy midrib above, both sides less hairy with age, edges rolled under or not, tips pointed or rounded. **FLOWERS** plants male or female, flowers in catkins, blooming before leaves unfold. Catkins 1–2.5 in. long,

stamens 2, hairy or not, styles to 0.02 in. long, stigmas longer than style, catkin scales brown or blackish. **FRUIT** capsule, pear-shaped, hairy. **ECOLOGY** shade intolerant, grows on streambanks, forest openings, lakeshores, and disturbed areas in lowland, steppe, and montane areas. The similar *S. sitchensis* has solitary stamen and shiny hair on leaf bottoms.

Salix ×sepulcralis
SALICACEAE
WEEPING WILLOW
Non-native, locally common, blooms all spring, to 40 ft. Streambanks, disturbed, low to mid elevation

Tree, stems, branches, and twigs drooping, yellow or yellowish green, becoming yellowish brown with age, branches brittle at the base. **LEAVES** deciduous, alternate, stalked, stipules leafy or absent, blade oval or lance-shaped, 4–8 in. long, both sides with whitish bloom and sparsely long-hairy to non-hairy, glossy above, edges toothed, tips pointed. **FLOWERS** plants usually either male or female, blooming as the leaves unfold. Flowers in catkins, male catkins 1–2 in. long,

stamens 2, female catkins about 1 in. long, styles to 0.08 in. long. **FRUIT** capsule, stalked, 0.04–0.08 in. long. **ECOLOGY** grows along riverbanks, disturbed areas, wet or dry places, lowland to montane. Hybrid between *S. babylonica* and *S. alba*. Cultivar 'Chrysocoma' has catkins with both male and female flowers.

Salix sessilifolia
SALICACEAE
NORTHWEST SANDBAR WILLOW, SOFT-LEAVED
WILLOW

Native, locally common, blooms late spring–mid
summer, 10–17 ft. Streambanks, low elevation
Shrub, stems erect, colony-forming, twigs reddish
brown, densely long-hairy. **LEAVES** deciduous, alternate, blade linear, oval, or lance-shaped, 1–4 in. long,
3–7 times longer than wide, hairy without whitish
bloom below, dull green and sparsely long-hairy above,
edges smooth or toothed, tips pointed. **FLOWERS** plants
male or female, flowers in catkins, blooming as or
after the leaves unfold. Catkins 1–3 in. long, stamens
2, styles to 0.03 in. long, stigmas to 0.04 in. long, catkin scales yellow, sometimes brown. **FRUIT** capsule,
pear-shaped, hairy. **ECOLOGY** grows on sandbars, along
streams or in floodplains. The similar *S. melanopsis*
and *S. exigua* have shorter styles and stigmas; *S. melanopsis* grows in montane to subalpine areas. Rare in
Washington.

Salix sitchensis
SALICACEAE
SITKA WILLOW

Native, common, blooms early spring, 3–27 ft. Bog/fen/
wetland, lake/pond, streambanks, low to high elevation
Shrub or tree, bark gray to brown, branches mostly
brittle, twigs yellowish to reddish brown, densely
hairy. **LEAVES** deciduous, alternate, lance- to egg-
shaped, 1–3 in. long, 2–4 times longer than wide,
green and sparsely hairy above, densely satiny-hairy
below, edges smooth, tips pointed. **FLOWERS** plants
male or female, flowers in catkins, blooms before or as
the leaves unfold. Catkins 1–3 in. long, stamen 1, ovary
hairy, style 0.03 in. long, catkin scales light to dark
brown, long-hairy. **FRUIT** capsule, pear-
to egg-shaped, densely satiny-hairy.
ECOLOGY shade intolerant, grows in
open areas in moist to wet forests, floodplains, along streams and lakes, and in
disturbed areas. The similar *S. bebbiana*
has more pronounced pointy leaf tips; *S.
scouleriana* lacks satiny hair on leaf bottoms, prefers drier habitats.

Salix tracyi
SALICACEAE
TRACY'S WILLOW
Native, locally common, blooms mid spring, 3–20 ft. Lake/pond, streambanks, serpentine, west-side forest, low elevation
Shrub, multi-stemmed, twigs brown, reddish, or yellowish, velvety hairy, less so with age. **LEAVES** deciduous, alternate, oval to strap-shaped, 2–4 in. long, 2–4 times longer than wide, hairy or not and glossy above, mostly white or white/rusty hairy below, edges smooth, wavy, or toothed, often rolled under, tips pointed. **FLOWERS** plants male or female, flowers in catkins, blooming right before or as the leaves unfold. Male catkins 0.7–1 in. long, stamens 2, anthers purple turning yellow, female catkins 0.7–1.7 in. long, ovary smooth, catkin scales all brown or bicolor, hairy below. **FRUIT** capsule, pear-shaped, smooth. **ECOLOGY** grows along lakeshores, streambanks, and in floodplains, in sandy or rocky soils, often in serpentine, at low elevation.

Salix vestita
SALICACEAE
ROCK WILLOW, FALSE MOUNTAIN WILLOW
Native, scattered, blooms mid summer, 1–5 ft. Streambanks, meadows, subalpine, high elevation
Shrub, erect, not clump-forming, twigs yellowish to grayish brown, hairy. **LEAVES** deciduous, alternate, roundish to egg-shaped, 1–3 in. long, 1–2.5 times longer than wide, leathery, shiny, hairy or not above, hairy or not and sometimes waxy below, edges toothed or not, tips rounded or notched. **FLOWERS** plants male or female, flowers in catkins, blooming as or after the leaves unfold. Catkins 0.5–2 in. long, stamens 2, ovary hairy, style to 0.02 in. long, catkin scales tan, densely long-hairy. **FRUIT** capsule, pear-shaped, hairy. **ECOLOGY** grows in open forests, wet meadows, and rocky streambanks, at higher but rarely alpine elevations. Rare in Washington.

Salix wolfii
SALICACEAE
WOLF'S WILLOW, IDAHO WILLOW
Native, rare, blooms late spring, 2–7 ft. Bog/fen/
wetland, streambanks, subalpine, high elevation
Shrub, erect, much-branched, twigs yellowish green
to reddish brown, hairy. **LEAVES** deciduous, alternate,
oval to lance-shaped, 1–2 in. long, 3–4.5 times longer
than wide, surfaces hairy, usually grayish-hairy below,
edges smooth, tips pointed.

FLOWERS plants male or female, flowers in catkins, blooming as the leaves
unfold. Catkins 0.5–1.5 in. long, stamens 2, ovary hairy or not, styles to 0.04
in. long, catkin scales brown to blackish, long-hairy. **FRUIT** capsule, pear-
shaped, hairy or not. **ECOLOGY** grows in
bogs, wet meadows, and streambanks at
higher elevations.

Smilax californica
SMILACEAE
CALIFORNIA GREENBRIER
Native, locally common, blooms mid–late
spring, 7–17 ft. Streambanks, west-side forest,
east-side forest, low to mid elevation
Vine, stems often climbing, prickles flexible, to 0.5 in.
long, sometimes absent near stem ends. **LEAVES** evergreen, alternate, egg-shaped, 1.5–4.5 in. long, surfaces dull green, non-hairy, veins prominent, edges
smooth, tips pointed, tendrils mostly 2 per leaf stalk.
FLOWERS in drooping, rounded clusters at leaf axils,
unisexual, male and female flowers on the same plant,
green, tepals 6, 0.1–0.2 in. long. **FRUIT** berry, black,
egg-shaped to round. **ECOLOGY** grows
on streambanks and seeps in ponderosa pine and mixed evergreen forests,
in sun to partial shade, from low to mid
elevation.

Smilax jamesii
SMILACACEAE
ENGLISH PEAK GREENBRIER
Native, rare, blooms mid spring–mid summer, 7–10 ft. Streambanks, west-side forest, east-side forest, mid elevation

Vine, herbaceous, rhizomatous, stems annual, smooth, shiny, prickles absent. **LEAVES** deciduous, alternate, triangular to egg-shaped, 2–3 in. long, dark green above, whitish waxy below, edges smooth to wavy, tips pointed, tendrils many. **FLOWERS** in ball-like clusters in leaf axils, unisexual, male and female clusters on same plant, flowers green, tepals 6, to 0.1 in. long. **FRUIT** berry, egg-shaped, blue. **ECOLOGY** grows in streambanks, on shorelines, and in alder thickets in montane conifer forests. Endemic to California.

Solanum douglasii
SOLANACEAE
GREENSPOT NIGHTSHADE, DOUGLAS' NIGHTSHADE
Native, common, blooms all year, to 7 ft. Coastal, west-side forest, low to mid elevation

Subshrub, erect, much-branched, hairy, hairs curved. **LEAVES** deciduous, alternate, egg-shaped, 0.5–3.5 in. long, edges toothed, tips pointed. **FLOWERS** in flat-topped clusters, flowers saucer-shaped, lobes > tube, petals white, lavender-tinged, or lavender, 0.5 in. wide, stamens 0.1–0.15 in. long. **FRUIT** berry, black. **ECOLOGY** grows along the coast and in canyons, sagebrush communities, forests, and woodlands, in shade to partial shade conditions. All parts of plant toxic.

Solanum parishii
SOLANACEAE
PARISH'S NIGHTSHADE
Native, locally common, blooms mid spring–
mid summer, to 3.3 ft. Chaparral, west-side
forest, east-side forest, low to mid elevation
Subshrub, much-branched, stems ridged, sparsely
hairy to non-hairy. **LEAVES** deciduous, alternate, oval to
lance-shaped, 1–3 in. long, stalk absent, edges mostly
wavy, tips pointed. **FLOWERS** in loose, stalked clusters,
flowers saucer-shaped, petals mostly bluish purple
with a green and white eye, about 1 in. across, sepals
green, 0.2 in. long. **FRUIT** berry, green, to 0.5 in. long.
ECOLOGY grows in chaparral, pine-oak woodlands, and
pine forests. All parts of
plant toxic.

Solanum umbelliferum
SOLANACEAE
BLUEWITCH NIGHTSHADE
Native, locally common, blooms early spring–
mid summer, 12–35 in. Chaparral, west-side
forest, east-side forest, low to mid elevation
Shrub or subshrub, much-branched, hairy.
LEAVES deciduous, alternate, oval to egg-shaped,
0.5–1.5 in. long, edges wavy. **FLOWERS** in flat-topped
clusters, flowers saucer-shaped, petals blue to purple
with green eye, 0.5–1 in. wide. **FRUIT** berry, about 0.5
in. wide. **ECOLOGY** grows in mixed evergreen forests,
shrubfields, and chaparral from low to mid elevation.
All parts of plant toxic.

Solanum xanti
(*Solanum tenuilobatum*)
SOLANACEAE
CHAPARRAL NIGHTSHADE
Native, common, blooms late winter–spring,
16–36 in. Disturbed, chaparral, west-side forest,
east-side forest, low to high elevation
Subshrub, stems erect to trailing, much-branched,
hairy and glandular-hairy, hair unbranched.
LEAVES deciduous (drought), alternate, lance- to egg-
shaped, 1–3 in. long, surfaces hairy and glandular-hairy, edges smooth or wavy, tips pointed.
FLOWERS in flat-topped clusters in leaf axils, flowers
nodding, saucer-shaped, 0.5–1 in. across, lobes < tube,

petals blue to lavender (rarely white)
with green spots, stamen to 0.2 in. long.
FRUIT berry, round, 0.5 in. across, green,
drying brownish. **ECOLOGY** grows in
chaparral, oak woodlands, conifer forests, and disturbed areas. All parts of
plant toxic.

Styrax redivivus
(*Styrax officinalis* var. *redivivus*)
STYRACACEAE
CALIFORNIA SNOWDROP BUSH, STORAX,
DRUG SNOWBELL
Native, locally common, blooms all spring, 3–13 ft.
Chaparral, east-side forest, low to mid elevation
Shrub, stems stiff, dark grayish brown. **LEAVES** deciduous, alternate, roundish to egg-shaped, 1–3.5 in. long,
shiny green above, mostly grayish-hairy below, edges
smooth, tips rounded. **FLOWERS** single or in small
clusters at branch ends, flowers fragrant, bell-shaped,
white, sepal lobes 6–9, brownish yellow, different sizes,
petals 5- to 10-lobed, anthers bright yellow.

FRUIT capsule, 0.4–
0.6 in. long, tan,
hairy when mature.
ECOLOGY grows in
chaparral and pon-
derosa pine forests.
Endemic to California.

Tamarix parviflora
TAMARICACEAE
SMALLFLOWER TAMARISK
Non-native, common, blooms all spring, 7–13 ft.

Lake/pond, streambanks, disturbed, low elevation
Shrub or tree, branches slender, arching. **LEAVES** deciduous, alternate, small and scalelike, lance- to egg-
shaped, to 0.1 in. long, overlapping, edges smooth, tips
pointed. **FLOWERS** in numerous, narrow clusters produced on previous year's growth, flowers small, sepals
and petals 4, petals pink. **FRUIT** capsule,
0.15 in. long. **ECOLOGY** grows in streambanks, seeps, lakeshores, and other wet
areas in warm, dry habitats. Somewhat
tolerant of drought and tolerates saline
soils, excreting excess salt. Seeds are
short-lived. Resprouts from the root
crown after fire. Invasive.

Tamarix ramosissima
TAMARICACEAE
SALTCEDAR

Non-native, scattered, blooms mid spring–mid summer, 5–27 ft. Streambanks, disturbed, low elevation

Shrub or tree, erect to spreading, branches slender, arching. **LEAVES** deciduous, alternate, small and scale-like, lance-shaped, to 0.1 in. long, overlapping, surfaces grayish green, edges smooth, tips pointed.
FLOWERS in drooping, branched clusters, flowers small, sepals and petals 5, petals pink to purplish, sepal edges toothed, stamens 5. **FRUIT** capsule. **ECOLOGY** invasive Asian import, grows in streambanks, dry washes, and other wet areas in warm, dry habitats. Tolerates saline soils, excreting excess salt, forming crusts on the leaves. Leaves turn golden yellow. Resprouts from the root crown after fire.

Daphne laureola
THYMELAEACEAE
SPURGE LAUREL

Non-native, locally common, blooms late winter–early spring, 2–6 ft. Disturbed, west-side forest, low elevation

Shrub, many-stemmed, leaves arranged spirally around the stem. **LEAVES** evergreen, alternate, oval to lance-shaped, 1.5–5 in. long, surfaces glossy, dark green, edges smooth, tips pointed. **FLOWERS** clusters in leaf axils, flowers bisexual or female only, fragrant, bell-shaped, sepals pale green, petals absent.
FRUIT berry, 1-seeded, black, egg-shaped, to 0.5 in. across, toxic to humans. **ECOLOGY** invasive escapee from cultivation, shade tolerant, grows in disturbed areas and moist lowland forests. Fruit eaten and dispersed primarily by birds.

Ulmus americana
ULMACEAE
AMERICAN ELM

Non-native, scattered, blooms late winter–early spring,
70–117 ft. Streambanks, disturbed, low elevation

Tree, crown open, main branches arching, grace-
ful, bark gray, splitting into curved, diamond-shaped
ridges, branches lack warty growths, twigs brown,
hairy or not. **LEAVES** deciduous, alternate, oval to egg-
shaped, 3–5.5 in. long, green, hairy or not below, tufts
of hair in vein axils below, edges doubly toothed, tips
pointed. **FLOWERS** in small, drooping clusters, flowers
before the leaves unfold, bisexual, bell-shaped, greenish white, sepal lobes 7–9, lobe edges fringed, stamens
reddish, petals absent. **FRUIT** samara, egg-shaped,
yellowish white, sometimes reddish-tinged, edges
fringed. **ECOLOGY** grows in streambanks, shorelines,
valley bottoms, and disturbed areas, often spreading
by root suckers. Long-lived (up to 300 years) and fast
growing, this treasured eastern North American native
has been decimated by Dutch elm disease, a fungus
spread by bark beetles.

Ulmus procera (*Ulmus minor*)
ULMACEAE
ENGLISH ELM
Non-native, locally common, blooms early–mid spring, to 133 ft. Disturbed, low elevation

Tree, crown open, bark grayish brown, ridged, outer layers flaking, older branches with warty growths, twigs reddish brown, hairy. **LEAVES** deciduous, alternate, lance- to egg-shaped, 2–4.5 in. long, dark green above, paler and with tufts of hair in vein axils below, edges doubly toothed, tips pointed. **FLOWERS** in small clusters in leaf axils of old wood, flowers before the leaves unfold, bisexual, sepals united, with 5–8 shallow lobes, green, reddish purple, or tan, petals absent. **FRUIT** samara, heart-shaped, pale green to tan, tip notched, edges smooth except hairy near tip. **ECOLOGY** European import, grows in disturbed places, often near old plantings, spreads by root suckers.

Ulmus pumila

ULMACEAE

SIBERIAN ELM

Non-native, locally common, blooms late winter–spring, 25–100 ft. Streambanks, disturbed, low to mid elevation

Tree, crown open, bark gray to brown, furrowed, ridges interlaced, older branches lacking warty growths, twigs grayish brown, hairy or not. **LEAVES** deciduous, alternate, oval to lance-shaped, 1–2.5 in. long, dark green and non-hairy above, paler and with tufts of hair in vein axils below, edges singly toothed, tips pointed. **FLOWERS** in small clusters in leaf axils, flowers before the leaves unfold, bisexual, bell-shaped, sepals with 4–5 unequal lobes, greenish, petals absent. **FRUIT** samara, rounded, tan to whitish, tip notched, edges smooth. **ECOLOGY** Asian import, grows in streambanks, washes, roadsides, and other disturbed places.

Vitis californica
VITACEAE
CALIFORNIA WILD GRAPE, CALIFORNIA GRAPE
Native, locally common, blooms mid–late
spring, 7–67 ft. Streambanks, west-side forest,
east-side forest, low to mid elevation

Woody vine, stems hairy when young, less so with age.
LEAVES deciduous, alternate, roundish to heart-shaped,
2.5–5 in. long, surfaces hairy, edges 3- to 5-lobed or
not, toothed, tips mostly rounded. **FLOWERS** in clusters along stem opposite the leaves, flowers unisexual,
often on different plants, greenish yellow. **FRUIT** berry,
purple with whitish waxy coating, palatable.
ECOLOGY grows in riparian forests, shrub thickets,
along streambanks, and near seeps, from low to mid

elevation. Can damage trees if it gets
into the canopy. Used extensively in the
wine industry as rootstock.

See Vitaceae with compound leaves,
page 409

Viburnum edule
ADOXACEAE (CAPRIFOLIACEAE)
HIGHBUSH CRANBERRY, MOOSEBERRY
Native, locally common, blooms late spring–
mid summer, 1.5–8 ft. Bog/fen/wetland,
streambanks, meadows, west-side forest,
east-side forest, low to mid elevation
Shrub, erect, somewhat straggly, multi-stemmed,
rhizomatous, bark reddish to gray, twigs non-hairy.
LEAVES deciduous, opposite, mapleleaf-shaped, 1–4
in. long, hairy below, shallowly 3-lobed, edges sharply
toothed, tips pointed, fall color bright red.
FLOWERS in flat-topped clusters, stalked with 2 leaves
beneath, flowers all alike, funnel-shaped, petals white,
stamens shorter than floral tube.
FRUIT berrylike, roundish, orange to red,
palatable, tart. ECOLOGY grows in moist
forests, streambanks, and in swampy
areas, from lowland to mid-montane.

See Adoxaceae with compound leaves,
page 410

Viburnum ellipticum
ADOXACEAE (CAPRIFOLIACEAE)
OVAL-LEAVED VIBURNUM, WESTERN
VIBURNUM
Native, locally common, blooms mid–late spring, 3–10
ft. Chaparral, west-side forest, low to mid elevation
Shrub, erect, bark reddish or grayish brown, branches
slender, twigs warty, grayish green or reddish.
LEAVES deciduous, opposite, oval to roundish, 1–3 in.
long, shiny dark green above, paler and hairy below,
edges toothed, tips rounded. FLOWERS in flat-topped
clusters at stem ends, flowers bisexual, funnel-shaped,
whitish, petals and sepals 5, stamens showy, longer
than floral tube, odor unpleasant. FRUIT berrylike, oval,
red, becoming black with
age. ECOLOGY grows in
oak woodlands, pine for-
ests, and chaparral, from
low to mid elevation. Rare
in California.

Viburnum opulus var. *americanum*
(*Viburnum trilobum*)
ADOXACEAE (CAPRIFOLIACEAE)
AMERICANBUSH CRANBERRY
Native, scattered, blooms late spring–mid
summer, 3–13 ft. Streambanks, west-
side forest, low to mid elevation

Shrub or tree, multi-stemmed, bark smooth, gray, twigs tan to gray, non-hairy. **LEAVES** deciduous, opposite, stalk with linear bracts with blunt or glandular tips and several glandular hairs, taller than wide, duck-foot-shaped, 1.5–5 in. long, usually hairy below, deeply 3-lobed, edges toothed or not, tips pointed, fall color yellow to red-purple. **FLOWERS** in flat-topped clusters, stalked with 2 leaves below, flowers funnel-shaped, petals white, flowers on cluster edge larger and sterile, inner flowers fertile and smaller, stamens of fertile flowers extend beyond the petals. **FRUIT** berry, oval to roundish, reddish orange to red, palatable, tart. **ECOLOGY** grows in moist forests and streambanks, swamps and other wet habitats. Var. *opulus*, a commonly cultivated non-native, is distinguished by bracts on leaf stalks that are wider than tall, with pointed tips and glandular hairs. The similar *V. edule* has shallowly lobed leaves, lacks sterile flowers, and has stamens < petals.

Carpobrotus chilensis

(*Mesembryanthemum chilense*)

AIZOACEAE

SEA FIG

Non-native, locally common, blooms all
year, 6–12 in. Coastal, low elevation

Shrub, prostrate, mat-forming, bark gray, splits to
reveal dark brown inner bark, stems up to 7 ft. long.
LEAVES evergreen, succulent, opposite, triangular,
1.5–3 in. long, edges rounded, surfaces green with
a whitish waxy coating, edges smooth, tips pointed.
FLOWERS single at stem ends, asterlike, petals many,
purplish rose, to 2 in. across. **FRUIT** berrylike, fleshy,
oval to roundish, to 1 in. long, green to yellowish,
seeds many. **ECOLOGY** invasive African
import, grows on rocky bluffs, dunes,
salt marshes, beaches, and other coastal
habitats. Reproduces by seed and stem
fragmentation.

Carpobrotus edulis

AIZOACEAE

HOTTENTOT FIG

Non-native, locally common, blooms all
year, 6–12 in. Coastal, low elevation

Shrub, prostrate, mat-forming, bark leathery, stems up
to 10 ft. long. **LEAVES** evergreen, succulent, opposite,
triangular, 2–4.5 in. long, 3-angled, surfaces green,
whitish waxy coating absent, edges finely toothed, tips
pointed. **FLOWERS** single at stem ends, asterlike, petals
many, yellow, to 4 in. across. **FRUIT** berrylike, fleshy,
club-shaped to roundish, to 1.5 in. long, yellowish,
seeds many. **ECOLOGY** invasive African import, grows
on sand dunes, in estuary edges, beaches, and other
coastal habitats. Reproduces by seed and
stem fragmentation, hybridizes with *C.
chilensis*.

Draperia systyla
BORAGINACEAE
VIOLET DRAPERIA

Native, locally common, blooms late spring–
early summer, 4–16 in. Rocky sites, west-side
forest, east-side forest, low to high elevation
Subshrub, stems slender, erect or trailing, rooting at
the nodes. **LEAVES** deciduous, opposite, egg-shaped,
0.5–3 in. long, edges smooth, tips pointed. **FLOWERS** in
rounded clusters at stem ends, flowers funnel-shaped,
to 0.5 in. long, petals white, pink, or lavender, outer
surface hairy, style 1. **FRUIT** capsule, round, long-hairy.
ECOLOGY grows in forests, rocky slopes, and crevices.
Endemic to California.

Calycanthus occidentalis
CALYCANTHACEAE
WESTERN SWEETSHRUB, SPICEBUSH

Native, locally common, blooms early
spring–mid summer, 3–10 ft. Lake/pond,
streambanks, low to mid elevation
Shrub, erect, rounded shape, bark grayish brown, scaly
with age, twigs brown, hairy when young.
LEAVES deciduous, opposite, lance- to egg-shaped,
2–6 in. long, surfaces green and usually hairy, edges
smooth, tips rounded or pointed. **FLOWERS** single at
branch ends, to 2 in. across, tepals red, 1–2.5 in. long,
hairy, tips rounded, bracts green. **FRUIT** capsule-like,
bell-shaped, brown and somewhat woody at maturity,
holding numerous achenes,
persistent on plant.
ECOLOGY grows in streambanks, pond edges, and
moist canyon slopes in
shady areas from low to mid
elevation.

Lonicera cauriana (Lonicera caerulea)
CAPRIFOLIACEAE
SWEETBERRY HONEYSUCKLE, BLUEFLY
HONEYSUCKLE
Native, locally common, blooms late spring–mid
summer, 0.7–7 ft. Bog/fen/wetland, lake/pond,
streambanks, meadows, mid to high elevation
Shrub, erect, bark brown, flaking. **LEAVES** deciduous,
opposite, oval to egg-shaped, 1–2.5 in. long, surfaces
short-hairy, edges smooth, tips rounded.
FLOWERS paired in leaf axils, bell-shaped, to 0.5 in.
long, petals cream to yellow, ovaries of flower pair
appear fused, bracts small, lance-shaped. **FRUIT** berry,
red, joined pair, edible. **ECOLOGY** grows in moist soils
on streambanks, lake-
shores, pond edges, wet
meadows, and bogs from
mid to high elevation.

Lonicera ciliosa
CAPRIFOLIACEAE
ORANGE HONEYSUCKLE, WESTERN TRUMPET
HONEYSUCKLE
Native, common, blooms late spring–mid
summer, to 20 ft. West-side forest, east-
side forest, low to mid elevation
Vine, woody, stems climbing or creeping.
LEAVES deciduous, opposite, oval, 1.5–4 in. long, surfaces light green, non-hairy, edges fringed with hair,
tips rounded or pointed. **FLOWERS** in clusters at stem
tips, cluster with oval cup- to disk-shaped fused leaves
below, flowers trumpet-shaped, petals orange to reddish, 1–1.5 in. long, tube 3–4 times longer than the
lobes. **FRUIT** berry, orange
to red, about 0.5 in. across,
inedible, may be toxic.
ECOLOGY grows in open
to shady forests, in forest
edges and openings, and in
shrub thickets, shade tolerant but produces more flowers in sunny locations.

Lonicera conjugialis
CAPRIFOLIACEAE
PURPLE HONEYSUCKLE
Native, locally common, blooms late spring–
early summer, 2–6 ft. Streambanks, west-side
forest, subalpine, mid to high elevation

Shrub, stems erect, slender. **LEAVES** deciduous, opposite, oval to egg-shaped, 1–3 in. long, surfaces hairy,
edges smooth, tips rounded or pointed.

FLOWERS paired at the end of stalks from the leaf axils,
flowers trumpet-shaped, fragrant, petals wine-red, to
0.3 in. long, lobes longer than the tube. **FRUIT** berry,
oval to roundish, contains 2 fused ovaries, bright red,
shiny, to 0.5 in. long, inedible, may be toxic.

ECOLOGY grows along streams, in moist forests, and on
open slopes in montane to subalpine areas.

Lonicera hispidula
CAPRIFOLIACEAE
HAIRY HONEYSUCKLE, PINK HONEYSUCKLE
Native, common, blooms late spring–mid summer,
3–20 ft. West-side forest, low to mid elevation
Woody vine, ground creeper, climbs adjacent plants,
twigs hollow, waxy when young. **LEAVES** semi-
evergreen, opposite, oval to egg-shaped, 1–3 in. long,
surfaces glandular, usually hairy, waxy below, edges
smooth, tips rounded. **FLOWERS** in clusters at branch
ends as well as in leaf axils, 2 leaves fused below forming a cup- to disk-shaped structure, flowers trumpet-shaped, petals pink-tinged yellow to pink, 0.5–0.7
in. long, lips = or > tube, hairy within. **FRUIT** berry,
round, red, to 0.5 in. across, inedible.
ECOLOGY grows in open to shady forests,
along forest edges and openings, and in
shrub thickets from the coast to montane areas.

Lonicera interrupta
CAPRIFOLIACEAE
CHAPARRAL HONEYSUCKLE
Native, locally common, blooms mid spring,
3–10 ft. Chaparral, west-side forest, east-
side forest, low to mid elevation
Woody vine, stems climbing or sprawling, twigs waxy,
non-hairy. **LEAVES** deciduous, opposite, oval to round,
1–1.5 in. long, surfaces non-hairy, often waxy, edges
smooth, tips rounded, leaf pairs at stem ends fused.
FLOWERS in narrow, elongate clusters, bell-shaped, 0.5
in. long, petals cream to pale yellow, non-hairy.
FRUIT berry, red, edible but bitter. **ECOLOGY** grows in
chaparral, oak woodlands, and pine forests on slopes,
ridges, and flood-
plains from low to
mid elevation.

Lonicera involucrata
CAPRIFOLIACEAE
BLACK TWINBERRY, BEARBERRY HONEYSUCKLE,
BUSH HONEYSUCKLE
Native, common, blooms mid spring–mid summer,
1.7–17 ft. Coastal, bog/fen/wetland, lake/pond,
streambanks, subalpine, low to high elevation
Shrub, erect, bark gray, shredding, twigs 4-angled,
greenish, non-hairy. **LEAVES** deciduous, opposite, oval
to lance-shaped, 2–5.5 in. long, non-hairy above, usually hairy below, especially along the veins, edges
smooth, tips pointed. **FLOWERS** in pairs on stalks from
leaf axils, flowers trumpet-shaped, petals yellow or
yellow tinged with red or orange, hairy,
bracts beneath leaflike, 4, glandular-hairy.
FRUIT berry, purplish black, paired, bracts
beneath reddish, inedible, poisonous.
ECOLOGY grows in moist forests, wetlands,
and streambanks from coastal to high montane areas.

Lonicera tatarica
CAPRIFOLIACEAE
TATARIAN HONEYSUCKLE
Non-native, scattered, blooms all
spring, 5–10 ft. Streambanks, disturbed,
meadows, low to mid elevation
Shrub, erect, multi-stemmed, bark grayish brown,
ridged, branches long and arching, hollow, twigs reddish brown, 3-angled. **LEAVES** deciduous, opposite, egg-
shaped, 1–2.5 in. long, surfaces green, hairy or not,
paler below, edges smooth, tips pointed.
FLOWERS in pairs in leaf axils, leaves not fused into
cup beneath flowers, fragrant, petals white or pink,
becoming yellowish with age, 0.5 in. long, tube slightly
shorter than lobes, paired ovaries not
fused. **FRUIT** berry, round, red, orange,
or yellow, inedible, possibly toxic.
ECOLOGY invasive Asian import, grows
in disturbed places, moist pastures,
streambanks, forest edges, low to mid
elevation.

Lonicera utahensis
CAPRIFOLIACEAE

UTAH HONEYSUCKLE, RED TWINBERRY

Native, locally common, blooms mid spring–mid summer, 2–7 ft. Bog/fen/wetland, west-side forest, east-side forest, subalpine, low to high elevation

Shrub, erect, branches slender, twigs smooth. **LEAVES** deciduous, opposite, oval to egg-shaped, 1–3 in. long, non-hairy above, can be hairy below, edges smooth, tips rounded. **FLOWERS** in pairs on stalks from the leaf axils, flowers funnel-shaped, lobes short, petals cream to yellow, 0.5–1 in. long. **FRUIT** berry, red, pair fused at base, to 0.5 in. across, edible. **ECOLOGY** grows in open forests, meadows, valley bottoms, and shrub-steppe, often in wet or moist places, low to high elevation.

Symphoricarpos albus
CAPRIFOLIACEAE

COMMON SNOWBERRY

Native, common, blooms late spring–early summer, 1.7–10 ft. Meadows, west-side forest, east-side forest, low to mid elevation

Shrub, erect, rhizomatous, colony-forming. **LEAVES** deciduous, opposite, oval to egg-shaped, mostly 0.5–1 in. long, sometimes sparsely hairy beneath, edges mostly smooth, occasionally with a few rounded lobes (more common on young plants), tips pointed. **FLOWERS** in leaf axils and in small clusters at stem tips, flowers bell-shaped, about as long as wide, petals pink to white, hairy inside, style short, to 0.12 in. long. **FRUIT** berry, white, to 0.5 in. long, inedible, persistent on the shrub through winter, consumed by wildlife when little else is available. **ECOLOGY** grows in dry meadows, shrubfields, forests and forest openings, leafs out in early spring.

Symphoricarpos mollis

(*Symphoricarpos hesperius, Symphoricarpos mollis* var. *hesperius*)
CAPRIFOLIACEAE
CREEPING SNOWBERRY, TRAILING SNOWBERRY
Native, locally common, blooms late spring–mid summer, to 2 ft. Meadows, west-side forest, east-side forest, low to high elevation

Shrub, trailing along the ground, roots at the nodes, rhizomatous, twigs sparsely hairy. **LEAVES** deciduous, opposite, oval to egg-shaped, 0.5–1 in. long, hairy or not above, hairy below, edges smooth, sometimes toothed or lobed (more common on young plants), tips pointed. **FLOWERS** in small clusters at stem tips, and at times in upper leaf axils, flowers bell-shaped, small, about as long as wide, reddish pink with white outside, hairy within, style short, to 0.1 in. long. **FRUIT** berry, round, white, to 0.3 in. long, inedible. **ECOLOGY** prefers sunny, dry sites in forested communities, grows on slopes, ridges, often on gravelly or sandy soils.

Symphoricarpos occidentalis

CAPRIFOLIACEAE
WESTERN SNOWBERRY
Native, locally common, blooms late spring–mid summer, 1–3 ft. Streambanks, meadows, low to mid elevation

Shrub, erect, rhizomatous, thicket-forming, branches slender. **LEAVES** deciduous, opposite, oval to egg-shaped, 1–3 in. long, usually hairy below, edges smooth or few-toothed, tips pointed. **FLOWERS** in upper leaf axils and in clusters at stem tips, flowers bell-shaped, often wider than long, light pink, style long, to 0.3 in., = or > petals. **FRUIT** berry, round, white, to 0.4 in. across, inedible. **ECOLOGY** grows in moist soils, streambanks, lakeshores, floodplains, and meadows.

Symphoricarpos oreophilus
(*Symphoricarpos rotundifolius*)
CAPRIFOLIACEAE
MOUNTAIN SNOWBERRY
Native, common, blooms late spring–mid
summer, 1.7–5 ft. Meadows, east-side
forest, subalpine, mid to high elevation
Shrub, erect, branches spreading to sometimes trailing, trailing stems will root, generating new shoots.
LEAVES deciduous, opposite, oval to egg-shaped, mostly
0.5–1.5 in. long, hairy or not, edges smooth, tips
pointed. **FLOWERS** in upper leaf axils and in small clusters at stem tips, flowers bell-shaped, longer than wide,
pink to white, somewhat hairy inside, style short, to
0.15 in. long. **FRUIT** berry, oval, white, to
0.5 in. long, persistent on shrub, inedible. **ECOLOGY** grows in dry meadows,
shrubfields, forests and forest openings, on sandy or rocky soils, one of the
earliest shrubs to leaf out in spring.
The similar *S. albus* has larger leaves,
flowers as wide as long, and is found at
lower elevations.

Euonymus occidentalis
CELASTRACEAE
WESTERN BURNING BUSH, WESTERN WAHOO
Native, rare, blooms mid–late spring, 6–20 ft.
Streambanks, west-side forest, low to mid elevation
Shrub, erect to climbing, branches slender, non-hairy.
LEAVES deciduous, opposite, egg- to lance-shaped, 2–5.5
in. long, surfaces green, non-hairy, edges toothed, tips
pointed. **FLOWERS** saucer-shaped, in 1- to 5-flowered
drooping clusters in leaf axils, petals 5, greenish to
purplish brown. **FRUIT** capsule, seeds covered by fleshy,
orangish red aril. **ECOLOGY** grows in shady forests,
streambanks, and Garry oak savannas from
low to mid elevation. Locally common in
California.

Paxistima myrsinites
(*Pachystima myrsinites*)
CELASTRACEAE
OREGON BOXWOOD, MYRTLE BOXWOOD
Native, common, blooms late spring–early summer, 1–3 ft. West-side forest, east-side forest, subalpine, low to high elevation

Shrub, erect to creeping, stems much-branched, reddish brown, non-hairy. **LEAVES** evergreen, opposite, lance-shaped, 0.5–1 in. long, surfaces glossy green, non-hairy, edges toothed, tips pointed or rounded. **FLOWERS** single or clustered in leaf axils, petals 4, egg-shaped, maroon, stamens 4, alternate with petals. **FRUIT** capsule, seeds 1–2, dark brown, largely covered by whitish, fleshy aril.

ECOLOGY grows on forest slopes, ridgetops, ravines, and in shrub communities, from low to subalpine areas.

Cornus glabrata
CORNACEAE
BROWN DOGWOOD, SMOOTH DOGWOOD
Native, locally common, blooms mid–late spring, 1–20 ft. Streambanks, west-side forest, east-side forest, low to mid elevation

Shrub or small tree, thicket-forming, bark grayish or reddish brown, twigs reddish. **LEAVES** deciduous, opposite, oval to lance-shaped, 1–2 in. long, hairy, 3–4 lateral vein pairs, edges smooth to wavy, tips pointed. **FLOWERS** in rounded clusters at branch tips, sepals and petals 4, sepal lobes triangular, pale green, petals white, to 0.2 in. long, fragrance spicy sweet. **FRUIT** berrylike stone fruit, bluish or white. **ECOLOGY** grows in forests, chaparral, and grasslands, along streambanks, seeps, and in other moist places.

See *Cornus* with whorled leaves, page 351

Cornus nuttallii
CORNACEAE
PACIFIC DOGWOOD
Native, scattered, blooms mid–late spring,
7–75 ft. Streambanks, west-side forest,
east-side forest, low to mid elevation

Tree, sometimes shrublike, bark blackish brown,
smooth to ridged, twigs purplish gray, hairy, becoming smooth with age. **LEAVES** deciduous, opposite,
oval to egg-shaped, 1.5–4 in. long, dark green and
sparsely hairy above, paler and hairy below, edges
smooth, tips pointed, fall color bright orange, red, or
purplish. **FLOWERS** in headlike clusters, each with 4–7
showy bracts, bracts oval, 1–3 in. long, white or pinkish, petals 4, greenish white, tips sometimes purple,
about 0.1 in. long. **FRUIT** berrylike stone fruit, bright
red, unpalatable, bitter. **ECOLOGY** grows along streambanks and in both coniferous and hardwood forests.
Shade tolerant, relatively drought tolerant, limited
cold hardiness. Seeds are dispersed by
birds and other animals that consume
the fruit. Resprouts after fire or logging. May reflower in autumn. Affected
by anthracnose, a fungal disease that
causes brown spots on the leaves, twig
death, and cankers on the trunk. Provincial flower of British Columbia.

Cornus sericea (*Cornus stolonifera*)
CORNACEAE
RED-OSIER DOGWOOD

Native, common, blooms late spring–early summer, 5–20 ft. Bog/fen/wetland, streambanks, west-side forest, east-side forest, low to mid elevation

Shrub, thicket-forming, twigs bright red to purplish, becoming grayish with age. **LEAVES** deciduous, opposite, oval to egg-shaped, 2–4 in. long, hairy or not, green above, paler beneath, 4–7 lateral vein pairs, edges smooth, tips pointed. **FLOWERS** in flat-topped clusters at branch tips, sepals and petals 4, petals

white, to 0.2 in. long. **FRUIT** berrylike stone fruit, white or bluish, unpalatable, bitter. **ECOLOGY** grows on streambanks, in swamps, bog edges, shorelines, and forests from low to montane elevation. The similar *C. glabrata* has leaves 1–2 in. long with 3–4 vein pairs.

Cornus sessilis

CORNACEAE

BLACKFRUIT DOGWOOD, WESTERN CORNELIAN
CHERRY, MINER'S DOGWOOD

Native, locally common, blooms early–mid
spring, to 15 ft. Streambanks, west-side forest,
east-side forest, low to mid elevation

Shrub or small tree, stems gray or yellowish brown.
LEAVES deciduous, opposite, oval to egg-shaped, 2–3.5
in. long, hairy below, edges smooth, tips pointed.
FLOWERS in small headlike clusters, few-flowered with
4 bracts, bracts about 0.5 in. long, brownish with yellow edges, shed soon after flowering, sepals and petals
4, petals about 0.1 in. long, yellowish. **FRUIT** berrylike
stone fruit, oval, shiny purplish black when mature.
ECOLOGY grows along streambanks in shade or part
shade, usually in forest communities. Fruit highly
prized by birds. Endemic to California.

Shepherdia argentea
ELAEAGNACEAE
SILVER BUFFALOBERRY, THORNY BUFFALOBERRY
Native, locally common, blooms mid spring–early summer, 7–20 ft. Lake/pond, streambanks, mid elevation

Shrub or small tree, erect, thicket-forming, branches often spine-tipped, twigs silvery scaly. **LEAVES** deciduous, opposite, oblong to lance-shaped, 1–2 in. long, both sides silvery scaly, edges smooth, tips rounded. **FLOWERS** in dense clusters in leaf axils and side branches, male and female flowers on separate plants, male flowers often bloom before the leaves unfold, flowers yellowish brown, petals absent, sepal lobes 4, spreading or erect, stamens 8. **FRUIT** berrylike, yellowish to red, oval, palatable, sour. **ECOLOGY** grows along streambanks, springs, and ponds, sometimes also on slopes, from the foothills to montane areas. Introduced in British Columbia, otherwise native.

Shepherdia canadensis
ELAEAGNACEAE
RUSSET BUFFALOBERRY, SOAPBERRY,
SOOPOLALLIE
Native, locally common, blooms mid–late
spring, 3–13 ft. West-side forest, east-
side forest, low to high elevation

Shrub, erect, twigs brownish, scaly, not spine-tipped.
LEAVES deciduous, opposite, lance- to egg-shaped,
0.5–2.5 in. long, green above, whitish scaly with brown
patches below, edges smooth, tips pointed.
FLOWERS in few-flowered clusters in leaf axils, male
and female flowers on separate plants, flowers brownish, petals absent, sepal lobes 4, spreading in male
flowers, erect in females, stamens 8.
FRUIT berrylike, oval, red, edible but
bitter. **ECOLOGY** grows in forest understories and openings, often in sandy
or rocky soils, adds nitrogen to the soil
through bacteria-filled nodules in its
roots. Native Americans ate the fruit.
Rare in California.

Cassiope lycopodioides
ERICACEAE
CLUBMOSS MOUNTAIN HEATHER, GROUND
PINE HEATHER
Native, rare, blooms mid summer, 2–7 in. Meadows,
alpine, subalpine, mid to high elevation

Shrub, stems trailing to somewhat erect, forms loose
mats. **LEAVES** evergreen, opposite, scalelike, linear
to lance-shaped, to 0.1 in. long, somewhat overlapping, appressed, not grooved on lower (outward-facing) surface, surfaces hairy, edges thin, nongreen, tips
of young leaves with curled hairs. **FLOWERS** single or
few in leaf axils, stalks 0.5 in. long, flowers nodding,
bell-shaped, white, 0.25–0.3 in. long, sepals reddish,
anthers tipped by 2 bristles.
FRUIT capsule, round, about 0.1 in.
across. **ECOLOGY** grows in rock crevices, meadows, rocky slopes, often near
water. Usually high elevation.

See Ericaceae with alternate leaves, page
154; whorled leaves, page 351

Cassiope mertensiana
ERICACEAE
WHITE HEATHER, MERTENS' MOUNTAIN
HEATHER, MOSS HEATHER
Native, common, blooms mid summer, 2–12 in.
Meadows, alpine, subalpine, high elevation

Shrub, mat-forming, stems hairy, glandular, or neither. **LEAVES** evergreen, opposite, overlapping and concealing stem, egg- to lance-shaped, 0.1–0.2 in. long, grooved at base on lower (outward-facing) surface, edges smooth. **FLOWERS** solitary in leaf axils, stalks hairy or not, flowers nodding, bell-shaped, petals white, 0.25–0.3 in. long, sepals reddish, anthers tipped by 2 bristles. **FRUIT** capsule, round, to 0.15 in. across.

ECOLOGY grows in meadows, forest slopes, and shrubfields, subalpine to alpine. The similar *C. lycopodioides* has thin, nongreen leaf edges and young leaves near stem tips with curled hairs.

Cassiope tetragona
ERICACEAE
WHITE ARCTIC MOUNTAIN HEATHER, FOUR-
ANGLED MOUNTAIN HEATHER
Native, locally common, blooms mid summer, 2–12 in. Meadows, alpine, subalpine, high elevation

Shrub, somewhat erect, mat-forming, stems 4-angled, hairy. **LEAVES** evergreen, opposite, scalelike, lance-shaped, 0.15 in. long, overlapping and appressed, grooved and hairy on lower (outward-facing) surface, edges fringed with hair, tips pointed. **FLOWERS** single or few in leaf axils, stalks 0.5–1 in. long, flowers nodding, bell-shaped, white to pinkish, 0.2–0.4 in. long, sepals reddish, anthers tipped by 2 bristles. **FRUIT** capsule, round, to 0.2 in. across. **ECOLOGY** grows in meadows, shrubfields, and rocky slopes, alpine, subalpine. Ours is var. *saximontana*.

Kalmia microphylla

(*Kalmia polifolia, Kalmia occidentalis*)
ERICACEAE
WESTERN SWAMP LAUREL, BOG LAUREL,
ALPINE LAUREL
Native, locally common, blooms late spring–
mid summer, 2–32 in. Bog/fen/wetland,
meadows, west-side forest, east-side forest,
alpine, subalpine, low to high elevation
Shrub, spreading, rooting at branch nodes.
LEAVES evergreen, opposite, oval to lance-shaped, 0.5–
1.5 in. long, dark green and non-hairy above, grayish,
densely hairy below, tips pointed or rounded.
FLOWERS in small clusters (1–12 flowers) at stem
ends, flowers saucer-shaped, petals pink to purplish, sepals pink or light green, edges
hairy, stamens 10. **FRUIT** capsule,
round, non-hairy, about 0.2 in. across.
ECOLOGY grows in bogs and wet meadows. Var. *occidentalis* is taller, grows
at lower elevations; var. *microphylla* is
smaller, found at high elevation. Both
varieties are poisonous, containing
andromedotoxin.

Kalmia procumbens (*Loiseleuria procumbens*)

ERICACEAE
ALPINE AZALEA
Native, locally common, blooms mid summer,
to 4 in. Bog/fen/wetland, meadows, alpine,
subalpine, mid to high elevation
Shrub, stems trailing, short- or non-hairy, mat-
forming. **LEAVES** evergreen, opposite, lance-shaped to
oval, 0.1–0.3 in. long, surfaces bright green, hairy or
not above, short-hairy below, edges rolled under, tips
rounded, stalks partially enclosing stem.
FLOWERS in small clusters or single at stem ends, flowers bell-shaped, 0.1–0.2 in. long, light to deep pink or
white, joined ½ total length, sepals red, stamens 5.
FRUIT capsule, egg-shaped, non-hairy.
ECOLOGY grows on dry to moist alpine
slopes in heath communities, and
in bogs at higher latitudes. Rare in
Washington.

Garrya buxifolia
GARRYACEAE
DWARF SILKTASSEL, BOXLEAF SILKTASSEL
Native, locally common, blooms late winter–
spring, to 10 ft. Serpentine, chaparral,
west-side forest, low to mid elevation
Shrub, bark grayish brown, twigs yellowish brown.
LEAVES evergreen, opposite, oval to egg-shaped, 0.5–
2.5 in. long, yellowish green and hairy or not above,
densely white-hairy below, hair straight or wavy, edges
smooth, tips pointed or rounded. **FLOWERS** in drooping
narrow clusters, plants male or female, petals absent,
sepals joined, bractlike, hairy, stamens 4. **FRUIT** berry-

like, round, reddish to bluish
purple, non-hairy to sparsely
hairy at the tip. **ECOLOGY** grows
only in serpentine soils or rocks,
in forests and chaparral from
low to mid elevation.

Garrya congdonii
GARRYACEAE
**CHAPARRAL SILKTASSEL, INTERIOR SILKTASSEL,
CONGDON'S SILKTASSEL**
Native, locally common, blooms late winter–
early spring, 5–10 ft. Serpentine, chaparral,
west-side forest, low to mid elevation
Shrub, rounded, ball-like form. **LEAVES** evergreen,
opposite, oval to egg-shaped, 0.5–3 in. long, surfaces
flat or curved, yellowish green above, densely white-
hairy below, hair fine and wavy, edges often wavy, tips
pointed or not. **FLOWERS** in drooping narrow clusters,
plants male or female, petals absent, sepals joined,
bractlike, hairy, stamens 4. **FRUIT** berrylike, roundish,

dark purple to black-
ish, hairy.
ECOLOGY grows in
chaparral, oak wood-
lands, and shrub-
fields, usually in ser-
pentine or heavy clay
soils.

Garrya elliptica
GARRYACEAE
WAVYLEAF SILKTASSEL

Native, locally common, blooms winter–early spring,
  7–23 ft. Coastal, west-side forest, low to mid elevation
Shrub or tree, bark grayish brown, twigs green and
hairy, becoming brown and smooth with age.
LEAVES evergreen, opposite, oblong to egg-shaped, 2–3
in. long, leathery, dark green and non-hairy above,
densely white-hairy beneath, edges wavy, tips rounded.
FLOWERS in drooping linear clusters, plants male or
female, petals absent, sepals joined, bractlike, long-
hairy, stamens 4. **FRUIT** berrylike, round, purplish blue,
densely silky-hairy. **ECOLOGY** grows in sand dunes,
coastal bluffs, forests, and chaparral,
often in sand or sandy soils, low to mid
elevation.

Garrya fremontii
GARRYACEAE
FREMONT'S SILKTASSEL, BEARBRUSH

Native, scattered, blooms winter–early
  spring, 3–10 ft. Serpentine, chaparral, west-
  side forest, low to mid elevation
Shrub, bark gray with lighter stripes, twigs sparsely
hairy to smooth, brownish purple. **LEAVES** evergreen,
opposite, oval to egg-shaped, 1.5–3 in. long, shiny
dark green above, paler and sometimes sparsely hairy
below, edges smooth, tips pointed. **FLOWERS** in drooping, narrow clusters, plants male or female, petals
absent, sepals joined, bractlike, male flower bracts
hairy or not, female bracts long-hairy, stamens 4.
FRUIT berrylike, round, purple, sparsely
hairy to smooth at maturity.
ECOLOGY grows in chaparral and forests, often in rocky soils, tolerant of serpentine, low to mid elevation. Resprouts
after fire and other disturbances.

Philadelphus lewisii
HYDRANGEACEAE
LEWIS'S MOCK-ORANGE, WESTERN SYRINGA
Native, locally common, blooms late spring–
mid summer, 5–10 ft. Streambanks, west-side
forest, east-side forest, low to mid elevation
Shrub, erect, bark reddish brown to gray, shed in
strips, twigs gray, hairy or not. **LEAVES** deciduous,
opposite, oval to egg-shaped, 1–3 in. long, promi-
nently 3-veined from the base, hairy or not above, at
least sparsely hairy below, edges smooth or toothed,
tips pointed. **FLOWERS** fragrant, in clusters at branch
ends, petals 4, white, oblong, 0.5–1 in. long, sepals 4,
green, lobes lance-shaped with pointed tips, stamens
25–40, unequal. **FRUIT** capsule, woody
when mature, 0.5 in. long, ends pointed.
ECOLOGY grows in seasonally moist
sites with well-drained soils, such as the
bases of cliffs and talus slopes, streambanks, draws, seeps, and springs in
shrub-steppe or forest communities.

Whipplea modesta
HYDRANGEACEAE
WHIPPLEVINE, YERBA DE SELVA, MODESTY
Native, common, blooms mid–late spring, to 4
in. Rocky sites, west-side forest, mid elevation
Subshrub, stems trailing, somewhat woody, bark grayish brown, peeling in strips. **LEAVES** deciduous or persistent, opposite, oval to egg-shaped, 0.5–1.5 in. long,
surfaces hairy, edges smooth or toothed, tips pointed.
FLOWERS in clusters at the end of short, erect stems,
petals 4–6, white, sepal lobes white, stamens showy,
8–12, white. **FRUIT** capsule, round, separating into
1-seeded segments. **ECOLOGY** grows in dry rocky places
within conifer forests, coastal scrub, or chaparral, also
found on stream-
banks, low to mid
elevation.

Clinopodium douglasii
(*Satureja douglasii*)
LAMIACEAE
YERBA BUENA

Native, locally common, blooms spring–
summer, 4 in. Chaparral, west-side forest,
east-side forest, low to mid elevation

Subshrub, mat-forming, stems sparsely hairy.
LEAVES deciduous, opposite, egg-shaped to round, 0.5–
1.5 in. long, surfaces sparsely hairy, edges toothed, tips
rounded. **FLOWERS** usually single in leaf axils, tubular with liplike lobes, 0.3–0.4 in. long, petals white to
purplish, sepals to 0.3 in. long, stamens 4, the lower
pair at least as long as the upper pair. **FRUIT** nutlet, 4
per flower, shiny brown.
ECOLOGY grows in shady,
dry to mesic forests, chaparral, and rocky shrub
thickets; dried leaves used
to make tea.

Lepechinia calycina
LAMIACEAE
WHITE PITCHER SAGE, WOODBALM

Native, common, blooms all spring, 2–5 ft.
Chaparral, east-side forest, low to mid elevation

Aromatic shrub, hairs long, branched, not glandular,
glands if present either short-stalked or stalkless.
LEAVES deciduous, opposite, lance- to egg-shaped,
1.5–5 in. long, surfaces grayish green, edges smooth
to toothed, tips pointed. **FLOWERS** in narrow clusters at
stem ends, flower stalks to 0.5 in. long, bracts shorter
than flower, flowers tubular with 2 liplike lobes, white,
sepals green, hairy, lobes 5, inflated. **FRUIT** nutlets, surrounded by round, persistent sepals, hairy.
ECOLOGY grows
on rocky slopes
in chaparral, oak
woodlands, and
pine forests. Pre-
fers sun to partial
shade. Endemic to
California.

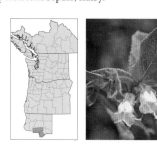

Monardella odoratissima
LAMIACEAE
WESTERN MOUNTAIN BALM, COYOTE MINT,
MOUNTAIN MONARDELLA

Native, locally common, blooms late spring–mid
summer, 4–20 in. Rocky sites, west-side forest,
east-side forest, subalpine, mid to high elevation
Subshrub, mound-forming, aromatic, stems hairy,
sometimes glandular. **LEAVES** deciduous, opposite,
oval to lance-shaped, 0.5–1.5 in. long, surfaces green
to grayish, often purplish-tinged, hairy or not, tips
rounded. **FLOWERS** in dense, flat-topped clusters at
stem ends, bracts beneath clusters 0.3–1 in. long, flowers tubular with lobes, lobes about ½ as long as tube,
petals pinkish purple to whitish, sepals
hairy, stamens 4. **FRUIT** nutlet.
ECOLOGY grows in dry to wet places, on
rocky slopes and meadows, in forests
and sagebrush communities from mid
elevation to subalpine areas. Rare in
British Columbia.

Monardella odoratissima ssp. *pallida*
LAMIACEAE
MOUNTAIN MONARDELLA, PALLID MOUNTAIN
MONARDELLA

Native, locally common, blooms all summer,
6–18 in. Rocky sites, east-side forest,
subalpine, mid to high elevation
Subshrub, mound-forming, aromatic, stems hairy,
sometimes glandular. **LEAVES** deciduous, opposite, oval to lance-shaped, 0.5–1.5 in. long, surfaces
green to grayish, often purple-tinged, hairy or not,
tips rounded. **FLOWERS** in dense, flat-topped clusters
at stem ends, bracts beneath flowers 0.5–1 in. long,
bent back, flowers tubular with lobes, lobes about ½
as long as tube, petals
white, occasionally lav-
ender to purplish, sepals
hairy, stamens 4. **FRUIT**
nutlet. **ECOLOGY** grows
in dry to wet places, on
rocky slopes, and in for-
ests from mid elevation to
subalpine areas.

Monardella purpurea
LAMIACEAE
SISKIYOU MONARDELLA, SERPENTINE
MONARDELLA

Native, uncommon, blooms late spring–early
summer, 4–16 in. Rocky sites, serpentine,
chaparral, west-side forest, low to mid elevation
Subshrub, stems erect, purplish, mostly non-hairy.
LEAVES deciduous, opposite, leathery, oval to lance-
shaped, 0.5–1.2 in. long, surfaces deep purple to green,
edges sometimes toothed. **FLOWERS** in dense clusters
at stem end, purplish bracts beneath, flowers about
0.5 in. long, tubular, lobed, lobes > ½ as long as tube,
sepals glandular, sometimes hairy, purple, petals
reddish pink to purple,
stamens 4. **FRUIT** nut-
let. **ECOLOGY** grows on
rocky slopes, forests, and
chaparral, often in ser-
pentine-derived soils or
related substrates. Rare
in Oregon.

Monardella sheltonii
(*Monardella villosa* ssp. *sheltonii*)
LAMIACEAE
SHELTON'S MONARDELLA

Native, locally common, blooms all summer, 6–18 in.
Rocky sites, serpentine, chaparral, low to mid elevation
Subshrub, erect, rhizomatous, stems non-hairy.
LEAVES deciduous, opposite, lance- to egg-shaped, 0.5–
1.5 in. long, non-hairy above, velvety short-hairy below,
edges smooth or toothed, tips pointed.
FLOWERS in dense, flat-topped clusters at stem ends,
bracts beneath cluster 0.3–0.7 in. long, flowers tubular with lobes, petals purple, sepals hairy, stamens 4.
FRUIT nutlet. **ECOLOGY** grows in rocky, open areas in
forests, oak woodlands, and chaparral,
often in serpentine.

Monardella stebbinsii
LAMIACEAE
FEATHER RIVER MONARDELLA, STEBBINS'
MONARDELLA

Native, rare, blooms mid summer, 6–18 in. Rocky sites, serpentine, chaparral, mid elevation

Subshrub, rhizomatous, mat-forming, stems white velvety-hairy, hairs >0.01 in. long. **LEAVES** deciduous, opposite, egg-shaped, 0.5–1 in. long, relatively thick, surfaces grayish with purple blotches, hairy above, hairy and glandular-hairy below, edges smooth, tips blunt. **FLOWERS** in dense, flat-topped clusters at stem ends, bracts beneath cluster lance-shaped, glandular-hairy, purple-tinged, flowers tubular with lobes, petals pink, sepals glandular-hairy, stamens 4. **FRUIT** nutlet.

ECOLOGY restricted to serpentine substrates, grows on dry rocky slopes in chaparral and open forest communities. Endemic to California.

Monardella villosa (*Monardella siskiyouensis*)
LAMIACEAE
COYOTE MINT, SISKIYOU COYOTE MINT

Native, uncommon, blooms all summer, to 20 in. Chaparral, west-side forest, east-side forest, low to mid elevation

Subshrub, erect, stems grayish, densely short-hairy, some hairs glandular. **LEAVES** deciduous, opposite, lance- to egg-shaped, 0.5–1 in. long, glandular-hairy beneath, edges smooth or toothed, tips pointed or not. **FLOWERS** in headlike cluster, clusters one or more at stem end, leaflike green bracts beneath, flowers tubular, petals white, pink, or purple, sepals glandular-hairy, stamens 4, extending beyond petals.

FRUIT nutlet.

ECOLOGY grows in chaparral and oak woodlands from low to montane areas.

Salvia dorrii
LAMIACEAE
PURPLE SAGE

Native, scattered, blooms mid–late spring, 4–28 in.
Rocky sites, shrub-steppe, low to mid elevation
Shrub, erect, mounded, branches rigid, scent minty
sage. **LEAVES** deciduous, opposite, oval to spoon-
shaped, 0.5–1 in. long, surfaces densely silvery hairy,
edges smooth, tips mostly rounded. **FLOWERS** tiered
clusters with leafy, often purplish bracts, flowers tubular with liplike lobes, petals blue to vio-
let, rarely white, stamens protuding
from the floral tube, pollen sac 1.
FRUIT nutlet, gray to reddish brown.
ECOLOGY grows in rocky places in sagebrush communities, pinyon-juniper
woodland, and on talus slopes, from low
to mid elevation.

Salvia sonomensis

LAMIACEAE
CREEPING SAGE, SONOMA SAGE
Native, locally common, blooms early
spring–mid summer, to 16 in. Chaparral,
east-side forest, low to mid elevation

Subshrub, sprawling to creeping, mat-forming, stems
square. **LEAVES** deciduous, opposite, oval, lance-, or
egg-shaped, 1–2.5 in. long, greenish-hairy above,
densely white-hairy below, edges finely toothed, tips
rounded. **FLOWERS** in tiered clusters on leafless flower
stalks, flowers tubular with liplike lobes, lower lobe
larger than upper, petals blue, lavender, or deep purple,
stamens protuding from the floral tube. **FRUIT** nutlet,
brown. **ECOLOGY** grows
in chaparral, oak wood-
lands, and ponderosa
pine forests.

Linnaea borealis

LINNAEACEAE (CAPRIFOLIACEAE)
TWINFLOWER
Native, common, blooms late spring–mid
summer, 2–4 in. West-side forest, east-side
forest, subalpine, low to high elevation

Subshrub, stems creeping along the ground as well
as forming short upright shoots, somewhat hairy and
often glandular. **LEAVES** evergreen, opposite, egg-
shaped to round, 0.3–1 in. long, dark green and shiny
above, paler beneath, non-hairy or hairy only on edges
and veins, edges often with rounded lobes near leaf tip.
FLOWERS fragrant, growing in pairs at stem tips, trumpet-shaped with 5 rounded lobes, 0.4–0.6 in. long, nodding, petals white to pink. **FRUIT** nutlet,
hairy and glandular. **ECOLOGY** grows in
open to shady forests, shrubfields, moist
to dry sites, often on decaying wood,
from low to subalpine elevation.

Mimulus aurantiacus (*Diplacus aurantiacus*)
PHRYMACEAE (SCROPHULARIACEAE)
ORANGE BUSH MONKEYFLOWER
Native, common, blooms mid spring–early summer,
0.3–5 ft. Coastal, rocky sites, low to mid elevation
Shrub, erect to spreading, twigs hairy or not.
LEAVES deciduous (summer), opposite, linear to lance-
shaped, 1–2 in. long, surfaces shiny dark green, non-
hairy above, hairy and mostly glandular below, edges
smooth, often rolled under, tips mostly pointed.
FLOWERS 2–4 in upper leaf axils, broadly trumpet-shaped, 1–1.5 in. long, sepals tubular, non-hairy,
petals orange to yellowish orange, edges ruffled, with
tubular base and liplike lobes, lower lip splotched.
FRUIT capsule, to 1 in. long, seeds many.
ECOLOGY grows on rocky slopes, coastal
cliffs, and disturbed areas in a wide
range of plant communities, low to
montane elevation.

Mimulus aurantiacus var. *grandiflorus*
(*Diplacus grandiflorus, Mimulus bifidus*)
PHRYMACEAE (SCROPHULARIACEAE)
SLENDER MONKEYFLOWER, LARGEFLOWER
BUSH MONKEYFLOWER
Native, common, blooms mid spring–early
summer, 0.3–5 ft. Rocky sites, chaparral,
east-side forest, low to mid elevation
Shrub, erect to spreading, twigs hairy or not.
LEAVES deciduous (summer), opposite, linear to oval,
0.5–3.5 in. long, surfaces shiny dark green, non-hairy,
edges smooth, flat, or rolled under, tips mostly pointed.
FLOWERS 1–2 in leaf axils, stalked, broadly trumpet-shaped, 1.5–2.3 in. long, sepals tubular, green,
non-hairy, petals pale yellow
or orange, edges ruffled, with
tubular base and liplike lobes,
lower lip splotched.
FRUIT capsule, to 1 in. long,
seeds many. **ECOLOGY** grows
on rocky slopes in canyons
and hillsides within chaparral, oak woodlands, and pine
forests.

Keckiella breviflora

PLANTAGINACEAE (SCROPHULARIACEAE)
BUSH BEARDTONGUE, YAWNING
BEARDTONGUE

Native, common, blooms mid spring–mid summer, 2–7 ft. Chaparral, east-side forest, low to high elevation
Subshrub or shrub, erect to spreading, stems slender, grayish green. **LEAVES** deciduous (summer), opposite, lance-shaped, 0.5–1.5 in. long, surfaces grayish green, edges toothed, tips pointed. **FLOWERS** in open clusters at stem ends, flowers 2-lipped, white, cream, or rose-tinged, purple- or pink-lined, 0.5–0.7 in. long, upper lip longer than rest of flower. **FRUIT** capsule.
ECOLOGY grows on rocky slopes in chaparral, oak woodlands, pine forests, from low to high elevation.

Keckiella corymbosa

PLANTAGINACEAE (SCROPHULARIACEAE)
REDWOOD KECKIELLA

Native, locally common, blooms mid summer–autumn, 1–2 ft. Rocky sites, west-side forest, east-side forest, low to mid elevation
Shrub, erect, mat-forming, stems hairy or not. **LEAVES** deciduous (summer), opposite, lance- to egg-shaped, leaf base triangular, 0.5–1.5 in. long, surfaces dark green, edges smooth to 3- to 5-toothed, tips rounded. **FLOWERS** in open clusters at stem ends, flowers 2-lipped, bright pink to red, 1–1.5 in. long. **FRUIT** capsule, oval. **ECOLOGY** grows on rocky slopes and cliffs in woodland and forest communities.

Keckiella lemmonii
PLANTAGINACEAE (SCROPHULARIACEAE)
LEMMON'S KECKIELLA
Native, common, blooms mid summer,
2–5 ft. Rocky sites, west-side forest, east-
side forest, low to high elevation
Shrub, erect, stems slender, unbranched.
LEAVES deciduous (summer), opposite, lance- to
egg-shaped, 0.5–2.5 in. long, surfaces green, edges
toothed, tips pointed. **FLOWERS** in branched clusters,
stalked, flowers 2-lipped, purplish brown, to 0.5 in.
long, lower lip pale yellow with darker lines, upper lip
shorter than rest of flower. **FRUIT** capsule.
ECOLOGY grows on rocky slopes in conifer and mixed
evergreen forests and
oak woodlands, lower
to high elevation.

Penstemon barrettiae
PLANTAGINACEAE (SCROPHULARIACEAE)
BARRETT'S PENSTEMON
Native, rare, blooms late spring, 8–16 in.
Rocky sites, low to mid elevation
Subshrub, stems much-branched, non-hairy.
LEAVES evergreen, opposite, clustered near plant base,
lance- to egg-shaped, 0.5–3 in. long, leathery or succulent, surfaces bluish or grayish green, non-hairy, edges
smooth to toothed, tips pointed. **FLOWERS** 1–2 in leaf
axils, snapdragon-shaped, pinkish to reddish purple,
about 1.5 in. long, anthers densely woolly-hairy.
FRUIT capsule, narrow, about 0.5 in. long.
ECOLOGY endemic to the Columbia River Gorge, growing in crevices in basalt cliffs, talus, and
occasionally along roadsides, low to mid
elevation.

Penstemon davidsonii
PLANTAGINACEAE (SCROPHULARIACEAE)
DAVIDSON'S PENSTEMON
Native, locally common, blooms early–
mid summer, 2–6 in. Rocky sites, alpine,
subalpine, mid to high elevation

Subshrub, mat-forming. LEAVES evergreen, opposite, oval to round, 0.2–0.5 in. long, surfaces glossy dark green, non-hairy, edges smooth or toothed, tips mostly rounded. FLOWERS few-flowered clusters at stem tips, snapdragon-shaped, bluish purple to purple, 1–1.5 in. long, anthers woolly-hairy. FRUIT capsule, oval, to 0.5 in. long. ECOLOGY grows on rocky slopes, ledges, and rock outcrops, from mid elevation to alpine. Around Steens Mountain, look for var. *praeteritus*, with flowers about 2 times larger than other varieties, rare in Oregon.

Penstemon fruticosus
PLANTAGINACEAE (SCROPHULARIACEAE)
SHRUBBY PENSTEMON

Native, common, blooms mid spring–mid
summer, 6–16 in. Rocky sites, east-side forest,
shrub-steppe, low to high elevation

Shrub, stems erect to trailing, multi-branched, reddish
brown. **LEAVES** evergreen, opposite, lance-shaped, 0.5–
1.5 in. long, 2–10 times longer than wide, surfaces non-
hairy, edges smooth or toothed, tips pointed.
FLOWERS few-flowered clusters at stem tips, flowers
snapdragon-shaped, 1–2 in. long, bluish lavender to
purplish, anthers woolly-hairy. **FRUIT** capsule.
ECOLOGY grows on rocky slopes and in open forests
from lower elevations to subalpine
areas.

Penstemon newberryi
PLANTAGINACEAE (SCROPHULARIACEAE)
MOUNTAIN PRIDE

Native, locally common, blooms mid summer, 5–12 in.
Rocky sites, alpine, subalpine, mid to high elevation

Subshrub, mat-forming. **LEAVES** evergreen, opposite,
egg-shaped, 0.5–1.5 in. long at base of plant, shorter
upward, edges toothed, tips pointed.
FLOWERS few-flowered clusters at stem ends, flowers
snapdragon-shaped, glandular, crimson to rose-
red, 0.75–1.5 in. long, anthers woolly-hairy, mostly
extend beyond petals. **FRUIT** capsule. **ECOLOGY** grows
on rock outcrops and talus slopes, montane to alpine,
California to Nevada, more inland than var. *berryi*,
with smaller flowers,
narrower throat, and
exserted stamens.

Penstemon newberryi var. *berryi*
PLANTAGINACEAE (SCROPHULARIACEAE)
BERRY'S PENSTEMON, BERRY'S MOUNTAIN PRIDE
Native, locally common, blooms all summer, 5–12 in.
Rocky sites, alpine, subalpine, mid to high elevation
Subshrub, mat-forming. **LEAVES** evergreen, opposite,
egg-shaped, 0.5–1.5 in. long at base of plant, shorter
upward, edges toothed, tips pointed.
FLOWERS in few-flowered clusters at stem ends, flowers
snapdragon-shaped, glandular, rose-red, 1–1.5 in. long,
throat wide, >0.3 in. across, long-hairy within, anthers
woolly-hairy, shorter than petals.
FRUIT capsule. **ECOLOGY** grows on rock outcrops

and talus slopes, higher elevations, in
Oregon south, more toward coast
in California. Distinguish this variety
from the straight species by its larger
flowers, with wider throat and stamens
within petals.

Penstemon rupicola
PLANTAGINACEAE (SCROPHULARIACEAE)
ROCK PENSTEMON, CLIFF PENSTEMON
Native, locally common, blooms late spring–mid
summer, 2–5.5 in. Rocky sites, west-side forest,
east-side forest, subalpine, low to high elevation
Subshrub, sometimes forming large mats.
LEAVES evergreen, opposite, roundish to egg-shaped,
0.3–1 in. long at base of plant, shorter upward, surfaces
often waxy, hairy or not, edges toothed, tips rounded.
FLOWERS few-flowered clusters at stem ends, flowers
snapdragon-shaped, glandular-hairy, hot pink to violet, 1–1.5 in. long, anthers woolly-hairy. **FRUIT** capsule.
ECOLOGY grows on cliffs, ledges, and rocky slopes, usu-

ally montane but in the Columbia River
Gorge at low elevation. Hybridizes with
P. davidsonii and *P. newberryi* where
ranges overlap.

Leptosiphon nuttallii
(*Linanthus nuttallii*, *Linanthastrum nuttallii*)
POLEMONIACEAE
NUTTALL'S LINANTHUS
Native, common, blooms late spring–mid
summer, 4–12 in. Rocky sites, serpentine, east-
side forest, subalpine, low to high elevation
Subshrub, stems either unbranched or with few
branches, hairy. **LEAVES** deciduous, opposite but can
seem whorled, mostly 5(9) linear lobes, each lobe 0.1–
0.5 in. long, somewhat flexible, often with a bundle of
smaller leaves in the axils, surfaces non-hairy to hairy,
grayish to greenish, tips pointed, spiny. **FLOWERS** in
clusters at stem ends, flowers trumpet-shaped, lobes
white, tube yellowish to white, sepals smaller or equal
to floral tube, loosely joined by membranous webbing.
FRUIT capsule. **ECOLOGY** grows in forest openings and
rocky slopes. Ssp. *howellii* has shorter (to 0.3 in. long),
densely hairy, grayish leaves, often found on serpentine, rare in California.

See Polemoniaceae with alternate leaves, page 222

Phlox aculeata
POLEMONIACEAE
SAGEBRUSH PHLOX, PRICKLY-LEAVED PHLOX
Native, locally common, blooms mid spring,
2.5–6 in. Shrub-steppe, mid to high elevation
Subshrub or herbaceous, mat-forming, stems clustered, branched. **LEAVES** deciduous, opposite, linear, 0.5–1.5 in. long, crowded, firm, surfaces deep
green, smooth or glandular-hairy, edges smooth, tips
pointed. **FLOWERS** 1–3 at stem ends, trumpet-shaped,
petals white to pink or blue, sepals glandular-hairy,
tube bulged near base. **FRUIT** capsule. **ECOLOGY** grows
in shrub-steppe communities, often with sagebrush,
on rocky or sandy slopes and flats, tolerant of alkaline
soils, from mid to high elevation.

Phlox adsurgens
POLEMONIACEAE
WOODLAND PHLOX, NORTHERN PHLOX
Native, locally common, blooms late spring,
4–12 in. West-side forest, mid elevation
Subshrub, trailing to sprawling, rhizomatous, stems
glandular-hairy. **LEAVES** deciduous, opposite, oval to
egg-shaped, 0.5–1 in. long, surfaces non-hairy, edges
smooth, tips pointed. **FLOWERS** in flat-topped clusters
at stem ends, flowers trumpet-shaped, tube 0.5–1 in.
long, petals pink marked with white, tube and sepals
glandular-hairy, style 0.25–0.5 in. long, several times
longer than stigmas. **FRUIT** capsule. **ECOLOGY** grows
on slopes in conifer and mixed evergreen forests in the
mountains.

Phlox austromontana
POLEMONIACEAE
WESTERN MOUNTAIN PHLOX
Native, locally common, blooms mid
spring–early summer, 2–4 in. Rocky sites,
shrub-steppe, mid to high elevation
Subshrub, erect, forms loose cushions or mats, not
glandular. **LEAVES** deciduous, opposite, stiff, lance-

shaped, 0.2–0.6 in. long, hairy above,
mostly non-hairy below, tips sharply
pointed. **FLOWERS** single at stem ends,
flowers trumpet-shaped, membrane
between sepals curved near base, petals white, sometimes pink or lavender,
lobes rounded. **FRUIT** capsule.
ECOLOGY grows in rocky areas in
woodlands, forests, and sagebrush
communities.

Phlox caespitosa

(*Phlox rigida, Phlox douglasii* ssp. *rigida*)
POLEMONIACEAE
CLUSTERED PHLOX, CLUMPED PHLOX, TUFTED
PHLOX

Native, locally common, blooms mid spring, 2–6 in.
East-side forest, shrub-steppe, low to high elevation
Subshrub, erect to mat-forming, often glandular-hairy
in part. **LEAVES** deciduous, opposite, firm, linear, 0.2–
0.5 in. long, edges sometimes fringed with hair near
base, tip sharply pointed. **FLOWERS** single at stem ends,
trumpet-shaped, petals pink, white, or pale lavender,
tube less than twice as long as sepals, sepals thickened,
joined with flat membranes. **FRUIT** capsule.

ECOLOGY grows on rocky, open slopes, usually in ponderosa pine forests, also found in juni-
per woodlands and in shrub-steppe.

Phlox colubrina

POLEMONIACEAE
SNAKE RIVER PHLOX

Native, locally common, blooms early–mid spring,
4–20 in. Rocky sites, low to mid elevation
Subshrub, erect to spreading, stems branched, non-
hairy. **LEAVES** deciduous, opposite, linear, 1–3 in. long,
flexible, surfaces grayish green, non-hairy, edges
smooth, tips pointed. **FLOWERS** stalked, in leaf axils
and at stem ends, single or small leafy clusters, trumpet-shaped, petals unnotched, pink or white, style to
0.1 in. long, often shorter than stigmas, sepals smooth.
FRUIT capsule. **ECOLOGY** endemic along the Snake
River and its tributaries, growing on rocky banks,
slopes, rock outcrops, and in crevices,
often in basalt. The similar *P. speciosa*
has notched petals and is often hairy or
glandular-hairy.

Phlox diffusa
POLEMONIACEAE
SPREADING PHLOX

Native, common, blooms mid spring, 2–6 in.
Rocky sites, west-side forest, east-side forest,
alpine, subalpine, mid to high elevation

Subshrub, taprooted, mat-forming. **LEAVES** deciduous,
opposite, linear to lance-shaped, 0.2–1 in. long, surfaces non-hairy, edges with cobwebby hairs near the
base, tips pointed. **FLOWERS** single at stem ends, trumpet-shaped, petals pink, white, or light blue, tube less
than twice as long as sepals, sepals hairy, joined by flat
membranes. **FRUIT** capsule, seeds mostly 3.
ECOLOGY grows on forested or rocky slopes from mid
elevation to alpine areas.

Phlox hirsuta
POLEMONIACEAE
YREKA PHLOX

Native, rare, blooms mid spring, 2–6 in.
Rocky sites, serpentine, mid elevation

Subshrub, stems open, trailing to erect, with coarse,
stiff hairs. **LEAVES** deciduous, opposite, oval to lance-
shaped, 0.5–1 in. long, rigid, surfaces densely hairy,
hair coarse and stiff, tips pointed. **FLOWERS** in few-flowered, flat-topped clusters, trumpet-shaped, petals
bright pink to white, style 0.2–0.3 in. long, longer
than stigmas, sepals glandular-hairy, joined by curved
membranes. **FRUIT** capsule. **ECOLOGY** grows in serpentine-derived soils on open, rocky slopes and ridges,
with western juniper, Jeffrey pine
and/or ponderosa pine. Endemic to
California.

Phlox longifolia
POLEMONIACEAE
LONGLEAF PHLOX

Native, common, blooms late spring–early
summer, 4–16 in. Meadows, east-side forest,
shrub-steppe, low to mid elevation
Subshrub, stems erect to trailing, hairy or not.
LEAVES deciduous, opposite, linear, 0.5–3 in. long, tips
pointed. FLOWERS in leafy clusters, trumpet-shaped,
petals purplish, pink, or white, lobes unnotched, style
long, 0.2–0.6 in. long, much longer than stigmas.
FRUIT capsule. ECOLOGY grows in dry, often rocky
places, in shrub-steppe and forests, lowland to montane. The similar *P. speciosa* has notched petals and
style to 0.1 in. long, mostly
shorter than stigmas.

Phlox speciosa
POLEMONIACEAE
SHOWY PHLOX

Native, common, blooms mid spring, 6–16 in. East-
side forest, shrub-steppe, low to mid elevation
Subshrub or shrub, erect, glandular-hairy or hairy,
rarely non-hairy. LEAVES deciduous, opposite, linear
to lance-shaped, 0.5–3 in. long, edges smooth, tips
pointed. FLOWERS in leafy clusters, trumpet-shaped,
petals light pink to white, lobes notched, style short,
to 0.1 in. long, mostly shorter than stigmas, sepals
glandular-hairy, joined by flat membranes. FRUIT capsule. ECOLOGY grows in shrub-steppe, dry forests, and
grassy slopes, often with sagebrush or ponderosa pine,
from low to montane areas. Rare in
British Columbia.

Phlox viscida
POLEMONIACEAE
STICKY PHLOX
Native, locally common, blooms all spring, 2–8 in. Rocky sites, shrub-steppe, mid elevation
Subshrub, erect or trailing, stems often creeping below ground, mostly glandular-hairy. **LEAVES** deciduous, opposite, linear to lance-shaped, 0.5–1.5 in. long, somewhat crowded, edges smooth, tips pointed. **FLOWERS** in leafy clusters, odor unpleasant, trumpet-shaped, petals pink, purple, or white, style 0.2–0.4 in. long, several times longer than stigmas, sepals glandular-hairy, joined by flat membranes. **FRUIT** capsule. **ECOLOGY** grows in rocky or gravelly areas, often thin soils, in shrub-steppe, meadows, and pine forests.

Ceanothus arcuatus
RHAMNACEAE
ARCHING CEANOTHUS
Native, locally common, blooms all spring, 1–3 ft. Rocky sites, serpentine, west-side forest, mid to high elevation
Shrub, erect to spreading, stems arching, stiff, bark gray, twigs grayish brown to brown, with waxy coating. **LEAVES** evergreen, opposite, oval to egg-shaped, to 0.5 in. long, dull green and non-hairy above, paler and sometimes hairy below, edges smooth, tips rounded. **FLOWERS** in small clusters, <0.5 in. long, flowers small, petals and sepals 5, white to pale blue. **FRUIT** capsule, ridged, white, horns present, slender, to 0.1 in. long. **ECOLOGY** grows on rocky slopes, including serpentine substrates, in conifer and mixed evergreen montane forests.

See *Ceanothus* with alternate leaves, page 225

Ceanothus cuneatus
RHAMNACEAE
BUCKBRUSH, WEDGELEAF CEANOTHUS
Native, common, blooms late winter–early
spring, 3–10 ft. Coastal, chaparral, west-side
forest, east-side forest, low to mid elevation
Shrub, stems erect to arching, twigs brown or grayish
brown, rigid, hairy or not. LEAVES evergreen, opposite, oval to roundish, 0.2–1 in. long, tapering to the
base, dull green and non-hairy above, paler, hairy or
not below, edges smooth or toothed, tips rounded or
few-toothed. FLOWERS small, in dense rounded clusters, 0.5–1 in. long, petals and sepals white, blue, or
lavender. FRUIT capsule, round, short horns on top.
ECOLOGY grows in sandy
flats, chaparral, forests,
and coastal scrub. Var.
fascicularis, rare in California, has blue or lavender flowers and clusters
of narrower leaves in the
main leaf axils.

Ceanothus jepsonii
RHAMNACEAE
JEPSON'S CEANOTHUS
Native, locally common, blooms early–mid
spring, 1.7–5 ft. Rocky sites, serpentine, chaparral,
west-side forest, low to mid elevation
Shrub, erect, twigs brown, rigid. LEAVES evergreen,
opposite, oval to egg-shaped, 0.5–1 in. long, shiny
light green to yellowish green and non-hairy above,
pale with short patches of hair below, edges with 7–15
spine-tipped teeth, wavy, sometimes rolled under, tips
rounded or pointed. FLOWERS small, in rounded clusters, sepals and petals 6–8, white to bluish violet, scent
musky. FRUIT capsule, round, with short horns, wrinkled. ECOLOGY grows on open, serpen-
tine slopes and ridges, often where hot
and sunny, in coastal scrub, chaparral,
and pine and oak woodlands. White
flowers usually in eastern part of the
range, blue in the west. Endemic to
California.

Ceanothus pinetorum
RHAMNACEAE
COVILLE CEANOTHUS, KERN CEANOTHUS,
KERN PLATEAU CEANOTHUS

Native, rare, blooms mid–late spring, 0.5–3 ft.

East-side forest, subalpine, mid to high elevation Shrub, erect to spreading, mat- to mound-forming, twigs reddish brown, hairy or not. **LEAVES** evergreen, opposite, roundish, 0.5–1 in. long, <2 times longer than wide, shiny green and non-hairy above, paler and minutely hairy below, edges with spine-tipped teeth, tips rounded. **FLOWERS** in clusters at stem ends and upper leaf axils, to 1 in. long, flowers small, petals and sepals 5, pale blue to bluish lavender. **FRUIT** cap-

sule, lobed or not, brown, horns present, erect, wrinkled. **ECOLOGY** grows on rocky to gravelly, often granitic soils, slopes and flats in openings in conifer forests, montane to subalpine. The similar *C. prostratus* has leaves mostly >2 times longer than wide. Endemic to California.

Ceanothus prostratus
RHAMNACEAE
PROSTRATE CEANOTHUS, MAHALA MAT,
PINEMAT
Native, locally common, blooms mid spring–
early summer, to 1 ft. Chaparral, west-side
forest, east-side forest, mid elevation

Shrub, stems trailing, mat-forming, rooting at the
nodes, twigs reddish brown, hairy. **LEAVES** evergreen, opposite, lance- to egg-shaped, 0.5–1 in. long,
mostly >2 times longer than wide, shiny dark green
above, edges with 3–9 sharp-tipped teeth near tip,
tips rounded. **FLOWERS** in rounded clusters 0.5–1 in.
long, flowers small, petals and sepals 5, blue, lavender, or purple. **FRUIT** capsule, round-
ish, red, ridged, horns short, wrinkled.
ECOLOGY forms dense mats in sun or
partial shade in ponderosa pine, red fir,
or chaparral communities.

Ceanothus pumilus
RHAMNACEAE
SISKIYOU MAT, DWARF CEANOTHUS
Native, locally common, blooms mid–late
spring, to 20 in. Serpentine, chaparral, west-
side forest, low to mid elevation

Shrub, mat- or mound-forming, twigs reddish brown.
LEAVES evergreen, opposite, lance- to egg-shaped, 0.2–
0.5 in. long, dull green and non-hairy above, paler and
with tiny patches of hair below, edges toothed, tips
rounded. **FLOWERS** small, in rounded clusters about 0.5
in. long, sepals and petals pale blue to lavender.
FRUIT capsule, red, roundish, ridged, with 3 short
horns. **ECOLOGY** grows on rocky serpentine slopes and
flats in chaparral and conifer forests,
and with *Quercus garryana* var. *breweri*
in the Siskiyou region.

Cephalanthus occidentalis
RUBIACEAE
COMMON BUTTONBUSH
Native, locally common, blooms mid spring–
late summer, 7–33 ft. Bog/fen/wetland, lake/
pond, streambanks, low to mid elevation
Shrub, erect, base of plant often swollen, bark gray
or brown, branches green to brown. **LEAVES** deciduous, opposite or whorled, oval to egg-shaped, 3–8 in.
long, surfaces non-hairy, edges smooth, tips pointed.
FLOWERS in ball-shaped, dense clusters, bisexual, tubular, white to yellowish, sepals and petals 4. **FRUIT** nutlets, reddish brown. **ECOLOGY** grows on streambanks,
shorelines, marshes, bogs, and other wet places from
low to mid elevation.

Acer circinatum
SAPINDACEAE (ACERACEAE)
VINE MAPLE

Native, common, blooms early–mid spring, 3–26 ft.

West-side forest, east-side forest, low to mid elevation Tree or shrub, typically with multiple, spreading trunks and sprawling branches, often reclining and rooting, sometimes forming extensive colonies. **LEAVES** deciduous, opposite, roundish, 7- to 9-lobed, 1–2.5 in. long, hairy beneath, veins hairy above, edges toothed, lobes and teeth pointed, fall color gold to bright red (in sunny spots). **FLOWERS** in few-flowered flat-topped clusters, flowers male or bisexual, saucer-shaped, sepals 4–5, reddish, petals white, shorter than sepals, stamens 8–10. **FRUIT** samara, in pairs, wings of the pair spreading at about a 180-degree angle, reddish brown, non-hairy. **ECOLOGY** shade tolerant, grows in moist forests and forest openings, along streambanks, in draws, often underneath other tree species.

See Sapindaceae with compound leaves, page 417; see *Acer* with compound leaves, page 417

Acer glabrum
SAPINDACEAE (ACERACEAE)
TORREY MAPLE, MOUNTAIN MAPLE
Native, common, blooms mid spring,
3–30 ft. Streambanks, west-side forest,
east-side forest, mid elevation

Shrub or small tree, bark gray to reddish purple, twigs reddish, non-hairy. **LEAVES** deciduous, opposite, heart-shaped, blade 1–2 in. long, usually <2.5 in. wide, 3- to 5-lobed, edges toothed, lobe and teeth tips rounded, green above, paler beneath, somewhat leathery, both sides glandular-hairy or not, tips rounded. **FLOWERS** in flat-topped clusters in leaf axils, blooming as the leaves unfold. Male and female flowers on separate or the same plant, flowers saucer-shaped, petals and sepals each mostly 5(4–6), yellowish green, stamens usually 10, styles 2. **FRUIT** samara, in pairs, wings of the pair <90-degree angle, greenish brown, non-hairy. **ECOLOGY** grows in forest understories, streambanks, canyons, and on rocky slopes in montane areas.

Acer glabrum var. *douglasii*
SAPINDACEAE (ACERACEAE)
DOUGLAS MAPLE
Native, common, blooms mid spring, 3–30
ft. East-side forest, low to mid elevation

Shrub or small tree, bark gray to reddish purple, twigs reddish, non-hairy. **LEAVES** deciduous, opposite, heart-shaped, 1–5.5 in. long, usually >2.5 in. wide, 3- to 5-lobed, edges sharp-toothed, green above, paler beneath, both sides glandular-hairy or not, tips pointed. **FLOWERS** in flat-topped clusters in leaf axils, blooming as the leaves unfold. Male and female flowers on separate plants or on the same plant, flowers saucer-shaped, petals and sepals each mostly 5(4–6), yellowish green, stamens usually 10, styles 2. **FRUIT** samara, in pairs, wings of the pair <90-degree angle, greenish brown, non-hairy. **ECOLOGY** grows in forest understories, streambanks, valleys, and on rocky slopes from low to montane elevation.

Acer macrophyllum
SAPINDACEAE (ACERACEAE)
BIGLEAF MAPLE

Native, common, blooms early–mid spring,
50–100 ft. Streambanks, west-side forest,
east-side forest, low to mid elevation

Tree, crown rounded and spreading, bark grayish brown, ridged, branches smooth, greenish. **LEAVES** deciduous, opposite, outline round, 4–12 in. wide, edges deeply 5-lobed, lobe edges also lobed, dark green above, paler beneath, both sides short-hairy, tips pointed, fall color golden yellow. **FLOWERS** in drooping, elongated clusters, 10–50 flowers each, flowers bisexual or male only, both types on same plant, blooms before or as the leaves unfold. Flowers saucer-shaped, sepals and petals usually 5(4–6), about the same length, to 0.3 in. long, petals greenish yellow, stamens hairy near the base, styles 2. **FRUIT** samara, in pairs, wings of the pair <90-degree angle, golden yellow, hairy. **ECOLOGY** moderately shade tolerant, grows in forests, streambanks, draws, and canyons, from moist to arid areas. Distribution in the north is controlled by its cold hardiness, and in the south by its level of drought tolerance. Intolerant of prolonged flooding, suffering high mortality rates if floods last more than 2 months. Supports a variety of mosses, lichens, ferns, and other epiphytes on its trunk and branches in moist areas. Produces abundant amounts of seed that are dispersed by twirling through the air on their wings, germinating readily the following spring. Often killed by fire but resprouts from the root crown.

Buddleja davidii
SCROPHULARIACEAE (BUDDLEJACEAE)
BUTTERFLYBUSH
Non-native, scattered, blooms mid spring–mid
summer, 3–17 ft. Streambanks, disturbed, low elevation
Shrub, many-branched, can die back to ground in
cold climates, with star-shaped hairs. **LEAVES** deciduous to evergreen, opposite, lance- to egg-shaped,
2–12 in. long, dark green and sparsely hairy above,
densely white-hairy below, edges toothed or smooth,
tips pointed. **FLOWERS** in large clusters at stem ends,
flowers trumpet-shaped, lobes 4, purple with orange
eye, stamens inside tube. **FRUIT** capsule, brown, to 0.3
in. long. **ECOLOGY** invasive escapee from cultivation,
native to China, grows in forests, streambanks, roadsides, railroad tracks, and other disturbed places.

Stenotus acaulis (*Haplopappus acaulis*)
ASTERACEAE
STEMLESS GOLDENWEED
Native, common, blooms late spring–mid
summer, 1–8.5 in. Rocky sites, shrub-steppe,
alpine, subalpine, mid to high elevation
Subshrub, mat-forming, stems with withered, persistent leaves at base. **LEAVES** basal, on short stems,
linear to lance-shaped, 0.2–3.5 in. long, rigid, green,
edges fringed with short, stiff hairs, tips pointed.
FLOWERS aggregated into heads, heads mostly single at
the end of leafless stalks, 0.5–3 in. long, both ray and
disk flowers, petals yellow, bracts oval to lance-shaped,
sticky-glandular, tips pointed. **FRUIT** achene, hairy or
not. **ECOLOGY** grows in dry rocky areas
in shrub-steppe, open forest, and alpine
meadows, from mid elevation to alpine.

See Asteraceae with alternate leaves,
page 113; compound leaves, page 374

Stenotus lanuginosus
(*Haplopappus lanuginosus*)
ASTERACEAE
WOOLLY GOLDENWEED, WOOLLY STENOTUS
Native, uncommon, blooms mid spring–mid
summer, 1.5–12.5 in. Meadows, east-side forest,
shrub-steppe, subalpine, low to high elevation
Subshrub, forming low tufts, stems densely hairy,
glandular or not. **LEAVES** deciduous, basal, linear to
lance-shaped, 1–4 in. long, floppy, surfaces grayish,
woolly hairy, hair sometimes in tufts, edges smooth,
tips pointed or rounded. **FLOWERS** aggregated into
heads, heads solitary at end of flower stalk, stalk leafy
or not, both ray and disk flowers, petals yellow, rays
showy, bracts mostly lance-shaped,
length similar, tips pointed.
FRUIT achene, short-hairy, hair tuft
white. **ECOLOGY** grows in rocky or gravelly soils in sagebrush, open forests, and
alpine meadows, low to high elevation.
Rare in California.

Cornus canadensis
CORNACEAE
BUNCHBERRY, DWARF DOGWOOD

Native, locally common, blooms late spring–early summer, 2–8 in. Bog/fen/wetland, west-side forest, east-side forest, low to high elevation Subshrub, rhizomatous, stems erect. **LEAVES** semi-evergreen, whorled at stem tip, can have opposite leaf-like bracts below, oval to egg-shaped, 1–3 in. long, edges smooth, tips pointed. **FLOWERS** in headlike clusters, cluster with 4 showy bracts, bracts egg-shaped, 0.5–1 in. long, white, pinkish, or purplish, petals 4, greenish white, about 0.04 in. long. **FRUIT** berrylike stone fruit, bright red, edible, sweet. **ECOLOGY** moist forests, bogs. Rare in California. Specimens with purple or purple-tipped white petals are now granted specific status as *C. unalaschkensis.*

See *Cornus* with opposite leaves, page 312

Empetrum nigrum
ERICACEAE (EMPETRACEAE)
CROWBERRY

Native, locally common, blooms mid spring–mid summer, to 6 in. Coastal, bog/fen/wetland, west-side forest, alpine, subalpine, low to high elevation Shrub, spreading, branches woolly-hairy, up to 1 ft. in length. **LEAVES** evergreen, in part whorls of 4 and in part alternate, needlelike, 0.2–0.3 in. long, surfaces glandular-hairy, green, central groove beneath, edges rolled under, tips pointed. **FLOWERS** 1–2 in leaf axils, either bisexual or male, small, purplish brown, stamens 3. **FRUIT** berrylike, purplish black, edible but some consider the taste unpleasant. **ECOLOGY** grows in bogs, coastal bluffs, subalpine forests and alpine slopes. Fruit relished by bears and other wildlife. Rare in California.

See Ericaceae with alternate leaves, page 154; opposite leaves, page 317

Eriogonum caespitosum
POLYGONACEAE
MATTED BUCKWHEAT, CUSHION DESERT
BUCKWHEAT, CUSHION ERIOGONUM
Native, common, blooms late spring–early
summer, 1–4 in. Rocky sites, shrub-steppe,
subalpine, mid to high elevation

Subshrub, mat-forming. **LEAVES** persistent, basal,
oval to egg-shaped, 0.1–0.5 in. long, surfaces usually grayish-hairy. **FLOWERS** in round, dense clusters,
unbranched and lacking bracts, flowering stem leafless, flowers unisexual, male and female flowers on
separate plants, cup-shaped, stalk present, tepals to
0.5 in. long in female flowers, to 0.2 in. long in males,
yellow to pinkish, outer surface hairy.
FRUIT achene, brown. **ECOLOGY** grows
in sandy to rocky soils, in shrub-steppe
and conifer forests, montane.

See Polygonaceae with alternate leaves,
page 223; *Eriogonum* with alternate
leaves, page 223

Eriogonum compositum
POLYGONACEAE
NORTHERN BUCKWHEAT, HEARTLEAF
BUCKWHEAT
Native, common, blooms late spring–mid summer,
8–16 in. Rocky sites, shrub-steppe, low to high elevation

Subshrub or herbaceous, erect to spreading,
clump-forming. **LEAVES** deciduous, basal, lance-,
heart-, or egg-shaped, 1–10 in. long, hairy and greenish above, white-woolly hairy below, edges smooth,
tips pointed. **FLOWERS** in flat-topped clusters with
leafy bracts beneath, floral stalk 8–20 in. long, flowers
mostly bisexual, cup-shaped, pale to bright yellow or
cream, tepals about 0.2 in. long, outer surface mostly
non-hairy, stalk present, to 0.06 in. long.
FRUIT achene, light brown, to 0.2 in.
long. **ECOLOGY** cliffs, talus, and gravelly
or sandy slopes in sagebrush communities, montane forests, and oak woodlands. Uncommon in California.

Eriogonum congdonii
POLYGONACEAE
CONGDON'S BUCKWHEAT

Native, rare, blooms all summer, 6–20 in. Rocky
sites, serpentine, west-side forest, mid elevation
Subshrub, spreading to erect. **LEAVES** deciduous, basal,
oval, 0.2–1 in. long, olive-green, hairy or not above,
white-hairy below, edges rolled under. **FLOWERS** in
branched, flat-topped clusters, flowering stem green,
mostly non-hairy, flowers cup-shaped, 0.2 in. long,
stalk present, tepals bright yellow, non-hairy.
FRUIT achene, light brown. **ECOLOGY** grows on serpentine slopes and outcrops, in conifer forests, and with
manzanitas. Endemic to California. The similar *E. ter-
natum* is mat-forming and has wider
leaves and hairy flowering stems.

Eriogonum douglasii
POLYGONACEAE
DOUGLAS' ERIOGONUM, DOUGLAS'
BUCKWHEAT

Native, common, blooms late spring–mid
summer, 1.5–6 in. Rocky sites, east-side forest,
shrub-steppe, subalpine, low to high elevation
Subshrub, mat-forming. **LEAVES** deciduous, basal, linear to spatula-shaped, 0.2–1 in. long, greenish, grayish,
or white-hairy above, gray or white-hairy below, edges
smooth. **FLOWERS** in rounded clusters, bracts below
absent, flowering stem usually has a whorl of leaves at
midlength, flowers cup-shaped, 0.2–0.4 in. long, stalk
present, tepals lemon-yellow, cream, purplish, or pinkish red, hairy to rarely not.
FRUIT achene, light brown, hairy.
ECOLOGY grows in sandy to rocky soils
in the sagebrush steppe, juniper woodlands, and open conifer forests.

Eriogonum elatum
POLYGONACEAE
TALL BUCKWHEAT

Native, locally common, blooms all summer, 12–32 in. Rocky sites, shrub-steppe, low to high elevation Subshrub, erect, stems slender to stout, hairy or not. **LEAVES** deciduous, basal, stalks spreading-hairy, lance- to egg-shaped, 1.5–6 in. long, both surfaces greenish and mostly hairy, edges smooth, tips pointed. **FLOWERS** in loose, open, flat-topped clusters, branches with linear bracts, flowers cup-shaped, about 0.1 in. long, stalk absent, tepals white to cream, sometimes aging reddish, tepal outer surface hairy. **FRUIT** achene, light brown, to 0.2 in. long, non-hairy.

ECOLOGY grows on open, dry slopes, ridges, and rocky areas, in sage-brush and forest communities.

Eriogonum flavum (*Eriogonum piperi*)
POLYGONACEAE
ALPINE GOLDEN BUCKWHEAT, YELLOW BUCKWHEAT, GOLDEN ERIOGONUM

Native, locally common, blooms all summer, 2–12 in. Rocky sites, alpine, subalpine, mid to high elevation Subshrub, mat-forming. **LEAVES** deciduous, basal, linear to lance-shaped, 1–3 in. long, greenish or gray-ish-hairy above, white- or grayish-hairy beneath, tips pointed. **FLOWERS** in rounded, branched clusters with leafy bracts beneath, flowering stem leafless, hairy, flowers cup-shaped, 0.2 in. long, stalk present, tepals pale to bright yellow, outer surface hairy. **FRUIT** achene, brown. **ECOLOGY** grows in rocky areas in montane grasslands to alpine ridges.

Eriogonum heracleoides
POLYGONACEAE
PARSNIP-FLOWERED BUCKWHEAT, CREAMY
ERIOGONUM, WYETH'S BUCKWHEAT
Native, common, blooms late spring–mid
summer, 4–24 in. Rocky sites, shrub-steppe,
subalpine, low to high elevation
Subshrub, erect, mat-forming. LEAVES deciduous,
basal, linear to lance-shaped, 1–2 in. long, 4–15 times
longer than wide, surfaces hairy, grayish to greenish, edges smooth. FLOWERS in branched, flat-topped
clusters, flowering stem often with a whorl of bracts at
midlength, flowers cup-shaped, 0.2–0.4 in. long, stalk
present, tepals white, cream, or yellowish, outer surface non-hairy. FRUIT achene, light to
dark brown. ECOLOGY grows in shrub-
steppe, dry forest openings, and ridges
from lower elevations to subalpine.

Eriogonum hirtellum
POLYGONACEAE
KLAMATH MOUNTAIN BUCKWHEAT
Native, rare, blooms mid summer, 4–12 in. Rocky sites,
serpentine, west-side forest, mid to high elevation
Subshrub, erect, stems non-hairy. LEAVES deciduous, basal, oval, lance-, or egg-shaped, 0.2–1 in. long,
surfaces mostly with short, stiff hairs, edges smooth.
FLOWERS in ball-shaped clusters, branched, 5 semi-
leafy bracts beneath, flowering stalk leafless, flowers
cup-shaped, stalk present, 0.1 in. long, tepals bright
yellow, white-hairy on outer surface, stamens protrude
beyond tepals. FRUIT achene, brown, hairy at the tip.
ECOLOGY grows on serpentine outcrops and slopes
in oak woodlands and conifer forests.
Endemic to California.

Eriogonum latifolium
POLYGONACEAE
COAST BUCKWHEAT
Native, common, blooms all year,
8–28 in. Coastal, low elevation
Subshrub, erect to spreading, mat-forming.
LEAVES deciduous, basal, oblong to egg-shaped, 1–2 in. long, greenish or not, hairy or not above, densely white- to tan-hairy below, edges smooth or wavy. **FLOWERS** in ball-shaped to open clusters, branched, 3 leafy bracts beneath, flowering stalk leafless, flowers cup-shaped, 0.1 in. long, stalk absent, tepals white, pink, or reddish, non-hairy, stamens protrude beyond tepals. **FRUIT** achene, brown, non-hairy. **ECOLOGY** grows near the coast, in sandy flats, slopes, and bluffs within sagebrush scrub and grassland communities.

Eriogonum libertini
POLYGONACEAE
DUBAKELLA MOUNTAIN BUCKWHEAT
Native, rare, blooms mid summer, 2–8 in. Rocky sites, serpentine, chaparral, west-side forest, mid elevation
Subshrub, spreading, mat-forming. **LEAVES** deciduous, basal, oblong to oval, 0.2–0.5 in. long, greenish, sparsely hairy above, densely white-hairy below, edges smooth. **FLOWERS** in ball-headed clusters, unbranched, 3 leafy bracts beneath, flowering stem with whorl of leafy bracts at midlength, flowers cup-shaped, to 0.3 in. long, stalk present, tepals bright yellow, outer surface sparsely hairy. **FRUIT** achene, light brown, hairy at tip. **ECOLOGY** restricted to serpentine substrates, in chaparral, oak woodlands, and conifer forests. Endemic to California.

Eriogonum lobbii
POLYGONACEAE
LOBB'S BUCKWHEAT
Native, locally common, blooms mid summer,
1–12 in. Rocky sites, shrub-steppe, alpine,
subalpine, mid to high elevation
Subshrub, stems trailing, sometimes mat-forming.
LEAVES deciduous, basal, roundish to egg-shaped,
0.5–1.5 in. long, greenish, hairy above, densely hairy
below, edges smooth, tips rounded. **FLOWERS** in dense,
rounded clusters, branched, leafy bracts beneath, flowering stem leafless, hairy, flowers cup-shaped, 0.2 in.
long, stalk present, tepals white to rose, non-hairy, stamens protrude beyond tepals. **FRUIT** achene, brown,
non-hairy. **ECOLOGY** grows in gravelly to
rocky areas in shrub-steppe and conifer
forests. Rare in Oregon.

Eriogonum marifolium
POLYGONACEAE
MARUMLEAF BUCKWHEAT
Native, locally common, blooms late spring–mid
summer, 2–20 in. West-side forest, east-side
forest, alpine, subalpine, mid to high elevation
Subshrub, mat-forming. **LEAVES** deciduous, basal, oval
to egg-shaped, 0.1–1 in. long, green above, grayish-
or brownish-hairy below, sparsely hairy to non-hairy
above. **FLOWERS** in rounded, branched clusters with
short leafy bracts beneath, flowering stem leafless,
hairy or not, flowers unisexual, male and female flowers on separate plants,
flowers bell-shaped, 0.1
in. long, stalk present,
pale to deep yellow, red-
dish with age, non-hairy.
FRUIT achene, brown.
ECOLOGY grows in conifer forests to rocky alpine
slopes.

Eriogonum niveum
POLYGONACEAE
SNOW BUCKWHEAT, SNOW ERIOGONUM
Native, common, blooms all summer,
8–24 in. Rocky sites, east-side forest,
shrub-steppe, low to mid elevation
Subshrub or herbaceous, mat-forming or erect.
LEAVES deciduous, basal, oval to egg-shaped, 0.5–2.5
in. long, both surfaces grayish-hairy, edges smooth,
tips rounded or pointed. **FLOWERS** in much-branched,
open clusters with leafy bracts, flowering stems and
bracts grayish-hairy, tepals separate, cream, pink, or
rarely yellow, to 0.2 in. long, stalk absent. **FRUIT** achene,
brown, non-hairy. **ECOLOGY** grows in rocky or sandy

soils in shrub-steppe
communities and
forest openings. The
similar *E. strictum*
has open or dense
flower clusters, leafy
bracts absent.

Eriogonum nudum
POLYGONACEAE
NAKED BUCKWHEAT, BARESTEM BUCKWEAT,
NAKED ERIOGONUM
Native, common, blooms all summer, 0.3–5 ft.
Rocky sites, subalpine, low to high elevation
Subshrub, erect. **LEAVES** deciduous, basal, oval to lance-
shaped, 0.5–2.5 in. long, stalk 2–4 times longer than
blade, greenish with tufts of hair above, grayish-hairy
below, edges wavy. **FLOWERS** in loose, open, flat-topped
clusters with narrow, leafy bracts beneath, flowering
stem leafless, flowers cup-shaped, 0.1 in. long, stalk
absent, tepals white, pinkish, or yellow, mostly non-
hairy, with feathery bracts beneath. **FRUIT** achene,

brown, non-hairy. **ECOLOGY** grows in
various habitats and elevations, usually
in rocky or sandy soils. Some varieties
rare in Oregon and California.

Eriogonum ochrocephalum
POLYGONACEAE
WHITEWOOLLY BUCKWHEAT

Native, rare, blooms late spring–mid summer, 2–18 in. Rocky sites, shrub-steppe, mid to high elevation Subshrub, matted to spreading, white woolly-hairy. **LEAVES** deciduous, mostly basal, oval, lance-, or egg-shaped, 0.5–1 in. long, surfaces grayish green, densely white-hairy, edges smooth, tips rounded. **FLOWERS** in ball-shaped clusters at end of leafless stems, flowers cup-shaped, to 0.1 in. long, stalk absent, tepals light yellow, non-hairy, stamens protrude beyond tepals. **FRUIT** achene, light brown. **ECOLOGY** grows in volcanic or clay soils on dry slopes within pinyon-juniper woodlands and sagebrush communities.

Eriogonum ovalifolium
POLYGONACEAE
OVAL-LEAVED BUCKWHEAT

Native, common, blooms late spring–mid summer, 1–8 in. Meadows, rocky sites, shrub-steppe, alpine, subalpine, mid to high elevation Subshrub, mat-forming. **LEAVES** deciduous, basal, oval, lance-, or diamond-shaped, 0.1–2.5 in. long, surfaces white- or greenish-hairy, edges sometimes brownish. **FLOWERS** in dense, round clusters, mostly unbranched, flowering stem leafless, hairy, flowers often unisexual, cup-shaped, 0.2 in. long, stalk absent, non-hairy, tepals separate, white, cream, yellow, pink, or red, outer ones broader than the inner. **FRUIT** achene, brown. **ECOLOGY** grows in rocky areas, meadows, and forests, from montane to alpine elevation. The similar *E. strictum* has branched, less dense flower clusters.

Eriogonum ovalifolium var. *nivale*
POLYGONACEAE
CUSHION BUCKWHEAT

Native, locally common, blooms all summer, to 5 in. Rocky sites, alpine, subalpine, high elevation Subshrub, mat-forming. **LEAVES** deciduous, basal, round, 0.1–0.3 in. long, surfaces white or silvery-hairy, edges sometimes brownish. **FLOWERS** in dense, round clusters, unbranched, flowering stems leafless, hairy, flowers often unisexual, 0.2 in. long, stalk absent, non-hairy, tepals separate, white, pink, or red, outer ones broader than the inner. **FRUIT** achene, brown. **ECOLOGY** grows in rocky areas, meadows, and forests from montane to alpine elevation.

Eriogonum ovalifolium var. *purpureum*
(*Eriogonum ovalifolium* var. *celsum*)
POLYGONACEAE
PURPLE CUSHION BUCKWHEAT

Native, common, blooms late spring–mid summer, 2–8 in. Rocky sites, alpine, subalpine, mid to high elevation Subshrub, mat-forming. **LEAVES** deciduous, basal, oval, spatula-, or egg-shaped, 0.2–1 in. long, surfaces hairy, hairs tangled, edges not brownish. **FLOWERS** in dense, round clusters, unbranched, flowering stem leaf-less, hairy, flowers often unisexual, 0.2 in. long, stalk absent, non-hairy, tepals separate, white, pink, or pur-ple, outer ones broader than the inner. **FRUIT** achene, brown. **ECOLOGY** grows in rocky or sandy areas, mead-ows, and forests, higher elevations.

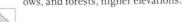

Eriogonum pendulum
POLYGONACEAE
WALDO BUCKWHEAT

Native, rare, blooms mid–late summer, 8–20 in. Rocky
sites, serpentine, west-side forest, low elevation
Subshrub or shrub, erect to scraggly. **LEAVES** deciduous, basal, oval to lance-shaped, 1–1.5 in. long, greenish with tufts of hair above, grayish-hairy beneath,
edges smooth. **FLOWERS** in open, branched clusters
with narrow, leafy bracts at the forks, stem leafless,
hairy, flowers cup-shaped, 0.2 in. long, tepals white,
outer surface hairy. **FRUIT** achene, brown, hairy.
ECOLOGY grows in rocky, serpentine areas in conifer
forests, oak woodlands, and sagebrush communities.

Eriogonum pyrolifolium
POLYGONACEAE
ALPINE BUCKWHEAT, SHASTA BUCKWHEAT,
DIRTY SOCKS

Native, locally common, blooms all summer, 1–8 in.
Rocky sites, alpine, subalpine, mid to high elevation
Subshrub, erect, mat-forming. **LEAVES** deciduous,
basal, oval to diamond-shaped, 0.5–1.5 in. long,
non-hairy above, woolly-hairy or not beneath, edges
smooth. **FLOWERS** in clusters, with 2 linear bracts, to
1 in. beneath, flowering stems leafless, flowers cup-
shaped, 0.2 in. long, stalk short, tepals white, greenish,
pink, or red, outer surface hairy, some hairs glandular.
FRUIT achene, brown, hairy at tip. **ECOLOGY** grows on
rocky slopes, meadows,
and forests. Var. *pyrolifo-
lium*, which has non-hairy
leaf surfaces, is rare in
California and Oregon.

Eriogonum siskiyouense
POLYGONACEAE
SISKIYOU BUCKWHEAT

Native, rare, blooms all summer, 2–8 in. Rocky
sites, serpentine, west-side forest, high elevation
Subshrub, mat-forming. **LEAVES** deciduous, basal,
round to spatula-shaped, to 0.3 in. long, olive-green
and sparsely to non-hairy above, white- or greenish-hairy beneath, rarely both surfaces non-hairy.
FLOWERS in round, dense clusters, flowering stems
non-hairy with a whorl of leafy bracts at midlength,
flowers cup-shaped, 0.2 in. long, stalk short, tepals
yellow, outer surface non-hairy. **FRUIT** achene, light
brown, non-hairy. **ECOLOGY** grows on serpentine
slopes and rock outcrops
in conifer forest and manzanita communities.
Endemic to California.

Eriogonum sphaerocephalum
POLYGONACEAE
ROUND-HEADED BUCKWHEAT, ROCK
BUCKWHEAT

Native, common, blooms late spring–early summer,
2–16 in. Shrub-steppe, low to high elevation
Subshrub, spreading to erect. **LEAVES** deciduous, basal,
lance- to spatula-shaped, 0.5–1 in. long, sparsely hairy
or not above, usually grayish-hairy beneath, edges
sometimes rolled under. **FLOWERS** in several round,
stalked clusters with a whorl of leaves at the base, rest
of flowering stem leafless, flowers cup-shaped, 0.3 in.
long, stalk present, 0.1 in. long, tepals yellow, white,
cream, or pinkish, tepal outer surface mostly hairy.
FRUIT achene, light brown.
ECOLOGY grows in gravelly and sandy
soils in sagebrush communities, grasslands, and dry conifer forests.

Eriogonum strictum
POLYGONACEAE
STRICT BUCKWHEAT

Native, common, blooms late spring–mid summer, 4–20 in. Rocky sites, shrub-steppe, subalpine, low to high elevation

Subshrub, mat-forming. **LEAVES** deciduous, basal, oval to egg-shaped, 0.2–1 in. long, greenish- or grayish-hairy above, grayish-hairy below, edges smooth, tips rounded or pointed. **FLOWERS** in open or dense clusters, little-branched, leafy bracts absent, tepals separate, cream, pink, or yellow, to 0.2 in. long, stalk absent, outer tepals wider than the inner. **FRUIT** achene, brown, non-hairy.

ECOLOGY grows in rocky or sandy areas within shrub-steppe communities and in forest openings. Var. *greenei*, rare in California, has white-hairy leaves, flowers white to pink. The similar *E. niveum* has many-branched clusters with leafy bracts.

Eriogonum ternatum
POLYGONACEAE
TERNATE BUCKWHEAT

Native, uncommon, blooms all summer, 4–10 in. Serpentine, west-side forest, mid elevation

Subshrub to herbaceous, mat-forming. **LEAVES** deciduous, basal, oval to egg-shaped, to 0.5 in. long, hairy or not above, brownish-hairy below. **FLOWERS** in branched, flat-topped clusters, flowering stem leafless, hairy, flowers cup-shaped, 0.2 in. long, stalk present, tepals bright yellow, non-hairy. **FRUIT** achene, light brown. **ECOLOGY** grows on serpentine slopes and outcrops, in conifer forests, and with manzanitas. Rare in California. The similar *E. congdonii* is not mat-forming and has narrower leaves and non-hairy flowering stems.

Eriogonum thymoides
POLYGONACEAE
THYMELEAF BUCKWHEAT

Native, common, blooms mid spring, 2–12 in. Rocky sites, shrub-steppe, mid elevation

Subshrub, erect to spreading. **LEAVES** deciduous, basal, linear to spatula-shaped, 0.1–0.5 in. long, straight-hairy above, woolly-hairy below, edges rolled under, tips rounded. **FLOWERS** in rounded, dense clusters, floral stalk with whorl of leafy bracts at midlength, flowers mostly unisexual, male and female flowers on separate plants, cup-shaped, to 0.2 in. long, stalk present, tepals yellow, white, or reddish, long, downward-facing hairy. **FRUIT** achene, brown, hairy near the tip. **ECOLOGY** grows in sandy to gravelly, often volcanic, substrates in sagebrush communities, on slopes, ridges, and rock outcrops.

Eriogonum umbellatum
POLYGONACEAE
SULPHUR BUCKWHEAT, SULPHUR ERIOGONUM, SULPHUR FLOWER

Native, common, blooms all summer, 0.3–4 ft. Rocky sites, east-side forest, shrub-steppe, alpine, subalpine, low to high elevation

Subshrub, mat-forming or erect. **LEAVES** deciduous, basal, oval, egg-, or spatula-shaped, 0.5–1.5 in. long, greenish, hairy or not above, mostly grayish-hairy below, tips rounded or pointed. **FLOWERS** in rounded, branched clusters with leafy bracts beneath, flower stalks sometimes with leafy bracts at midlength, flowers usually unisexual, cup-shaped, 0.2 in. long, stalk present, tepals cream, yellow, or pinkish, non-hairy. **FRUIT** achene, brown. **ECOLOGY** habitat and elevation variable, rocky slopes, ridges, forests, and in shrub-steppe.

Eriogonum umbellatum var. *dichrocephalum*

(*Eriogonum umbellatum* var. *aridum*)
POLYGONACEAE
BICOLOR SULPHUR BUCKWHEAT
Native, common, blooms mid summer,
4–12 in. East-side forest, shrub-steppe,
subalpine, mid to high elevation
Subshrub, mat-forming. **LEAVES** deciduous, basal, oval,
0.5–1 in. long, greenish, hairy or not above, grayish-
hairy below. **FLOWERS** in rounded, branched clusters
with leafy bracts beneath, flower stalks leafless, flowers
unisexual, cup-shaped, 0.2 in. long, stalk present,
tepals cream, pale yellow, or whitish, non-hairy.
FRUIT achene, brown. **ECOLOGY** grows
in sandy to gravelly soils, shrub-steppe,
conifer forests, to subalpine areas.

Eriogonum umbellatum var. *hausknechtii*

POLYGONACEAE
HAUSKNECHT'S BUCKWHEAT
Native, common, blooms all summer, 2–6 in.
Shrub-steppe, subalpine, mid to high elevation
Subshrub or herbaceous, mat-forming. **LEAVES** deciduous, basal, oval, 0.2–0.5 in. long, olive-green, hairy or
not above, whitish-hairy below. **FLOWERS** in rounded,
branched clusters with leafy bracts beneath, flower
stalks leafless, flowers unisexual, cup-shaped, 0.2 in.
long, stalk present, tepals bright yellow, non-hairy.
FRUIT achene, brown. **ECOLOGY** grows in gravelly or
sandy soils, within shrub-steppe, and conifer forests.

Eriogonum wrightii
POLYGONACEAE
BASTARD-SAGE, WRIGHT'S BUCKWHEAT
Native, locally common, blooms mid summer–
autumn, 2–16 in. Rocky sites, chaparral,
east-side forest, low to high elevation
Subshrub or shrub, matted to erect, much-branched,
branches and stems mostly white-hairy. **LEAVES** deciduous, basal, oval to lance-shaped, 0.05–1 in. long,
surfaces hairy or not, edges sometimes rolled under,
tips pointed or rounded. **FLOWERS** in clusters along
the branches, flowers cup-shaped, stalk absent, tepals
white, pink, or reddish, non-hairy, stamens longer
than tepals. **FRUIT** achene, brown, non-hairy.
ECOLOGY grows on gravelly flats or rocky slopes within
chaparral, oak or conifer forests, and sagebrush
communities.

Douglasia laevigata
PRIMULACEAE
SMOOTH DOUGLASIA
Native, locally common, blooms late spring–
mid summer, 0.5–3 in. Coastal, rocky sites,
alpine, subalpine, low to high elevation
Subshrub, rhizomatous, mat-forming. **LEAVES** deciduous, basal, appear whorled, oblong to lance-shaped,
0.2–1 in. long, surfaces non-hairy, edges smooth,
toothed, often fringed with hair, tips rounded or
pointed. **FLOWERS** in flat-topped clusters at the end
of a leafless stalk, flowers funnel-shaped, petals dark
pinkish red to lavender, sepals star-shaped hairy or
smooth. **FRUIT** capsule, round. **ECOLOGY** grows on
rocky slopes, ledges, and cliffs, from
lowland to alpine. The similar *D. nivalis*
has densely hairy leaf surfaces. Rare in
British Columbia.

Douglasia nivalis
PRIMULACEAE
SNOW DOUGLASIA, SNOW DWARF-PRIMROSE
Native, locally common, blooms mid spring–mid
summer, 1–3 in. Rocky sites, east-side forest, shrub-
steppe, alpine, subalpine, low to high elevation
Subshrub, mat-forming. **LEAVES** deciduous, basal,
appear whorled, linear to lance-shaped, 0.5–1 in. long,
surfaces grayish green, densely hairy, edges smooth
or toothed, tips rounded or pointed. **FLOWERS** in flat-
topped clusters at the end of leafless stalks, flowers
2–8, funnel-shaped, petals red to purplish red, sepals
star-shaped hairy or smooth. **FRUIT** capsule, round.
ECOLOGY grows on rocky slopes, ridges, roadcuts, from
sagebrush areas to alpine. Often blooms
soon after snowmelt. The similar *D.
laevigata* has non-hairy leaf surfaces.
Endemic to Washington.

Primula suffrutescens
PRIMULACEAE
SIERRA PRIMROSE
Native, locally common, blooms mid summer,
2–6 in. Alpine, subalpine, high elevation
Subshrub, rhizomatous, mat-forming. **LEAVES** evergreen, basal, wedge- to spoon-shaped, 0.5–1.5 in. long,
succulent, surfaces glossy green, non-hairy, edges
toothed near tip, tips rounded. **FLOWERS** in small clusters, stalks leafless, flowers trumpet-shaped, 0.5–1
in. across, sepals lance-shaped, petals glandular, reddish pink with yellow throat. **FRUIT** capsule, roundish. **ECOLOGY** grows in granitic soils on rocky slopes
and rock crevices in subalpine forests and rocky alpine
habitats. Endemic to
California.

Galium multiflorum
RUBIACEAE
SHRUBBY BEDSTRAW
Native, uncommon, blooms late spring–mid
summer, 6–14 in. Meadows, rocky sites,
shrub-steppe, mid to high elevation
Subshrub, rhizomatous, stems erect, hairy or not.
LEAVES deciduous, in whorls of 4, lance- to egg-shaped,
one pair larger than the other, tips sharply pointed.
FLOWERS in few-flowered branched clusters at stem
ends, flowers unisexual, male and female flowers on
separate plants, flowers small, somewhat bell-shaped,
petals 4, whitish to pink. **FRUIT** nutlet, densely long-
hairy, hairs straight. **ECOLOGY** grows in rocky places
within dry forests and sagebrush, at mid
elevation and above.

Galium porrigens
RUBIACEAE
CLIMBING BEDSTRAW
Native, locally common, blooms early spring–
mid summer, 2–5 ft. Chaparral, west-side
forest, shrub-steppe, low to mid elevation
Vine, climbing or sprawling, with curved prickles, stems squarish, short-hairy. **LEAVES** deciduous,
in whorls of 4, linear to oval, 0.1–0.7 in. long, surfaces short-hairy, edges toothed or not, tips rounded
or pointed. **FLOWERS** in leaf axils, unisexual, male
and female flowers on separate plants, flowers small,
disk-shaped, petals 4, yellow to reddish. **FRUIT** berry,
non-hairy. **ECOLOGY** grows in chaparral, oak woodlands, and pine forests, from low to mid
elevation.

Galium serpenticum
RUBIACEAE
**MANY-FLOWERED BEDSTRAW, INTERMOUNTAIN
BEDSTRAW**
Native, locally common, blooms all summer, to 1
ft. Meadows, serpentine, west-side forest, east-
side forest, subalpine, mid to high elevation
Subshrub, clumped, somewhat hairy. **LEAVES** deciduous, in whorls of 4, oval to lance-shaped, <0.5 in. long,
tips pointed. **FLOWERS** male and female flowers on separate plants, male flowers in branched clusters, female
solitary in leaf axils, flowers small, saucer-shaped, petals 4, pale yellow or whitish. **FRUIT** nutlet, long-hairy.
ECOLOGY grows on ridgetops, forests, and rocky slopes
from montane to subalpine areas. Ssp.
scotticum, a serpentine endemic of ponderosa pine forests with flat leaf tips
and cup-shaped flowers, is rare in California; ssp. *warnerense*, with bent leaf
tips and flat flowers, grows in subalpine
meadows and rocky areas and is rare in
California and Oregon.

Rhus glabra

ANACARDIACEAE

SMOOTH SUMAC, SCARLET SUMAC, WESTERN SUMAC

Native, common, blooms mid spring–mid summer, 3–10 ft. Streambanks, meadows, east-side forest, low to mid elevation

Shrub, erect, rhizomatous, thicket-forming, bark brownish gray, smooth, milky sap released when cut. **LEAVES** deciduous, alternate, pinnately divided into 7–29 leaflets, leaflets oval to lance-shaped, 2–5 in. long, dark green above, whitish beneath, edges toothed, tips pointed. **FLOWERS** in dense, pyramid-shaped clusters at stem ends, male and female flowers on separate plants, flowers pale yellow, petals and sepals 5, petals hairy inside. **FRUIT** berrylike, flattened sphere, red, hairy, edible. **ECOLOGY** grows on streambanks, rocky slopes, grasslands, shrubfields, and dry forests, lowland to montane. Often used as an ornamental for its vibrant fall color. Resprouts after fire.

See Anacardiaceae with simple leaves, page 111; see *Rhus* with simple leaves, page 111

Rhus trilobata (Rhus aromatica)
ANACARDIACEAE
SKUNKBUSH SUMAC, FRAGRANT SUMAC
Native, common, blooms mid spring–early summer,
2–8 ft. Streambanks, disturbed, meadows, rocky
sites, shrub-steppe, low to mid elevation

Shrub, erect, crown rounded, thicket-forming, bark
grayish brown, twigs hairy when young, skunky odor
released when twigs or leaves are damaged.
LEAVES deciduous, alternate, palmately divided into 3
(sometimes 5) leaflets, leaflets egg-shaped, 0.5–1 in.
long, shiny green above, hairy below, edges smooth,
toothed or lobed, tips mostly rounded. **FLOWERS** in
small clusters near stem ends, blooms before the
leaves unfold, flowers mostly unisexual and on different plants, flowers yellowish green, petals and sepals
5, petals hairy inside. **FRUIT** berrylike, round, reddish
orange, hairy and sticky, palatable, tart.
ECOLOGY grows on rocky slopes, streambanks, sand
dunes, sagebrush scrub or steppe, oak woodlands,
and disturbed areas, lowland to montane. Resprouts
after fire. The similar *Toxicodendron diversilobum* lacks
the skunky odor and has white berries and non-hairy
petals.

Toxicodendron diversilobum
(Rhus diversiloba)
ANACARDIACEAE
POISON-OAK

Native, common, blooms mid spring–mid summer, 3–50 ft. Meadows, west-side forest, east-side forest, low to mid elevation

Shrub or vine, rhizomatous, colony-forming, milky sap released when damaged. **LEAVES** deciduous, alternate, palmately divided into 3 (sometimes 5) leaflets, leaflets round to egg-shaped, 1–3 in. long, middle leaflet larger, shiny bright green and non-hairy above, paler and short-hairy beneath, edges smooth or lobed, tips mostly rounded. **FLOWERS** in spreading to drooping clusters in leaf axils, flowers mostly unisexual and on different plants, flowers small, sepals 5, green, petals 5, yellow. **FRUIT** berrylike, round, white, hairy or not, poisonous. **ECOLOGY** habitat variable, grows in

sun or shade, forests, streambanks, bluffs, open rocky slopes, lowland to montane. All plant parts contain urushiol. Although this resin can be life-threatening, most people suffer only from rashes or blisters after contact. Do not touch this plant or the similar *T. rydbergii*. Uncommon in British Columbia.

Toxicodendron rydbergii
(*Rhus radicans*)
ANACARDIACEAE
WESTERN POISON-IVY
Native, common, blooms mid spring–early
summer, 1–7 ft. Streambanks, meadows,
east-side forest, low to mid elevation

Shrub, erect or sprawling, sometimes vinelike, colony-
forming, milky sap released when damaged.
LEAVES deciduous, alternate, palmately divided into
3 leaflets, leaflets egg-shaped, 2–6 in. long, shiny
bright green above, paler beneath, non-hairy, edges
smooth, wavy, or somewhat toothed to lobed, tips
pointed. **FLOWERS** in dense clusters in leaf axils, flowers mostly unisexual and on different plants, flowers
small and yellowish, sepals and petals 5. **FRUIT** berrylike, round, white, non-hairy, remains
on plant through the winter, poisonous. **ECOLOGY** habitat variable, forests, streambanks, seeps, roadsides,
open rocky slopes, lowland to montane. Urushiol, which causes skin irritation, is found throughout the plant.
Do not touch this plant or the similar *T.
diversilobum*.

Artemisia absinthium
ASTERACEAE
WORMWOOD, ABSINTHE, COMMON
WORMWOOD

Non-native, common, blooms mid summer–
autumn, 1.3–4 ft. Disturbed, meadows, east-side
forest, shrub-steppe, low to mid elevation

Subshrub or herbaceous, fragrant, erect, stems grayish green, densely to sparsely hairy, hair gray to white.
LEAVES deciduous, alternate, egg-shaped, lower leaves
1–3 in. long, 2–3 times pinnately divided into leaflets, surfaces grayish green, densely white-hairy, tips
rounded. Upper leaves smaller, divided or not, tips
sharply pointed. **FLOWERS** aggregated into heads, nodding in leafy, branched clusters, all disk flowers fertile,
petals yellow, outer flowers female only, inner bisexual, hairy between flowers. **FRUIT** achene, non-hairy.
ECOLOGY European import, grows on disturbed sites,
often near human settlements, from low to mid elevation. Widely cultivated medicinal herb, contains
absinthal, a neurotoxic oil used to flavor absinthe liquor.

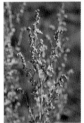

See Asteraceae with simple leaves, page 113, basal
leaves, page 350

Artemisia frigida
ASTERACEAE
PRAIRIE SAGEWORT

Native, common, blooms all summer, 4–16 in.
Meadows, shrub-steppe, low to high elevation

Subshrub, mound-forming, aromatic, stems grayish
green to brown, sparsely hairy. **LEAVES** persistent, alternate, egg-shaped, 0.2–0.5 in. long, silvery gray, 2–3
times pinnately divided into trident-like leaflets, surfaces densely white-hairy, tips pointed. **FLOWERS** aggregated into heads, heads nodding, clustered, all disk
flowers fertile, outer flowers female only, inner flowers
bisexual, petals yellow, hair present between flowers.
FRUIT achene, smooth. **ECOLOGY** prefers gravelly, well-
drained soils, grows in
meadows, open forest,
shrub-steppe, and sandy
places from low to high
elevation.

Artemisia michauxiana
ASTERACEAE
MICHAUX'S MUGWORT, LEMON SAGEWORT

Native, locally common, blooms all summer, 0.7–3.3 ft. Rocky sites, alpine, subalpine, mid to high elevation
Aromatic subshrub, stems several, green, mostly non-hairy, scent spicy-sweet lemony. **LEAVES** deciduous, alternate, pinnately twice-divided into linear leaflets, 0.5–4.5 in. long, bright green and non-hairy above, densely white-hairy below, tips pointed.
FLOWERS aggregated into heads, heads nodding to erect in narrow clusters at stem ends, all disk flowers fertile, outer flowers female only, inner flowers bisexual, petals yellow. **FRUIT** achene, non-hairy. **ECOLOGY** grows in wet meadows, on talus slopes, and in rock crevices, usually at mid to high elevation. The similar *A. tilesii* has no lemony scent, and *A. ludoviciana* is grayish green.

Artemisia pycnocephala
ASTERACEAE
BEACH WORMWOOD

Native, locally common, blooms late spring–mid summer, 1–3 ft. Coastal, low elevation
Subshrub or herbaceous, spreading, clump-forming, stems whitish gray, densely hairy. **LEAVES** persistent, alternate, 1–3 in. long, 2–3 times pinnately divided into linear leaflets, surfaces grayish green, densely hairy, tips pointed. **FLOWERS** aggregated into heads, heads in narrow, leafy clusters, bracts egg-shaped, hairy, all disk flowers, outer ring female only, fertile, inner flowers functionally male, sterile, petals pale yellow. **FRUIT** achene, non-hairy. **ECOLOGY** grows on beaches in sandy or rocky soils. Rare in Oregon.

Artemisia spinescens
(*Picrothamnus desertorum*)
ASTERACEAE
BUDSAGE
Native, locally common, blooms all spring,
4–12 in. Shrub-steppe, mid elevation

Aromatic shrub, mounded, stems many-branched, some branches spine-tipped. **LEAVES** deciduous (summer), alternate, stalks to 1 in. long, palmately divided into 3–5 linear to spoon-shaped leaflets, leaflets to 0.2 in. long, grayish green, densely hairy. **FLOWERS** aggregated into heads, heads in flat or ball-shaped clusters, all disk flowers, petals yellow. **FRUIT** achene, 1-seeded, long-hairy. **ECOLOGY** grows in deserts and other arid shrub communities, tolerant of salty soils.

Berberis aquifolium (*Mahonia aquifolium*)
BERBERIDACEAE
TALL OREGON-GRAPE, SHINING OREGON-GRAPE

Native, common, blooms winter–mid spring, 0.5–7 ft. West-side forest, east-side forest, shrub-steppe, low to high elevation

Shrub, erect to spreading, often scraggly, rhizomatous, bark yellowish brown. **LEAVES** evergreen, alternate, pinnate, leaflets 5–9, oval to egg-shaped, 1–3 in. long, 2 times longer than wide, shiny green above, paler and somewhat shiny below, 1 main vein from leaflet base (pinnately veined), edges spiny-toothed, tips pointed. **FLOWERS** in dense, rounded clusters, flowers bowl-shaped, bright yellow, sepals and petals in 6s. **FRUIT** berry, purplish blue with a waxy coating, to 0.4 in. long, edible, tart. **ECOLOGY** open forests, shrub-steppe, often in sunny areas, lowland to montane. State flower of Oregon.

Berberis aquifolium var. *dictyota*
(*Mahonia dictyota, Berberis dictyota*)
BERBERIDACEAE
JEPSON'S OREGON-GRAPE, SHINING NETVEIN
BARBERRY
Native, common, blooms all spring, 1.7–6.7 ft.
Chaparral, east-side forest, mid elevation
Shrub, erect, bark brown or purplish. **LEAVES** ever-green, alternate, pinnate, leaflets 5–9, oval to egg-shaped, 1–3.5 in. long, dull green and waxy above, dull green below, 1–3 veins from leaflet base (palmately veined), edges crinkled with 6–10 spine-tipped teeth per side, to 0.2 in. long. **FLOWERS** in dense, rounded, branched clusters, flowers bowl-shaped, bright yellow, sepals and petals in 6s. **FRUIT** berry, bluish purple, waxy or not, to 0.3 in. long, edible, tart. **ECOLOGY** grows in rocky areas in forests and chaparral, montane. Endemic to California.

Berberis nervosa (Mahonia nervosa)

BERBERIDACEAE

LOW OREGON-GRAPE, DULL OREGON-GRAPE

Native, common, blooms late winter–spring, 4–24 in.
West-side forest, east-side forest, low to mid elevation
Shrub, erect, rhizomatous, bark yellowish brown.
LEAVES evergreen, alternate, pinnately divided into
9–21 leaflets, leaflets lance- to egg-shaped, 1–3 in.
long, surfaces dull green, veins 4–6 from the leaflet
base (palmately veined), edges spiny-
toothed, tips pointed. **FLOWERS** in long,
narrow clusters, up to 7 in. long, flowers
bowl-shaped, bright yellow, sepals and
petals in 6s. **FRUIT** berry, purplish blue
with a waxy coating, to 0.4 in. long, edible, tart. **ECOLOGY** open to shady conifer
forests, often in rocky areas, lowland to
montane.

Berberis pinnata (*Mahonia pinnata*)
BERBERIDACEAE
WAVYLEAF BARBERRY, CALIFORNIA BARBERRY
Native, locally common, blooms late winter–
spring, 1–5.7 ft. Coastal, chaparral, west-
side forest, low to mid elevation

Shrub, erect, bark grayish brown. **LEAVES** evergreen,
alternate, pinnate, leaflets 7–11, oval to egg-shaped,
1–2.5 in. long, <2 times longer than wide, shiny green
above, similar beneath, 1 midvein from leaflet base,
edges mostly wavy, spiny-toothed. **FLOWERS** in dense,
branched clusters, bowl-shaped, bright yellow, sepals
and petals in 6s. **FRUIT** berry, bluish purple with a waxy
coating, to 0.3 in. long, edible, tart. **ECOLOGY** grows in
oak woodlands, conifer forests, chapar-
ral, rocky areas, coastal to montane.

Berberis repens
(*Berberis aquifolium* var. *repens*, *Mahonia amplectens*)
BERBERIDACEAE
**TRAILING OREGON-GRAPE, CREEPING
OREGON-GRAPE**
Native, common, blooms late spring–early
summer, 0.5–3 ft. Chaparral, west-side forest,
east-side forest, low to mid elevation

Shrub, stoloniferous, stems trailing. **LEAVES** evergreen,
alternate, pinnate, leaflets 5–9, egg-shaped, 1–3.5 in.
long, dull or shiny green above, dull green and sometimes waxy below, 1 midvein from leaflet base, edges
with small spiny teeth, tips pointed. **FLOWERS** in dense,
rounded, branched clusters, flowers bowl-shaped,
bright yellow, sepals and petals in 6s.
FRUIT berry, bluish purple with a waxy
coating, to 0.4 in. long, edible, tart.
ECOLOGY grows in forests, chaparral,
rocky areas, lowland to montane. The
similar *B. aquifolium* is rarely trailing,
has leaves 2 times longer than wide and
edges with longer spiny teeth.

Acacia dealbata
FABACEAE
SILVER WATTLE
Non-native, locally common, blooms late winter–
early spring, 50–100 ft. Disturbed, low elevation
Tree, twigs ridged, silvery blue, hairy. **LEAVES** evergreen,
alternate, stalked, frond-like, to 7 in. long, grayish green
to green, pinnately twice-divided, primary leaflets 6–30
pairs, 0.5–2 in. long, secondary leaflets 15–70 pairs, linear, 0.1–0.2 in. long. **FLOWERS** gathered in dense heads,
heads grouped in clusters about 7 in. long, flowers yellow to cream-colored, petals and sepals 4–5, small, stamens many and showy. **FRUIT** pod, reddish brown to
black, 1–3 in. long, smooth. **ECOLOGY** invasive Australian import, grows in riparian areas, for-
est edges, roadsides and other disturbed
areas, usually in lowland areas. Spreads
by rhizomes and long-lived seeds,
resprouts readily, and may have allelopathic effect on nearby plants.

See Fabaceae with simple leaves, page
184

Amorpha californica
FABACEAE
**CALIFORNIA FALSE INDIGO, CALIFORNIA
INDIGOBUSH**
Native, locally common, blooms mid
spring–mid summer, 3–12 ft. Chaparral,
east-side forest, low to high elevation
Aromatic shrub, erect to spreading, stems white-
hairy, glandular-hairy, also with sessile blister-like
glands, prickles absent, scent reminiscent of pine-
apple or lavender. **LEAVES** deciduous, alternate, 4–12
in. long, stalks glandular-hairy, pinnately divided into
15–33 leaflets, leaflets oval to egg-shaped, 0.5–1 in.
long, surfaces short-hairy, sessile glands yellowish,
edges smooth, tips rounded or notched.
FLOWERS in erect cluster at stem tips,
3–8 in. long, flowers tubular, sepals
greenish aging purplish red, glandular,
petal 1, surrounding pistil and stamens,
burgundy, stamens 10. **FRUIT** pod, 0.2
in. long, tan, hairy, glandular.
ECOLOGY grows in chaparral, forests,
and oak woodlands, in open to shaded
places.

Amorpha fruticosa
(*Amorpha dewinkeleri, Amorpha occidentalis*)
FABACEAE
DESERT INDIGOBUSH, WESTERN FALSE INDIGO, DESERT FALSE INDIGO
Non-native, locally common, blooms early–mid summer, 5–20 ft. Bog/fen/wetland, streambanks, low to mid elevation
Shrub, thicket-forming, twigs green, hairy. **LEAVES** deciduous, alternate, 6–16 in. long, pinnately divided into 11–21 leaflets, leaflets oval, 1–2 in. long, green, hairy below, edges smooth, tips rounded. **FLOWERS** in dense, narrow clusters at stem tips, flowers purple, petal 1, sepals joined, lobes narrow, stamens yellow, longer than petal. **FRUIT** pod, curved, 3–4 in.

long, glandular, non-hairy, seeds mostly 2. **ECOLOGY** grows along streambanks, in draws and canyons, lowland to mid elevation. Native to the eastern United States.

Cytisus scoparius
FABACEAE
SCOTCH BROOM
Non-native, common, blooms late spring–early summer, 1–10 ft. Disturbed, meadows, west-side forest, low to mid elevation
Shrub, erect, bark greenish brown, smooth, twigs green, 5-sided. **LEAVES** deciduous, alternate, pinnately divided into 3 leaflets or not, leaves and leaflets egg-shaped, 0.2–1 in. long, green, mostly non-hairy, edges smooth, tips pointed. **FLOWERS** single in leaf axils, sometimes in 2s or 3s, flowers pea-like, about 1 in. long, yellow or purplish, style curved. **FRUIT** pod, black, 1–1.5 in. long, non-hairy except on the seams.

ECOLOGY invasive, grows in disturbed, open sunny sites and along roadsides and also undisturbed areas, lowland to montane. Reproduces primarily by its hardy, long-lived seed.

Genista monspessulana
FABACEAE
FRENCH BROOM
Non-native, locally common, blooms early
spring–mid summer, 3–10 ft. Disturbed,
meadows, west-side forest, low elevation

Shrub, erect, stems green, mostly silvery hairy, less
so with age. **LEAVES** evergreen, alternate, pinnately
divided into 3 leaflets, leaflets lance- to egg-shaped,
about 0.5 in. long, green, non-hairy above, hairy below,
edges smooth, tips rounded or pointed. **FLOWERS** in
dense clusters in leaf axils, flowers pea-shaped, 0.5 in.
long, light yellow, sepals bell-shaped, lobes 2 above,
hairy, style bent at tip. **FRUIT** pod, 0.5–1 in. long, reddish brown to black, hairy.

ECOLOGY an invasive escapee from cultivation, found in disturbed areas, roadsides, grasslands, and forests in the lowlands. The similar *Cytisus scoparius* has
simple leaves on upper branches, less
hairy leaves and pods, and its style is
curved at the middle, not bent at tip.

Lupinus arboreus
FABACEAE
TREE LUPINE, YELLOW BUSH LUPINE
Non-native, locally common, blooms spring–
summer, 3–7 ft. Coastal, low elevation

Subshrub or shrub, erect, stems and branches hairy.
LEAVES deciduous, alternate, pinnately divided into
5–11 leaflets, leaflets lance-shaped, 1–2.5 in. long,
green to grayish, hairy or not, tips pointed.
FLOWERS in large upright clusters at stem ends, flowers pea-like, yellow, sometimes white or bluish, sepals
hairy. **FRUIT** pod, brown to blackish, about 0.5 in.
long, hairy. **ECOLOGY** invasive, often on coastal bluffs,
beaches, sand dunes, and disturbed areas but can
occur inland. Not native
north of San Francisco.

Pickeringia montana
FABACEAE
CHAPARRAL PEA
Native, locally common, blooms mid
spring–mid summer, 2–7 ft. Chaparral,
east-side forest, low elevation

Shrub, erect to spreading, rhizomatous, branches stiff, twigs spine-tipped. **LEAVES** evergreen, alternate, oval to egg-shaped, 0.5–1 in. long, simple or pinnately divided, leaflets 2–3, surfaces short-hairy or not, edges smooth, tips rounded or pointed. **FLOWERS** in clusters, in leaf axils and stem tips, flowers pea-shaped, 0.5 in. long, bright pink to purple, stamens 10, filaments free. **FRUIT** pod, 1–2.5 in. long, constricted between seeds. **ECOLOGY** grows in chaparral, oak woodlands, and conifer forests. Rarely sets fruit, mostly reproduces vegetatively. Resprouts following fire. Endemic to California.

Robinia pseudoacacia

FABACEAE
BLACK LOCUST

Non-native, scattered, blooms mid spring,
40–83 ft. Disturbed, meadows, low elevation

Tree, erect, bark brown and smooth, becoming furrowed with age, twigs reddish brown, with paired
thorns at the nodes. **LEAVES** deciduous, alternate, entire
leaf 8–14 in. long, pinnately divided into 11–21 leaflets, leaflets oval to lance-shaped, 1–1.5 in. long, green
above, paler beneath, edges smooth, tips pointed.
FLOWERS in drooping clusters in leaf axils, clusters
4–5.5 in. long, flowers pea-like, fragrant, petals white,
sepals hairy. **FRUIT** pod, light brown, 2.5–4 in. long.

ECOLOGY grows near abandoned settlements, roadsides, streambanks, and
slopes, lowland. Shade intolerant, fast
growing, and short-lived, it spreads by
seed or root suckers and resprouts after
disturbance. Planted as a shade tree,
for erosion control, or as a windbreak in
arid lands.

Sesbania punicea
FABACEAE
RATTLEBOX
Non-native, locally common, blooms late
spring–late summer, 5–13 ft. Streambanks,
disturbed, meadows, low elevation

Tree or shrub, erect, thicket-forming, bark grayish
to reddish brown, lenticels prominent, twigs reddish
brown. **LEAVES** deciduous, alternate, pinnately divided
into 20–34 leaflets, leaflets oval, 0.5–1 in. long, dark
green above, paler below, edges smooth, tips rounded.
FLOWERS in drooping clusters, 5- to 15-flowered,
pea-shaped, orangish red. **FRUIT** pod, 1.5–3 in. long,
brown, winged, rattles if shaken. **ECOLOGY** invasive

South American import,
grows along roadsides,
streambanks, shorelines,
and other moist places,
often planted as an
ornamental.

Sphaerophysa salsula (*Swainsona salsula*)
FABACEAE
ALKALI SWAINSONPEA, RED BLADDER-VETCH
Non-native, locally common, blooms mid spring–mid
summer, 1–5 ft. Disturbed, meadows, low elevation

Subshrub, erect, stems one to several, sparsely hairy.
LEAVES deciduous, alternate, pinnately divided into
15–25 leaflets, leaflets oval to egg-shaped, 0.2–1 in.
long, green, non-hairy above, hairy below, edges
smooth, tips rounded. **FLOWERS** loose clusters in leaf
axils, flowers pea-like, about 0.5 in. long, orangish red
to pinkish brown. **FRUIT** pod, inflated, round to egg-
shaped, about 0.5 in. long, smooth. **ECOLOGY** invasive,
grows in disturbed, low-lying places, such as roadsides

and the edges of farm
fields. Prefers alkaline
soils.

Ulex europaeus
FABACEAE
GORSE

Non-native, locally common, blooms early spring–mid summer, 3–10 ft. Coastal, disturbed, low elevation Shrub, erect, clump-forming, densely branched, branches greenish, 5-sided, tips spiny. **LEAVES** ever-green, alternate, pinnately divided into 3 linear leaflets when young, becoming spinelike and simple with age, rigid, 1–2.5 in. long. **FLOWERS** single in leaf axils near branch tips, flowers pea-like, petals yellow, sepals yellow and hairy. **FRUIT** pod, black, gray, or brown, hairy, about 1 in. long. **ECOLOGY** invasive European import, grows in sandy or rocky soils, old fields, coastal bluffs, pastures, and disturbed places in lowland areas. Highly flammable.

Juglans hindsii (*Juglans californica* var. *hindsii*)
JUGLANDACEAE
NORTHERN CALIFORNIA BLACK WALNUT, HIND'S WALNUT

Native, locally common, blooms mid spring, 23–77 ft. Streambanks, west-side forest, low elevation Tree, crown spreading, bark gray, ridged and scaly, trunk single, twigs green to reddish brown, buds oval, flattened, to 0.3 in. long. **LEAVES** deciduous, alternate, pinnately divided into 13–21 leaflets, leaflets lance-shaped, 2.5–5 in. long, surfaces green, tufts of hair in vein axils below, edges toothed, tips pointed. **FLOWERS** unisexual on same plant, small, male flowers in yellowish green catkins, 2.5–6 in. long, on last year's twigs, female flowers 1–3 on short stalks of current year's twigs. **FRUIT** nut enclosed in husk, round, 1.5–2 in. across, surface smooth to shallowly grooved, edible.

ECOLOGY grows with black cottonwood and willows in riparian forest communities, streambanks, floodplains, and in disturbed areas. Hybridizes with other walnut species. Lives to about 300 years of age, intolerant of cold and drought. Rare in California.

Chamaebatia foliolosa
ROSACEAE
MOUNTAIN MISERY, BEARCLOVER, SIERRA
MOUNTAIN MISERY

Native, common, blooms mid spring–mid summer,
8–24 in. Meadows, east-side forest, mid elevation
Aromatic shrub, rhizomatous, thicket-forming, bark
dark reddish brown, densely branched. **LEAVES** evergreen, alternate, fernlike, 1–4 in. long, pinnately
divided into 8–17 leaflets per side, leaflets lobed,
sticky-glandular. **FLOWERS** in branched, few-flowered
clusters at stem ends, flowers sticky, petals 5, white,
roundish, 0.2–0.4 in. long, sepals 5, stamens many,
pistil mostly 1, ovary hairy. **FRUIT** achene, egg-shaped,
brownish black. **ECOLOGY** grows in open
ponderosa pine or mixed conifer forest in mountainous areas. Moderately
shade tolerant but abundance decreases
in dense, shady forests. Resprouts following fire. Endemic to California.

See Rosaceae with simple leaves, page
235

Chamaebatiaria millefolium
ROSACEAE
DESERT SWEET, FERN BUSH

Native, locally common, blooms late
spring–mid summer, 1–7 ft. Rocky sites,
shrub-steppe, mid to high elevation
Aromatic shrub, erect, multi-stemmed, bark gray,
smooth, twigs brown. **LEAVES** evergreen, alternate,
fernlike, 1–3 in. long, pinnately divided into 8–15 leaflets per side, leaflets lobed, sticky-glandular and hairy.
FLOWERS in branched, many-flowered clusters, to 8
in. long at stem ends, flowers saucer-shaped, petals 5,
white, roundish, 0.2 in. long, sepals 5, glandular-hairy,
stamens many, pistils mostly 5. **FRUIT** podlike capsule,
reddish brown, hairy.
ECOLOGY grows on open,
rocky slopes, sagebrush
scrub, in juniper or pine
forests, often on top of
basalt lava beds.

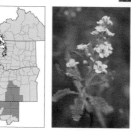

Dasiphora fruticosa
(Potentilla fruticosa, Pentaphylloides floribunda)
ROSACEAE
SHRUBBY CINQUEFOIL
Native, common, blooms all summer, 1–5 ft.
Meadows, alpine, subalpine, mid to high elevation
Shrub, erect to spreading, stems hairy when young, becoming non-hairy with age, bark reddish brown, shredding. **LEAVES** deciduous, alternate, pinnately divided into mostly 5(3–7) leaflets, leaflets linear to oval, 0.2–1 in. long, grayish green, hairy, edges rolled under. **FLOWERS** in small clusters at stem ends or solitary in leaf axils, flowers saucer-shaped, petals 5, pale to bright yellow, oval to egg-shaped, 0.2–0.5 in. long, sepals hairy, pistils many. **FRUIT** achene, light brown, hairy, to 0.1 in. long. **ECOLOGY** grows in meadows, rocky slopes, and bogs, montane to alpine areas.

Rosa acicularis
ROSACEAE
PRICKLY ROSE

Native, common, blooms mid summer, 1–5 ft. Streambanks, meadows, west-side forest, east-side forest, low to high elevation

Shrub, slender, stems erect to arching, prickles many, slender, straight, length varies, can be absent on new twigs. **LEAVES** deciduous, alternate, pinnately divided into 5–7 leaflets, leaflets oval to egg-shaped, 0.5–2 in. long, green and mostly non-hairy above, paler and hairy below, edges mostly doubly toothed, teeth tips mostly gland-tipped. **FLOWERS** usually single, can be in small clusters, flowers saucer-shaped, 2–3 in. across, petals 5, pink to reddish pink, sepals 5, 0.5–1 in. long, smooth, lance-shaped with long, pointed tips. **FRUIT** achenes surrounded by fleshy hip, deep red to purplish, round, oval, or pear-shaped, 0.5–1 in. long, smooth, sepals present, edible. **ECOLOGY** grows in dry or wet open forests, streambanks, on rocky or grassy slopes.

Rosa bridgesii (*Rosa yainacensis*)
ROSACEAE
PYGMY ROSE, CASCADE ROSE
Native, locally common, blooms late spring–
mid summer, 4–32 in. Meadows, rocky sites,
east-side forest, mid to high elevation

Shrub or dwarf shrub, rhizomatous, stems with thorns
paired at nodes, stout, straight, to 0.5 in. long, other
prickles few. LEAVES deciduous, alternate, pinnately
divided into 5–7 leaflets, leaflets oval to egg-shaped,
mostly 0.5–1 in. long, surfaces finely hairy, sometimes
glandular, edges doubly toothed, teeth glandular-
tipped, leaflet tips rounded. FLOWERS single or in small
clusters, flowers saucer-shaped, petals 5, 0.5–1 in. long,
pink to red, sepals 5, edges smooth, persistent.
FRUIT achenes surrounded by fleshy hip, bright red,
oval to round, to 0.5 in. across, mostly smooth, sepals
present, edible. ECOLOGY grows in rocky areas and in
open conifer forests, more common at mid-montane
elevation. Can act as a groundcover.

Rosa californica

ROSACEAE

CALIFORNIA ROSE

Native, locally common, blooms spring–autumn, 3–8 ft. Streambanks, meadows, low to mid elevation Shrub, erect, rhizomatous, sometimes thicket-forming, stems with few to many stout, curved thorns, thorns often absent on flowering stems. **LEAVES** deciduous, alternate, pinnately divided into 5–7 leaflets, leaflets oval, 0.5–2 in. long, sparsely hairy to smooth above, hairy and glandular below, edges mostly singly toothed. **FLOWERS** in flat-topped clusters, flowers saucer-shaped, petals 5, pink, 0.5–1 in. long, sepals hairy and often glandular, edges smooth. **FRUIT** achenes surrounded by fleshy hip, bright red, round to oval, 0.3–1 in. long, edible. **ECOLOGY** grows in wooded areas in streambanks to mid elevation. The similar *R. pisocarpa* has few straight thorns and nonglandular leaflets.

Rosa canina
ROSACEAE
DOG ROSE
Non-native, locally common, blooms late
spring–early summer, 3–13 ft. Disturbed,
meadows, low to mid elevation

Shrub, rhizomatous, sometimes thicket-forming,
stems erect or arching, with stout, curved thorns.
LEAVES deciduous, alternate, pinnately divided into
5–7 leaflets, leaflets oval to egg-shaped, 0.5–1.5 in.
long, mostly not hairy or glandular below, edges
either singly or doubly toothed, teeth often gland-
tipped. **FLOWERS** single or in flat-topped clusters,
flowers saucer-shaped, petals 5, white to pinkish, to
1 in. long, sepals not glandular-hairy,
edges lobed, deciduous after flowering.
FRUIT achenes surrounded by fleshy
hip, bright red, round to egg-shaped, to
about 1 in. long, sepals usually absent,
edible. **ECOLOGY** European import,
grows along roadsides, in disturbed
areas, and around homesteads, hips
commonly used in teas.

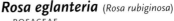

Rosa eglanteria (*Rosa rubiginosa*)
ROSACEAE
SWEETBRIER ROSE, SWEET-BRIER
Non-native, locally common, blooms late
spring–early summer, 3–10 ft. Disturbed,
meadows, low to mid elevation

Shrub, often thicket-forming, stems with stout, curved
thorns, mature stems olive-green. **LEAVES** deciduous,
fragrant, alternate, pinnately divided into 5–7 leaflets,
leaflets oval to round, 0.5–1 in. long, glandular-hairy
below, edges doubly toothed and gland-tipped.
FLOWERS solitary or in small flat-topped clusters, flowers saucer-shaped, petals 5, light to bright pink, 0.5–1
in. long, sepals glandular-hairy. **FRUIT** achenes surrounded by fleshy hip, bright red, round
to oval, to about 0.5 in. long, sepals present or absent, edible. **ECOLOGY** European import, grows in pastures, roadsides, and other disturbed areas, often
in drier places.

Rosa gymnocarpa
ROSACEAE
BALDHIP ROSE, WOOD ROSE
Native, common, blooms late spring–mid summer, 1–7 ft. West-side forest, east-side forest, low to mid elevation

Shrub, stems erect to spreading, thorns thin and straight, usually numerous but sometimes nearly absent, glandular hairs sometimes present.
LEAVES deciduous, alternate, pinnately divided into 5–9 leaflets, oval to egg-shaped, 0.5–1.5 in. long, non-hairy, edges doubly toothed, teeth tips glandular.
FLOWERS usually single at branch ends, can be in clusters of 2–4, flowers saucer- or bowl-shaped, petals 5, pink, to 0.5 in. long, sepals 5 and deciduous soon after flowering. **FRUIT** achene surrounded by fleshy hip, orange to bright red, oval to pear-shaped, to 0.5 in. long, sepals absent, edible.
ECOLOGY grows in forests and shrub thickets, shade tolerant, hybridizes with other roses.

Rosa multiflora
ROSACEAE
MULTIFLORA ROSE, RAMBLER ROSE
Non-native, locally common, blooms all spring, 7–17 ft. Disturbed, meadows, low elevation

Shrub, climbing or trailing, thicket-forming, stems erect to arching, thorns paired or not, stout, curved, can be absent on current year's growth. **LEAVES** deciduous, alternate, pinnately divided into 7–9 (usually) leaflets, leaflets oval to egg-shaped, 1–2 in. long, surfaces hairy and glandular, edges singly toothed, teeth often gland-tipped, base of leaf stalk fringed with hair.
FLOWERS in large clusters, 20–100 flowers, flowers saucer-shaped, petals 5, white to pinkish, 0.3–0.5 in., sepals lance-shaped, variably persistent.
FRUIT achenes surrounded by fleshy hip, red to purplish, round to egg-shaped, to 0.3 in. across, sepals often absent, edible. **ECOLOGY** Japanese import, thrives in sun, tolerates shade, grows in forests, disturbed places, along streambanks.

Rosa nutkana
ROSACEAE
NOOTKA ROSE
Native, common, blooms late spring–early summer, 1.7–10 ft. Coastal, meadows, west-side forest, east-side forest, low to mid elevation
Shrub, rhizomatous, sometimes thicket-forming, stems with paired stout, straight thorns at the nodes. **LEAVES** deciduous, alternate, pinnately divided into 5–7 leaflets, leaflets oval to egg-shaped, 0.5–3 in. long, edges singly or doubly toothed. **FLOWERS** usually single at branch ends, flowers saucer-shaped, petals 5, pink, 1–1.5 in. long, sepals lance-shaped, 0.5–1.6 in. long,

persistent. **FRUIT** achenes surrounded by fleshy hip, deep red to purplish, round to pear-shaped, 0.5–1 in. long, edible. **ECOLOGY** grows in open forests, shrub thickets, shorelines, and streambanks, hybridizes with other roses, hips good source of vitamin C.

Rosa pisocarpa
ROSACEAE
CLUSTERED WILD ROSE, PEAHIP ROSE
Native, common, blooms late spring–mid
summer, 3–7 ft. Coastal, streambanks,
meadows, low to mid elevation

Shrub, rhizomatous, sometimes thicket-forming,
stems with few paired thorns at leaf base, straight,
prickles otherwise present or not. **LEAVES** deciduous,
alternate, pinnately divided into 5–9 leaflets, leaflets
oval to egg-shaped, 0.5–1.5 in. long, surfaces not glandular, edges singly toothed, nonglandular.
FLOWERS in flat-topped clusters, flowers saucer-shaped,
petals 5, pink, 0.5–1 in. long, sepals lance-shaped, to
0.5 in. long, glandular-hairy,

persistent. **FRUIT** achenes
surrounded by fleshy hip,
reddish purple, round to
pear-shaped, 0.2–0.5 in.
long, sepals present, edible. **ECOLOGY** grows in
shady, moist shrub thickets,
streambanks, and swamps.

Rosa spithamea
ROSACEAE
COAST GROUND ROSE, DWARF ROSE
Native, locally common, blooms mid spring–mid
summer, to 20 in. Coastal, chaparral, west-side
forest, east-side forest, low to mid elevation

Shrub or dwarf shrub, erect, rhizomatous, not thicket-
forming, thorns few to many, straight. **LEAVES** deciduous, alternate, pinnately divided into 5–9 leaflets, leaflets oval, 0.5–1 in. long, surfaces smooth, edges doubly
toothed, teeth glandular. **FLOWERS** in small clusters or
single, flowers saucer-shaped, petals 5, pink to red, to
0.5 in. long, sepals glandular, persistent. **FRUIT** achenes
surrounded by fleshy hip, round, about 0.5 in. long,
glandular-hairy, edible. **ECOLOGY** grows
in dry forests and chaparral, often more
floriferous and vigorous after fire.

Rosa woodsii var. *ultramontana*
ROSACEAE
PEARHIP ROSE, WOODS' ROSE, PRAIRIE ROSE
Native, locally common, blooms late spring–
early summer, 2–7 ft. Streambanks, meadows,
east-side forest, low to high elevation

Shrub, thicket-forming, stems with paired thorns at
the base of each leaf, plus smaller, thinner prickles
throughout, especially on younger stems, sometimes
nearly absent on older stems. **LEAVES** deciduous, alternate, pinnately divided into 5–9 leaflets, leaflets oval
to egg-shaped, 0.5–2 in. long, edges singly toothed,
teeth not gland-tipped. **FLOWERS** in flat-topped clusters
at branch ends, flowers saucer-shaped, petals 5, pink,
0.5–1 in. long, sepals lance-shaped,
0.5–1 in. long, not glandular-hairy,
persisent. **FRUIT** achenes surrounded
by fleshy hip, deep red, round to oval,
0.2–0.5 in. long, edible. **ECOLOGY** grows
in moist spots within dry forests, in
streambanks, and around ponds from
lowland to subalpine elevation.

Rubus arcticus ssp. *acaulis*
(*Rubus acaulis*)
ROSACEAE
ARCTIC BLACKBERRY, DWARF RASPBERRY,
NAGOONBERRY
Native, locally common, blooms late spring–mid
summer, 6 in. Bog/fen/wetland, meadows, east-side
forest, alpine, subalpine, mid to high elevation
Subshrub, rhizomatous, thorns absent. **LEAVES** deciduous, alternate, palmately divided into 3 leaflets, leaflets egg-shaped, 0.5–2 in. long, hairy or not above,
hairy below, edges toothed, tips pointed or rounded.
FLOWERS single or in clusters of 2–3, flowers saucer-shaped, petals 5, pink to reddish, 0.3–0.7 in. long,
sepals hairy, not glandular, bent back. **FRUIT** berry, red
to purplish, round, about 0.5 in. across,
edible, tasty. **ECOLOGY** grows in bogs,
meadows, and other wet places. Rare in
Washington.

See *Rubus* with simple leaves, page 255

Rubus armeniacus
(*Rubus bifrons*, *Rubus discolor*)
ROSACEAE
HIMALAYAN BLACKBERRY
Non-native, common, blooms mid
spring–early summer, to 10 ft. Disturbed,
meadows, low to mid elevation
Shrub, erect to arching, stems 5-angled, sometimes
rooting at tips, thicket-forming, thorns stout, curved.
Each stem lives for 2 years, 1st year vegetative, 2nd
flowering. **LEAVES** evergreen or deciduous, alternate,
palmately divided (mostly) into 5 leaflets (1st year) or 3
(2nd year), egg-shaped, 2–5 in. long, non-hairy above,
grayish-hairy beneath, edges toothed, tips pointed.
FLOWERS in clusters at stem ends or in leaf axils,
stalks nonglandular, flowers bisexual, cup-shaped,
petals 5, white to pinkish, sepals bent back, densely
hairy. **FRUIT** berry, black, non-hairy, roundish, about
1 in. long, edible, tasty. **ECOLOGY** invasive Eurasian
import, grows in sun or partial shade along roadsides, in clearings, and other disturbed, often moist
sites from low to mid elevation.

Rubus idaeus
ROSACEAE
RED RASPBERRY
Native, common, blooms late spring–mid summer, 1.5–10 ft. Streambanks, meadows, west-side forest, east-side forest, low to mid elevation
Shrub, erect to arching, bark yellowish brown, exfoliating, stems live for 2 years, thorns straight, numerous to almost absent. **LEAVES** deciduous, alternate, palmately divided into 3–5 leaflets, leaflets lance- to egg-shaped, 1–4 in. long, surfaces variably hairy, greenish above, sometimes grayish below, edges doubly toothed, tips pointed. **FLOWERS** in small clusters at stem ends or in leaf axils, flowers bowl-shaped, petals 5, white, to 0.3 in. long, sepals bent back, hairy and often glandular.

FRUIT berry, red, to 0.5 in. across, edible, sweet. **ECOLOGY** grows in shrub thickets, open forests, rocky slopes, from low to mid elevation. Scores of cultivars are grown commercially.

Rubus laciniatus
ROSACEAE
CUTLEAF BLACKBERRY, EVERGREEN BLACKBERRY

Non-native, locally common, blooms late spring–mid summer, 2–6 ft. Disturbed, meadows, low to mid elevation

Shrub, stems erect to arching, 5-angled, rooting at tips, thicket-forming, thorns stout, curved. **LEAVES** evergreen, alternate, palmately divided (mostly) into 3 leaflets, leaflets triangular, again divided or lobed, green above, hairy or not, densely hairy below, edges irregularly toothed, tips pointed. **FLOWERS** in flat-topped clusters, flowers bisexual, disk-shaped, petals 5, tips lobed, pinkish to white, sepals bent back, densely hairy and prickly. **FRUIT** berry, black, oval, about 1 in. long, edible, tasty. **ECOLOGY** invasive, shade intolerant, grows in disturbed, often cutover and/or burned sites, young forests, and roadsides.

Rubus leucodermis
ROSACEAE
BLACKCAP RASPBERRY, BLACK RASPBERRY, WHITEBARK RASPBERRY

Native, common, blooms mid spring–mid summer, 3–10 ft. Disturbed, meadows, west-side forest, east-side forest, low to mid elevation

Shrub, erect, stems at times arching and rooting at the tip, waxy, thorns stout, curved. Each stem lives for 2 years, 1st year vegetative, 2nd flowering. **LEAVES** deciduous, alternate, palmately divided into 3(5) leaflets, leaflets lance- to egg-shaped, 1–3 in. long, non-hairy above, woolly hairy beneath, edges doubly toothed, tips pointed. **FLOWERS** in small flat-topped clusters at stem ends and leaf axils, flowers bowl-shaped, sepals hairy, bent back, petals 5, shorter than sepals, white. **FRUIT** berry, reddish purple to black, finely hairy, to 0.5 in. across, edible, tasty. **ECOLOGY** grows in disturbed areas, open forests, and fields. The similar *R. idaeus* has red fruit and straight thorns.

Rubus pedatus
ROSACEAE
STRAWBERRY BRAMBLE, FIVE-LEAVED BRAMBLE, DWARF BRAMBLE
Native, common, blooms late spring–early summer, 4 in. West-side forest, east-side forest, subalpine, low to high elevation

Subshrub, stems trailing, stoloniferous, rooting at the nodes, prickles absent. **LEAVES** deciduous, alternate, palmately divided into 5 leaflets (or 3, but then lower 2 deeply lobed), leaflets egg-shaped, 0.5–1 in. long, surfaces non-hairy except on veins below, edges doubly toothed, tips pointed. **FLOWERS** single, stalked, flowers saucer-shaped, petals 5, white, sepals bent back, often toothed at tip. **FRUIT** berry, red, about 0.5 in. across, non-hairy, edible, tasty. **ECOLOGY** grows in moist forests and mossy areas. The similar *R. lasiococcus* has simple 3-lobed leaves and hairy berries, and *R. arcticus* ssp. *acaulis* has pink to reddish petals.

Rubus pubescens
ROSACEAE
DWARF RED BLACKBERRY, TRAILING RASPBERRY
Native, locally common, blooms late spring–mid summer, 6–20 in. Bog/fen/wetland, streambanks, meadows, mid elevation

Subshrub, rhizomatous, vegetative stems trailing, hairy, prickles absent. **LEAVES** deciduous, alternate, palmately divided into 3 leaflets, egg-shaped, 1–2.5 in. long, hairy or not above, hairy below, edges singly or doubly toothed, tips pointed. **FLOWERS** single or few-flowered clusters, bisexual, flowers saucer-shaped, petals 5, white to rarely pinkish, 0.2–0.5 in. long, sepals hairy and often glandular, bent back. **FRUIT** berry, dark red, round, about 0.5 in. across, edible, sweet. **ECOLOGY** grows in bogs, wet meadows, streambanks, and forests in the mountains.

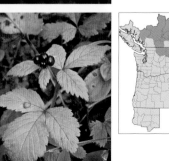

Rubus spectabilis
ROSACEAE
SALMONBERRY
Native, common, blooms early spring, 3–13
ft. Streambanks, west-side forest, east-
side forest, low to mid elevation

Shrub, erect, rhizomatous, thicket-forming, stems yellowish brown, lower stem with numerous straight prickles, few to none on upper stem. **LEAVES** decidu-ous, alternate, palmately divided into 3 leaflets, leaf-lets egg-shaped, 1.5–3.5 in. long, edges doubly toothed and sometimes lobed, tips pointed. **FLOWERS** single to few-flowered clusters on short side branches, flow-ers nodding, saucer-shaped, sepals hairy with pointed tips, petals pink to reddish purple. **FRUIT** berry, red, yellow, or yellowish pink, edible but not especially tasty. **ECOLOGY** shade toler-ant, grows in moist forests, swampy places, stream-banks, and other wet areas.

Rubus ursinus
ROSACEAE
**TRAILING BLACKBERRY, DEWBERRY, PACIFIC
BLACKBERRY**
Native, common, blooms mid spring–mid
summer, to 20 in. Disturbed, meadows, west-side
forest, east-side forest, low to mid elevation

Subshrub, stems trailing, hairy when young, prickles slender, slightly curved. **LEAVES** deciduous, alternate, palmately divided (mostly) into 3 leaflets, leaflets oval to egg-shaped, 1–4 in. long, sparsely to densely hairy below, edges doubly toothed and sometimes lobed, tips pointed. **FLOWERS** in small, flat-topped clusters, flowers unisexual, male and female flowers on separate plants, flowers saucer-shaped, petals 5, white, sepals 5, lobed, woolly hairy and glandu-lar, sometimes prickly.

FRUIT berry, black, non-hairy, oval to roundish, about 0.5 in. long, edible, tasty. **ECOLOGY** grows in open forest, cleared or otherwise disturbed areas, and streambanks.

Sorbus aucuparia
ROSACEAE
EUROPEAN MOUNTAIN ASH
Non-native, scattered, blooms late spring,
17–50 ft. Disturbed, meadows, west-
side forest, low to mid elevation

Tree, crown oval to rounded, bark gray, smooth when young, becoming cracked and split with age, branches ascending and spreading, twigs hairy becoming smooth, grayish brown. **LEAVES** deciduous, alternate, pinnately divided (mostly) into 11–15 leaflets, often more than 13, leaflets oblong to lance-shaped, 1–2.5 in. long, dull dark green above, paler below, edges toothed to near leaf base, tips pointed. **FLOWERS** in flat-topped, dense clusters, flowers small, malodorous, petals 5, roundish, to 0.2 in. long, white, stamens 15–20, styles 2–3. **FRUIT** pome, round, orange to bright red, waxy coating absent, to 0.5 in. across, edible, sour. **ECOLOGY** European import, it and its cultivars grow near home-steads, along roadsides, disturbed areas, and open forests. Fruit often made into jelly, high in vitamin C; highly desirable to birds, who in turn disseminate the seeds.

Sorbus californica
ROSACEAE
CALIFORNIA MOUNTAIN ASH

Native, locally common, blooms late spring–early summer, 3–13 ft. Rocky sites, west-side forest, east-side forest, subalpine, mid to high elevation Shrub, erect, stems and branches grayish brown. **LEAVES** deciduous, alternate, pinnately divided into 7–11 leaflets, leaflets oblong to egg-shaped, 1–1.5 in. long, shiny green above, hair when present reddish brown, edges toothed, tips pointed. **FLOWERS** in rounded dense clusters, flowers small, petals 5, egg-shaped, to 0.2 in. long, white. **FRUIT** pome, oval to round, bright red with a waxy coating, to 0.4 in. across. **ECOLOGY** grows in moist forests, rock outcrops, talus slopes, and into subalpine habitats.

Sorbus scopulina
ROSACEAE
CASCADE MOUNTAIN ASH, GREENE'S MOUNTAIN ASH, ROCKY MOUNTAIN MOUNTAIN ASH
Native, common, blooms late spring–mid summer, 3–17 ft. West-side forest, east-side forest, subalpine, low to high elevation

Shrub or small tree, stems hairy when young, bark yellowish to grayish red. **LEAVES** deciduous, alternate, pinnately divided into 9–13 leaflets, leaflets oval to lance-shaped, 1–3 in. long, shiny dark green and non-hairy above, sometimes hairy beneath, edges toothed, tips pointed. **FLOWERS** in flat-topped, many-flowered clusters, flowers small, petals 5, oval, to 0.2 in. long, white

to cream. **FRUIT** pome, round, orange to bright red, about 0.5 in. across, edible, tart. **ECOLOGY** grows in open moist forests, rocky slopes, streambanks, and other places. Fruit is desired wildlife forage.

Sorbus sitchensis
ROSACEAE
SITKA MOUNTAIN ASH, WESTERN MOUNTAIN ASH

Native, common, blooms late spring–mid summer, 3–13 ft. Meadows, west-side forest, east-side forest, subalpine, mid to high elevation

Shrub, erect, stems hairy when young, bark grayish red to reddish brown. **LEAVES** deciduous, alternate, pinnately divided into 7–11 leaflets, leaflets oval to egg-shaped, 1–2.5 in. long, mostly non-hairy above, often rusty-hairy beneath, edges partially toothed, tips rounded. **FLOWERS** in rounded, many-flowered clusters, flowers small, petals 5, egg- to diamond-shaped, to 0.2 in. long, white to cream. **FRUIT** pome, oval to round, red with a waxy coating, about 0.5 in. across, edible, tart. **ECOLOGY** grows in open moist forests, rocky slopes, streambanks, from montane to alpine elevation.

Ptelea crenulata
RUTACEAE
CALIFORNIA HOPTREE
Native, common, blooms mid spring, 7–15 ft.
East-side forest, shrub-steppe, low elevation
Shrub or tree, bark brown, smooth, twigs brown and glandular. **LEAVES** deciduous, alternate, pinnately divided into 3 leaflets, leaflets lance- to egg-shaped, 1–3 in. long, glandular, shiny green and non-hairy above, hairy below, edges smooth or scalloped, tips pointed.

FLOWERS in flat-topped clusters, flowers bisexual, star-shaped, petals 5 or 4, greenish white, fragrant. **FRUIT** samara, round, tan, seeds 2. **ECOLOGY** grows in sagebrush scrub or woodlands within the lower montane zone, often in moist areas of canyons or flats. Endemic to California.

Parthenocissus vitacea

(*Parthenocissus inserta*)
VITACEAE
WOODBINE, THICKET-CREEPER

Non-native, scattered, blooms mid spring–early
summer, 1–19 ft. Disturbed, meadows, low elevation
Woody vine, climbing or creeping, stems weak, tendrils lack adhesive tip. **LEAVES** deciduous, alternate,
palmately divided into 5 leaflets, lance- to egg-shaped,
2–5 in. long, glossy green above, paler beneath, edges
toothed, tips pointed. **FLOWERS** in clusters along
stems, opposite of leaves, flowers small, unisexual or
bisexual, greenish. **FRUIT** berry, deep
blue to black, to 0.5 in. wide, palatable.
ECOLOGY a fast grower, found along
roadsides, shrub thickets, open forests.

See Vitaceae with simple leaves, page
300

Sambucus nigra ssp. *cerulea*
(*Sambucus cerulea*, *Sambucus mexicana*)
ADOXACEAE (CAPRIFOLIACEAE)
BLUE ELDERBERRY
Native, common, blooms mid spring–early summer, 3–20 ft. Meadows, west-side forest, east-side forest, low to high elevation

Shrub or tree, erect, bark gray or brown, furrowed with age, twigs with waxy coating. **LEAVES** deciduous, opposite, pinnately divided into 5–9 leaflets, leaflets egg- to lance-shaped, 2–6 in. long, surfaces mostly non-hairy, edges finely toothed, tips pointed. **FLOWERS** in flat-topped clusters, flowers small, wheel-shaped, petals white to cream. **FRUIT** berry, powder blue (blackish

blue with white waxy coating), to 0.2 in. across, edible. **ECOLOGY** shade intolerant, grows in well-drained sites on open slopes, valley bottoms, near streams, and along roadsides from low to high elevation. Resprouts after burning; fire also stimulates seed germination.

See Adoxaceae with simple leaves, page 301

Sambucus racemosa
(*Sambucus racemosa* ssp. *pubens* var. *arborescens*)
ADOXACEAE (CAPRIFOLIACEAE)
RED ELDERBERRY, COASTAL RED ELDERBERRY
Native, common, blooms early spring–mid summer, 3–20 ft. Coastal, west-side forest, east-side forest, low to high elevation

Shrub or tree, erect, bark reddish brown. **LEAVES** deciduous, opposite, pinnately divided into 5–7 leaflets, leaflets oval to lance-shaped, 2–6 in. long, non-hairy above, non-hairy or hairy on veins below, edges finely toothed, tips pointed. **FLOWERS** in rounded to pyramidal clusters, 1–5 in. long, flowers small, wheel-shaped, petals white to cream.

FRUIT berry, round, red, about 0.2 in. across, edible when cooked. **ECOLOGY** tolerates partial shade, grows in moist places, meadows, forests, and streambanks.

Sambucus racemosa var. *melanocarpa*
(*Sambucus melanocarpa, Sambucus racemosa*
ssp. *pubens* var. *melanocarpa*)
ADOXACEAE (CAPRIFOLIACEAE)
BLACK ELDERBERRY

Native, common, blooms all spring, 3–10 ft. Meadows,
west-side forest, east-side forest, low to high elevation
Shrub or tree, erect, bark reddish brown. **LEAVES** deciduous, opposite, pinnately divided into 5–7 leaflets, leaflets oval to lance-shaped, 2–6 in. long, non-hairy above,
often hairy below, edges finely toothed, tips pointed.
FLOWERS in rounded to pyramidal clusters, 1.5–3 in.
long, flowers small, wheel-shaped, petals white to
cream. **FRUIT** berry, round, purplish black to black,
about 0.2 in. across, edible when cooked. **ECOLOGY** tolerates partial shade, grows in moist places, meadows,
forests, and streambanks.

Fraxinus dipetala
OLEACEAE
CALIFORNIA ASH, TWO-PETALED ASH, FLOWERING ASH
Native, common, blooms all spring, 5–20 ft. Streambanks, disturbed, chaparral, eastside forest, low to mid elevation

Shrub or tree, bark grayish brown, smooth to scaly, twigs gray. **LEAVES** deciduous, opposite, pinnately divided into 3–7 leaflets, leaflets roundish to egg-shaped, 1–2 in. long, dark green above, paler beneath, edges mostly toothed, tips rounded, leaflet stalks present. **FLOWERS** in dense, large clusters, blooming as the leaves unfold, flowers showy, fragrant, bisexual, sepals 4, green, petals 2, creamy white.
FRUIT samara, to 1.5 in. long.
ECOLOGY streambanks in chaparral and woodlands, also along roads, low to mid elevation. The similar *F. latifolia* has unisexual yellowish or green flowers, light green leaves with pointed tips, and ridged bark.

Fraxinus latifolia
OLEACEAE
OREGON ASH
Native, common, blooms all spring, 27–67
ft. Streambanks, meadows, west-side forest,
east-side forest, low to mid elevation

Tree, crown spreading or narrow, bark dark grayish brown, with narrow, interlocking ridges, twigs
stout, woolly-hairy, less so with age. **LEAVES** deciduous,
opposite, pinnately divided into 5–7 leaflets, leaflets
oval to egg-shaped, 2–4.5 in. long, light green above,
paler beneath, edges smooth or toothed, tips pointed.
FLOWERS in dense clusters on short stalks, blooming as
the leaves unfold, small, unisexual on separate plants,
male flowers yellow, female greenish. **FRUIT** samara,
1–2 in. long. **ECOLOGY** grows in meadows, swamps,
valley bottoms, streambanks, and other wet places,
also along roads and at times in drier forests. Prefers
deep, fertile soils and has an extensive,
shallow root system. Shade intolerant,
can withstand strong winds and floods.
Grows fast when young, growth slowing
thereafter, with a lifespan of about 250
years. Resprouts from the base after logging or fire. Rare in British Columbia.

Clematis hirsutissima
RANUNCULACEAE
SUGAR BOWLS, LEATHER-FLOWER
Native, locally common, blooms mid spring–
mid summer, 6–24 in. Meadows, east-side
forest, shrub-steppe, low to high elevation
Subshrub, erect, stems several, densely hairy to nearly
non-hairy. **LEAVES** deciduous, opposite, 2–4 times
pinnately divided into linear to lance-shaped leaflets,
leaflets 0.5–2.5 in. long, whole blade up to 5 in. long,
surfaces hairy, edges sometimes lobed, tips pointed.
FLOWERS single at stem tips, flowers bell- to urn-
shaped, 1–2 in. long, bisexual, dark brownish purple,
rarely pink or white, sepals 4, leathery, grayish-hairy
outside, non-hairy inside, petals absent. **FRUIT** achene,
roundish, hairy, with feathery beak to 3.5 in. long.
ECOLOGY grows in grasslands, meadows, sagebrush
steppe, and ponderosa pine and other open, grassy
forests.

Clematis lasiantha
RANUNCULACEAE
PIPESTEM CLEMATIS
Native, common, blooms winter–mid
spring, 10–13 ft. Streambanks, chaparral,
east-side forest, low to mid elevation

Vine, stems climbing or sprawling, woody, bark grayish brown, stringy, young stems hairy.
LEAVES deciduous, opposite, pinnately divided into 3–5
leaflets, leaflets egg-shaped, 0.5–2.5 in. long, hairy
or not above, hairy below, edges usually lobed and
toothed, tips rounded. **FLOWERS** mostly single in leaf
axils, sometimes in clusters of 3–5, flowers unisexual
or bisexual, sepals 4, pale yellow to white, hairy, oval to
egg-shaped, about 1 in. long,
petals absent, stamens and
pistils many. **FRUIT** achene,
egg-shaped, hairy, with
feathery beak to 2 in. long.
ECOLOGY grows in streambanks and on slopes in chaparral and ponderosa pine forests. Endemic to California.

Clematis ligusticifolia
RANUNCULACEAE
WESTERN WHITE CLEMATIS, VIRGIN'S BOWER
Native, common, blooms all summer,
10–67 ft. Streambanks, west-side forest,
east-side forest, low to high elevation

Vine, rhizomatous, stems climbing or sprawling,
woody, hairy or not. **LEAVES** deciduous, opposite, pinnately divided into 5–7 leaflets, leaflets lance- to egg-
shaped, 1–3.5 in. long, edges smooth, toothed, or
lobed, tips pointed. **FLOWERS** in densely 7- to 20-flow-
ered clusters in leaf axils, flowers male or female,
sepals 4, white to cream, lance- to egg-shaped, to 0.5 in.
long, petals absent, stamens and pistils many, female
flowers with sterile stamens.
FRUIT achene, oval, long-hairy, with
feathery beak about 1.5 in. long.
ECOLOGY grows along streambanks,
forest edges, moist slopes, scrub,
and cleared areas, from low to high
elevation.

Clematis occidentalis (*Clematis columbiana*)
RANUNCULACEAE
WESTERN BLUE CLEMATIS
Native, locally common, blooms mid
spring–mid summer, to 7 ft. East-side
forest, subalpine, low to high elevation
Vine, stems climbing or creeping. **LEAVES** deciduous,
opposite, pinnately divided into 3 leaflets, leaflets egg-
shaped, 1–4.5 in. long, surfaces hairy when young,
non-hairy with age, edges smooth to toothed, tips
pointed. **FLOWERS** single on stems in leaf axils, flowers
bisexual, bowl-shaped, blue to reddish purple, sometimes white, sepals 4, 1–2.5 in. long, surfaces hairy,
tips pointed, petals absent, stamens and pistils many,
sterile stamens present.
FRUIT achene, oval, hairy,
with feathery beak to 2.5
in. long. **ECOLOGY** grows
on shady, grassy forest
slopes, rock outcrops, and
cliffs from low to high
elevation.

Clematis vitalba
RANUNCULACEAE
TRAVELER'S JOY, OLD MAN'S BEARD
Non-native, locally common, blooms all summer,
to 40 ft. Disturbed, west-side forest, low elevation
Vine, climbing, woody, stem grooved, sparsely hairy.
LEAVES deciduous, opposite, pinnately divided into 5
leaflets, leaflets heart-shaped, to 3 in. long, hair present on veins below, non-hairy above, edges smooth
to toothed, tips mostly pointed. **FLOWERS** in densely
5- to 22-flowered clusters in leaf axils and stem ends,
flowers bisexual, sepals 4, white to cream, lance- to
egg-shaped, to 0.5 in. long, hairy above and below, petals absent, stamens and pistils many, sterile stamens
absent. **FRUIT** achene, hairy, with feathery beak about 1.5 in. long.
ECOLOGY Eurasian import, grows in
riparian areas, disturbed places, and forest edges at lower elevations. The similar *C. ligusticifolia* has unisexual flowers. Listed as a noxious weed in Oregon
and Washington.

Acer negundo
SAPINDACEAE (ACERACEAE)
BOXELDER
Native and non-native, scattered, blooms
early–mid spring, 40–67 ft. Streambanks,
disturbed, low to mid elevation

Tree, crown irregular, bark gray, smooth becoming furrowed with age, trunk often divided near the ground, twigs hairy or not, light brown. **LEAVES** deciduous, opposite, pinnately divided into 3(5–9) leaflets, leaflets egg- or lance-shaped, 1.5–4.5 in. long, edges lobed and toothed, surfaces hairy to non-hairy, tips pointed. **FLOWERS** male and female flowers on separate plants, blooming before or as the leaves unfold. Male inflorescences are dense clusters in leaf axils, female inflorescences are elongated drooping clusters. Flowers are light green, sepals and stamens 4–5, petals lacking, style 1. **FRUIT** samara, 1-seeded, in pairs, wings of the pair <90-degree angle, hairy.
ECOLOGY grows on streambanks, floodplains, open slopes, and disturbed areas, lowland to montane. Fast growing and relatively short-lived (75–100 years). Non-native in British Columbia, Washington, and Oregon, native in California; these last, often split into var. *californicum*, have velvety, dense spreading hair on leaves and stems.

See Sapindaceae with simple leaves, page 345; see *Acer* with simple leaves, page 345

Aesculus californica
SAPINDACEAE (HIPPOCASTANACEAE)
CALIFORNIA BUCKEYE
Native, common, blooms late spring–early summer, 12–40 ft. Chaparral, west-side forest, east-side forest, low to mid elevation

Shrub or small tree, crown rounded, bark silvery gray. **LEAVES** deciduous (summer), opposite, palmately divided into 5–7 leaflets, leaflets oblong to lance-shaped, 2.5–7 in. long, edges toothed, tips pointed. **FLOWERS** in long, narrow clusters at stem ends, flowers showy, petals white to pale pink, stamens extend beyond petals, anthers orange. **FRUIT** capsule, pear-shaped, leathery, seeds one to several. **ECOLOGY** grows in riparian areas and on dry slopes, in woodlands, forests, and chaparral. All parts of the plant are toxic to humans and other animals.

Staphylea bolanderi
STAPHYLEACEAE
SIERRA BLADDERNUT
Native, uncommon, blooms early–mid spring, 7–20 ft. Chaparral, east-side forest, low to mid elevation

Shrub or tree, erect, bark grayish brown, twigs non-hairy. **LEAVES** deciduous, opposite, palmately divided into 3 leaflets, leaflets roundish to egg-shaped, 1–2.5 in. long, surfaces non-hairy, edges finely toothed, tips pointed. **FLOWERS** in pendent clusters, flowers tubular, petals white, stamens 5, protrude beyond petals. **FRUIT** capsules, egg-shaped, 1–2 in. long, cream to white, inflated, tips horned. **ECOLOGY** grows on canyon walls in chaparral and woodland communities, often planted as an ornamental. Endemic to California.

Aralia nudicaulis

ARALIACEAE

WILD SARSAPARILLA

Native, common, blooms mid–late spring, 12–28 in.
Streambanks, east-side forest, low to mid elevation
Subshrub or herbaceous, stems very short, mostly
below ground, rhizomatous. **LEAVES** deciduous, basal,
solitary, pinnately twice-divided into leaflets, leaflets
oblong to egg-shaped, 2–5 in. long, surfaces green,
edges toothed, tips pointed. **FLOWERS** in several ball-
shaped clusters, stalk shorter than the leaf, flowers
small, greenish white, petals and sepals 5. **FRUIT** berry,
dark purple, edible but not very tasty. **ECOLOGY** grows
in shady, moist forests, streambanks, and floodplains,
lowland to montane. Root used medicinally by Native
Americans.

See Araliaceae with simple leaves, page 112

Ephedra viridis
EPHEDRACEAE
MORMON TEA, GREEN EPHEDRA
Native, locally common, blooms winter–early summer,
1–3 ft. Rocky sites, shrub-steppe, mid elevation
Shrub, erect, stems and branches green, mostly leafless, short-hairy. **LEAVES** ephemeral, simple and opposite if present, scales at base persistent, brownish, 0.1–
0.2 in. long. **CONES** male and female cones on separate
plants, seed cones one to several at nodes, egg-shaped,
yellowish green to brown. **ECOLOGY** grows in sagebrush communities and juniper woodlands in rocky or
sandy soils.

Opuntia ×columbiana

CACTACEAE

GRIZZLYBEAR PRICKLYPEAR CACTUS

Native, locally common, blooms late spring–early summer, 4–10 in. Rocky sites, shrub-steppe, low elevation

Shrub, mat-forming, stems flattened, jointed, segments egg-shaped, spines in clusters, present throughout stems, longer spines mostly 1, 1–1.5 in. long, smaller spines >0.1 in. long, tufts of barbed hair at base of spines. **LEAVES** mostly absent, ephemeral, small if present. **FLOWERS** single, emerge from previous year's growth, unstalked, tepals erect, many, yellow, 1–2 in. long, stamens many, filaments reddish or white. **FRUIT** top- or barrel-shaped, <2 times longer than wide, spiny, to 1 in. long. **ECOLOGY** grows on basalt outcrops, cliffs, sandy areas, grassy slopes, sagebrush steppe. The similar *O. fragilis* usually has more than 1 long spine per cluster, short spines not >0.1 in., and pear-shaped fruits. Rare in British Columbia.

Opuntia fragilis
CACTACEAE
BRITTLE PRICKLYPEAR CACTUS
Native, locally common, blooms late spring–
early summer, 2–8 in. Coastal, meadows,
shrub-steppe, low to mid elevation

Shrub, mat-forming, stems flattened to somewhat rounded, jointed, forming segments, spines in clusters, longer spines 2–7, 0.5–1.5 in. long, grayish to brownish, short spines 0–3, 0.05–0.1 in. long, tufts of barbed hair at base of spines. **LEAVES** mostly absent, ephemeral, small if present. **FLOWERS** single, emerge from previous year's growth, unstalked, tepals erect, many, yellow, sometimes red at the base, about 1 in. long, stamens many, filaments reddish or white. **FRUIT** pear-shaped, tan, spiny, about 0.5–1 in. long, seeds many. **ECOLOGY** grows on rock outcrops, dry grassy slopes, with sagebrush, and in juniper woodlands, on sandy or gravelly soils. Rare in California.

Pediocactus nigrispinus
(*Pediocactus simpsonii* var. *robustior*)
CACTACEAE
HEDGEHOG CACTUS
Native, locally common, blooms late
spring–early summer, 1–10 in. Rocky sites,
shrub-steppe, low to mid elevation

Herbaceous, stems unjointed, rounded, 3–5 in.
wide, ribbed, single or clustered, spines smooth,
hard, in clusters spirally arranged along stem, longer central spines 4–11, 0.3–1 in. long, yellowish
to reddish brown, smaller marginal spines 15–35,
whitish, to 0.5 in. long. **LEAVES** absent.
FLOWERS grouped near stem tips, flowers
unstalked, tepals erect, many, bright pink, purplish, yellowish green or white, 0.4–1 in. long,
edges smooth, wavy, or toothed, stamens many,
style 1. **FRUIT** roundish, to 0.5 in. long, green with
red, seeds many, gray to black. **ECOLOGY** grows in
arid areas in lithosols, in sagebrush communities,
grasslands, and forests. Rare in Oregon.

ABOUT THE PHOTOGRAPHS

Most field guide users start with the photographs, matching characteristics of the plant in front of them with the pictures in the book. I worked hard to photograph the plants in a way that makes identification as accurate as possible, while simultaneously employing the artist's tools of composition, light and shadow, and point of view. One or more key characters of the species are illustrated in each photo.

The photographs were made over a period of 16 years, although the majority were created in two intensive field seasons. I drove over 40,000 miles, with repeated trips across the Northwest to capture many of the plants in both flower and fruit. Most photos were made within a short walk of a road, but some of those roads were little more than tracks left by all-wheel-drive vehicles. I was guided to locations by herbarium records provided by botanists who came before me.

I worked in all kinds of weather and lighting conditions, from bright midday sun to dense coastal fog to rain. I held an umbrella over my camera on more than one occasion. With so many plants and locations spread over such a wide area I did not have the luxury of waiting for perfect conditions. Most of the time I used whatever light was available, modifying it with a reflector or diffuser for the close-up images. I battled wind. I sought vantage points that let me separate specimen from background. While all my subjects were firmly rooted, that didn't make them easy.

The great majority of the photographs were made with Canon digital single-lens reflex cameras. A few originated on 35mm slide film. I used a variety of lenses from 16mm ultra wide-angle to 400mm telephoto. Three lenses were the workhorses: 24–105mm, 100mm macro, and 70–200 mm. I almost always work with my camera on a tripod.

Once field photography was complete I selected the best views of each species from over 20,000 candidates. I made my selections using Adobe® Lightroom® and did most of the post-capture processing in the develop module of the same program to adjust density, color balance, and contrast.

ADDITIONAL PHOTOGRAPHY

All photographs in *Trees and Shrubs of the Pacific Northwest* are by Mark Turner with the exception of the following:

Zoya Akulova-Barlow: *Ribes menziesii* (fruit), page 208
Aaron Arthur: *Amorpha californica* (specimen), page 381
Tom Ballinger: *Sorbus californica* (flower), page 405
André Benedito: *Sesbania punicea* (flower), page 386
Jeff Bisbee: *Abies grandis* (cones), page 60; *Abies magnifica* (cones), page 62; *Picea glauca* (cones), page 70
Todd Boland: *Salix candida* (flower), page 270
Barry Breckling: *Ericameria arborescens* (flower), page 125; *Salix petrophila* (fruit), page 285; *Staphylea bolanderi* (flower, fruit), page 418
Robert L. Carr: *Rubus idaeus* (specimen), page 400
Joyce Cory: *Solanum douglasii* (fruit), page 292
Chris Earle: *Pinus flexilis* (cones), page 77
Mark Egger: *Salix vestita*, page 290
Jamie Fenneman: *Rubus pubescens* (fruit), page 402; *Salix discolor* (foliage), page 273; *Salix myrtillifolia* (foliage), page 284; *Salix pseudomyrsinites* (foliage), page 287
Jake Frank: *Artemisia tilesii*, page 118
Toshiko Gunter: *Tamarix ramosissima* (flower), page 296
Dale Hameister: *Ribes malvaceum* (fruit), page 207
James Holland: *Phlox austromontana*, page 336
Jason Hollinger: *Chrysolepis sempervirens* (flower), page 188
Donald House: *Rubus chamaemorus* (fruit), page 256

Melissa Hutchison: *Cassiope lycopodioides* (specimen), page 317
Tim Kellison: *Salix petrophila*, page 285
Brian Klinkenberg: *Vaccinium macrocarpon* (flower), page 179
Jukka-Pekka Korpi-Vartiainen: *Rubus arcticus* ssp. *acaulis* (fruit), page 399
Neal Kramer: *Primula suffrutescens* (flower, specimen), page 368
Ellen Kuhlmann: *Ribes lobbii* (fruit), page 206
Louis-M. Landry: *Gaultheria hispidula* (fruit), page 167
Matt Lavin: *Salix wolfii* (fruit), page 291
Ben Legler: *Cassiope lycopodioides* (habitat), page 317; *Viburnum ellipticum* (flower), page 301
Uli Lorimer: *Vaccinium macrocarpon* (flower), page 179
Joshua McCullough: *Salix candida* (specimen), page 270
Malcolm Manners: *Rosa acicularis* (fruit), page 391
Don Martyn: *Kalmia procumbens* (flower), page 319
Steve Matson: *Brickellia microphylla* (flower, specimen), page 123
Keir Morse: *Calystegia purpurata* (flower, specimen), page 148; *Monardella sheltonii*, page 325; *Ribes erythrocarpum* (fruit), page 203
Dan Mullen: *Salix discolor* (flower), page 273
Jessica O'Brien: *Viburnum ellipticum* (specimen), page 301
Jerry R. Oldenettel: *Tamarix ramosissima* (specimen), page 296

BIBLIOGRAPHY

Adams, Robert P. *Juniperus maritima*, the seaside juniper, a new species from Puget Sound, North America. *Phytologia* 89(3): 263–283. 2007.

Anderson, Michelle D. *Ceanothus velutinus*. Fire Effects Information System. USDA Forest Service, Rocky Mountain Research Station, Fire Sciences Laboratory. 2001. http://www.fs.fed.us/database/feis/.

———. *Rhus trilobata*. Fire Effects Information System. USDA Forest Service, Rocky Mountain Research Station, Fire Sciences Laboratory. 2004. http://www.fs.fed.us/database/feis/.

Arno, Stephen F., and Ramona P. Hammerly. *Northwest Trees*. Rev. ed. Seattle: Mountaineers Books, 2007.

Bailey, Robert G. *Description of the Ecoregions of the United States*. Fort Collins, Colo.: USDA Forest Service, 1995. http://www.fs.fed.us/land/ecosysmgmt/ecoreg1_home.html. Accessed 17 November 2004.

Baldwin, Bruce G., et al., eds. *The Jepson Manual: Vascular Plants of California*. 2nd ed. Berkeley: University of California Press, 2012.

Bannick, Paul. *The Owl and the Woodpecker*. Seattle: Mountaineers Books, 2008.

Begnoche, Don. *Siskiyou Sundays: A Tour of Southwestern Oregon*. Ashland, Ore.: Don Begnoche, 1999.

Biek, David. *Flora of Mount Rainier National Park*. Corvallis: Oregon State University Press, 2000.

Boyd, Robert, ed. *Indians, Fire, and the Land in the Pacific Northwest*. Corvallis: Oregon State University Press, 1999.

British Columbia Ministry of Forests. *Ecosystems of British Columbia*. Special report series ISSN 0843-6452: 6. Victoria: Crown Publications, 1991.

Brayshaw, T. Christopher. *Catkin Bearing Plants (Amertiferae) of British Columbia*. Occasional papers of the British Columbia Provincial Museum no. 18. Victoria: British Columbia Provincial Museum, 1976.

Britton, Nathaniel L., and H. Addison Brown. *An Illustrated Flora of the Northern United States and Canada Volumes I and II*. New York: Dover Publications, 1970.

Buckingham, Nelsa M., et al. *Flora of the Olympic Peninsula*. Seattle: Northwest Interpretive Association, Washington Native Plant Society, 1995.

Burke Museum of Natural History and Culture. *University of Washington Herbarium Image Collection*. Seattle: University of Washington. http://biology.burke.washington.edu/herbarium/imagecollection.php. Accessed 25 January 2013.

Burns, Russell M., and Barbara H. Honkala, eds. *Silvics of North America*. Vols. 1 and 2. Agricultural Handbook no. 654. Washington, D.C.: USDA Forest Service, 1990.

Calflora: Information on California plants for education, research and conservation, based on data contributed by dozens of public and private institutions and individuals, including the Consortium of Calif. Herbaria. Berkeley: The Calflora Database. http://www.calflora.org/. Accessed 25 January 2013.

Callahan, Frank. Hind's walnut (*Juglans hindsii*) in Oregon. *Kalmiopsis* 15:42–52. 2008.

Camp, Pamela, and John G. Gamon, eds. *Field Guide to the Rare Plants of Washington*. Seattle: University of Washington Press, 2011.

Campbell, Christopher S. *Amelanchier Systematics and Evolution.* http://sbe.umaine.edu/amelanchier/. 2010.

Clark, Lewis J. *Wild Flowers of the Pacific Northwest.* Madeira Park, B.C.: Harbour Publishing, 1998.

Cooke, Sarah Spear, ed. *A Field Guide to the Common Wetland Plants of Western Washington and Northwestern Oregon.* Seattle: Seattle Audubon Society, 1997.

Cook, Thea, and Scott Sundberg, eds. *Oregon Vascular Plant Checklist.* Version 1.2. 2011. http://www.oregonflora.org/checklist.php. Accessed 25 January 2013.

Cope, Amy B. *Abies magnifica, Abies procera, Pinus muricata.* Fire Effects Information System. USDA Forest Service, Rocky Mountain Research Station, Fire Sciences Laboratory. 1993. http://www.fs.fed.us/database/feis/.

Cope, Edward A. *Muenscher's Keys to Woody Plants.* Ithaca, N.Y.: Cornell University Press, 2001.

Crane, M. F. *Arctostaphylos uva-ursi.* Fire Effects Information System. USDA Forest Service, Rocky Mountain Research Station, Fire Sciences Laboratory. 1991. http://www.fs.fed.us/database/feis/.

Cronquist, Arthur, et al. *Vascular Plants of the Intermountain West, U.S.A.* Vol. 1. New York and London: Hafner Publishing Company, 1972.

Demarchi, Dennis A. *An Introduction to the Ecoregions of British Columbia.* Wildlife Branch, Ministry of Environment, Lands and Parks. Victoria, B.C., 1996. http://www.env.gov.bc.ca/wld/documents/techpub/rn324.pdf. Accessed 25 January 2013.

Douglas, G. W., et al., eds. *Illustrated Flora of British Columbia.* 8 vols. Victoria: B.C. Ministry of Environment, Lands and Parks and B.C. Ministry of Forests, 1998–2002.

eFloras. *Acacia dealbata, Lonicera tatarica, Salix fragilis.* Flora of China. St. Louis, Missouri: Missouri Botanic Garden and Harvard University Herbaria. 2008. http://www.efloras.org. Accessed in 2012.

Esser, Lora. *Cupressus bakeri.* Fire Effects Information System. USDA Forest Service, Rocky Mountain Research Station, Fire Sciences Laboratory. 1994. http://www.fs.fed.us/database/feis/.

Ertter, Barbara. *Native California Roses.* 2001. http://ucjeps.berkeley.edu/ina/roses/roses.html.

Flora of North America Editorial Committee, eds. 1993–. *Flora of North America North of Mexico.* 16+ vols. New York and Oxford. http://www.eflora.org/. Accessed 25 January 2013.

Franklin, Jerry F., and C. T. Dyrness. *Natural Vegetation of Oregon and Washington.* Corvallis: Oregon State University Press, 1988.

Fross, David, and Dieter Wilken. *Ceanothus.* Portland, Ore.: Timber Press, 2006.

Fryer, Janet L. *Pinus albicaulis.* Fire Effects Information System, USDA Forest Service, Rocky Mountain Research Station, Fire Sciences Laboratory. 2002. http://www.fs.fed.us/database/feis/.

———. *Pinus balfouriana.* Fire Effects Information System, USDA Forest Service, Rocky Mountain Research Station, Fire Sciences Laboratory. 2004. http://www.fs.fed.us/database/feis/.

———. *Quercus douglasii.* Fire Effects Information System, USDA Forest Service, Rocky Mountain Research Station, Fire Sciences Laboratory. 2007. http://www.fs.fed.us/database/feis/.

———. *Artemisia nova.* Fire Effects Information System, USDA Forest Service, Rocky Mountain Research Station, Fire Sciences Laboratory. 2009. http://www.fs.fed.us/database/feis/.

———. *Quercus wislizeni.* Fire Effects Information System, USDA Forest Service, Rocky Mountain Research Station, Fire Sciences Laboratory. 2012. http://www.fs.fed.us/database/feis/.

Gilkey, Helen M., and Patricia L. Packard. *Winter Twigs*. Corvallis: Oregon State University Press, 2001.

Gucker, Corey L. *Cornus nuttallii*. Fire Effects Information System, USDA Forest Service, Rocky Mountain Research Station, Fire Sciences Laboratory. 2005. http://www.fs.fed.us/database/feis/.

———. *Salix discolor, Prunus andersonii, Pinus jeffreyi*. Fire Effects Information System, USDA Forest Service, Rocky Mountain Research Station, Fire Sciences Laboratory. 2007. http://www.fs.fed.us/database/feis/.

Habeck, R. J. *Pinus lambertina*. Fire Effects Information System, USDA Forest Service, Rocky Mountain Research Station, Fire Sciences Laboratory. 1992. http://www.fs.fed.us/database/feis/.

Harris, James G. and Melinda Woolf Harris. *Plant Identification Terminology: An Illustrated Glossary*. Spring Lake, Utah: Spring Lake Publishing, 1994.

Hauser, A. Scott. *Cercis orbiculata*. Fire Effects Information System, USDA Forest Service, Rocky Mountain Research Station, Fire Sciences Laboratory. 2006. http://www.fs.fed.us/database/feis/.

Hickman, James C., ed. *The Jepson Manual: Higher Plants of California*. Berkeley: University of California Press, 1993.

Hitchcock, C. Leo, and Arthur Cronquist. *Flora of the Pacific Northwest*. Seattle: University of Washington Press, 1973.

Hitchcock, C. Leo, et al. *Vascular Plants of the Pacific Northwest*. 5 vols. Seattle: University of Washington Press, 1955–69.

Hosie, Robert C. *Native Trees of Canada*. 8th ed. Don Mills, Ontario: Fitzhenry and Whiteside Limited, 1979.

Howard, Janet L. *Eriodictyon californicum, Chrysolepis sempervirens, Chamaebatia foliolosa, Pinus sabiniana, Pinus attenuata, Quercus lobata*. Fire Effects Information System, USDA Forest Service, Rocky Mountain Research Station, Fire Sciences Laboratory. 1992. http://www.fs.fed.us/database/feis/.

———. *Tetradymia glabrata*. Fire Effects Information System, USDA Forest Service, Rocky Mountain Research Station, Fire Sciences Laboratory. 2002. http://www.fs.fed.us/database/feis/.

———. *Artiplex canescens*. Fire Effects Information System, USDA Forest Service, Rocky Mountain Research Station, Fire Sciences Laboratory. 2003. http://www.fs.fed.us/database/feis/.

Jensen, Edward C., and Charles R. Ross. *Trees to Know in Oregon*. Extension Circular 1450. Corvallis: Oregon State University Extension Service and Oregon Department of Forestry, 1995.

Johnson, Kathleen A. *Rhus glabra*. Fire Effects Information System, USDA Forest Service, Rocky Mountain Research Station, Fire Sciences Laboratory. 2000. http://www.fs.fed.us/database/feis/.

Jolley, Russ. *Wildflowers of the Columbia Gorge*. Portland: Oregon Historical Society Press, 1988.

Justice, Douglas. Leaf shape in Rocky Mountain maple, *Acer glabrum* Torr. *Menziesia: Native Plant Society of British Columbia Newsletter* 7(3): 4–6. Summer 2002.

Kauffmann, Michael Edward. *Conifer Country: A Natural History and Hiking Guide to 35 Conifers of the Klamath Mountain Region*. Kneeland, Calif.: Backcountry Press, 2012.

Kershaw, Linda J., et al. *Plants of the Rocky Mountains*. Edmonton, Alb.: Lone Pine Press, 1998.

Klinkenberg, Brian, ed. *E-Flora BC: Electronic Atlas of the Plants of British Columbia*. Lab for Advanced Spatial Analysis, Department of Geography, University of British Columbia, Vancouver. 2013. http://www.geog.ubc.ca/biodiversity/eflora/. Accessed 25 January 2013.

Kruckeberg, Art. *Geology and Plant Life: The Effects of Landforms and Rock Types on Plants*. Seattle: University of Washington Press, 2002.

Lyons, Chess, and Bill Merilees. *Trees, Shrubs*

and *Flowers to Know in British Columbia and Washington*. Redmond, Wash.: Lone Pine Publishing, 1995.

Mallek, Chris R. Fire history, stand origins, and persistence of MacNab cypress, northern California, USA. *Fire Ecology* 5(3): 100–199. 2009.

McMurray, Nancy E. *Chrysolepsis chrysophylla*. Fire Effects Information System, USDA Forest Service, Rocky Mountain Research Station, Fire Sciences Laboratory. 1989. http://www.fs.fed.us/database/feis/.

———. *Adenostoma fasciulatum, Heteromeles arbutifolia*. Fire Effects Information System, USDA Forest Service, Rocky Mountain Research Station, Fire Sciences Laboratory. 1990. http://www.fs.fed.us/database/feis/.

Mansfield, Donald H. *Flora of Steens Mountain*. Corvallis: Oregon State University Press, 2000.

Marshall, Ian B., and Peter H. Schut. *A National Ecological Framework for Canada*. Ottawa, Ont.: Ecosystems Science Directorate, Environment Canada and Research Branch, Agriculture and Agri-Food Canada, 1999. http://sis.agr.gc.ca/cansis/nsdb/ecostrat/intro.html. Accessed 25 January 2013.

Mason, Georgia. *Guide to the Plants of the Wallowa Mountains of Northeastern Oregon*. Eugene: University of Oregon Press, 2001.

Mathews, Daniel. *Cascade-Olympic Natural History: A Trailside Reference*. 2nd ed. Portland, Ore.: Raven Editions, 1999.

Meyer, Rachelle. *Ceanothus leucodermis*. Fire Effects Information System, USDA Forest Service, Rocky Mountain Research Station, Fire Sciences Laboratory. 2011. http://www.fs.fed.us/database/feis/.

Mitchell, Alan. *Trees of Britain and Northern Europe*. London: HarperCollins, 1978.

Morin, Nancy R., and Judith M. Unger, eds. Botanical news *Neviusia cliftonii. Flora of North America Newsletter* 6(4): October to December 1992.

NatureServe Explorer: An Online Encyclopedia of Life. Version 7.1. Arlington, Va.: NatureServe. http://www.natureserve.org/explorer. 2010.

Nellessen, J. E. *Viburnum opulus* L. var. *americanum* (Mill) Ait (American cranberrybush). USDA Forest Service, Rocky Mountain Region. http://www.fs.fed.us/r2/projects/scp/assessments/viburnum opulusvaramericanum.pdf. 2006.

Newsholme, Christopher. *Willows*. Portland, Ore.: Timber Press, 1992.

Oregon Flora Project. *Oregon Flora Project Plant Atlas*. Corvallis: Oregon State University Department of Botany and Plant Pathology. http://www.oregonflora.org/atlas.php. 2010.

Parish, Roberta, et al., eds. *Plants of Southern Interior British Columbia*. Vancouver: Lone Pine Press, 1996.

Pavek, Diane S. *Fremontodendron californicum*. Fire Effects Information System, USDA Forest Service, Rocky Mountain Research Station, Fire Sciences Laboratory. 1993. http://www.fs.fed.us/database/feis/.

Peck, Morton E. *A Manual of the Higher Plants of Oregon*. 2nd ed. Portland: Binfords and Mort, 1961.

Phipps, James B. Introduction to the red-fruited hawthorns (*Crataegus*, Rosaceae) of western North America. *Canadian Journal of Botany* 76:1863–1899. 1998.

Phipps, James B., and Robert J. O'Kennon. New species of *Crataegus* (Rosaceae) from western North America, *C. okennonii, C. okanaganensis*, and *C. phippsii. SIDA* 18:169–191. 1998.

———. New taxa of *Crataegus* (Rosaceae) from the northern Okanagan-Southwestern Shuswap diversity center. *SIDA* 20:115–144. 2002.

———. A review of *Crataegus* series *Rotundifoliae* (Rosaceae) in western Canada. *SIDA* 21:65–77. 2004.

Plants of Pacific Northwest: Interactive Keys and Color Photos. CD-ROM. Pendleton, Ore.: Flora ID Northwest, 2001.

Pojar, Jim, and Andy MacKinnon, eds. *Plants*

of the Pacific Northwest Coast. Redmond, Wash.: Lone Pine Publishing, 1994.

Quinn, Ronald D., and Sterling C. Keeley. *Introduction to California Chaparral.* Berkeley: University of California Press, 2006.

Reddell, Greg. The Crater Lake currant. *Nature Notes from Crater Lake* 32–33. 2001–02.

Reeves, Sonja L. *Ceanothus cordulatus.* Fire Effects Information System, USDA Forest Service, Rocky Mountain Research Station, Fire Sciences Laboratory. 2006. http://www.fs.fed.us/database/feis/.

Rosario, Lynn C. *Acer negundo.* Fire Effects Information System, USDA Forest Service, Rocky Mountain Research Station, Fire Sciences Laboratory. 1988. http://www.fs.fed.us/database/feis/.

Rowntree, Lester. *Flowering Shrubs of California and Their Value to the Gardener.* Stanford, Calif.: Stanford University Press, 1939.

Scher, Jannette S. *Larix occidentalis.* Fire Effects Information System, USDA Forest Service, Rocky Mountain Research Station, Fire Sciences Laboratory. 2002. http://www.fs.fed.us/database/feis/.

Seiler, John, et al. *Prunus cerasus* fact sheet. Virginia Technology Department of Forest Resources and Environmental Conservation. 2011. http://dendro.cnre.vt.edu/dendrology/syllabus/factsheet.cfm?ID=860.

Simonin, Kevin A. *Atriplex confertifolia.* Fire Effects Information System, USDA Forest Service, Rocky Mountain Research Station, Fire Sciences Laboratory. 2001. http://www.fs.fed.us/database/feis/.

Simpson, Charlene, et al. *Vascular Plants of Lane County, Oregon.* Eugene: Emerald Chapter, Native Plant Society of Oregon, 2002.

Stearns, William. *Botanical Latin.* Newton Abbott, Devon, U.K.: David & Charles, 1991.

——. *Stearn's Dictionary of Plant Names for Gardeners.* London: Cassell, 1994.

Stuart, John D., and John O. Sawyer. *Trees and Shrubs of California.* Berkeley: University of California Press, 2001.

Taylor, Jennifer L. *Populus fremontii.* Fire Effects Information System, USDA Forest Service, Rocky Mountain Research Station, Fire Sciences Laboratory. 2000. http://www.fs.fed.us/database/feis/.

Taylor, Ronald J. *Northwest Weeds: The Ugly and Beautiful Villains of Fields, Gardens, and Roadsides.* Missoula, Mont.: Mountain Press Publishing, 1990.

——. *Sagebrush Country: A Wildflower Sanctuary.* Missoula, Mont.: Mountain Press Publishing, 1992.

Taylor, Ronald J., and George W. Douglas. *Mountain Plants of the Pacific Northwest.* Missoula, Mont.: Mountain Press Publishing, 1995.

Tirmenstein, Debra. *Juniperus occidentalis.* Fire Effects Information System, USDA Forest Service, Rocky Mountain Research Station, Fire Sciences Laboratory. 1999. http://www.fs.fed.us/database/feis/.

Turner, Nancy J. *Food Plants of Coastal First Peoples.* Vancouver: University of British Columbia Press, 1995.

Uchytil, Ronald J. *Picea glauca.* Fire Effects Information System, USDA Forest Service, Rocky Mountain Research Station, Fire Sciences Laboratory. 1991. http://www.fs.fed.us/database/feis/.

U.S. Environmental Protection Agency. *Level III Ecoregions.* http://www.epa.gov/wed/pages/ecoregions/level_iii.htm. Accessed 17 November 2004.

——. *Primary Distinguishing Characteristics of Level III Ecoregions of the Continental United States, July 2010.* ftp://ftp.epa.gov/wed/ecoregions/us/Eco_Level_III_descriptions.doc. Accessed 16 July 2013.

U.S. Fish and Wildlife Service. Recovery plan for *Phlox hirsuta* (Yreka phlox). Sacramento, Calif. 2006.

University of Washington Herbarium. *Consortium of Pacific Northwest Herbaria.* Seattle: University of Washington. http://www.pnwherbaria.org/index.php. Accessed 25 January 2013.

——. *Washington Flora Checklist.* Seattle:

University of Washington. http://biology
.burke.washington.edu/herbarium/
waflora/checklist.php. Accessed 25 January 2013.

USDA Forest Service. *Rubus bartonianus*:
state review for Wallowa-Whitman National
Forest and Baker Resource Area, Vale
District BLM. Portland, Ore.: U.S. Forest
Service Region 6. 2010.

———. *Woody Plant Seed Manual.* Revision of
USDA agricultural handbook 650. 1974.
http://www.nsl.fs.fed.us/wpsm.

USDA, NRCS. *The PLANTS Database.*
National Plant Data Team, Greensboro,
N.C. 27401-4901 USA. 2013. http://plants.
usda.gov. Accessed 25 January 2013.

Washington Natural Heritage Program and
United States Department of the Interior
Bureau of Land Management. *Field Guide
to Selected Rare Vascular Plants of Washington.* http://www1.dnr.wa.gov/nhp/refdesk/
fguide/htm/fgmain.htm. Accessed 25 January 2013.

Washington State Department of Ecology.
Major Ecoregions of Washington State.
http://www.ecy.wa.gov/apps/watersheds/
maps/state/level3_ecoregions.html.
Accessed 25 January 2013.

Weber, William A. *Rocky Mountain Flora.*
Boulder: University Press of Colorado, 1976.

Wheeler, D. L., and T. Atzet. *Guide to Common Forest Plants, Rogue River, Siskiyou, and
Umpqua National Forests.* Oregon: Pacific
Northwest National Parks and Forest Association, 1987.

Whitson, Tom D., ed. *Weeds of the West.* New-
ark, Calif.: Western Society of Weed Science and the Western United States Land
Grand Universities Cooperative Extension
Services, 1992.

Wirth, Christian, et al. Black spruce meets
white spruce: dispersal, postfire establishment and growth in a warming climate.
Ecological Monographs 78(4): 489–505.
2008.

Zlatnik, Elena. *Juniperus osteosperma.* Fire
Effects Information System, USDA Forest
Service, Rocky Mountain Research Station,
Fire Sciences Laboratory. 1999. http://www.
fs.fed.us/database/feis/.

Zouhar, Kris. *Tamarix* spp. Fire Effects
Information System, USDA Forest Service,
Rocky Mountain Research Station, Fire
Sciences Laboratory. 2003. http://www.
fs.fed.us/database/feis/.

———. *Spartium junceum.* Fire Effects Information System, USDA Forest Service,
Rocky Mountain Research Station, Fire
Sciences Laboratory. 2005. http://www.
fs.fed.us/database/feis/.

CONVERSION TABLE FOR METRIC MEASUREMENTS

FEET	METERS
0.25	0.08
0.3	0.1
0.5	0.15
1	0.3
1.5	0.5
2	0.6
2.5	0.8
3	0.9
4	1.2
5	1.5
6	1.8
7	2.1
8	2.4
9	2.7
10	3.0
12	3.6
15	4.5
18	5.4
20	6.0
25	7.5
30	9.0
35	10.5
40	12
45	13.5
50	15
60	18
70	21
75	22.5
80	24
90	27
100	30
125	37.5
150	45
175	52.5
200	60

INDEX

Main species entries are in **bold type**. Species only mentioned in the descriptions are in roman type.

ABOUT THE AUTHORS

MARK TURNER is a professional photographer who specializes in gardens and native plant environments. He combines a strong sense of photographic design, attention to detail, curiosity about both native and garden plants, and more than 30 years of exploring native plants in their environments. His work in the award-winning *Wildflowers of the Pacific Northwest* has been widely praised.

ELLEN KUHLMANN is a professional botanist with extensive experience with Northwest flora. She has a background in fire ecology, rare plant research, and plant community ecology. She worked for the U.S. Forest Service for many years, and for six years was the project manager for Seeds of Success, Washington Rare Plant Care and Conservation (Rare Care), a program sponsored by the Royal Botanic Gardens, Kew. She has written many scientific and general-interest articles on native plants.

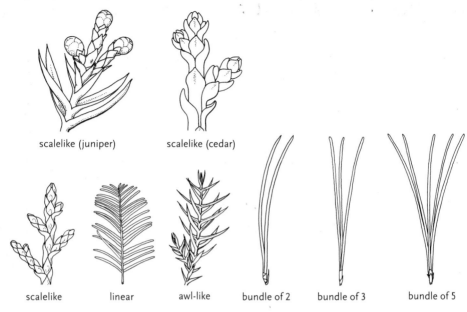

scalelike (juniper) scalelike (cedar)

scalelike linear awl-like bundle of 2 bundle of 3 bundle of 5

CONIFERS

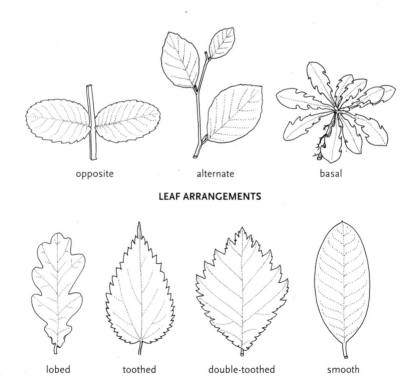

opposite alternate basal

LEAF ARRANGEMENTS

lobed toothed double-toothed smooth

LEAF EDGES